SURRY COUNTY, NORTH CAROLINA COURT MINUTES

VOLUMES I & II

1768-1789

By
Mrs. W. O. Absher

SOUTHERN HISTORICAL PRESS, INC.
c/o The Rev. Silas Emmett Lucas, Jr.
P.O. Box 738
Easley, South Carolina 29641-0738

ISBN 0-89308-554-5

INTRODUCTION

Surry County was formed in 1771 from Rowan County. It is bounded on the north by the Virginia line. In 1777 parts of Surry and the District of Washington were taken to form Wilkes Co. Stokes County was formed in 1789 from Surry, and in 1849 Forsyth County was formed from Stokes. Yadkin County was formed in 1850 from Surry. Ashe County was formed in 1799 from Wilkes, and in 1859 Alleghany County was formed from Ashe. Thus, from 1771 - 1778, these Surry County records covered the present day counties of Ashe, Alleghany, Wilkes, Surry, Yadkin, Stokes and Forsyth; from 1777 to 1787 the counties of Surry, Yadkin, Stokes and Forsyth. The county seat is Dobson, North Carolina.

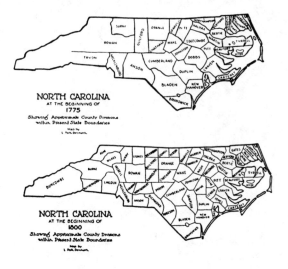

NORTH CAROLINA
AT THE BEGINNING OF
1775
Showing Approximate County Divisions
within Present State Boundaries
Map by
L. Polk Denmark

NORTH CAROLINA
AT THE BEGINNING OF
1800
Showing Approximate County Divisions
within Present State Boundaries
Map by
L. Polk Denmark

SURRY COUNTY, NORTH CAROLINA

COURT MINUTES
(1768-1785)

VOL. I

THE COURT MINUTES recorded on microfilm do not begin until 1779. There is no record of the Minutes prior to this date to be found in the State Archives. It is assumed those for this period are lost. However, in the State Archives in File C.R. 92.325.1-Civil Action Papers of Surry County (1768-1806) are loose papers which have been abstracted and used in this work in order to give what information there is in this file for the missing period.

23 January 1768

Promissory Note from Thomas EASON to Hugh DENNUM; Wm. BROOKS, security.

3rd Tuesday February-11th year Reign
Lord George Third-Court held Gideon WRIGHTS

Present: Jacob BONN, Gidion WRIGHT, Robert WALKER, Esqrs.

Jurors upon oath present that Sarah GWIN, Parish Saint Jude on 30th May 1769 "being moved and seduced by instigation of the Devil" did commit the henious crime of fornication.

3rd Tuesday August-11th year Reign
Lord George Third-Court held Gideon WRIGHTS

Present: Jacob BOND, Chas. McANELLEY, Gideon WRIGHT, Moses MARTIN, Esqrs.

Jurors present on oath that Elizabeth WARD on 30 May 1768 did commit the henious crime of fornication.

Present: Jacob BOND, Charles McANALLY, John DUNCAN, Esqrs.

Jurors upon oath present that Lucretia COMBS, on 30th April 1770 did commit henious crime of fornication.

Hezekiah WRIGHT on 13th August 1770 did with force and arms take one certain mair, goods and chattels of some person unknown.

William ROBISON, Planter, on 30th July 1770 did take one grey horse, goods and Chattels some person unknown.

3rd Tuesday February-12th year Reign
Lord George Third

Present: Jacob BOND, Gideon WRIGHT, Edward RIGGS, Esqrs.

Juriors present on oath that William ROBISON of Parrish of Saint Jude, Planter, did on 10 January 1769 with force and arms did committ henious crime fornication upon one certain Charity KENNEDY.

Present: Jacob BOND, Charles McANALLY, Robert WALKER, Justices.

Jurors upon oath present that Samuel CARTER on 10th May 1771 did commit hineous crime fornication on body Susannah PIPES. Witnesses: Jabez JARVIS and George MORRIS; Jesse BENTON, Clerk Court; W. AVERY, Attorney.

1

August Court 1771

Lord George the Third commands Sheriff, Surry County to summons (blank) to appear before Justices of Inferior Court of Pleas and Quarter Sessions. Jesse BENTON, Clerk Court.

11 August 1771. The KING vs Joseph PHILLIPS; Valentine VANHOZER in behalf of said PHILLIPS.

12 August 1771. The KING vs Andrew BOHANNAN to answer charge Tresspass, Assault and Battery against him.

12 August 1771. The KING vs Joseph PHILLIPS; Valentine VANHOZAR and John REED on behalf of said PHILLIPS.

20 August 1771. Reubin RIGGS vs Gerrett GROSS; Jacob WILLIAMS on behalf of said RIGGS.

Jurors on oath present that William RIDENS, Planter, on 20 April 1771 did assault one Peter MOYER.

That William VENABLES, Laborer, on 20 August 1771 did assault one Samson BRASILL.

That William BOYLS, Yeoman, on 20 August 1771 did assault Samson BRASILL.

That Levy JONES, Laborer, on 20 March 1771 did beat and falsely imprison one William ROBISON.

That Lemuel JONES on 20 April 1771 did beat William ROBISON.

11 September 1771

Committee of Arbitrators, to wit: Moses MARTAIN, Nathaniel Mc-CARROL and Barney FARE to determine sartain contravarsy betwixt Thomas FIZPATRICK and Nathan DILLON in suit for a note given for payment in either six pounds, ten shillings in money or Liquer. DILLION to pay FIZPATRICK twenty two gallons and 1 half of M---ch--ble wiskey and FIZPATRICK to pay court costs.

9 October 1771

Newman BLACKBURN bound unto Gray BYNUM, 24 pounds North Carolina money to be paid by 15 October next. Witnesses: Foster SAMUELL, Robert HILL, John (X) BOOLE.

Third Tuesday November-12th year
Reign King George Third

Present: Jacob BONN, Charles McANNALLY, Robert WALKER, Justices.

Jurors upon oath present that William LOGANS on 9 November 1771 did assault William VENABLES.

That Thomas FLOYD, Planter, on 17 November 1771 did take one dark Brindle Dog, goods and chattles of Sarah BOWIN.

Summons Charles WADDLE to answer to indictment for a Misdemeanor in office 20 November 1771.

10 January 1772

Jurors on oath present David GORDON on 10 January 1772 did take one Bell, goods and chattels of some person unknown. W. AVERY, Attorney.

Sheriff to summons on 12 February 1772 William AWLS to answer bill indicted against him for trespass.

2

On 18 February 1772 Richard MURPHEY on behalf Thomas CODY in case The KING vs Thomas CODY.

On 18 February 1772 William SHEPPERD, John ARMSTRONG and Gideon WRIGHT on behalf Frederick GREEN in case Wm. BOYLES vs said GREEN.

On 19 February 1772 Judy PICKET to answer indictment crime of fornication.

On 29 February 1772 Francis RUNELS (Reynolds) maketh oath David PRESTON is indebted to him, ordered to attach estate of said PRESTON for enough money to satisfy said RUNELS. Signed by Edward RIGGS.

MEMO: From Jesse BENTON to Jo. WILLIAMS; to KING vs Judy PICKET February 1772; R. RIGGS and Jonathan STAMPER to pay; to KING vs Thomas FLANERY August 1772; Wm. NAUL and John PIPES to pay; to KING vs Charles CATES August 1774; to State vs Grenberry PATTERSON August 1774; to KING vs Frederick COX; to KING vs D. ALLEN: to KING vs Thomas PETTIT February 1775; to KING vs Joseph EASON May 1775; Major WILLIAMS, please issue Exrs. for ye above and all others which you think ought now to be paid with memo. for Sheriff not to levy if appears money is paid. Cast up BOYLES account of fees and charge him at selling price this fall; John ARMSTRONG is to have 7 barrels of corn at selling price.

Third Tuesday August-12th year
Reign King George Third

Present: Jacob BOND, Gideon WRIGHT, Robert WALKER, Esqrs.

Jurors on oath present Thomas FLANERY on 2 May 1772 did take one black mare, goods and chattels of Thomas TURNER.

Sheriff to summons William HALL, Esq., David BRYANT, James COYLE on behalf Jonathan OSBURN vs Wm. ROBERSON 3 May 1772.

James BROWN, Wm. HALL and Wm. DALTON on behalf KING vs Charity KENNADAY 12 May 1772.

Thomas GILES to answer to Lawrence SMITH plea Trespass 12 May 1772.

John HARDY and Volentine AUSTON on behalf John JARVIS vs John SCRITCHFELD 18 May 1772.

Andrew VANNOY to answer bill indicted against him for crime fornication 19 May 1772.

John REED, Noble LADD and Thomas LAGFORD to shew cause whey they failed attending as jurors at February Court 19 May 1772.

William HALL, Wm. DALTON and Henery MENADUE on behalf Wm. FORKNER in case Elijah SMALLWOOD vs William FORKNER 3 May 1772.

Charles CATE to answer unto Wm. STAFFORD plea tresspass 18 August 1772.

John HAMILTON, Planter, and Robert LANIER, Merchant, to answer to Benj. PETTIE plea trespass 18 August 1772.

Jesse BROWN, John HALBERT, John BOWLS, Arthur DENTON on behalf William BUTLER vs William BOWLS 10 August 1772.

George WILSON to answer Whitfield WILSON plea trespass 20 August 1772.

Jesse WALTON to answer indictment against him for tresspass 20 August 1772.

Jurors upon oath present Sarah BARRET on 12 August 1772 did take one red pide cow, property of Oze Moss.

3

Charles McANNALLY, Planter, on 13 July 1772 did with one John COOLY conspire to assault one Rebecca YOUNG.

Thomas FLANERY, Labourer, together with one John FLANERY on 24 July 1772 did take one sorrel mare (duly taken in Execution by Jonathan STAMPER, Constable in suit Abraham HOWARD, Pltf.) out of possession of said STAMPER.

Abigail BARRAT (wife of Nathaniel BARRET) did on 13 June 1772 take one red pide cow, property of Oze MOSS.

25 September 1772

Joseph HUGHES complains before William COLVARD, one of his Majestys Justices of Pease, that John COLE is indebted to him in 7 pounds, 11 shillings, 9 pence; said John COLE hath privatly removed himself out of this county or so absconded; ordered estate said John COLE be attached and sold in value sufficient to satisfy said HUGHES.

2 October 1772

Articles Agreement between Wm. SHEPPERD and Charles ALLEN; Chainged their notes for 50 pounds payable in following manner: Agreed to run their horses against one another, to wit: Sorrel Stallion of SHEPPERDS and Geldin called Inperter of said ALLEN; two miles at one heet according to Rules of Raceing - said two miles to be within Old Field wherein Reas Peaths (Race Paths) now is nigh Johnstons falls on Yadkin River. SHEPPERDS stallen to carrey him or his weight. ALLENS geldin Inperter to carry James JETT or his weight. Colo. Gideon WRIGHT shall deliver them both to the winder of said race. Signed by William SHEPPERD and Charles ALLEN. Witnesses: John ARMSTRONG and Garden HAMILTON.

4 January 1773

Jacob VENDERMAN, Michael FRY and David DAVIS give bond to Martin ARMSTRONG, high Sheriff, for appearance said VENDERMAN at suit of Wm. HILL at next Inferior Court Pleas and Quarter Session to be held at Gideon WRIGHTS. Witness: Benjamin PRIME.

26 January 1773

Presley LOVINS and Antony MORGAIN bound unto Marten ARMSTRONG, high Sheriff for appearance said Presley LOVING next court answer to John BARRAT, Senr., plea trespass. Witness: Reuben RIGGS.

February Court 1773

Jurors upon oath present John REDEFURD, Labourer, on 25 January 1773 did enter the quiet and peaceable possession of one Bethany HAIS (male).

Angus ALEXANDER, Planter, on 9 January 1773, did retail, sell and disperse Spiritous Liquor by a smaller and lesser quantity than a quart, to wit: two pints run and one bowl of Toddy, without first obtaining a License for that purpose.

26 February 1773, suit brought by Jesse ALEXANDER (?) vs David PRESTON, sundry goods not sufficient to satisfy pltf.

Francis REYNOLDS, Pltf. vs David PRESTON, Deft., Sheriff returned, levied on sundry goods not sufficient to satisfy Pltf.; attachment by Jonathan STAMPER, constable.

13 March 1773, John ARMSTRONG, Thomas POINDEXTER and Hezekiah

WRIGHT bound unto Edward HERRING in case Garrot GROSS attachment against Estate Edward HERRING returned next court. Witness: Malcum CURREY.

MEMO: Jesse BENTON, C. C. James CARSON vs John and Joseph ENGLAND. Thomas CARSON witness for pltf. February 7, 1773 to 5 days attended and 40 miles; May 1774 for 3 days, 40 miles; August for 4 days, 40 miles.

14 May 1773

William FORSTER promise to pay WILSON and TATE before 1 August next. Witnesses: Nathaniel MOXLEY, John CARRINE (?).

MEMO: Serch for Wm. WOOLFS Inventory returned May Court (74) found; Serch Lucey GENTRY. administration bond May (74) found; Nicholas EVANS, deceased, Inventory November (74); Inventory David WALKER, estate serch for and found; 2 bills of Sale from Ben PRIME to Geo. PARRIS serch for February (75); serch for account current of Margarett ZINZ Estate.

14 August 1774

Summons Richard CHEEK to answer to John REED plea of trespass.

12 September 1774

Richard CHEEK and William HALL bound unto William SHEPPARD, High Sheriff for Richard CHEEKS appearance at next Court to be held for county in Richmond second Tuesday November next to answer to John REEDS plea he render unto said CHEEKS 20 pounds. Witness: John WIL-S (?).

29 September 1774, Promissory Note from Thomas EASON to Matthew WARNOCK; William CARMICHAEL, Security.

November 1774

MEMO: From William SHEPPERD to Jesse BENTON. Clerks fees in full PIPES vs JARVIS and PIPES vs ALLIN; F. HAMILTON vs Wm. SCOTT; M. WARNOCK vs D. HUFFINDS; John HARMOND vs William PILGRIM; WAGGONER vs Thomas EASON; William and Moses JOHNSON vs Jeffrey JOHNSON; John ARMSTRONG vs John NOLAND; Reuben RIGGS vs Garrot GROSS; MONTGOMERY vs HUSBANDS by Robert LANIER; by Matthew BROOKS.

15 November 1774

Samuel MORE and Malcum CURRY bound unto Wm. SHEPPERD, High Sheriff for Samuel MORES appearance next court to answer Johnston RUTLEG pleas damage. Witness: Martin ARMSTRONG.

17 November 1774

Summons Samuel MOORE, Planter, answer Johnston RUTLEDGE why he did with force and arms assault, wound, maim and ill treat said RUTLEDGE.

1 December 1774

George ROBERTS and Abraham CRESON bound unto Wm. SHEPPERD, Sheriff, for George ROBERTS appearance next court.

Court House in Richmond to answer LANIER and WILLIAM plea trespass. Witness: John HARRISON.

10 May 1775

Summons Jabez JARVIS and Reuben RIGGS on behalf Edward RIGGS vs William SHEPPERD.

Abraham CRESON vs Adnorirum ALLIN, judgment. John WILLIAMS, Attorney.

Hugh CAIN vs Joseph MURPHEY.

11 September 1775

Case Thomas FIZPATRICK vs Nathan DILLON. Both have agreed to discontinue said suit and further agreed to refer said suit to Moses MARTAIN, Nathaniel McCARROL and Barney FAIR as umpires. Witnesses: Smith (X) HUTCHENS and Robert SCOTT.

12 May 1778

Ordered goods and chattels, lands and tenements of Adornirum ALLIN (at Court held 10 August 1772 at Richmond, Abraham CRESON recovered against him for debt) be attached for monies to be brought next court.

Ordered goods and chattels Hugh CAIN (at court Richmond, Joseph MURPHEY recovered against him) be attached for monies to be brought next court.

Ordered summons William SHEPPERD, Robert LANIER, Joseph WILLIAMS, Matthew BROOKS, John WILSON, John ARMSTRONG and Samuel CUMMINGS, gentlemen, to answer to Richard CASWELL, Esquire, Governor of North Carolina, plea that they render unto him the sum one thousant pounds Sterling Money of Great Britain which to him they owe and unjustly detained from him.

13 August 1778

Joseph JOHNSON and Jabez JARVIS are bound unto Wm. COOK for said Joseph JOHNSONS Cavet and entry of land maid by Wm. COOK. Witness: Joseph WINSTON.

(END OF CIVIL ACTION PAPERS)

(THE FIRST PAGE OF THE MICROFILM from which these abstracts have been taken is blurred and has no beginning of a day of court. The film states the minutes begin in 1779.)

------ surrendered by bail James MARTIN and afterwards produced Richard (blurred) Esqr. and Reubin MATTHEWS, security, who are bound for the appearance of the said William REYNOLDS that he do not depart without leave of the Court.

Wm. HANKINS, Esqr. qualified as Justice of Peace.

James COFFEE delivered up the body of Daniel WELLS.

11th - Wednesday (no year)

Present: John HUDSPETH, William HALL, Michael HOWZER, William HANKINS, Esqrs.

Ordered Charles WADDAL, overseer, road leading from Surry Court house to Allins Iron Works, beginning at Yellow Banks; thence to his house.

Ordered Samuel HAGGARD, overseer, road from Charles WADDALS to

Younger COLEMANS.

Ordered Reubin RIGGS, overseer, road from (blurred) COLEMANS to his house.

Ordered William HANKINS, overseer, road from Reubin RIGGS to Iron Works Road.

Ordered Ferry Rates as follows: Waggon and Team 12/6; Cart and Team 8/0; Man and Horse 2/0; Foot Man 1/0; Horse per Head 1/0; Cattle per head 1/0; Hogs and Sheep per head 0/6.

Ordered Abraham POWELL, overseer, road in room William AMY.

Ordered John McKINNEY, overseer, road from Osborns Mill to Virginia Line.

Ordered Surveyor lay off residue Entry Alexander MARTIN lying on Dan River near mouth Seven Islands so as not to include Plantations of John and George SLATEN.

James REAVIS records his mark.

Ordered James REAVIS Mill be recorded as publick Mill on N. fork Deep Creek.

Ambrous BLACKBURN being no Freeholder, ordered he be excused attending as a Grand Juror.

Letters of Administration on Estate Samuel DUNLAP, deceased, granted Margaret DUNLAP, widow and Relict of deceased; John DUNLAP produced copy Nuncupative Will. Robert WARNOCK and James DAVIS, securities. Inventory returned by said Margaret.

William REYNOLDS and Daniel WELLS appeared and both acquitted.

Deed from Lewis and Barbara LIMEBURG to Benjamin LIMEBURG 200 acres; oath Christian SMITH.

Deed from William SPARKS to Matthew SPARKS.

Ordered Letters of Administration on Estate Phillip DAVIS, deceased, granted Leticia DAVID, widow and relict; David DAVIS and Thomas EVANS, securities.

Thursday 12th

Present: John HUDSPETH, William MERIDETH, Richard VARNAL, Esqrs.

Last Will and Testament. Benjamin PAINIEL proved oath William HILL; Letters of Administration granted John HALBERT.

Ordered Alexander BURGE pay no more than single tax for 1778 because he was not given proper notice.

Ordered a Didimus Potestatum issued Henry County, Virginia to take deposition Robert BOWMAN and Peter BOWMAN in caviat to be tried between John SIMMONS, Caviator and Joseph CLOUD.

Ordered John SHOUB, overseer, road in room Jacob BLUM.

Thomas GALLION surrendered himself and gave bond to keep the children from being chargeable to the county.

Adam MITCHELL records his mark.

Ordered Joseph BURKETT and William BUTLER pay on single tax 1778.

Matthew BASS, John Thomas LONGINO and David (or Daniel) GRAVES took oath of allegiance and oath of Deputy Sheriff.

Friday 13th

Present: William SHEPPARD, Robert WALKER, William HARDIN, Esqrs.

John HUDSPETH vs William STAFFORD. Jury: John CHILDRESS, James DAVIS, John DUNLAP, Michael FRY, Henry FRY, Charles WADDLE, William HARRISON, Levi SPEER, Andrew SPEER, John WILLIAMS, Hezekiah WRIGHT, Samuel MORELY, Junr.

Charles PATTERSON vs Marble STONES (it looks like) same jury.

Jonas GRIFFITH vs Richard LANKFORD; same jury.

John GRIFFITH vs Richard LANKFORD; same jury.

Godfrey MILLER vs Richard LANKFORD: same jury.

William COOK vs Richard LANKFORD: same jury.

Frederick MILLER qualified as Justice of Peace.

Ordered John COE be released of fine 3 pounds imposed on him for his non-attendance as a Talisman at August Term 1778.

Ordered new road begin where Peters Creek old road crosses Guilford County line; thence to where new road crosses Peters Creek road leads from Virginia line to mouth Snow Creek and following appointment, view said road: William MEREDETH, Joseph GIBSON, John GIBSON, Edmond HOLT, Joseph REED, Hugh HOLTON, John FOLKNER, John WILKINS, John ROBERSON, Williamson MAYO, John ROGERS, John ROAS, Thomas DUGGONS and Samuel SHULL.

Deed from Ambrous BLACKBURN to Mack SHIP; oath Gray BYNUM.

Ordered Matthew WARNOCK, overseer, road in room Wm. CARMICHAEL and clear most convenient way round them hills between John CARMICHAELS and Moses MARTINS.

Ordered Joseph CARTER, overseer, road in room David MARTIN, dec'd.

Ordered following attend next court as Jurors 2nd Monday in February: Hezekiah WRIGHT, Gideon WRIGHT, John CONNEL, John LANE, David MELTON, William RIDENS, Benjamin PETTIT, John HORN, Senr., Volentine MARTIN, Job MARTIN, Robert ELROD, Jacob HOWZAR, Abraham PAG--(?), Mathew MARKLIN, William PETTICOAL (Petticord), Alexander MOORE, James DOAK, Reubin MATTHEWS, Richard LAWRANCE, John ROBERTS, Matthew DAVIS, Stephen CLAYTON, Joel HALBERT, George DEATHERAGE, Joseph CLOUD, Lazarous TILLY, John SLATTEN, Frederick COX, Alexander JONES, and Thomas CARDWELL. Signed by order of Justices: Joseph WINSTON, William MERIDETH, and Robert WALKER.

8 February 1779
Court House in Richmond

Present: John HUDSPETH, William MEREDITH.

9 February 1779

Present: John HUDSPETH, William HALL, William MEREDITH, William DOBSON, Esqrs.

Last Will and Testament. Thomas FISHER proved oath Wm. HALL; James FISHER, quallified as administrator.

Inventory Estate, Roger TURNER, deceased, returned by Elias TURNER, Exexr.

Inventory Estate, Issac GARRISON, deceased, returned by Benjamin WATSON, Administrator.

Account sale, Estate, John ROTHROCK, returned by Gabriel WAGGONER, Admr.

Account part, Estate, Tyree GLEN, deceased, returned by John BLACKWELL, guardian orphans said Tyree GLEN.

Ordered Samuel WAGGONER, Seth COFFIN and Barnabas FAIR appraise Estate Isaac GARRISON, deceased.

Deed from David STEWARD to John LYNCH, acknowledged.

Bill of Sale from James REYNOLDS to James SANDERS; oath John HUDSPETH.

John ENDSLEY, one securities Administrator Estate James ENDSLEY, deceased, asked to be released from his securityship and John CUMMINS, who hath married Jane ENDSLEY, Widow and Admrx. of deceased, intered into bond with Barnabas FAIR and Wm. DOBSON.

Ordered John CUMMINS appointed guardian of Hugh, John, Mary, Andrew and Jane ENDSLEY, orphans of James ENDSLEY, deceased; Barnabas FAIR and William DOBSON, securities.

Grand Jury: Gideon WRIGHT, foreman, John CONNEL, William RIDENS, Robert ELROD, David MELTON, John HORN, Senr., Reubin MATTHEWS, Joseph MARTIN, Valentine MARTIN, William LANE, Frederick COX, Alexander JOICE (Joyce), and Thomas CARDWELL.

Abraham CRESON and Henry WAGGONER enters themselves securities for Richard JACKS appearance next court.

Ordered Abraham CRESON be bound with security to produce negro woman named Jane SCOTT who lives with him and claims her freedom at next court; motion made by Colo. OSBORN.

Deed from Martha McGEE to James MATTHEW; oath William HALL.

Inventory Estate, Benjamin PANNIEL returned by John HALBERT, Exec.

Inventory Estate, Phillip DAVIS, deceased, return by Administrator.

10 February 1779

Present: William HALL, William DOBSON, Thomas JOHNSON, Esqrs.

William GRAY, one administrator Estate James ENDSLEY, deceased, produced account sale Estate.

Frederick GREEN and Benedictus ALDERSON fined for contempt; bound to good behavior with George HOWZAR, secruity for ALDERSON; John HOLCOMB security for GREEN.

On motion, Colo. OSBORN, ordered Elizabeth McBAIN be taken out of possession John Thomas LONGINO and delivered to Sarah McBAIN to be carried to Guilford County to be dealt with at discretion of Court in said County; Sarah McBAIN'S security, Colo. Robert LANIER.

Ferry Rates: Loaded waggon and team 1:10:0; Empty Waggon and Team 0:18:0; Loaded Cart and Team 0:18:0; Empty Cart and Team 0:12:6; Man and Horse 0:3:0; Foot Man 0:2:0; Hoggs and Sheep per head 0:1:0; Single Horse 0:2:0.

11 February 1779

Present: Charles McANALLY, Matthew MOORE, Robert WALKER, Esqrs.

Ordered Robert WALKER, Esqr. and Samuel CUMMINS appointed commissioners to provide and agree with workman to erect Stocks and Whiping Post in town Richmond and call upon County Trustee for money for expense of same.

Ordered Didimus Potestatum issued respecting Jane SCOTT, a supposed free Negro in possession of Abraham CRESON, concerning her freedom.

Ordered Didimus Potestatum issue in Caviat Joseph WILLIAMS against

9

Samuel CUMMINS.

Ordered Samuel FRANCIS, overseer, road in room William BOYLES.

Ordered Jacob SPEER, overseer, road from Fortees Creek to Rowan County line and hands from Cresons old place and waters of Turners Creek work thereon.

Ordered William VARNAL, overseer, road in room Matthew BASS.

Ordered Robert SPEERS Mill already built on Little Yadkin be deemed a publick Mill.

Ordered Terry BRADLEY have leave to build to a water Grist Mill on Snow Creek near Colo. MARTINS; deemed publick mill.

Ordered Brazalia ROSE, now 15 years old, orphan of Brasalia ROSE, deceased, be bound to Robert SPEER until he arrives age 21 to learn art and mistry of a carpenter and at end apprenticeship be given set carpenters tools and suit woolen clothes and learn him to read, wright and cypher.

Order citation against Mary NOWLEN produce her children and show cause why they not be bound out to some suitable trade and employment agreeable to law.

Ordered following attend next Superior Court in Salisbury for District of Salisbury 15 March next as Jurors: Tragott BAGGE, Matthew BROOKS, Benjamin YOUNG and John LYNCH.

Ordered following attend next County Court second Monday May as Jurors: James GLEN, Seth COFFIN, Stephen CLAYTON, Absolem BOSTICK, Barnabas FAIR, Samuel WAGGONER, Noble LADD, Senr., Thomas EVANS (cooper), Michael FRY, Lathan FOLGER, James GAMBLE, Abraham CRE-SON, Simon HADLEY, James DOAK, Richard LAWRENCE, Charles WORD, Hugh ARMSTRONG, George LASH, John HARVEY, Andrew SPEER, Joseph BURKE, John CHILDRESS, William HEAD, Robert WALKER, Junr., John HANNAH (Blues Creek), John PINKLEY (Binkley), Henry SHORES, Matthew WARNOCK, John BLALOCK, James SANDERS.

Joseph WINSTON entered 200 account in Surry County on waters Town Fork adjacent David DAVIS land and myself.

Nicholas DULL (Doll?) Administrator estate Jacob BLACK and Barabara BLACK, deceased, produced account settlement said estate.

On motion Robert WARNOCK, ordered entry taker delay issue warrant survey to Joseph EASON until next court it appearing EASON has taken illegal measures on Caviat Robert WARNOCK vs Mary EASON.

Ordered following view and mark road from Phillip COLDEASURES to Richmond Town: Matthew BROOKS, Joseph WILLIAMS, Robert LANIER, Benjamin STEWART, Joseph STEWART, Gideon WRIGHT, Joseph PHILLIPS, Martin HOWZAR, John LYNCH, Thomas SMITH, Phillip HOWARD, George LASH, John MILLER, Joseph MILLER, Frederick MILLER, Phillip COLDEASURE, Francis KIDNOW, George SPRINKLE, Leander HUGHES, James SHORT, John HARVEY, Senr., Thos. JOHNSON.

Ordered William WALLACE, overseer, road in room John ALLEN.

Ordered James SHORT, overseer, road from Richmond to Wachovia Tract.

Joseph WINSTON entered 200 acres both sides Mulberry Field Road adjacent lines Edward MOORE, Simon GROSE, Thomas HOWELL, John GROSE 12 February 1779; also 100 acres both sides Redd Bank Creek adjacent Abraham MARTIN and including Thomas BOTHURNS (?) claim 7 November 1778.

Ordered Adam MITCHELL, overseer, road in room Matthew WARNOCK and clear road round them hills between John CARMICHAELS and

10

Moses MARTINS.

Jury made their report view road from Guilford line to where new road from Virginia line to mouth Peters Creek old road.

Ordered Joseph REED, overseer, same.

Collectors in Districts of Capt. James SHEPPARD, Capt. HARDIN and Capt. ROWARK has not appeared; they stand charged with whole amounts of their collections.

Saturday 13 July 1778

Present: Joseph WINSTON, Robert WALKER, William MERIDETH, Esqrs.

Ordered Joseph READ, Constable in room Joseph GIBSON.

Ordered Thomas LOYD, overseer, road from Grassey Creek to Court House.

Account valuation of several Estates (not named) of 100 pounds and upwards for year 1778; MARTINS, DOBSONS, JARVIS'S, SANDERS, BYNUMS, HICKMANS, MOSLEYS, HOUZARS, CAMPLINS (?), Hardins Districts.

Also, account taxes due from each District to County Treasurer of Salisbury, tax included.

Also, account taxes due from each District in county to County Trastee (a list is given in pounds, shillings, and pence for each above.)

2nd Monday May 1779
Richmond Court House

Present: John HUDSPETH, Robert WALKER, Micajah CLARK, William SHEPPERD, Esqrs.

Deed from Rachel HOGGALL, (or Hockkett), widow Nathaniel HOCKKETT (?) to John (blurred) 500 acres; oath James GAINES and Thomas LANKFORD.

Deed from John and Agnes DYCKES to James GAINS 203 acres and 107 acres; oath John DYCKES.

Deed from John DYCKES to Thomas LANKFORD, 100 acres.

Deed from Thomas ROGERS and Jean ROGERS to Edwin HICKMAN, 117 acres; oath George DEATHERAGE.

Ordered Henry PARISH, overseer, road in room John COLE.

Tuesday 11 May 1779

Present: John HUDSPETH, Wm. HANKINS, William MEREDITH, Esqrs.

Ordered Samuel JONES, overseer, road in room Philip SHOUSE.

Ordered Robert WARNOCK, overseer, road in room Adam MITCHEL.

Ordered John BLACKBURN , overseer, road in room Thomas EVANS.

Ordered James BLACKWELL, overseer, road in room John COE.

Power of Attorney from John GREEN to Thomas BURKE; oath Joseph WINSTON.

Deed from John GREEN by his Attorney Thomas BURKE to Robert LANIER; oath Philip HOLCOMB.

Deed from Robert LANIER to Robert HARRIS, 200 acres; oath LANIER.

Nathaniel WILLIAMS, Esq. qualified as Attorney at Law.

William HEAD and Benjamin WATSON qualified as Justice of Peace.

Joshua and Palmer CRITCHFIELD took Oath of Allegiance.

Ordered Letters of Administration, Estate, John GRIFFITH granted Elizabeth GRIFFITH, widow and relict; Martin ARMSTRONG and Samuel FREEMAN, securities; said Elizabeth qualified.

Ordered Letters of Administration, Estate, David MARTIN, deceased be granted Mary MARTIN and Salathial MARTIN; Chas. McANNALY and John CARTER, securities.

Ordered appraisement, Estate, Isaac GARRISON, deceased.

Ordered Seth COFFIN and Lathem FOLGER, Jurors, be excused from duty.

Ordered copy oath and certificate for Joseph CLOUD, Junr. to act as Deputy Surveyor in this county be recorded.

Wednesday 12 May 1779

Present: Martin ARMSTRONG, Robert LANIER, John HUDSPETH, Thomas JOHNSON, Esqr.

Ordered Elijah GALLASPY, overseer, road in room Abraham HOWARD.

Ordered Jacob SPEER, overseer, road crossing Deep Creek near Creson; also road from Shallowford to Cresons.

Ordered James GLEN, overseer, road from Court House road crossing Yadkin at Glens ford to Brookes old place.

Ordered Joseph BURKE, overseer, Brooks road from Forbis's Creek to the Chesonutt Hill.

Ordered Jacob FEREE, overseer, road from Chesnutt Hill to the Iron Works Road.

Ordered following view road out of road leads from Richmond to Allins Iron Works, crossing Yadkin at White Rock into road leads from Richmond to Salisbury near Deep Creek: Jabez JARVIS, James YORK, Thomas JOHNSON, James LINZY, John MOORE, Amos LONDON, John ENGLAND, Moses BAKER, Robert AYRS, John SUMMERS, Samuel HAGWOOD, Richard CHILDRESS, Joseph ENGLAND, Weightman SUMMERS, Spence BOELING, Thomas CARSON, Thomas GILES, Aron SPEER, Philip HOLCOMB, William RIDENS, Junr.

Ordered Philip GREEN, overseer, road in room Frederick MILLER, Esq.

Ordered following view road from Philip COLDEASURES to Surry Court House: Matthew BROOKS, Benjamin STEWART, Gideon WRIGHT, Martin HOWZAR, Philip HOWARD, John M(blurred), Joseph MILLER, Frederick MILLER, George SPRINKLE, Leander HUGHES, James SHORT, John HARVEY, Senr., John SNEAD, Robert WALKER, Esq., James BAGGET, John GILBERT, Robert TATE, Thomas SMITH, Philip COLDEASURE, John LYNCH.

Ordered Matthew MARKLAND, overseer, road in Muddy Creek District.

Last Will and Testament. Lorenz VOGLER proved oath Simon SNIDER; Nicholas BEAKET, Exerc. qualified and Letters of Administration granted.

Inventory Account, settlement Estate, Ambrous BLACKBURN returned by Ambrous BLACKBOURN, Administrator.

LANIER & WILLIAMS vs WAGONER & BROOK. Jury: James GLEN, Andrew SPEER, Joseph BURK, John HANNAH, James SANDERS, Thomas EVANS, John BLALOCK, John CHILDRESS, Henry SHORE, Malcum CURRY, John PINKLEY (Brinkley), Robert WALKER, Junr.

LANIER & WILLIAMS vs Robert TAYLOR and Benj. WATSON; same jury.

Abraham CRESON vs Isham WESTMOND; same jury.

12

Abraham CRESON vs Thomas LAXON; same jury.

LANIER & WILLIAMS vs Thomas HEATH; same jury.

Abraham CRESON vs Nathaniel WOODROUGH; same jury.

John ELSBERRY qualified as Justice of Peace.

Ordered bond from Thomas SMITH to Sarah SMITH be recorded.

Ordered Mary NOLIN enter into security for four securities to keep her children from being chargable to County and she be of good behaviour towards the State.

Thursday 13 May 1779

Present: Martin ARMSTRONG, Robert LANIER, Benjamin WATSON, Esqrs.

Ordered Henry COOK, overseer, Sandy Ridge Road from Thomas STINTONS to Guilford County line.

Ordered following view road from Rowan line near Moses MITCHELS to Wilkes County line near Hambling Store: Reubin CLEMMENTS, Junr., Butler ROBERTSON, Reubin CLEMENTS, Charles STEWARD, Jesse CLEMENTS, George WOOTEN, James SANDERS, John SANDERS, James SANDERS, Junr., Richard WOOTEN, Henry WARD, John WARD, Joseph MYERS, George STEWART, Isaac ELLESBERRY, Thomas WRIGHT, Lewis ELLIOTT.

Ordered Thomas ADDIMAN, overseer, road in room James GLEN.

Ordered Ferry Rates as follows: Loaded Waggon and Team 2:0:0; Empty Waggon and Team 1:10:0; Loaded Cart 1:10:0; Empty Cart 1:0:0; Man and Horse 0:4:0; Foot Man 0:2:8; Single Horse and Cattle per head 0:2:8; Hoggs and Sheep per head 0:1:4.

William WILEY vs PATTERSON AND PARIS. Jury: James GLEN, James SANDERS, John BLALOCK, John HANNAH, Henry SHORE, Robert WALKER, Junr., Andrew SPEER, Joseph BURKE, Joseph PHILIPS, Charles BRUCE, Hezekiah WRIGHT, James SHORT.

James BRANDON vs James CONDON; same jury.

Matthew TROY vs Adam LASH; same jury.

Ordered George BLACK, orphan of Jacob BLACK, deceased, aged 9 years be bound to John CROUSE til he comes of age 21 to learn art and Mistery of Blacksmith and be given blacksmith tools at end of said time.

Ordered Robert LANIER'S allowance for settlement, Estate, Elijah SKIDMORE to be paid by Charles BRUCE.

Ordered Lisha WILLIAMS (LT) Constable in room John REAVIS.

Ordered Samuel STROPP Constable in room Adam WOOLF, resigned.

John HUDSPETH, Esq. elected Sheriff by majority of four.

Ordered on motion Nathaniel WILLIAMS and Spruce McCAY, Esqrs, the Sheriff is to bring "in the body" of Jean SCOTT, detained in prison in his custody to be tried; signed by Joseph WINSTON, Wm. DOBSON and Benjamin WATSON. Jean SCOTT appeared, alledged she was detained by Abraham CRESON as a Slave, when in fact she was Free Born and prays she might be at liberty.

Ordered Jean SCOTT be freed from her Bondage and the children of said Jean be bound as Orphans: Sarah age 10, Prisilla age 8, Keziah age 6 and Happy SCOTT age 2½ years be bound to John HUDS-PETH until they arrive at 18 years and learn to read, spin, knit and weave.

Ordered Jemima SCOTT, aged 4½ be bound to Joseph WILLIAMS til 18 years to learn same.

Friday 14 May 1779

Present: John HUDSPETH, Joseph WINSTON, William DOBSON, Robert WALKER.

Ordered Thomas JOHNSON, John HARVEY, Philip HOWARD, John COLVARD, Philip CULDEASURE, Leander HUGHES, Thomas SMITH, Joseph HAWKINS, William THORNTON, Joseph STEWARD, Benjamin STEWARD, Matthew BROOKS, Joseph MILLER, Richard THOMERSON, John SNEED, Robert WALKER, James BADGIT, John LYNCH, Gideon WRIGHT, Joseph PHILIPS, George SPRINKLE view road from Philip CULDEASURES or Dutch Meeting House to Surry Court House.

Ordered Casper FISHER, overseer, road in room Henry SPOONHOUR in Bathany District.

Court proceeded to lay off county into Districts and Appointed Justices and Constables "to warn in" the persons, etc: Capt. BYNUMS: Joseph WINSTON, Esq., John COOLEY and John HALBERT; Capt. SMITHS: George HOWZAR, Esq., Samuel STROOP and John SHARPE, Junr.; Capt. Elijah SMALLWOODS: Wm. HALL, Esq., Thomas COKER and Elijah SMALLWOOD; Capt. James SHEPPERDS: Robert WILLIS, Esq., Wm. UNDERWOOD and Edmund KERBY; Capt. HICKMANS: William MEREDITH, Esq., Joseph REED and Reubin DODSON; Capt. WOODRIDGES: John ELSBERRY, Esq., John WILLIAMS and James DOYAL; Capt. Wm. SHEPPERDS: Wm. SHEPPERD, Esq., Roger GIDDINS and John SNEED; Capt. MOSBYS: Thomas SMITH, Esq., John HARVEY, Junr. and John HARVEY; Capt. Salathial MARTINS: Wm. HANKINS, Esq., Wm. Nicholas COOK and Abel COBB; Capt. CAMPORLINS: Charles McANALLY, Esq., Jesse McANALLY and John MORGAN; Capt. Joshua COX'S: Matthew MOORE, Esq., Lewis CONNER and George DEATHERAGE; Capt. Job MARTINS: Wm. HEAD, Esq., John Thomas LONGINO and Job MARTIN; Capt. BREWERS: Samuel FREEMAN, Esq., Wm. FREEMAN and Jabez JARVIS; Capt. Wm. DOBSONS: Wm. DOBSON, Esq., Jacob Joseph SCOTT and William WALKER.

Ordered following attend next County Court 2nd Monday August as Jurors: John ROBERSON, Stephen CLAYTON, Wm. CARMICHALL, Wm. JAMES, Barnabas FAIR, Gabriel WAGGONER, Henry COOK, John COLVARD, George DEATHERAGE, James BROWN, James BAGGETT, Abraham MARTIN, Daniel CHANDLER, John JOINER, Simon HADLEY, John THOMSON, James DOAK, Elijah SMALLWOOD, Doke HANNAH, Joseph BANNER, Abrham PECOCK, Samuel CUNNINGHAM, Philip SHOUSE, Younger BLACKBURN, Richard CHILDRESS, John HUTCHINS, Benjamin BURK, Thomas BRIGGS, John BOLES, John HARVEY.

Mary NOWLIN, brought from Jail, where she was comitted by William SHEPPERD, Esq. on suspecion of stealing, is discharged.

GORDON & STEWART vs George HOWZAR, Caviat.

John HUDSPETH, Robert LANIER and Joseph WINSTON, Esqrs. appointed to receive Tory Property.

Ordered Robert WALKER, Joseph HARRISON, Philip SHOUSE, John BINKLEY, Thomas BRIGGS, Gray BYNUM, Alexander MOORE, James FREEMAN, James ROSS, William CAMPBELL, Arthur DENTON, Frederick HELSIBECK, John SNEAD, Andrew FISLER, Abraham MARTIN, Thomas EVANS, Michael FRY, Joseph WINSTON, Edward EVANS, James CHARL(blurred), Valentine FRY, Henry FRY; jury to view road from Major WINSTONS to Court House.

Ordered Robert WALKER, Esq. have Licence keep Tavern in his now dwelling house in Richmond.

Ordered Peter HOWZAR have licence to keep Tavern at his now dwelling house in Bathany (Bethania).

Ordered Godfrey MILLER have Licence keep Tavern in his now dwelling house in Richmond.

Ordered Samuel CUMMINS have licence keep Tavern at this now dwelling house in Richmond. Signed by: John HUDSPETH, William MEREDITH, Mickel HAUSER, George HAUSER.

2nd Monday 9 August 1779
Richmond Court House

Present: Charles McANALLY, Robert WALKER, Macajah CLARK, Esqrs.

Ordered James MARTIN on Mill Creek, overseer, road in room John McANALLY.

10 August 1779

Present: Charles McANALLY, William MEREDITH, John HUDSPETH, William SHEPPERD, Esqrs.

Grand Jury: William JAMES, Barnabas FAIR, James BROWN, James PADGET, James DOAK, Jos. BANNER, Abel PECOCK, Philip SHOUSE, John HUTCHINS, John BOWLS, Samuel CUNNINGHAM, Stephen CLAYTON, Gabriel WAGGONER.

------(blurred) OSBORN, Esq., appointed State Attorney for Surry County.

Jesse McANALLY, John Thos. LONGINO, John COOLEY, James COFFEE appointed Constables.

Richard MURPHEY appointed Assessor in James SHEPPARDS District in room Edmund KERLEY, who is an inhabitant of Wilkes County.

David HUDSPETH qualified as Deputy Sheriff.

John HUDSPETH, Esq., produced commission from the Governor; appointed him Sheriff with Wm. MEREDITH, Joseph WILLIAMS, John BLALOCK, Giles HUDSPETH, David HUDSPETH, Wm. HUDSPETH, John WILLIAMS, Joseph PHILIPS, Robert LANIER, securities.

John HUDSPETH entered into Bond with above men as Collector of Public Taxes, etc.

Martin ARMSTRONG, Robert LANIER, Richard GOODE, Esqrs., appointed committee to receive and examine returns Assessors.

Wm. MEREDITH, Richard VARNAL and Charles McANALLY, Esqrs., appointed committee to receive and examine County Claims.

Richard GOODE, Esq. qualified as Justice of Peace.

Deed from William HALL and Thankful HALL, his wife to Richard LAWRENCE; oath Joseph LAWRENCE.

Ordered citation issued against David ROWARK for Extortion on Widow SUMMERS and others in execution of his office as Collector for his appearance to answer charges.

Ordered Dedimus Potestatum issued to Guilford County take reliquishment of Dower of John WALKERS wife to land conveyed by said WALKER to Matthew MOORE, Esq.

11 August 1779

Present: Charles McANALLY, Richard GOODE, Micajah CLARK, Esqrs.

Ordered Robert WILLIS, Esq. to receive tax in Capt. James SHEPPERDS District and Wm. HALL, Esq. in Smallwoods District and notify inhabitants to give in taxable property to Elijah SMALLWOOD and Richard MURPHEY.

15

Inventory Estate, David MARTIN, deceased, returned by Admr. Ordered sale postponed.

Ordered appraisement Estate, John GRIFFITH, deceased, returned by Wm. HALL, Elijah SMALLWOOD and James MATTHEWS be recorded.

James McKOIN, Admr. of James McKOIN, deceased, returned account of Estate.

Deed from Thomas JOHNSON to William JOHNSON.

Ordered following serve as Jurors next Superior Court in Salisbury for District 15 September next: Augustine BLACKBURN, Moses BAKER, Moses MARTIN and Abraham WINSCOTT.

Jonathan OSBORN vs William ROBERSON; Slander. Jury: Thomas BRIGGS, Hezekiah WRIGHT, Arthur DENTON, Solomon COKER, Henry HAND, Adam WOOLF, Frederick GREEN, Wyatt GARNER, David ROWARK, David OWEN, Josiah BROWN, John WILLIAMS.

Charles CATES vs William LAKEY; Slander; same jury.

David GORDON vs Sampson BRASWELL; Slander; same jury.

Peter BOWMAN vs John WELLS; same jury.

Jeremiah HARRISON vs Lewis CONNER; Debt; same jury.

Joseph HUGHES vs John HARDY, Adnirum ALLEN and Nicholas COOK; S/F. Jury do not find that the principal was dead before the S.F. was issued.

Alexander DOBSON vs Wm. McAFFEE; Debt; same jury.

The State vs Charles SNEED; Assault and Battery; same jury.

Matthew WARNOCK vs Wm. COCKER; same jury.

Ordered following attend next County Court as Jurors: Matthew WARNOCK, Roger TURNER, John ROBINSON (on Dan River), Leander HUGHES, Daniel CHANDLER, William WOOLDRIGE, Phil. WILSON, John RIDINS, Robert HARRIS, Robert AYERS, Richard COX, Olive ROBERTS, Abial COB, Elisha PEARCE, Richard NUNN, Elisha ROWARK, James TILLEY, Senr., Eddy HICKMAN, Senr., Abraham CRESON, James GAINS, Thomas HOWELL, James SANDERS, John WRIGHT, Robert HAZELET, Noble LAD, Senr., Jacob GLOOM (Blum), Peter HOUZAR, Martin HOUZAR, Joseph STEWART, Gideon WRIGHT.

12 August 1779

Present: Martin ARMSTRONG, Richard GOODE, Joseph WINSTON, Esqrs.

John HUDSPETH, Esqr., Sheriff, objects to sufficiency of Jail.

Ordered James GLEN be excused on paying single tax for 1779.

Ordered Clerk issue a HUE & CRY against Barnabas BAXTER who broke jail on night 11th Instant siting forth facts he was committed for.

Ordered citation issue against Mary NOWLIN to produce her three children: James, Sarah, and Susan, to show cause why they not be bound out.

On petition of Robert LANIER and sundry inhabitants. Ordered said LANIER have leave build Grist Mill on Dills Creek below Corneluis "old plantation on his own land."

On motion Colo. MARTIN; Joseph CLOUD, Deputy Surveyor, hath run out certain entry made by John DEATHERIDGE with entry taker contrary to location, whereby, Richard COX is much injured by survey. Ordered Surveyor forbear to return works of said survey until allegation farther inquired into.

John WELLS vs Andrew, Thomas and John FITZPATRICK. Jury: Richard CHILDRESS, David ROWARK, Leonard BRADLEY, Zacariah MARTIN, John WILLIAMS, Gideon BROWN, Ambrouse BLACKBURN, Benjamin FARMER, Wm. DAVID, Abraham CRESON, James Hampton.

The State vs James JOHNSON; Larceny; same jury; find not guilty.

Ordered David ROWARK appointed overseer, road in room Joshua COX.

Ordered jury view road leads from Richmond to Allens Iron Works and to cross Yadkin at White Rock; thence into road that leads from Richmond near Deep Creek, made return find it advantagus and following appointed overseers: Richard HORN from Iron Works Road to Yadkin River; Thomas JOHNSON from River to Riggs old road; Robert AYERS from Riggs road to Murpheys ford; Moses BAKER from Murpheys ford to Deep Creek.

Ordered hands of Moses MARTIN, Junr., James MARTIN, Moses MARTIN, Senr., William CLAYTON, Benjamin YOUNG, Absalom BOSTICK, Marble STONE, Terry BRADLEY, Samuel WARNOCK, James WHITE, Moses HAZLET, John DANIEL, Joseph MARTIN and Wm. WALKER work under Robert WARNOCK, overseer, from Dan River to Moses MARTINA.

Jury appointed view road from Major WINSTONS to Court House make report: turn out of old road just above BYNUMS; thence between Michael and Henry FRYS into old road below Abraham MARTINS; thence along old road to Henry HENDRICKS; thence turn off and run near Leonard MOUSERS; thence to Richmond following overseers keep same in repair: Thomas BRIGGS from Richmond to Leonard MOUSERS; Henry FRY from MOUSERS to Neatman Creek; John BLACKBURN from Neatman to Moses MARTINS.

Jury appointed view road from Phil CULLELEASURES to the Court House report as follows: begin at CULELEASURES; thence to run between the Plantation of William THORNTON and Frederick MILLER; thence to right of Matt Brooks crossing Stewarts Mill Creek between House of Joseph STEWART and his field on said Creek; thence to right Richard THOMERSONS, Jo. PHILIPS and widow PHILIPS; thence along ridge road to William SHEPPERDS; thence up river bank to Yellow Bank ford; thence on ridge to Court House Street and following be overseers: Philip COLELEASURE from his house to branch running through Major PHILIPS field; Richard THOMURSON from said branch to Court House.

Ordered claims to be paid as follows: John McANALLY, 2 catt scalps, 10 shilling; Joseph REED, Wm. Nichols COOK, Jesse McANALLY, constables, 8 pounds each; John WAGNOR, 1 wolf scalp, 1 pound; Robert WALKER, Junr., 4 days as Assessor, 4 pounds; Samuel STROOP, warning District, 8 pounds; Ambrous BLACKBURN, 4 woolf scalps, 4 pounds; Hardy RIDDICK, 1 woolf and 1 catt scalp, 1 pound, 5 shillings; Ezekial YOUNG, 2 Catt scalps, 10 shillings; John HALBERT, Assessor, 5 days, 25 pounds; William WALKER, Assessor, 5 days, 25 pounds; John SCHAUB, Assessor, 20 pounds; William SHEPPERD, 2 years as Sheriff, 140 pounds; Richard GOODE, 1 year as Sheriff, 150 pounds; Joseph WILLIAMS, as Clerk last year, 250 pounds; Joseph WILLIAMS, for blank books for Courts, use 8 pounds; James HAMPTON, as Juror September Court, 2 pounds, 7 shillings, 8 pence; John Thos. LONGINO, warning district, 8 pounds; Abial COBB, Assessor, 6 days, 30 pounds; Jabez JARVIS, Assessor, 6 days, 30 pounds.

Ordered Sheriff collect 3 shillings, 6 pence from each person for every 100 pounds they are assessed in order to defray Continges of County 1779.

2nd Monday 8th November 1779
Richmond Court House

Present: Matthew MOORE, Wm. MEREDITH, Robert WALKER, Esqrs.

Deed from John CHADWELL and Bathunia, his wife to Absalom BOSTICK 174 acres; oath Elizabeth BOSTICK.

Ordered Noble LADD, Senr. be excused attending as Juror this term.

Ordered John FLEMING overseer, road in room Charles WORD.

Ordered Reubin GEORGE overseer, road in room John ROGERS.

Ordered following view road from David MORROWS to Salem Town: Thomas ELMORE, Seth COFFIN, Wm. DOBSON, George HOLBROOK, John HANNAH, John CUMMINS, Robert JOHNSTON, John TEAGUE, Jonathan HARREL, William WALKER, Robert WALKER, Joseph PATTERSON, Trustum BARNARD, Joseph THORNBERRY, Barnabas FARE, Richard LINVIL.

9 November 1779

Present: William MEREDITH, Richard GOODE, Matthew MOORE, Benjamin WATSON, Esqrs.

Deed from Nathaniel McCARROL to George CARTER (very dim film); oath James COFFEE.

Power of Attorney from Leven COOPER to Henry SPEER; oath Wyatt GARNER.

Ordered Letters of Administration granted Sarah CARMICHAEL, widow and relict of William CARMICHAEL, deceased, and entered into bond with Richard GOODE, Absalom BOSTICK, securities.

Inventory, Estate, Wm. CARMICHAEL, deceased, returned by said Sarah, Admrx.

Ordered Patrick LOGAN be excused from fourfold tax and pay only single tax.

Ordered Grimes HOLCOMB be excused from fourfold tax and pay only single tax.

Ordered Stephen JEAN, overseer, road in room Thomas DUNNIGAN.

Ordered Henry BURCH, overseer, road in room John DENNY.

Ordered Sheriff sell Hogshead tobacco attached by John COOLEY at suit John BRADLEY vs John CHADWELL.

10 November 1779

Present: Richard GOODE, William MEREDITH, Richard VARNAL, Benjamin WATSON, Esqrs.

William MEREDITH, Esq., appointed County Trustee for ensuing year; Charles McANALLY and Richard GOODE, securities.

William DONALD got acquitted of an accusation laid against him by Colo. William PRESTON of Virginia.

Ordered Matthew BROOKS guardian of Matthew PRICE in room Samuel KERBY; securities: Gideon WRIGHT, John HUDSPETH, Nathanial WILLIAMS.

Thomas SMITH, Richard GOODE, Richard VARNEL, Esqrs. appointed committee examine list taxables and settle with county trustee.

Ordered William McFEE be cleared from paying tax; he being object of pitty and no person to work for him.

Ordered John CARTER overseer, road in room David Martin, deceased.

Ordered Zachariah MARTIN overseer, road from Yellow Banks ford leading to Shallowford in room Wm. HEAD.

Ordered following view road from waggon road that leads from

18

Richmond up Yadkin River where Thomas BIARD (?) lives or near there; thence to Settlement of Toms Creek; thence to Dan River at Widow LANKFORDS; thence to Virginia line: David ROWARK, John Cunningham (?), Richard COX, James GIBSON, George DEATHERAGE, William BARBAGH (?), William VARNAL, David CLARK, Garrel GIBSON, Henry BURCH, William RAMSEY, James HOOPER, Benjamin DENNY, Elisha PEARIS, James MARTIN, Abraham COOLEY.

Ordered Michael RUNNELS, overseer, road in room John DENNY.

Ordered Matthew BROOKS, overseer, road leads from Richmond to Phillip CULDEUSURES from his own house to Joseph PHILLIPS branch.

11 November 1779

Present: Richard GOODE, Richard VARNAL, Benjamin WATSON.

Ordered James SHEPPERD pay only single tax 1779.

John HARPER, a young man being returned (supposed to be a vagrant) to Maj. John ARMSTRONG as a Continental Soldier, but said HARPER brought properly before Court. Ordered released and Maj. ARMSTRONG discharge him from Regiment.

Ordered Matthew BASS, constable in Wm. SHEPPERDS District.

Deed of Gift from Thomas COKER to Ann COKER acknowledged.

Ordered Robert WALKER, Esq., overseer all streets and public roads within half mile of Court House.

Ordered following view road from Richmond to Poindexters Ferry; thence into road leads to Shallowford near Zachariah MARTINS: John SNEAD, Godfrey MILLER, Samuel CUMMINS, James SHORT, Job MARTIN, Valentine MARTIN, Zachariah MARTIN, Wm. HEAD, Thomas FLOYD, Auther SCOTT, James BADGETT, William SHEPPERD, Gideon WRIGHT, Malcum CURRY, Matthew BASS.

Ordered citation issue against Jurors did not appear, except those that got excused.

Ordered the Gun taken from Phillip ROBERTS be delivered to John HUDSPETH, Sheriff, to keep "her" until further orders.

15 February 1780
Richmond

Present: Robert WALKER, Richard VARNAL, George HOWZAR, Michael HOWZAR, William SHEPPERD, Esqrs.

Deed from William SHEPPERD and Elizabeth, his wife, to Robert WALKER: oath said SHEPPERD.

Deed from Augustine BLACKBURN to John APPLETON; oath said BLACKBURN.

Ordered people called Moravians, Quakers, Mononist and Dunkards pay only single County Tax 1779.

Ordered Anthony DEARING have leave to build Water Grist Mill on South fork of Beaver Island Creek and be deemed publick mill.

Thomas TINSLEY has leave build water Grist Mill at Great Falls of Beaver Island Creek which will be deemed publick mill.

Spruce McCAY, Esq. appointed States Attorney Protempore.

David NOWLIN appointed Constable in room Matthew MOSS.

William MEREDITH, Richard VARNAL, William SHEPPERD, Esqrs. appointed committee to re-examine property, etc. 1779.

19

Last Will and Testament. Robert COOK, deceased, oath Hardy RID-
DICK and Thomas COLLINS; Ambrouse BLACKBOURN and Thomas EVANS,
Execrs. qualified.

Admr. Estate, Martin ROMINGER, deceased, granted Elizabeth ROMIN-
GER and Henry SPOONHOUR; Henry SHORE and Michael HOUZAR, Junr.,
securities. Letters of Administration issued accordingly.

Ordered Joseph GARRISON, Henry HAMPTON, James HAMPTON, Robert
HARRIS, John ROBERSON, William BOSTICK, John CUMMINS, Robert
HAZLET, Geo. LASH, Thomas HOWELL to be fined 50 pounds for fail-
ing to appear as Jurors.

Samuel WRIGHT who failed to appear as Juror last term, ordered
to pay costs.

16 February 1780

Present: Richard GOODE, William DOBSON, Richard VARNAL, William
SHEPPERD, Esqrs.

Grand Jury: Ambrouse BLACKBOURN, Matthew WARNOCK, Richard LIN-
VELL, David MORROW, Peter HAUZAR, Leander HUGHES, Daniel CHANDLER,
James SANDERS, John WRIGHT, Job MARTIN, Hezekiah WRIGHT, Fredrick
COX, James FREEMAN, John MERRIL.

Matthew WARNOCK and Daniel CHANDLER failed to appear as Jurors
last term are fined.

Account, Sale Estate, William CARMICHAEL, deceased, returned by
Admr.

Last Will and Testament. Nathaniel McCARROL, deceased; oath
William HILL; Letters of Administration to Isbell McCARREL, widow
and relict of deceased with Joseph WINSTON and James CHARLES,
securities.

Inventory, Estate, Martin ROMINGER, deceased, returned by Admr.

Mark HARDIN, overseer, road in room Amos LADD.

Ordered John SHELTON, overseer, road in room Reubin DOBSON.

Deed from Moses MARTIN to Wm. CLAYTON, 150 acres; oath Wm. HILL.

Deed from Moses MARTIN to John MARTIN; oath Wm. HILL.

Ordered Joseph REAVIS, being charged of begitting a bastard mail
child on body Mary GALLION by her own oath before William HEAD,
Esq., stands chargable with maintenance of same; James REAVIS
and John WILLIAMS, securities.

17 February 1780

Present: Charles McANALLY, Thomas JOHNSON, George HAUZAR, Esqrs.

Deed from Spencer BALL to William DANIEL.

Bill of Sale from Thomas PETTIT to John SNEED; oath said PETTIT.

Ordered following attend next Superior Court in Salisbury for
District, Salisbury 15th March next: William SHEPHERD, Jacob
STONE, Robt. HARRIS, Henry HERBST (?).

Ordered Samuel DYAR have leave to build water Grist Mill on Little
Fishes River below Henry NORMANS; deemed a publick mill.

Sarah CARMICHAEL, widow and relict of William CARMICHAEL, deceased,
and claimed her Right of Dower of all deeded and entered lands
which he died possessed of.

Ordered Absalom BOSTICK, Mark HARDIN and Charles McANALLY chosen by said Sarah and Joseph CARMICHAEL, be empowered to lay off said Dower.

State vs John QUINN; Petty Larceney; Jury: William RIDGE, David BURK, John GILBERT, Henry SPEER, Thomas PETTIT, Robert TATE, Thomas BRIGGS, Zachariah MARTIN, Thomas FLOYD, Christopher STENTON, Matthew BASS, John WAGNOR.

Matthew BROOKS, Joseph PHILLIPS, Richard VARNAL appointed commissioners dispose confiscated property.

Ordered following appointed to serve as Jurors next Court: Adam THOMPSON, John QUINN, George HAUZAR, Henry SMITH, John BINKLEY, Aaron LISBY, Lazaros TILLEY, Joshua COX, Jack HUMPHRIS, Edward MOORE, David REAVIS, John ENGLAND, Robert AYERS, Joseph PHILLIPS, Henry SHORE, James HOWELL, Thomas HOWELL, Reuben GEORGE, Jesse GEORGE, Charles HOLDER, Joseph BURK, Peter ROTHROCK, Philip GREEN, Jesse COUNCIL, John GILES, Henry SPEER, David LINVILL, Andrew HANNAH, James GAMBLE.

18 February 1780

Present: Joseph WINSTON, Robert WALKER, William DOBSON, Richard VARNAL, William SHEPPERD, Esqrs.

Charles McANALLY, Esq. Corner, resigned his office; Robert WALKER Esqr. appointed Corner with Robert LANIER and Joseph WINSTON, securities.

Ordered County Trustee pay 25 dollars a day to all Expresses sent within County and producing certificate from Commanding Officer of his performance of Service, etc.

Henry BARTON, overseer, road in room William VENABLE.

Ordered Benjamin ALLIN overseer road in room John CARTER.

Ordered John SANDERS overseer road from John Allins Mill to Mulberry Field road.

Ordered following appointed to view road from David MORROWS to Salem Town: William WALKER, Richard IINVILLE, John HANNAH, John LOVE, William LOVE, George HOLBROOK, William DOBSON, Jonathan HARROLD, Hugh McKILLIP, John KIMMON, Abraham POWELL, William BEASON, John TEAGUE, Seth COFFIN, Trustum BARNARD.

Ordered John HORN, Junr. charged with Bastard mail child on body May WALKER by her own oath before William DOBSON and Benjamin WATSON, Esqr. be chargable for its maintenance.

By oaths of Henry SPOONHOUR, Michael HOWZAR and Joseph WINSTON; William BOWLES stands charged through mistake with 609 pounds too much assessment on his Estate; Ordered tax not be collected. Signed by: Jo. WILLIAMS, Clerk, Robert LANIER, Jo. WINSTON and Richard VARNAL.

8 May 1880
Richmond

Present: Robert WALKER, Esq.

9 May 1780

Present: Joseph WINSTON, William MEREDITH, George HAUZAR, Esqrs.

Gray BYNUM has leave build water Grist Mill on Big Neatman Creek on his own land; deemed publick Mill.

Inventory, Estate, Robert COOK, deceased, returned by Execrs.

Administrator of Estate, Matthew SANDERS, deceased, granted Matthew SANDERS, eldest son of deceased; Matt BROOKS, security. Admr. qualified according to law.

Grand Jury: Robert AYRES, foreman; John GILES, Philip WILSON, Aron LISBY, Lazarus TILLEY, Joshua COX, John HUMPHRIES, Edward MOORE, Joseph PHILLIPS, Henry SHORE, James HOWELL, Thomas HOWELL, Reuben GEORGE, Joseph BURKE.

Robert HAZLET cited to shew why failed to appear two last terms Court as Juror.

Ordered Edwin HICKMAN be cited show cause why he failed to attend as Juror.

Thomas HOWELL cited appear for not attending court as Juror.

John McCAY, servant boy of Robert WALKER, brought before Court and complained his master had used him with too much severity which fact WALKER acknowledged.

Ordered in future WALKER shall find John McCAY during his servitude good, wholesome diat, clothing, washing and lodging and give him unreasonable correction at no time.

Thomas GALLION summoned as Garnishee declares what property he has belonging to Valentine SLIDER, he has 30 dollars and no more.

James GLEN; same; has 20 shillings Old Proclamation Money and no more.

Abraham CRESON; same; has 20 shillings and no more.

Deed from Robert DOAK to John ROBERTS; oath James MATTHEWS.

Deed from John LYNCH to Robert LANIER, 170 acres; oath said LYNCH.

Ordered Gabriel SCOTT, a Free Mulatto Boy, bound Wm. Terrel LEWIS.

Ordered Younger BLACKBURN overseer road in room Ambrous BLACKBOURN.

Ordered Robert LANIER overseer road in room William WALLACE.

Ordered Zachariah MARTIN overseer road in room William HEAD.

Ordered Spencer BREEDING overseer Iron Works Road from Double Creek to Fishes River road.

Ordered Alexander MOORE overseer road from Town fork to Quaker road.

10 May 1780

Present: Joseph WINSTON, George HAUZAR, Richard VARNAL, Esqrs.

John B. COLVARD appointed Constable Mosbys District.

Michael HOWZAR, Junr. appointed Constable in room Samuel STROOP, resigned.

Ordered Adam THOMPSON, John QUINN, David REAVIS, John ENGLAND, Charles HOLDER, Jesse COUNCIL be fined 50 pounds for not appearing as Jurors.

Matthew MOORE, Esq. unanimously elected Sheriff.

Ordered Clerk be empowered to employ Express to carry orders to several Justices, etc.

William CRAUSS overseer road in room Casper FISHER.

Ordered John DYER overseer road in room Henry Parish.

Ordered Wm. FREEMAN overseer road in room John HORN.

Ordered Mark HARDIN, Absalom BOSTICK, Joshua TILLEY, Terry BRADLEY, Joseph CARMICHAEL, John CARMICHAEL, Moses MARTIN, Robert WARNOCK, James MARTIN, Amos LADD, Moses HAZELETT, Morgan DAVIS, John MARTIN, Thomas EVANS (Mill Creek) view road from Guilford line crossing Dan River at Bosticks and into old Moravian road below Moses MARTINS; also old road from Guilford line crossing Carmichaels ford.

Court to lay off Districts, appointed Justices and Constables and Assessors as follows: Capt. WOOLDRIGES: John Ellsberry, John WILLIAMS, John Wright; Capt. MOSBEYS: Thomas JOHNSON, John B. COLVARD, Samuel MOSBY, Junr.; Capt. Henry SMITHS: Frederick MILLER, Michael HOUZAR, Junr., Matthew BROOKS; Capt. SCOTTS: William HEAD, John Thomas LONGINO, John MARTIN; Capt. GIDDIONS: Micajah CLARKE, James JASON, Hugh ARMSTRONG; Capt. HALBERTS: Joseph WINSTON, John COOLEY, Ambrous BLACKBOURN; Capt. FREEMANS: Samuel FREEMAN, John MOORE, Jabez JARVIS; Capt. CLOUD: Micajah CLARK, David GRAVES, Reubin DODSON; Capt. William BOSTICKS: Wm. DOBSON, John Jacob SCOTT, Henry HAMPTON; Capt. Absalom BOSTICKS: Charles McANALLY, Jesse McANNALLY, Joshua TILLEY; Capt. MEREDITHS: William MEREDITH, Joseph REID, John CHILDRESS; Capt. MARTINS: William COOK, Wm. Nichols COOK, Wm. Terrel LEWIS; Capt. SHERPHEDS: Robert WILLIS, William BURCH, Benjamin BURCH; Capt. HORNS: Robert WALKER, Roger GIDDINS, Malcum CURRY.

Ordered following Jurors serve August Term next: Roger TURNER, John COE, Robert FORBIS, Samuel ARNOLD, John CRANE, John ALLEN, Richard HORN, John HANKINS, Joseph GARRISON, Henry HAMPTON, Absalom BOSTICK, John WAGNON, Joseph BANNER, William CAMBELL, James GAMBALL, Andrew HANNAH, George HOLBROOK, William HICKMAN, Thomas CARROLL, Colo. James MARTIN, James MARTIN (Ferry), David HUMPHRISS, Spencer BALL, William CARTER, Robert HARRIS, John FLEMINS, Charles HOLDER, David REAVIS, John ENGLAND, Jacob STONER. Signed by Jo. WILLIAMS, Clerk; Martin ARMSTRONG, Jo. WINSTON, Richard GOODE, William MEREDITH.

14 August 1780
Richmond

Present: Matthew MOORE, William SHEPPERD, Micajah CLARK, Esqrs.

Deed from James BRUCE and Mary, his wife to Wm. Hargus GRAY, 240 acres; oath Henry SPEER.

Deed from Samuel MOSBY and Herucia, his wife to Samuel MOSBY, Junr.; oath Nathaniel WILLIAMS.

15 August 1780

Present: Richard GOODE, Benjamin WATSON, George HAUZAR, Esqrs.

Last Will and Testament. Benjamin BOWLES, deceased, proved path William COOK and John BURCH; John BOWLS, one Execr. qualified.

Deed from Valentine FREY and Barbara, his wife to Jacob PETREE; oath Adam WOOLF.

Deed from William DANIEL to Macajah CLARKE; oath said DANIEL.

Power of Attorney from William BOSTICK to Littlebery BOSTICK acknowledged.

William COOK, Esq. qualified as Justice of Peace.

David CLARK appointed Constable in Richard VARNALS District.

Traugott BAGGE, Samuel CUMMINS, John HUDSPETH, Joseph WINSTON appointed Inspectors of Money; CUMMINS and HUDSPETH qualified.

William HALL, William COOK, Benjamin WATSON, Esqrs. appointed committee of claims; also lay county tax.

Henry KERBY overseer road in room William BOYLES.

Wyatt GARNER summond last court as Garnishee at suit Thomas PHELPS vs Valentine SLIDER, being sworn, declares to have 30 shillings old Proclamation money and one bushel corn in his hands and no more; Matthias STEELMAN declares he has one dollar and no more.

Charles HOLDER cited to show cause why failed to attend as Juror.

Burwell BREWER bound 3,000 pounds appear as an evidence at Salisbury Superior Court next to give testimony against Elophalet JARVIS.

Ordered Gray BYNUM, Fredrick MILLER, James GLENN and Robert HARRIS appointed Jurors to serve next Superior Court held at Salisbury.

Ordered following appear to serve as Jurors next county court: Gideon WRIGHT, Jon MARTIN, Matthew BROOKS, Amrous BLACKBOURN, William JAMES, Richard LAWRENCE, James DOAK, Samuel MOSBY, Junr., Philip HOWARD, George LASH, Adam WOOLF, Henry SHORES, James GAMBELL, John HANNAH, Andrew SPEER, William RUTLEDGE, Thomas CLANTON, William FREEMAN, James BADGET, Reubin SHORE, John BURCH, Abial COBB, Richard MURPHEY, Reubin DODSON, Richard COX, William HICKMAN, William SHELTON, Almon GUINN, Matthew WARNOCK, Malcum CURRY.

16 August 1780

Present: Matthew MOORE, Richard GOODE, Benjamin WATSON, Esqrs.

James QUILLIN and Joseph POWELL took Oath of Allegiance to State.

An application of James GLEN for a pass for his Wife to pass and repass to Broad River in Cambdon to see her Brother.

Ordered road whereon Thomas LOYD is overseer be turned by said LOYDS Plantation as now stands marked for better comuniencey of crossing Grassey Creek.

Ordered Robert WALKER, Junr. overseer road in room Abraham POWELL.

Gabriel JONES appointed Constable in room Jacob John SCOTT, resigned.

James CRESON appointed Constable in room James GIDDINS.

Children of Samuel FRANCIS likely to suffer for want proper care; Ordered James COFFEE, Constable, deliver them to John HORN to care for until next Court.

Ordered Major Richard GOOD appointed to take in list of taxables HOLBROOKS District in place Major WINSTON who is in the Service.

Ordered William COOK, Esq. in MARTINS District in place Robert LANIER now in Camp.

Ordered Charles McANALLY, Esq. in MEREDETHS District in place Capt. MEREDITH now in Service.

Matthew BROOKS and Joseph PHILLIPS two commissioners of confiscated property having made a Tender of their proceedings in office, etc.

Admr. Estate, William HOLT, deceased, granted Francis HOLT; Reubin DODSON and Jo. CLOUD, securities; Admr. qualified.

Matthew MOORE, Esq. produced commission from Governor appointed him Sheriff of Surry; William SHEPPERD, Samuel CUMMINS, William COOK, Benjamin WILSON, securities; Said MOORE qualified.

Matthew MOORE, Esq. present Sheriff, objects to suffcency of Jail.

Henry SNOW and William BREEDING, being charged with High Treason, Ordered sent Salisbury Superior Court for Tryal.

Whorton NUNN bound in recognization 50,000 pounds to appear at Salisbury Superior Court next; John PATRICK and John MOORE, securities for NUNN.

Ordered County Tax for year 1780 be 5/ on every 100 pounds.

Court Appointed Collectors for year 1780 as follows: WOOLDRIDGES District: Gibson WOOLDRIDGE; MOSBYS; John COLVARD; SMITHS: Matthew BROOKS; SCOTTS: John Thomas LONGINO; SMALLWOODS: Hugh ARMSTRONG; HALBERTS: John COOLEY; FREEMANS: John PARTICK; CLOUDS: Matthew MOORE, Wm. BOSTICKS: Augustine BLACKBOURN; Absalom BOSTICKS: John MORGAN; MEREDETHS: William MEREDITH; MARTINS: William Nichols COOK; SHEPPERDS: Benjamin BURCH; HORNS: Edward LINVILL.

Ordered following sums be allowed persons herein mentioned: John Jacob SCOTT, warning DOBSONS District, 3 years, 100 pounds; Roger GIDDINS warning SHERPHERDS District, 2 years, 66 pounds, 13 shillings, 4 pence; John HUDSPETH, Sheriff for extra services, 1 year, 1,000 pounds; Reubin MATTHEWS for 7 days attending Jail and Prisoners, 70 pounds; James DOAK, Assessor 2 years, 100 pounds; Matt. BASS taking prisoner from County to Virginia, 168 pounds; Matthew BASS warning District 33 pounds, 6 shillings, 8 pence; Stephen CROUDER carrying prisoner to Salisbury Jail and expenses 21 pounds, 16 shillings; Eli SCURRY, riding Express 2 days, 40 pounds; John Thomas LONGINO, riding Express 6 days and warning in SCOTTS District, 153 pounds, 6 shillings; Reubin MATTHEWS carring prisoners Salisbury, 100 pounds; Samuel McGRAW, riding Express 4 days to Virginia for Capt. GIDDINS, 80 pounds; Joseph WILLIAMS, Clerk, extra service 1 year, 1,200 pounds; Samuel CUMMINS for his Services for 5 years, 100 pounds. Signed by: Jo. WILLIAMS, Clerk; John HUDSPETH, Richard VARNAL and William COOK.

13 November 1780
Richmond

Present: Robert LANIER, Robert WALKER, Esqrs.

14 November 1780

Present: Martin ARMSTRONG, Robert LANIER, Robert WALKER, William SHEPPERD, Esqrs.

Power of Attorney from Wm. HALL to James DOAK; oath Thomas BALLARD.

Last Will and Testament; Charles WORK proved; oath James DOAK.

Last Will and Testament; John HUDSPETH, deceased, proved by parity of hands and other circumstances satisfactory to Court by Gibson WOOLDRIDGE; Ordered said WOOLDRIDGE qualified as Execr.

Last Will and Testament; Richard VARNEL, deceased, proved by Samuel HUMPHRIS; Robert COKER and Jesse BUMPS qualified as Execrs.

Malcom CURRY, Assessor in room Gideon WRIGHT in HORNS District.

Ordered Thomas SMITH, Esq. appointed, take list taxable property SCOTTS District in room William HEAD.

John UNDERHILL who formerly was security for Robert LYON and wife, Susannah, produced them to Court and he was released from his Recognizance. Said LYON and wife admitted to bail, in case can find it, till next court.

15 November 1780

Present: Robert LANIER, Richard GOODE, William COOK, Robert WALKER, William SHEPPERD, Esqrs.

Ordered Matthew BROOKS, Esqr. appointed commissioner in County to receive Specific Tax; Robert LANIER and William SHEPPERD, securities; 10,000 Spanish Milled Dollars.

Ordered Benjamin WATSON, Esq. appointed finish taking tax in HOLBROOKS District in place Major GOODS.

Ordered Joseph PHILLIPS, together with any other two commissioners, appointed see a building and finishing Court House and Jail in Surry County; Agreed with Godfrey MILLER to finish Jail immediately and borow money on faith of the County to defray expenses of same.

Francis HOLT, overseer, road in room John SHELTON.

Ordered following appointed Jurors to serve next court: Job MARTIN, Ambrous BLACKBURN, William JAMES, Richard LAWRENCE, Samuel MOSBY, Junr., Phil HOWARD, George LASH, James GAMBELL, John HANNAH, Andrew SPEER, Thomas CLANTON, William FREEMAN, James BADGET, Reubin SHORES, John BURCH, Abial COBB, Reubin DODSON, Richard COX, William HICKMAN, William SHELTON, Almond GUINN, Matthew WARNOCK, John SMITH, Robert FORBIS, Thomas WOODROUGH, Benjamin JOHNSON, and James SHEPPERD.

14 May 1781
Richmond

Present: Richard GOODE, Michael HOUSER, George HOUSAR, Esqrs.

Matthew MOORE, Esqr. chosen Sheriff unanimous consent whole Court.

Last Will and Testament. John HOLCOMB, deceased; oath Simon HADLEY and Thomas HADLEY, Junr.

Last Will and Testament. William SMITH, deceased; oath Matthew BROOKS and Basil RIDDLE.

Administrator of Estate, Thomas BOLES, deceased, granted Re(blurred) BOLES, wife deceased; William COOK and John BURK, securities; 100,000 pounds.

Inventory Estate, John HUDSPETH, deceased, by Airs HUDSPETH, Execr. Ordered Execr. of John HUDSPETH, deceased, have leave to employ person finish collection for 1779. Airs HUDSPETH, Exerc. took oath required by law.

Elizabeth GARRISON, widow and relict, Isaac GARRISON, deceased, relinquishes her right of Administrator. Ordered Letters of Administration issue to Benjamin WATSON; Auston BLACKBURN and Barnby FARE, securities.

Gabriel WAGGONER, Admr. John ROTHWELL, deceased, returned Inventory and Sale Estate.

Deed from John THOMPSON to Zachariah GR(blurred); oath Henry SPEER.

Deed from Jos. CARMICHAEL & Co. to John CARMICHAEL; oath Robt. WARNOCK.

Deed from Joseph CARMICHAEL to Robt. WARNOCK; oath Matthew WARNOCK.

Deed from George DEATHERIDGE to John DEATHERIDGE; oath James GAINES.

Deed from James ARMSTRONG to Hugh ARMSTRONG; oath James DOAK.

Deed from Jacob (film too blurred to read); oath Robert LANIER.

Deed from Robert LANIER to Thomas BALLARD; oath Robert LANIER.

26

Deed from Wm. BURRIS to George CARTER; oath Wm. BURRIS.

-- (blurred) Fratrum of United Brethren dated 12 November 1754, 1,000 acres lying on Gargales or Muddy Creek proved open Court by party of --(blurred).

Deed from Wm. HALL by his Attorney (blurred) to Charles SMITH; oath James DOAK.

Ordered John LYNCH have leave build Water Grist Mill and Saw Mill on Stewarts Creek on his own land.

Ordered George DEATHERIDGE has leave build Water Grist Mill on Great Creek of Dan; considered publick mill.

Ordered Grist Mill bought of Samuel VAUGHN by Isaac WRIGHT near Yellow Bank ford of Yadkin River be recorded as publick mill.

Mary RUTLEDGE of Capt. WOOLDRIDGE District, assessed fourfold; Ordered she pay only one fold tax.

Ordered that 700 pounds of total amount William THORNTON list for 1780 be taken off.

Ordered Martin ARMSTRONG, Robert LANIER, George HOUSER appointed committee examine list taxables.

David CLARKE appointed Collector in Hollow District in room Hugh ARMSTRONG resigned.

Ordered Collins HAMPTON appointed Constable in Hollow District; qualified.

Ordered Thomas BALDWIN appointed Constable Capt. MARTINS District in room Wm. N. COOK; also BALDWIN appointed collector of taxes; William Nichols COOK is removed.

John BUMPS, Hugh ARMSTRONG, William Terrel LEWIS, Esqrs. took oath Justice of Peace.

Ordered Dedimus Potestatum issue to Caswell County take deposition Absalom TATUM in case MOORE against ROWARK; notice given Deft.

Ordered following appointed Jurors next court: Job MARTIN, Malcum CURRY, William FREEMAN, James FREEMAN, John PATRICK, Nathaniel WOODROUGH, Olive ROBERTS, Reubin SHORES, James MATTHEWS, James DOAK, Robert HARRIS, George HUNTER, Frederick MILLER, James GAMBELL, Windle KRAUSE, Absalom BOSTICK, Matthew WARNOCK, Joseph CARMICHAEL, Mark HARDING, Joseph CLOUD, John SNEED, John DEATHER-IDGE; Aaron LISBY, Wiatt GARNER, Robert AYERS, John WILLIAMS (LG), Henry SPEER, John BLALOCK, Younger BLACKBURN, David MORROW.

(This page film very poor)
Richmond 9 day (blurred) third
year American Independence

Present: Richard VARNAL, Esqr. (since he is already deceased and from above year of Independence it is believed this blurred page on the film was perhaps in 1779; it is placed here because it is filmed here.)

Ordered ------ RICE (?) qualify as Deputy.

Spruce McCAY, Esqr. produced Licence from Samuel ASH and Samuel SPENCER, two Judges of Courts to Practice as an Attorney.

Last Will and Testament. Roger TURNER, deceased, proved oath Jacob SPEER. (Roger TURNER'S Inventory will be found recorded 9 February 1779 on abstract page 8.)

27

10th Tuesday (blurred)
Richmond

Present: John HUDSPETH, Richard VARNAL, William HALL, Esqr.

13 August 1781
Richmond

Present: Martin ARMSTRONG, Robert WALKER, Wm. MEREDITH, Esqrs.

Ordered that Matthew MOORE, Esq. Sheriff, be fined 3,000 pounds
Ni-Si for his non-attendance.

Admr. Estate, Frederick COX, deceased, granted Milly COX, wife
and relict said deceased; Reubin DODSON and Isaac JOYCE, securities.

14 August 1781

Present: Charles McANALLY, Martin ARMSTRONG, Benjamin WATSON,
Esqrs.

Deed from Charles FAIN to Joseph RAMEY; oath Henry SPEER.

Deed from William STEELMAN to Joseph WALKER; oath Matthias STEELMAN.

Deed from Mathias STEELMAN to Joseph WALKER; oath said MATHIAS.

Deed from John CHILDRESS to Samuel KERBY; oath Matt BROOKS.

Deed from Solomon NELSON to Elizabeth WARD.

Matthew MOORE, Esq. appeared by his Attorney that is out of his
power to give his attendance; fine of 3,000 pounds remitted to him.

Inventory Estate, James CHARLES, deceased, returned Oliver CHAR-
LES, Execr.

Depositions of David EVANS and James MARTIN respecting Nuncupetive
Will.

Estate, William CLAYTON recorded by consent Phil CLAYTON (blurred)
to said deceased; Administration granted Elizabeth CLAYTON, wife
and relict said deceased; Stephen and Philip CLAYTON, securities.

Last Will and Testament. Joseph MASTERS, deceased; oath Ephraim
McLIMORE and James SHAW; Ordered Letters Testament issue John
WRIGHT and Samuel ARNOLD who qualified.

Admr. Estate, Wm. RUTLEDGE, deceased, granted (blurred) RUTLEDGE,
wife and relict said deceased; James REAVIS and Ephraim McLIMOR,
securities. Inventory Estate returned by Admr.

Last Will and Testament. James SHEPPERD, deceased, proved oath
Thomas BARRON; Ordered Letters Testament granted Wm. and James
SHEPPERD, two of Execrs.

Being represented to Court that Roger and Elias TURNER, Execrs.
Last Will and Testament, Marmaduke KIMBROUGH, deceased, have removed and attached themselves to the Enemies of the U. S. by
taking up arms against same and not having discharged trust re-
posed in them by Testator, said Roger and Elias TURNER have for-
feited all right to said Executorship.

Ordered Admr. de Bonis be granted John ALLIN, husband of Mary,
late widow and relict of said Marmaduke KIMBROUGH; Samuel MOSBY
and Samuel MOSBY, Junr., securities.

Ordered Joseph WILLIAMS be appointed guardian to George KIMBROUGH,
Goldman KIMBROUGH, Ormon KIMBROUGH and Marduke KIMBROUGH, orphans
of Marmaduke KIMBROUGH, deceased, with Samuel MOSBY, Junr., and
Samuel MOSBY, Senr., securities.

Grand Jury: Absalom BOSTICK, foreman; Malcom CURY, John PATRICK, Reubin SHORE, James MATTHEWS, James DOAK, Windle CROUSE, Matthew WARNOCK, Joseph CARMICHAEL, Robert AYERS, John WILLIAMS, John BLALOCK, Ambrous BLACKBURN.

Letters of Administration, Estate, John HANN, deceased, granted Samuel MOSBY, Junr.; Joseph WILLIAMS and John ALLEN, securities.

Ordered Samuel MOSBY, Senr. appointed guardian to Susannah HANN and John HANN, orphans John HANN, deceased; John ALLIN and Joseph WILLIAMS, securities.

James REES, Esq., Attorney, admitted to practice law in Surry Co.

William UNDERWOOD, Gibson WOOLDRIDGE, Henry SPEER, Esqrs. qualified as Justices of Peace.

15 August 1781

Present: Richard GOODE, William MEREDITH, William DOBSON, Jesse BUMPS, Esqrs.

Deed from William WOOLDRIDGE and Martha, his wife, to Wm. Hargus GRAY; oath Henry SPEER.

Deed from Joseph WALKER to Andrew RUDOLPH; oath Henry SPEER.

Deed from John LEINBACK and Catharine, his wife, to Orphans of Jacob DEITZ, deceased; oath Henry SHORE.

Power of Attorney from Mary NOWLIN to James COFFEE; oath Thomas EVANS.

Deed from John LYNCH to David STEWART; oath said LYNCH.

Power of Attorney from Robert HARRISON to Matt BROOKS; oath Agnus PRICE.

Deed from Robert HARRISON by his attorney Matt BROOKS to Samuel KERBY; oath said Matthew BROOKS.

Ordered Thomas POINDEXTER, Anthony DEARING, Gray BYNUM and Frederick MILLER, Esqrs. appointed Juriors to serve next Superior Court at Salisbury for District Salisbury 15th September next.

Ordered following attend next court as Jurors: Lewis ELLIOTT, Isaac ELLSBURY, John SNEED, John DEATHERAGE, Charles DUDLEY, Thomas DUNNIGIN, William HICKMAN, William WEBB, John BRANSON, John CARMICHAEL, William BOSTICK, Senr., John HUTCHINS, Robert FORBIS, James HOWELL, Lemuel HARVEY, John HORN, William BURCH, Adam MITCHELL, Joel HALBERT, Adam SHOEMAKER, John BINKLEY, John MICKEY, Samuel HUMPHRIS, Joel GURLEY, Abial COBB, John PIPES, Junr., Levy PRUIT, Samuel RIGGS, Benjamin BURCK, Younger BLACKBURN.

Appraisement Estate, Warren WALKER, deceased, returned John MORGAN and Joshua TILLERY (Tilley).

Sarah CARMICHAEL, Admr. Estate, Wm. CARMICHAEL, deceased, exhibited current vouchers against said Estate.

Inventory Estate, Thomas BOWLS, deceased, returned by Admrx.

Licence granted Jacob BLUME to keep Tavern at his now Dwelling house in Bethabra; Joseph WILLIAMS and Alex. MARTIN, securities.

Licence granted Jacob MYARS to keep Tavern at his now dwelling House in Salem; Alex. MARTIN and Joseph WILLIAMS, securities.

Lewis WOOLF appointed Constable in room Michael HOWZAR, Junr., resigned.

Salathia MARTIN, Esq. qualified as Justice of Peace.

Ordered William MEREDITH, William T. LEWIS, Henry SPEER, Esqrs. committee of Claims to lay County Tax for 1781; also settle with Wm. SHEPPERD, Esqr., a former Sheriff.

Henry SPEER vs Robert SPEER. Jury: James SHEPPERD, Reubin DODSON, Charles DUDLEY, Joel LEWIS, Jonathan CLARKE, Airs HUDSPETH, Wm. FREEMAN, Phil HOLCOMB, John MARTIN, George HOLCOMB, Wyatt GARNER and Henry SHORE.

Henry AIRS vs Robert SPEER; same jury.

John MEREDETH has leave build water Grist Mill on Crooked Creek on his own land near Virginia line; deemed Publick Mill.

Ordered Robert WILLIS, Esq., overseer, road from the line to fork.

Ordered Rowland CORNELIUS, overseer, road from Thomas DAVIS to lower ford on Fishes River.

Ordered Christopher ISSBELL, overseer, road from ford on Fishes River to fork where Bakers old Hunting tract leaves road.

Ordered Richard MORRIS, overseer, road from Bakers old Hunting tract to Yadkin Road.

Ordered Younger BLACKBURN, overseer, road in room Ambrous BLACK-BURN.

Ordered Benjamin PARKS, William COOK, Junr., William McBRIDE, Olive ROBERTS, Wm. Nichols COOK, John PIPES, Junr., John HURT, Abraham DOWNEY, Zeanos BALDWIN, William COCKRAM, Humphrey COCKRAM, Michael BACIN, Gilbert KEEN, Nathaniel MORRIS, view road from near William HANKINS to new Meeting House near Michael BACONS.

Ordered Reubin DODSON, overseer, road from fork road at Head of Buffaloe to Wm. NELSONS.

Ordered Lazarous TILLEY, overseer, road from Wm. NELSONS to Finleys ford.

Ordered Thomas ALLEN, overseer, road from Allins Mill to fork road near Capt. COBBS.

Court proceeded to lay off Districts, appointed Justices take list of Taxables, Constables to warn Inhabitants and Assessors to assess taxable property in each District: Capt. MOSBYS: Henry SPEER, John COLVARD, Samuel MOSBY; Capt. AYRES: Thomas SMITH, John Thomas LONGINO, Robert AYRES; Capt. WOOLDRIDGES: Gibson WOOLDRIDGE, John WILLIAMS, John WRIGHT; Capt. MARTINS: Salathial MARTIN, Zeanos BALDWIN, Michael BACON; Capt. UNDERWOODS: Robert WILLIS, William BURCH, Benjamin BURCH; Capt. HUMPHRIS: Hugh ARMSTRONG, James JASON, James MATTHEWS; Capt. GAINS: Micajah CLARK, Joseph JONES, George DEATHERAGE; Capt. HICKMANS: William MEREDETH, Reubin GEORGE, Reubin DODSON; Capt. BOSTICKS: Charles McANALLY, John MORGAN, Constant LADD; Capt. HILLS: Richard GOODE, John COOLEY, Ambrous BLACKBURN; Capt. CUMMINS': Benjamin WATSON, Augus. BLACKBOURN, Drurey WATSON; Capt. BINKLEYS: Michael HOUZAR, Lewis WOOLF, Jacob BLUME; Capt. DYARS: William COOK, John MOORE, Alexander HAWKINS; Capt. LOVILS: William SHEPPERD, Roger GIDDINS, Samuel CUMMINS.

16 August 1781

Present: Martin ARMSTRONG, Joseph WINSTON, William COOK, William T. LEWIS, Salathial MARTIN, William UNDERWOOD.

Robert WALKER, Esq. Corner came into Court and resigned; William COOK, Esq. unanimously elected with Joseph WILLIAMS and William MEREDITH, securities.

James SHEPPERD appointed Commissioner of Confiscated Property in room Richard VARNAL, Esqr., deceased, with William SHEPPERD, William UNDERWOOD, James GAINS, William COOK, securities, sum 500,000 pounds.

Matthew BROOKS as Commissioner of confiscated Property gave return his proceedings.

Matthew MOORE, Esq., Sheriff, entered into bond with Wm. SHEPPERD, Samuel CUMMINS, William T. LEWIS and Wm. COOK, securities, sum 5,000 pounds.

Matthew MOORE, Esqr., Sheriff, objects to sufficiency of Jail.

James GAINS qualified as Deputy Sheriff.

Joseph PHILLIPS vs Robert SPEER. Jury: John SNEED, Joseph CLOUD, Reubin MATTHEWS, John HARPER, John MARTIN, Robert MOORE, Isaac GAMMON, Joel LEWIS, John MORGAN, James SHEPPERD, Samuel CUMMINS, and William HUGHLETT.

Henry SPEER vs James SIMPKINS; same jury.

Ordered Colo. Martin ARMSTRONG and Colo. Robert LANIER be impowered to contract with suitable persons to find provisions and other necessarys for Justices and other officers of Court during siting of same to be at their own private expence.

Ordered Robert WALKER has leave keep Tavern at his now dwelling house; Wm. Terril LEWIS, security.

Ordered Samuel CUMMINS has leave keep a Tavern at his now dwelling house; Joseph WILLIAMS, security.

Ordered George SPRINKLE overseer road in room Richard THOMERSON.

Ordered George GROCE overseer road from CULELEASURES to Major PHILLIPS.

Ordered Philip SHOUSE overseer road from Quaker road to within half mile of Richmond Town.

Ordered Perishable part Estate William HALL, deceased, be exposed to sale.

Committee of Claims and Laying County Taxes report as follows: County Tax 1781 be Six Pence in every pound; following sums be annexed and allowed herein mentioned: Assessors each day service 80 pounds; Constables for warning inhabitants 240 pounds; Sheriff Exoficio Services 4,000 pounds; Clerk of Court for Exoficio Services 6,000 pounds; Express per day 120 pounds; Samuel CUMMINS for furnishing Court with Candles to this date 250 pounds. Signed by: Jo. WILLIAMS, Clerk Court; William MEREDITH, Chairman; Henry SPEER and William T. LEWIS.

12 November 1781
Richmond

Present: Martin ARMSTRONG, Esq.

13 November 1781

Present: Martin ARMSTRONG, Henry SPEER, Gibson WOOLDRIDGE, Esqrs.

Admr. Estate Richard TALLIFERRO, deceased, granted Dorcas TALLIFERRO, wife and relict, said deceased; John TALLIFERRO and Wm. T. LEWIS, securities; sum 500 pounds. Ordered that Dorcas TALLIFERRO wife and relict Richard TALIFERRO, who fell in his countrys cause, be exempt from paying tax, she having a helpless family to support.

Inventory Estate, William CLAYTON, deceased, returned by Elizabeth CLAYTON, Exr.

Last Will and Testament. James GLEN, deceased; oaths James BLACKWELL and Joseph GENTRY; Patience GLEN, Execrx., quallified.

Admr. Estate, Samuel CUNNINGHAM, deceased, to Jane CUNNINGHAM, wife and relict said deceased; Joshua CRESON and Henry SPEER, securities.

Deposition, Thomas SPENCE taken before Wm. Terril LEWIS; it being Last Will and Testament.

Josiah KEEN, deceased, verbally; Letters of Administration Issued to Gilbert KEEN, Heir in Law to said deceased; Zeanos BALDWIN and Abial COBB, securities.

Christopher ZIGLAR has leave build Water Grist Mill on B(blurred) Creek on his own land; deemed a publick mill.

John CUNNINGHAM has leave build Water Grist Mill on Toms (?) Creek on his own land; deemed publick mill.

Richard RATLIFF made it appear he is a proper refugee from South Carolina; ordered he be released from paying any tax 1780.

Bill of Sale from Mark PHILLIPS to Jos. WILLIAMS and Samuel MOSBY; oath William WALLACE.

Deed from John McKINNEY and Eliazabeth, his wife, to James DOAK; oath James MATTHEW (2 deeds).

Power of Attorney from William STEPHENS to Timothy STAMPS; oath said STEPHENS.

Deed from Robert AYRES to Henry AYRES; oath Robert AYRES.

Deed from Robert AYRES to Joseph AYRES; oath Robert AYRES.

Deed from Solomon NELSON to Matthew COX; oath John HARRIS.

Deed from Solomon NELSON to Stokes YOMANS; oath John HARRIS.

Deed from Solomon NELSON to William ROGERS; oath John HARRIS.

Deed from Jos. CARMICHAEL to Peter PERKINS; oath William HILL.

Ordered Entry Taker and Surveyor transfer certain tract land of 200 acres; entered by Reubin RIGGS lying South side Yadkin River commonly known by name David RIGGS old place, in name of Wm. Terril LEWIS.

14 November 1781

Present: William COOK, Gibson WOOLDRIDGE, Henry SPEER, Esqrs.

On Resignation Anna Maria BONN, wife and relict Jacob BONN, deceased, on her part of right to Admr. on said Estate, Admr. granted Gottfrey BREZEL and John RIGHTS.

Inventory Estate, Fredrick COX, deceased, returned by Admrx.

Ordered Administrator Estate, Robert TURNER, deceased, granted Rhody TURNER, wife and relict said deceased; Andrew SPEER and John ALLEN, securities; sum 1,000 pounds.

Ordered the rent of Robert TURNER'S plantation for present year be restored to Rhody TURNER, wife and relict of said Robert.

Deed from John MORGAN to Richard WEBSTER: oath said MORGAN.

Deed from William WALKER to Richard WEBSTER; oath John MORGAN.

Deed from Hugh DENNUM to John GOODE; oath Charles McANALLY.

Ordered William PRATHER be not answerable for stray horse impressed from him; which was taken away by Torys in Arms against State.

Ordered William and Martha BEESLEY, orphans Reubin BEESLEY, deceased, choose Richard GOODE their guardian; Charles McANALLY and Wm. MEREDITH, securities.

Ordered Barna ROWARK appointed guardian to Molley HOLT, orphan Wm. HOLT, deceased; William MEREDITH and James GAINS, securities.

Ordered Samuel STROOP overseer road in room William STROOPS.

Ordered Crop made on Richard MURPHEYS plantation present year be restored to Keziah MURPHEY for benefit herself and family.

Joseph PHILLIPS commissioner of Confiscated Property be not chargable.

Ordered Fredrick HELSABECK, David OWEN, John BRINKLEY, Adam BINKLEY, George STEPHENS, Moses MARTIN, John WAGNON, Robert WALKER, Junr., William WALKER, Thomas WRIGHT, Delaney HERRIN, William QUILLIN, Robert WALKER, Senr., and Samuel CUMMINS view road from Guilford County line in old Moravian road; thence to John WAG (blurred); thence Adam BINKLEYS; thence to creek near Fredrick HELSEBECKS.

15 November 1781

Present: William UNDERWOOD, Gibson WOOLDRIDGE, William T. LEWIS, Esqrs.

Inventory Estate, John HANN, deceased, returned by Admr.; account sale Estate returned.

Committee appointed to settle with Admrx. of William CARMICHAEL, deceased, report balance 3,492 pounds; due from said Estate to Sarah SOUTHERLAND, Admrx.

Last Will and Testament. William HOWARD, deceased; oath Wm. ADKINS; Mary HOWARD and Samuel DYAR qualified as Execrs.

Committee appointed to settle with Admrx. Thomas RAY, deceased, report balance due from Admr. 2 pounds, 4 shillings, 1 pence.

Matthew BASS overseer road in room Robert COOKER.

Ordered Michael BACON overseer new marked road from Pipes Creek to Island ford and County line.

Ordered Olive ROBERTS overseer road from (blurred) Creek to fork below HANKINS.

Ordered Wm. Terril LEWIS, Salathial MARTIN, Gibson WOLDRIDGE appointed commissioners let to lowest bidder with workmen, bridge across Elkin Creek below Allins Iron Works.

Ordered John WRIGHT, Thomas WRIGHT, Samuel ARNOLD, John ELLSBERRY, George HOLCOMB, Philip HOLCOMB, John ENGLAND, Ambrous BRAMBLET, William PETTY, John SANDERS, Airs HUDSPETH, John WILLIAMS, John WILLIAMS (two are listed), James SANDERS, John (blurred) view road from William PETTYS to Yellow Bank Ford off Yadkin River.

Ordered Licence granted Lemuel HARVEY to keep Tavern at his now dwelling house in Richmond; Samuel CUMMINS and Reubin MATTHEWS, securities.

Ordered John Thomas LONGINO have leave keep Tavern at his dwelling house; Henry SPEER and Wm. COOK, securities.

Ordered John WILLIAMS have leave keep Tavern at his now dwelling house; Henry SPEER and Joseph WILLIAMS, securities.

Deed from James BADGET to William SHEPPERD; oath Wm. T. LEWIS.

Deed from Samuel CUMMINS to Joseph PHILLIPS; oath said CUMMINS.

Bill of Sale from Samuel BRIGGS to Wm. T. LEWIS; oath Wm. SHEPPERD.

Ordered certain order respecting transfer land in name Wm. Teril LEWIS be suspended til further enquery. Clerk cite ------- AYERS, his wife and son (not named); Matthew BROOKS, Henry SPEER and Wm. Terril LEWIS to appear and give information.

Ordered contract build Bridge across the Elkin be suspended; Wm. Terril LEWIS, Salathial MARTIN and Gibson WOOLDRIGE, commissioners to have let said bridge.

In settling exchange of Depreciation concerning Wm. SHEPPERD, Esq., former Sheriff; 4 member committee: Wm. Terril LEWIS, Gibson WOOLDRIDGE, Wm. UNDERWOOD and Robert WALKER, Esqrs. Wm. MERREDITH, Esq. refuses give his consent with other Justices and withdrew himself off the bench, etc; Joseph WILLIAMS, our Clerk not enter same on back SHEPPERDS condition, etc.

Samuel RIGGS vs Richard MURPHEY. Jury: Airs HUDSPETH, David ALLIN, John PATRICK, Phil HOLCOMB, Nichols COOK, Wm. HUGHLET, Geo. HOLCOMB, Ormand MORGAN, James GITTINS, Andrew MARTIN, Andrew COOKSEY, Joseph COOKER.

Ordered Grist Mill already built on Belews Creek on his own land, property William SOUTHERLAND be deemed publick mill.

Committee appointed to settle with William SHEPPERD, Esq. former Sheriff report: When Colo. SHEPPERD paid off greatest part claims against County he informs us that Torys has destroyed (?) which said SHEPPERD obliges himself to pay and he neglected to discharge some; find he is indebted to County in sum 149 pounds, 2 shillings, 11 pence. Colo. SHEPHERD paid agreeable to court for year 1774.

Ordered Mrs. Keziah MURPHEY and Joseph PHILLIPS appear concerning crop made on Richard MURPHEYS Plantation.

Ordered certain stray mare entered on Rangers Book by Robert TATE, be delivered to Matthew BROOKS as Commissioner of County; said TATE having behaved as an Ememy of the State.

Ordered following persons appointed Collectors: MOSBYS Dist: John COLVARD; AYRES Dist: John Thomas LONGINO; WOOLDRIDGES: John WILLIAMS; MARTINS: Michael BACON; UNDERWOODS: Benjamin BURCH; HUMPHRIS'S: John FLEMING; GAINS: James GAINS; HICKMANS: Reubin DODSON; BOSTICKS: John MORGAN; HILLS: John COOLEY; CUMMINS'S: Augustine BLACKBOURN; BINKLEYS: Matthew BROOKS; DYARS: John MOORE; LOUVILLS: Roger GIDDINS.

Ordered following attend next term court as Jurors: James HOWELL, Joseph RAMEY, William PETTIE, John SANDERS, Thomas POINDEXTER, Robery AYERS, Benjamin ALLEN, Olive ROBERTS, Richard TALLIEFERRO, Elijah SMALLWOOD, James DOAK, John FLEMING, Malcum CURRY, John HORN, Snr., Joshua COX, Joseph CLOUD, Edward HICKMAN, Senr., John DEATHERAGE, Reubin DODSON, William HICKMAN, Almond GUINN, Robert CRUMP, Younger BLACKBOURN, Thos. EVANS, William BOSTICK, Henry COOK, Frederick MILLER, Adam WOOLF, James FREEMAN and John BURCH.

Ordered Tavern Rates be settled as follows: Good West India Rum per gallon 1 pound; Continent Rum 12 shillings, 6 pence; Good Whiskey 12 shillings, 6 pence; Good proof Brandy 12 shillings, 6 pence; Good Beer well hopped per quart 6 pence; 1 quart Toddy, India Rum and loaf sugar 2 shillings; 1 quart Toddy, Continent Rum and loaf sugar 1 shilling, 6 pence; one quart Toddy, good wiskey or Brandy 1 shilling, 6 pence; Stabledge 24 hour with plenty fodder or hay 1 shilling; Corn or Oats per quart, 2 pence;

Breakfast with Hott Victuals and Tea or Coffee 1 shilling, 6 pence; Breakfast without Tea or Coffee 1 shilling; Dinner rost and boiled with Beer 1 shilling, 6 pence; Good pasturage 24 hour 8 shillings; Lodging per night with Clean Sheets 6 shillings; Good boiled cyder per quart 2 shillings; Cyder Royal per quart 2 shillings; Draught Cyder per quart 8 shillings; Matheglin per quart 1 shilling, 6 pence.   Signed by: Mark ARMSTRONG, Chas. McANALLY, Jo. WINSTON, Henry SPEER; Jo. WILLIAMS, Clerk Court.

11 February 1782
Richmond

Present: William SHEPPERD, Esq.

12 February 1782

Present: Joseph WINSTON, William COOK, Henry SPEER, Esqrs.

Deed from John DYKES and wife to Thomas GAINS; oath James GAINS and Thos. LANKFORD.

Deed from Alexander MOORE to John PETREE; oath Alex. MOORE.

Deed from Wm. DICKS and Susanah, his wife to Benjamin ISBELL; oath Thos. ISBELL.

Bond from Jason ISBELL and Edwin HICKMAN to Benj. ISBELL; oath Thos. ISBELL.

Bond from Adam TATE and Joseph CARMICHAEL to Almond GUINN; oath Andrew ROBERSON.

Thomas CRESON records his mark.

Last Will and Testament; William ARMSTRONG, deceased; oath James MEREDETH and Wm. MARTIN; John CHILDRESS, Execr. quallified.

Inventory Estate; Robert TURNER, deceased, returned by Rhody TURNER, Admrx.

Amount Sale Estate, Robert TURNER, deceased, returned by Sheriff and Admrx.

Nuncupitive Will; Solomon COKER, deceased, proved; oath Josiah BROWN; Joseph COKER and David POINDEXTER, Execrs. quallified.

Ordered Mary MOTTS, now aged six years, orphan of Mary MOTTS, bound to Alexander Moore til age 16 years to learn art and Mistry seemstriss.

Ordered Nansey JOLLEY, Orphan James JOLLEY, bound Anna BAKER for six years to learn art and mistry of a Spinster.

Ordered Lazarous BENTON, an aged infirm man having scarely any property, be exempt from paying taxes.

Ordered Anthony DEARING be excused from paying fourfold tax 1781.

Ordered James HOWARD be exempt from paying taxes and doing public duties.

Grand Jury: John FLEMING, foreman; William HICKMAN, John DEATH-ERAGE, Joshua COX, William BOSTICK, Reubn DODSON, Robert AYRES, Edwin HICKMAN, Malcum CURRY, Ayres HUDSPETH, Thomas SHIP, Thomas POINDEXTER, Adam WOOLF.

Court taking into consideration distressed situation of Catherine TURNER and Children, wife of Roger TURNER, a Traitor to his Country having attached himself to the Enemies of the United States, think it proper to direct Commissioners of Confiscated Estates to remit hire (her) estate to Catherine TURNER.

35

13 February 1782

Present: Joseph WINSTON, William SHEPPERD, George HOWZAR, William COOK, Esqrs.

Inventory Estate, Doctor Jacob BONN, deceased, returned by John RIGHTS.

Inventory Estate, James GLEN, deceased, returned by Execrx.

Ordered certain order November 1780 respecting probate Will Charles WORD, be reversed; said will not looked upon as Aughentically subscribed; Ordered Letters Admrx. granted Elizabeth WORD, wife and relict said deceased; James SHEPPARD and Wm. UNDERWOOD, securities.

Ordered sundry articles sold by Augustine BLACKBURN in consequence Jacob LOWREYS Tax for 1780 be restored to said JACOB as sale was illegally conducted.

Ordered Jacob LOWREY excused from fourfold tax for 1781.

Power of Attorney from Thomas SMITH to Samuel HUMPHRIES; oath Benj. HUMPHRIES.

Ordered Commissioners of confiscated property take into possession all property belonging to John MASH it appearing he has acted Innimican (un-American ?) to the State.

Ordered enquiry respecting Mrs. MURPHEYS rents be put off to future court.

Ordered Abejah ELMORE overseer road in room Jacob LOWREY.

Ordered Philip SHOUSE overseer road from Quaker road to within half mile of Richmond and Jacob SPOONHOUR, Adam FULK and Wm. MOORE'S hands work thereon.

Ordered William WEAVER overseer road in room Micheal REYNOLDS.

Ordered William DANIEL overseer road in room Stephen JEAN.

Ordered Joshua COX overseer road from Finleys ford on Dan River to William EASTS on waters Little Yadkin River.

14 February 1782

(No Justices)

Ordered Mrs. Elizabeth WRIGHT, wife of Gideon WRIGHT, who have taken up arms against this and the United States, on application to court for sustance of herself and children out of said husbands estate, be allowed use House and Plantation where she now lives and have possession of one Negro felow, one mare, colt, one milch cow, three yearlings and household furniture.

William HUGHLETT vs William UNDERWOOD; Assault and Battery; Jury: Daniel SHIP, Micheal REYNOLDS, Jeffery JOHNSON, Wm. JOHNSON, Joseph LAWRENCE, William VENABLE, George HOLCOMB, Thomas ELLIOTT, John COE, Thomas HUGHES, John WAGNON, David OWEN.

Micheal HENDERSON vs Jacob FERREE; same jury.

James EASON vs John SMITH; same jury.

Ordered collector in BOSTICKS District collect from Charles ANGLES, a single man.

Ordered James S(blurred), David ALLEN, Almon GUINN, Samuel MOSBY, Junr., appointed Jurors next Superior Court at Salisbury 15 March next.

Ordered following serve as Jurors next term: Younger BLACKBURN,

36

Joseph BANNER, William WAGGONER, John HALBERT, Micheal BACON, Thomas SPENCE, Al(blurred) MOORE, George DEATHERAGE, Anthony DEARING, Thomas HIGHSMITH, Stephen CLAYTON, John BURCH, William ELLIOR, John GARRETT, Samuel HUMPHRIES, Joseph RAMEY, James HOWELL, Joseph CLOUD, Jeffery JOHNSON, James BADGET, James BLACKWELL, Richard COX, Amos LADD, John FIELDER, Junr., Edward LOVILL, Henry KERBY, Joseph GIBSON, Thomas BRIGGS, Ambrous BRAMBLETT, Arthur SCOTT.

Ordered Christopher KIRSHNER be exempt from paying tax or doing public duties.

Ordered Preston HAMPTON deliver to Thomas FITZPATRICK following: one Bay Mare, three head sheep, one cow, three yards linen now in his possession, which articles Capt. Minor SMITH extorted from said FITZPATRICK. Ordered said SMITH be cited to answer for his conduct.

Ordered John MARTIN produce mulatta girl called Poll to be dealt with according to law.

Ordered Surveyor of MATTHEWS District not survey certain land lately transfered to Hall HUDSON, Thomas ROSS and Benjamin CORNE-LIUS, etc. Ordered said HUDSON, ROSS and CORNELIUS appear show cause why same not come under confiscation act.

15 February 1782

(No Justices)

Ordered Mrs. Keziah MURPHEY, wife of Richard MURPHEY, who has taken up arms against this and the United States, be allowed Horses, cattle, hogs, furniture for sustance of herself and children.

Bill of Sale from James BROWN and Solomon COKER to Samuel CUMMINS and William SHEPPERD; oath Wm. SHEPPERD.

Ordered road from FREEMANS to Richmond be turned leaving former road at Kerbys path to Saw Mill; thence down river to Poindexters Ferry road, Samuel KERBY, overseer.

Ordered Samuel CUMMINS overseer road in room Robert WALKER, Esq.

Inventory Estate, Samuel CUNNINGHAM, deceased, returned by Admr.; also Sale returned.

Ordered articles be allowed Elizabeth ROBERTS, wife and relict John ROBERTS, deceased; Cattle, stock, household furniture and rents and profits of her said husbands plantation; the said John ROBERTS having acted Inemican to the United States.

Ordered commissioners confiscated property deduct from Len FLINNS bond (account Negro wench he hired of Colo. WRIGHTS Estate which was out of his possession) 12 bushels corn; Matthew BROOKS, as Commissioner, not chargable.

Ordered William COOK, William T. LEWIS, Henry SPEER, Esqrs. let to lowest bidder to build bridge over Elkin Creek below Allins Iron Works.

Joseph WINSTON, Esq. resigned as Entry Taker; John Thomas LONGINO unanimously appointed to take charge said books till General Assembly make provision respecting entrying of Lands.

14 May 1782
Richmond

Present: Martin ARMSTRONG, George HOWZAR, Robert WILLIS, Esqrs.

37

Inventory Estate, Charles WORD, deceased, returned by Elizabeth
WORD, Admrx.

Nuncupetive Will, Philip CLAYTON, deceased; oath Benj. BANNER,
Elizabeth CLAYTON, Joseph BANNER, witnesses.

Ordered Letters of Administration issue Mary CLAYTON and William
CLAYTON; Joseph BANNER and Benj. BANNER, securities.

Administrator of Estate, William RIDENS, deceased, granted Milley
RIDENS, wife and relict said deceased; Thomas ADDIMAN and John
RIDENS, securities.

Last Will and Testament; William THOMPSON, deceased, exhibited;
after examination it is opinion of Court said Wm. THOMPSON was
not of sound and disposing memory when it was wrote and signed.

Ordered Letters of Administration be granted Ave THOMPSON, wife
and relict said deceased; Mark HARDIN and Matt BROOKS, securities.

Ordered Mrs. Jane HOWARD, wife and relict of Abraham HOWARD, who
have taken up arms against this State be allowed use his said
Plantation with stock and household furniture for sustance for
herself and children.

On motion Nathaniel WILLIAMS, Esq. certain indenture binding
Steward STEWARD to James TUCKER.

Ordered Mary WILSON, a free Mulatto girl, brought into county by
John MARTIN, be delivered unto Elizabeth CHAVES of Bladen County
to be returned to her parents.

Ordered Grist Mill already built by Na(blurred) JEAN on Toms
Creek on his own land be publick mill.

Ordered Water Grist Mill already built on Muddy Creek, the property Elijah STANDLEY, be deemed public mill.

Deed from Edward EVANS to William WHITE; oath James COFFEE.

Deed from Aaron SPEER to Thomas WILLIAMS; oath Robert AYRES.

Deed from Sarah LANKFORD and Thos. LANKFORD to Jos. SHIP; oath
Thomas SHIP.

Ordered John MICKEY overseer road in room Henry SHORE.

15 February 1782

Present: Martin ARMSTRONG, Charles McANALLY, Richard GOODE,
William DOBSON, Esqrs.

Deed from William RAMSEY and Jane, his wife, to James BRYSON; oath
William MEREDITH.

Deed from William RAMSEY and Jane, his wife, to Joel MA(blurred);
oath William MEREITH.

Ordered Andrew LOWRY and Cad. JONES be exempt paying fourfold
tax 1781.

Ordered David OWEN appointed Constable in Capt. LOVILLES District.

William MERREDITH appointed Sheriff for encusing year.

Charles McANALLY, Esq. unanumously appointed County Trustee;
Richard GOODE and Henry SPEER, securities.

Richard GOODE appointed Ranger; Charles McANALLY and Ben WATSON,
securities.

Elizabeth GIBSON vs Nathaniel WATSON; Jury: Joseph BANNER, William
WAGGONER, Alex. MOORE, Geo. DEATHERAGE, James BLACKWELL, Samuel
HUMPHRIES, Amos LADD, Edward LINVILL, Olive ROBERTS, Mark HARDIN,

George HOWZAR and Job MARTIN.

John GILBERT vs Warner SPOONHOUR; Slander; same Jury except John WILLIAMS in place of George HOWZAR.

Andrew LOWRY permitted to take Oath Allegiance to State.

Ordered Sundry articles mentioned in former Order directing them delivered to Thomas FITZPATRICK, be delivered said Thomas without delay; and Capt. Minor SMITH be released from citation.

Ordered Joseph EAST overseer road in room Thomas LOYD.

On resignation Elizabeth SPEER, wife and relict Robert SPEER, deceased, her right of Admr. on said husbands Estate; Admr. grant-ed to Andrew and Joshua SPEER; Robert AYRES and Henry SPEER, securities.

Job MARTIN, Robert LANIER, Samuel MOSBY, Junr., appointed appraise Estate of James GLEN, deceased.

Account Sale part Estate, Thomas RAY, deceased, returned by Char-les McANALLY, Esq.

Admr. Estate, Priscilla EDWARDS, deceased, granted Reuben GLOVER; Thomas GLOVER and Robert HARRISON, securities.

16 February 1782

Present: William MERREDITH, Benjamin WATSON, Richard GOODE, William COOK, Esqrs.

Deed from William WEBB to Daniel HUTHERSON; oath Reubin DODSON.

Ded--(?) to Virginia to examine Martha WEBB to relinquish her dower.

Samuel CUMMINS vs Joseph BUFFINGTON; Jury: Jason ISBELL, Reubin MATTHEWS, Jos. CARMICHAEL, Matthew BASS, Matthew WARNICK, John BRADLEY, Alex. MOORE, George DEATHERAGE, James BLACKWELL, George HOLCOMB, Amos LADD, and Edward LOVELL.

Jesse BENTON vs John JONES; same jury.

Godfrey MILLER vs Stephen WILLEFORD; same jury.

Samuel HENDERSON vs James THOMPSON; same jury.

Nicholas TULL vs Samuel ELRODE; same jury.

John DURHAM vs Patrick McKINNEY; same jury.

On motion Daniel EASLEY by his Attorney ordered certain gray mare now in possession John WILLIAMS, Constable, taken at instance David REAVIS to be delivered to said EASLEY as said mare is his property.

On resignation Rachel TATE, wife and relict Robert TATE, deceased, her right Admr. said husbands Estate; Admr. granted Godfrey MILLER; Samuel CUMMINS and George HOWZAR, Esors., Securities.

Ordered following be fined for their non-attendance as Jurors this Term: Younger BLACKBURN, John HALBERT, Micheal BACON, Thomas SPENCE, Anthony DEARING, Thomas HIGHSMITH, Stephen CLAYTON, Joseph RAMEY, James HOWELL, Jos. CLOUD, Jeffery JOHNSON, James BADGET, Richard COX, John FIELDER, Junr., Henry KERBY, Thomas BRIGGS, Ambrous BRAMBLET, Arthur SCOTT, John BURCH, William ELLIOTT, John GARRETT.

Peter IRONS charged of having in his possession a piece of Brass or Coper Mettle in likeness and similitude of ¼ of a Mordore; ordered said piece of mettle be by Sheriff nailed to Whiping Post.

William WHITE charged of conveying a Mulatto Boy called Stephen Cheavas out of this State and traded him away as a Slave, who was plundered from Bladen County in this State; ordered Wm. WHITE be bound over next Superior Court held Salisbury to answer for his conduct.

State vs William WHITE; bound next Superior Court answer to above charge.

State vs James GAINS and Edward LOVILL; bound for WHITES appearance.

Ordered following attend next term Court as Jurors: Younger BLACK-BURN, John HALBERT, Michael BACON, Thomas SPENCE, James HOWELL, Joseph CLOUD, Jeffrey JOHNSON, Anthony DEARING, Thomas HIGHSMITH, Stephen CLAYTON, Joseph RAMEY, James BADGET, Richard COX, John FIELDER, Junr., Henry KERBY, Thos. BRIGGS, Ambrous BRAMBLET, Arthur SCOTT, John BURCH, Wm. ELLIOT, John GARRETT, John WAGON, Fredr. MILLER, Esq., Jacob SHEPPERD, James McKOIN, Phil WILSON, Abraham WINSE (blurred), John LYNCH, Henry SHORES, John FORKNER.

17 February 1782

(No Justices)

George WATKINS vs Richard MORRIS; Jury: Alex MOORE, James BLACK-WELL, Samuel HUMPHRIS, Amos LADD, Edward LOVILL, Constant. LADD, George HOLCOMB, Charles DUDLEY, Mark HARDIN, James COFFEE, John BLACKWELL, and Phil HOLCOMB.

Matthew BROOKS vs William KIRKPATRICK; same jury.

Jacob FERREE vs John READ; same jury.

Richard MURPHEY vs Timothy TERRIL; same jury.

James CONDON vs William COOKER; same jury.

Gabriel WAGGONER, Admr. vs Urseley RAY; same jury.

Charles DUDLEY vs Henry PARRISH; same Jury except Wm. THORNTON instead Charles DUDLEY.

Ordered tract land whereon John COOK formerly lived be restored into possession of Wm. COOK, Esq. and court give up rent to Wm. COOK as rent is considered illegal by Court.

Ordered Resolve of General Assembly at Hillsborough respecting appointed Justices at Wake and Halifax Sessions 1781 be made public so those concerned may be satisfied that their appointments was not legal; being nominated by House of Commons only.

Ordered certain Negro fellow called Jacob, that Capt. Henry SPEER purchased of Francis BAKER be continued in said SPEERS possession.

Ordered County Trustee pay into hands Mrs. Rachael TATE six pounds to enable her to keep and maintain her same child until August Court.

Ordered certain order for appointed John Thomas LONGIO take care Entry officers Books be reversed.

Ordered Joseph WINSTON appointed take charge said books as Entry Taker.

Ordered Zachariah MARTIN overseer road in room Hezekiah WRIGHT, deceased.

Ordered Frederick HELSEBECK overseer road in room Thomas BRIGGS.

Ordered any person possession (possessing) a free Mulatto child aged about 5 years by name Staphen Chaves to bring forth said Stephen on demand by Elizabeth CHEAVES or other persons in her

behalf; she being the parent of said child; ordered copy above
order be given said Elizabeth when she has produced proper cred-
entials for herself and child being Free.

17 June 1782

(Special Session County Court for purpose laying Districts,
appointing Justices, receiving inventories of taxable property
and appointing Assessors for 1782.)

Present: Robert LANIER, Richard GOODE, Benjamin WATSON, William
DOBSON, Thomas SMITH, Esqrs.

Capt. MOSBYS: Robert LANIER, John HARVEY; Capt. BRINKLEYS: George
HAWZAR, Matt BROOKS; Capt. WRIGHTS: John ELLSBERRY, John WRIGHT;
Capt. MARTINS: Wm. COOK, Reuben SHORES; Capt. DYARS: Samuel FREE-
MAN, William FREEMAN; Capt. SHEPPERDS: Robert WILLIA, John TALLI-
FERRO; Capt. AYRES: Thomas SMITH, Job MARTIN; Capt. SMITHS: Martin
ARMSTRONG, Malcum CURRY; Capt. HUMPHRIS: Micajah CLARKE, Robert
HARRIS; Capt. COOKS: William DOBSON, William BOSTICK; Capt. HILLS:
Richard GOODE, James HAMPTON; Capt. BLACKBURN: Joseph WINSTON,
Ambrous BLACKBURN; Capt. BOSTICKS: Benjamin WATSON, Mark HARDIN;
Capt. HICKMANS: Charles McANALLY, Reuben DOTSON; Capt. GAINS:
William MEREDITH, George DEATHERAGE.

12 August 1782
Richmond, 7th year American Independance

Present: Martin ARMSTRONG, William DOBSON, William SHEPPERD,
William T. LEWIS, Esqrs.

Deed from William PHILIPS to John ROBERTS; oath William PHILIPS.

Deed from Joshua TILLERY and Susanah, his wife, to William SOUTH-
ERN; oath John MORGAN.

Deed from Henry SPEER, Attorney for Levin COOPER to John Butter-
worth COLVARD.

Deed from John THOMPSON to Thomas HOWELL; oath James and David
HOWELL.

Deed from Charles ANGLE to Litleberry STONE; oath Absalom BOSTICK.

Power of Attorney from Thomas DRAYTON to John ARMSTRONG; oath
Edward YARBROUGH.

Power of Attorney from Joseph STANDLEY and William STANLEY to
James SMITH; oath said William STANDLEY.

Grand Jury: Joseph CLOUD, foreman; Jacob SHEPERD, John WAGON,
John LYNCH, James HOWELL, Joseph RAMEY, Richard COX, John BURCH,
Anthony DEARING, Abraham WINSCOTT, Michael BACON, John FIELDER,
Junr., Ambrous BRAMBLET, and Arthur SCOTT.

Inventory Estate, Philip CLAYTON, deceased, returned by William
CLAYTON, Admr.

Amount Sale Estate, William CLAYTON, deceased, returned by Mary
RUTLEDGE, Admrx.

Inventory Estate, William THOMPSON, deceased, returned by Ave
THOMPSON, Admrx.; ordered perishable part estate be sold.

Admr. Estate, Matthias STEELMAN, Junr., granted Matthias STEELMAN,
John SKIDMORE and Abraham WINSCOTT, securities.

Admr. Estate, William FOWLER, deceased, granted Mary FOWLER, wife
and relict said deceased; John RING, Thomas WRIGHT and Richard
WOOD, securities.

Admr. Estate, James DOUTHIT, deceased, granted Mary DOUTHIT, wife and relict said deceased; Matthew MARKLAND and Richard THOMERSON, securities.

Last Will and Testament, Leonard MOSSER, deceased; oath Adam WOOLF, Execr.

Ordered John SPURLOCK be exempt from paying Poll Tax and doing public duties; he being exceeding Poor, Aged and Infirm.

Ordered Stephen CLAYTON be released of fine 3 pounds for his non-attendance as Juryman last term and be released from serving present term.

Ordered William SHEPPERD, William COOK, Samuel FREEMAN, Thomas SMITH, Esqrs. appointed committee receive lists Taxable 1782.

Ordered John DYCKES deliver to Peter SHEARMOUR certain Strawberry Roan Mare now in his possession, property of SHEAMOUR.

Ordered Edward SMITH has leave keep Tevern at Samuel FREEMANS Plantation in this county; Wm. FREEMAN and John PATRICK, securities.

William THOMPSON and Mary THOMPSON, orphans Wm. THOMPSON, deceased, choosed Edward THOMPSON, their guardian; Mark HARDIN and Absalom BOSTICK, securities.

Ordered Surveyor lay off one third land of Wm. THOMPSON, deceased, for widow, including Plantation whereon she now lives. Absalom BOSTICK, Mark HARDIN, Amos LADD appointed to direct surveyor.

Ordered John BONE, an orphan child, bound to Peter MOSSER for term 17 years from this date to learn art and mistry of a Weaver. MOSER agrees to teach him to read, write, cypher as _fare_ as the Double Rule of Three.

Ordered certain ladd named Henry SMITH who has run away from his master in Pittsylvania County, Virginia to be delivered into hands Sheriff til proper master _applyes_ for him.

14 August 1782

Present: Martin ARMSTRONG, Charles McANALLY, Robert LANIER, Benjamin WATSON, George HOUZAR, Esqrs.

Inventory Estate, William RIDINS, deceased, returned by Milley RIDINS, Admrx. Ordered perishable part estate be sold.

Inventory Estate, Priscilla EDWARDS, deceased, returned by Reuben GLOVER, Admr.

Ordered certain Deed of Lease and Release dated 27 and 28 October 1778 from James HUTTON conveying tract of Wachovia to Fredr. Wm. MARSHALL be admitted to record.

Deed from James BROWN and Sarah, his wife, to William APPERSON; oath James.

Deed from Thomas NORMAN to Matthew COX; oath Aaron KEMP.

Deed from Henry SHORE to William CAMPBELL; oath Henry SHORE.

Traugott BAGGE and Hugh ARMSTRONG quallified as Justices of Peace.

William MERREDITH, Esq. appointed Sheriff; James GAINS, Richard GOODE, Matthew MOORE, Charles McANALLY, securities.

Reubin DODSON admitted as Deputy Sheriff.

Wm. MERRIDETH, Esqr. Sheriff, objected to _sufficence_ of Jail.

Mark HARDIN, Junr. appointed Constable.

Jesse BUMPS overseer Hollow road leading from Toms Creek to

Virginia line.

Ordered John SNEED, Jesse BUMPS, Joshua COX, Matthew BASS, Charles DUDLEY, Thomas CUNNINGHAN, Salathiel MARTIN, Robert COOKER, Micajah CLARKE, Fredr. DESERN, William DENNEY, William BURRIS, Benjamin HUMPHRIS, Matthew MOORE, Edward LOVELL view road beginning on Double Creek of Dan River between Richard and Joshua COX'S; thence to Iron Works on Yadkin.

Accounts Debts due Estate Robert TURNER, deceased, returned by Admrtx.

Admr. Estate, Matthias BEATS, deceased, granted Mary BEATS, wife and relict said deceased; Daniel EASLEY and James SHORT, securities.

Ordered James HOWARD, poor pittifill young man be exempt paying Poll Tax and doing public duties.

William HUTHERSON has an infirm negroe wench; ordered he be excused from paying tax for her so long as she continues infirm.

Sarah BUTNER vs William COOK; Jury: William HUGHLET, Airs HUDS-PETH, Wm. SHELTON, Olive ROBERTS, Wm. DEAVENPORT, Sterling Mc-LIMORE, Henry SHORE, Charles DUDLEY, John DEATHERAGE, Reuben SHORE, Peter ELDER, and John BINKLY.

LANIER and WILLIAMS vs Philip WILSON; debt; same jury.

David GORDON vs Charles SNEED; same jury.

Sarah BOWEN vs Daniel CARTER; assault and battery; same jury.

Ordered James SANDERS, Robert HARRIS, Samuel FREEMAN, Esqrs., Robert WARNOCK, John CUMMINS, Salathiel MARTIN, Joseph WINSTON, Esqrs., appointed attend next Superior Court at Salisbury for District of Salisbury as Jurors.

15 August 1782

Present: Martin ARMSTRONG, Charles McANALLY, Benjamin WATSON, George HOUZAR, Tragott BAGGE, Esqrs.

John B. COLVARD quallified as Deputy Sheriff.

Inventory Estate, Robert SPEER, deceased, returned by Andrew and Robert SPEER, Admrs.

Inventory part Estate, James GLEN, deceased, returned by Execr.

GLENS Exectors vs Gideon WRIGHT; Jury: Jabez JARVES, Olive ROBERTS, Len BRADLEY, John HARVEY, Joseph COOKER, George DEATHER-AGE, Reuben MATTHEWS, John SHELTON, Rezia JARVIS, Wm. VENABLE, Constant LADD, and John BLALOCK.

GLENS Exectors vs Richard MURPHY; same jury except Geo. HOLCOMB instead Jabez JARVES.

Ordered whatever Commissioner of Confiscated property has done with any part of Gideon WRIGHTS Estate granted to his wife, is declared illegal.

Ordered Matthew BROOKS, a commissioner, be cited and answer for his conduct.

Ordered Robert WALKER, Samuel CUMMINS, Joseph PHILIPS appointed to lay off for Mary BEATS her right of Dower, including House and Plantation.

Ordered any persons having in their possession two free Mulatto children named Polly FREEMAN and Winney BLANKS, do forthwith deliver them on demand, said children being feloniously plundered and taken from their parents in Bladen County.

43

On motion Col. DUNN, seting forth Stephen BATTEN, young man late from Chathan County, and has been taken up when on his journey to Montgomery County, Virginia and ordered before magistrates and by them turned over into Continental Service as a Vagrant, it is ordered said Stephen permitted to oath on his journey as he is proven to be no Vagrant.

On motion of Matthew BROOKS, present County Commissioner to receive and give certificates for articles received by him from persons who are said to have acted Inimical to the State; ordered Matthew BROOKS grant no certificates, but deliver an account of all such articles received to Upper Board of Auditors of Salisbury District.

Justices of Court, Martin ARMSTRONG, Robert LANIER, Charles McANALLY, Robert WALKER, Benjamin WATSON, William COOK, George HAUZAR, Junr. and Traugott BAGGE, Esqrs. after mature deliberation, ordered the following persons be disquallified as acting Justices of Peace according to a resolve of last General Assembly 27 April 1782: William Terril LEWIS, Hugh ARMSTRONG, Jesse BUMPS, Salathiel MARTIN, Henry SPEER, Benjamin PARKS, Gibson WOOLDRIDGE, and William UNDERWOOD.

16 August 1782

Present: Martin ARMSTRONG, Charles McANALLY, Traugott BAGGE, Esqrs.

Ordered John HOLLAND and Philip GREEN appointed Constables in Krouses District.

Ordered Joseph JONES, Constable in Gaines District, be removed from office for deputing Archilas FARE to serve a precept and he be cited and answer above charge. Micajah CLARKE and Lewis CERTAIN to appear. Ordered citation issue vs Archelus FARE to appear next court to answer charge of a false return made by him on a summons James MARTIN against Lewis CERTAIN.

Ordered Ezekiel REYNOLDS be bound in sum 100 pounds for maintainance of bastard male child he fathered by Ann HOWARD; Roger GIDIONS and John BLACKWELL, securities.

John DIX vs Edward BRADLEY; Jury: Adam WOOLF, Reuben MATTHEWS, Samuel HUMPHRIS, Peter IRONS, Robert OBARR, James BROWN, Thomas FLYNN, Andrew SPEER, William FLYNN, George FLYNN, Robert AYRES, and Olive ROBERTS.

Daniel SHIP vs Henry LANKFORD; same jury.

Sarah LANKFORD vs John DYCKES; same jury.

Richard GOODE vs Valentine PERKINS; same jury.

Reubin DODSON vs John WILLIAMS; same jury.

William SHEPPERD vs Jacob McCRAW; same jury.

Thomas LANKFORD vs John LANKFORD, assault and battery; same jury.

John WILLIAMS vs Francis BAKER; same jury.

David REAVIS vs John REAVES; same jury.

Power of Attorney from William PATTERSON to Samuel CUMMINS; oath said PATTESON.

Ordered Geo. ABBERT overseer road in room Jacob SCOTT.

Ordered Micheal LASTER (?), overseer road in room Philip GREEN.

Ordered Peter YARREL, overseer road in room Charles HOLDER.

Ordered John BLAKE, overseer road in Maryland settlement in room Matthew MARKLAND.

Ordered John CONNELL, overseer road from Richmond leading towards Dan River as far as Muddy Creek; likewise from Richmond as *fare* as Little Yadkin.

Ordered following serve next court Richmond 2nd Monday in November as Jurors: Henry SHORE, Job MARTIN, Frederick MILLER, Esq., Daniel SCOTT, Samuel CROCKET, Wyatt GARNER, John SANDERS, George HOLCOMB, James BADGET, Moses MIERS, James DOAK, James MATTHEWS, Joshua COX, John DEATHERAGE, John SIMS, William HICKMAN, Younger BLACKBURN, Ambrous BLACKBURN, Absalom BOSTICK, Mark HARDIN, Wm. COOK, Capt. William McBRIDE, Petter SALLEY, John TEAGUE and Charles WHITLOCK.

Court appointed Collecters for year 1782: Capt. KROUSES: George HOUZAR, Jr.; Capt. LOVILLS: Malcom CURRY; Capt. WRIGHTS: John WILLIAMS; Capt. AYRES: John Thomas LONGINO; Capt. MOSBYS: John COLVARD; Capt. MARTINS: Wm. Nichols COOK; Capt. SHEPPERD: Rezia JARVIS; Capt. DYARE: John MOORE; Capt. HUMPHRIES: Robert HARRIS; Capt. HICKMANS: Reuben DODSON; Capt. BOSTICKS: Mark HARDIN, Junr., Capt. GAINS: George DEATHERAGE; Capt. COOKS: William DODSON; Capt. BLACKBURNS: Ambrous BLACKBURN; Capt. HILLS: John COOLEY.

17 August 1782

Present: Martin ARMSTRONG, Robert WALKER, Matt. MOORE, Traugott BAGGE.

Major Joel LEWIS informed court he has ·in his possession mullatto female child called Holday Ransome, suggested to be daughter Simon and Mary RANSOME of Bladen County; Ordered LEWIS furnish said child with reasonable supplys until delivered to her parents.

Colo. Wm. SHEPPERD informed court that Matthew BROOKS has impowered him to declare to Court that said Matthew BROOKS resigns to Court his office as Commissioner of Confiscated Estates and also as Commissioner of Specific Tax, which resignation is accepted.

Joseph PHILIPS resigned his appointment as Commissioner of Confiscated Estates which is also accepted.

Ordered James GAINS and Reuben DODSON be appointed Commissioners of Confiscated Estates in room said BROOKS and PHILIPS, resigned. Samuel CUMMINS and Matthew MOORE, securities for GAINS; Wm. MEREDITH and George DEATHERAGE, securities for DODSON.

Ordered Robert WALKER, Esq. appointed Commissioner of Specific Tax; William SHEPPERD and John ARMSTRONG, securities.

Ordered Reziah JARVIS and William Nichols COOK appointed Constables.

Ordered James SHEPPERD be suspended from office of Commissioner of Confiscated Estate for neglect of duty.

Ordered settlement of Wm. SHEPPERD for his collection as Sheriff made November 1781 not sufficient and not valid; said SHEPPERD to appear next Court and make another settlement satisfaction of Court.

Account Estate, Hezekiah WRIGHT was possessed of at or about time his death: 350 acres land, 6 horse creatures, 19 head cattle, 11 head sheep, 14 head hoggs, 2 beds and furniture, 2 potts, 7 plates, 3 dishes, 5 basons, 1 loom, 1 mans saddle and bridle, 1 set plow irons, 1 fluke plow, 3 pair Iron traces, half a waggon, 1 lock chain, 2 weeding hoes, 1 grubing hoe, 2 iron wedges, 1 pair saddle baggs, 2 geer, 1 small chest, 1 sack bagg, 1 field of oats, 50 barrels corn.

Account of sundries taken for use of Army and other purposes from
Catharine WRIGHT before and after decease of her husband, Hezekiah
WRIGHT: 2 beef cows taken by Virginia Soldier, 4 head cattle
taken by Mr. Matt BROOKS, half waggon and 1 pair geers taken by
Capt. MERRIDITH; 1 horse, 1 saddle and bridle taken by Capt. Wm.
CAMBELL; 1 field oats (200 bushels), 1 pair saddle baggs taken by
Capt. Wm. LEWIS; 1 sack bagg taken by Colo. SHEPPERD; 45 barrels
corn eaten by horses which was said belonged to the Public. On
application Catharine WRIGHT, widow and relict of Hezekiah WRIGHT,
deceased (who has taken up arms against this and the United States)
for a maintanance of herself and children ordered she allowed
rent said husbands plantation; also everything now in her possession.

Account sale Estate, Martin ROMINGER, deceased, returned by Henry
SPOONHOUR, Admr.

Deed from Jacob SPEER to Daniel MOSBY; oath Joseph WILLIAMS.

Deed from Joseph PHILIPS to Wm. SHEPPERD; oath Walter LEWIS.

Ordered John WILLIAMS, Abner GREENWOOD, George HOLCOMB, Airs
HUDSPETH, Fredrick LONG, James SANDERS, Thomas WRIGHT, Philip
HOLCOMB, John SANDERS, Robert AYRES, John ENGLAND, Jesse COUNCIL,
Ambrous BRAMBLETT, Carter HUDSPETH, Gibson WOOLRIDGE, Edward
CLANTON view road from Yellow Bank ford to Rowan County line near
Capt. SANDERS.

Ordered any order of Court for building bridge over Great Elkin
leading to Allens Iron Works at expense County, be resinded.

Ordered Matthew BROOKS, late Commissioner of Specific Tax furnish
Robert WALKER, present Commissioner with list persons who have
not paid.

Ordered Colo. Martin ARMSTRONG account with Court next November
for any money he may have received when Sheriff in collection of
taxes for purpose of building the present Court House.

Ordered certain mare entered by Benj. PETTIR on Rangers Book,
delivered by late Ranger to Wm. JOHNSON.

Ordered William SHEPPERD restore unto Robert ARMSTRONG (a person
taken up on Suspicion of being a Vagrant and having a counterfeit
pass but has been released by Justices of Peace), the horse,
saddle and bridle which was detained by Wm. SHEPPERD from said
Robert ARMSTRONG.

Report of Committee of Claims as follows: John WRIGHT, 10 days
assessing last three years, 4 pounds; Robert AYRES, 3 days, 1
pound, 40 shillings; Malcom CURRY, 4 days 1780 and 4 days 1781,
3 pounds, 40 shillings; John TALIFERRO, 6 days, 2 pounds, 8
shillings; Reubin DODSON, 5½ days; Constant LADD, 3 days; Mark
HARDIN, 4 days 1781, 5 days 1780; George DEATHERAGE, 16 days last
three years; Wm. FREEMAN, 4 days; Matthew BROOKS, 4 days; Job
MARTIN, 4 days; Jacob BLOOME, 3 days; Ambrous BLACKBURN, 6 days;
James HAMPTON, 4 days; Augustine BLACKBURN, 3 days; Reuben SHORES,
6 days; Joseph WILLIAMS, clerk for extra services; John Thomas
LONGINO for warning AYRES District; Samuel CUMMINS for extra
services; Michael HOWZAR warning in BINKLEYS District, 3 days;
Wm. MERREDITH, Sheriff, extra service; Richard THOMERSON, riding
Express and warning inhabitants; Samuel CUMMINS, Assessor; Joseph
WILLIAMS, clerk, for extra services.

11 November 1782
Richmond

Present: Martin ARMSTRONG, Robert WALKER, Traugott BAGGE, Esqrs.

Present: Martin ARMSTRONG, George HOWZAR, Traugott BAGGE, Esqrs.

Amount Sale Estate, Matthias STEELMAN, Junr., deceased, returned Matthias STEELMAN, Admr.

Last Will and Testament, Noble LADD, deceased, proved oath Andrew ROBINSON; Noble LADD, Execr. qualified.

Inventory Estate, Wm. FOWLER, deceased, returned Molley FOWLER, Admrx. ordered sale perishable part of estate.

Inventory part Estate, Robert SPEER, deceased, returned by Admr.

Adam BINKLEY, one of Execrs. Last Will and Testament, Leonard MOSER, deceased, qualified.

Admr. Estate, John FARGUSSON, deceased, granted Rebekah FARGISSON, wife and relict, deceased; Ambrous BLACKBURN and James BOLES, securities.

Inventory Estate, James DOUTHIT, deceased, returned by Admr.

Ordered John DUNN, Esqr. be appointed Attorney for State.

Grand Jury: Job MARTIN, foreman; Henry SHORE, Daniel SCOTT, Samuel CROCKET, Wyatt GARNER, John TEAGUE, Moses MEIRS, George HOLCOMB, John SIMS, James MATTHEWS, Peter SALLEY, Younger BLACK-BURN, Ambrous BLACKBURN, John HALBERT, and Samuel KERBY.

Deed from John BRASWELL and Hannah, his wife, to Joseph ALLEN; oath John Thomas LONGINO.

Deed from Jacob SALLEY to Joseph REED; oath William SOUTHERN.

Deed from Jacob KRUGER to John DOUB; oath Henry SPOONHOUR.

Deed from George GREEN and Lucy, his wife, to Francis GIDDENS: oath Chas. SNEED.

Bill of Sale from John DONELEY to Thos. DUNNINGAN; oath John DUNNINGAN.

Ordered James TILLEY, a cripled man, be exempt from paying Poll Tax.

Ordered Licence granted Edward YOUNG keep Tavern at his now Dwelling House; Joseph WILLIAM and Matthew MOORE, securities.

Ordered Lidia MOOT, orphan of Moses MOTT, aged 3 years be bound Samuel WAGGONER.

13 November 1782

Present: Martin ARMSTRONG, Charles McANALLY, Richard GOODE, William DOBSON, Hugh ARMSTRONG, Esqrs.

Ordered David ROSS appointed Constable Capt. LOVILLS District.

Ordered John SMITH appointed Constable in BLACKBURNS District in place James COFFEE, resigned.

Ordered John GOODNER excusted from paying 2/3 value Bay Horse entered with Ranger til next Court.

Last Will and Testament, Edward SHELTON, deceased; oath James HAMPTON and John APPLETON; Mary SHELTON and John APPLETON, Execrs. qualified.

Admr. Estate, Moses WILBURN, deceased, granted Martha WILBURN, wife and relict said deceased; James WILBURN and John TEAGUE, securities.

Inventory Estate, Philip WAGGONER, deceased, returned by Execr.

Ordered Sheriff expose sale perishable part Estate Charles WORD, deceased.

Deed from Thomas SMITH by his Attorney Samuel HUMPHRIES to David HUMPHRIES; oath Samuel HUMPHRIES.

Power of Attorney from Spencer BALL to (David) HUMPHRIES; oath Benjamin HUMPHRIES.

Deed from Spencer BALL to Micajah CLARK; oath Robert HARRIS.

14 November 1782

Present: Charles McANALLY, William DOBSON, Benj. WATSON, Esqrs.

Deed from David PAIN and Mary, his wife, to John REED; oath Jacob McCRAW.

Ordered an order of Survey in favour Adam TATE for land entered by Gray BYNUM.

Admr. Estate, John METALL, deceased, granted Rebekah METALL, wife and relict said deceased; James JONES and Jabez JARVIS, securities.

Last Will and Testament, Nathaniel SEIDEL, deceased, late County Northampton, Pennsylvania together with Codical; oath Fredrick William MARSHALL.

Ordered Joshua TILLERY appointed overseer from Dan River to Upper Sarra Town to Guilford line.

Ordered John HUCTHINS overseer road in room Henry COOK.

Ordered Charles DAVIS overseer road in room Isaac GARRISON.

Joseph HARRISON vs David OWEN; Jury: Arthur TATE, Barna HOWARD, James GIDDINS, Airs HUDSPETH, Joseph REAVIS, Thomas EVANS, John WAGGONER, Thos. COKER, William VENABLE, Thos. JONES, William PHILIPS, and James REAVIS.

William BOYD vs Francis HOLT, Junr.; assault and battery; same jury.

Ordered John MARTIN be fined 5 pounds for contempt Court; fine paid by Charles McANALLY, County Trustee.

James McKOIN also fined 5 pounds for Contempt Court, not serving as Juror when summond.

Daniel WRIGHT fined 10 pounds Ni Si Contempt in serving as Juror.

15 November 1782

Present: Charles McANALLY, Matthew MOORE, William DOBSON, Esqrs.

Ordered Admr. Estate, Gideon WRIGHT, deceased, granted Elizabeth WRIGHT, wife and relict said deceased; Samuel CUMMINS and Laughlin FLINN, securities.

Ordered Admr. Estate, James MARTIN, deceased, granted John MARTIN, Heir-at-law said deceased (Mary MARTIN, widow and relict having resigned her right); James GAINS and Matt. BROOKS, securities.

Ordered Rhody SPEERS, orphan Robert SPEERS, deceased, aged 3 years, 6 months be bound to Andrew SPEER according to law till 18 years.

Ordered Ann SPEER, orphan Robert SPEER, deceased, age 21 months, bound Andrew SPEER til 18 years.

John GILBERT being qualified concerning piece Brass in likeness of a quarter when he declared he received of John CALVIN as good money in payment debt; ordered said piece of Brass be nailed to Whiping Post by Sheriff.

State vs John TALIFERRO; Jury: Joseph PHILIPS, William HUGHLETT, John SUTTON, Etheldred SUTTON, James REAVES, Francis HOLT, Wm. CONNER, John HARPER, Abijah ELMORE, Natheniel WATSON, Stephen CROWDER, and Orman MORGAN.

William SHEPPERD made appearance according to order last Term for resettlement his public collection as Sheriff; said SHEPPERD and Joseph WILLIAMS being examined, Court found cause to discharge said order and allow his settlement.

Martin ARMSTRONG, Robert LANIER, Traugott BAGGE, Esqrs. appointed committee to settle with Matthew BROOKS, Joseph PHILIPS, James SHEPPERD, lage(?) Committee of Confiscated Property.

15 November 1782

Present: Martin ARMSTRONG, William DOBSON, William SHEPPERD, Matthew MOORE, Esqrs.

Ordered Clerk issue orders of Caveats to Sheriff to hold Jurys on all Caveats yet undertermined.

Ordered following work under Robert LANIER, overseer road: John ALLEN, Daniel HUDSPETH, Alexander DOUGLAS, William HOLLIMAN, Charles PARKER, Leander HUGHES, Thomas SMITH, Esq., William SHAMBLIN, Jacob ROBERSON, John LANCASTER, John SMITH, Thomas SMITH (cooper), John HAIXL, and Adam SPOON.

Ordered Joseph HOLDER overseer old Moravian Town road from Bridge to Mill.

Ordered Henry SPEER overseer road from Shallow ford to Edward MOORES and roads from Rowan County line and Shallowford to Deep Creek; all hands South side Deep Creek, as high as Edward MOORES work on same.

Ordered John BRUCE overseer road from Samuel CROCKETS as high as John McCOLLUMS; all hands fork Deep Creek, including hands of William Harguss GRAY work thereon.

Ordered Jiles HUDSPETH overseer road from Deep Creek to John RIDINS.

Matthew MOORE has leave build water Grist Mill on Mountain Creek on his own land; deemed public mill.

Ordered James SHEPPERD be not debared by order last Court for receiving from persons in consequence of he being Commissioner of Confiscated Estates.

Ordered part of certain order last term in favor Mrs. Catharine WRIGHT giving her rent said Husbands plantation, be resinded.

Ordered Settlement Colo. Martin ARMSTRONG concerning monies in his hands, be postponed.

Ordered David OWEN be suspended from Constable.

Ordered John GAINS appointed Constable in KROUSES District.

Ordered Admr. Estate, Abraham HOWARD, deceased, granted Jane HOWARD, wife and relict said deceased; Wm. Terril LEWIS and John WILLIAMS, securities.

Whereas Criminal Jail in Salisbury is deficient to keep Criminals, ordered Commanding Officer in County be empowered to call Militia to keep guard over any Prisoner that shall be committed to Jail of this county.

Ordered Samuel CUMMINS appointed furnish Jailor with provisions for all prisoners put in jail.

Ordered Committee appointed to settle with Matthew BROOKS, Joseph PHILIPS and James SHEPPERD, late Commissioner of Confiscated Estates, report find many debts yet unpaid in their accounts.

Ordered Court appoint three persons to make final settlement with them; Also, Exectors Richard VARNAL be cited to appear at same time as former Commissioner to render any amount Confiscated Property of his Estate.

Ordered Martin ARMSTRONG, Robert LANIER and Traugott BAGGE, make final settlement with above at Salem first Friday February next.

Ordered George EBERT, Adam WOOLF, Michael FREY, John FLEMING, James DOAK, James CALLIWAY, James BADGET, James FREEMAN, Jacob SHEPPERD, Philip HOWARD, Damuel MOSBY, John BRINKLEY, Wm. HICKMAN, Malcum CURRY, Theophilus FLYN, Henry SMITH, George HOUSER, Senr., Philip ROTHROCK, Peter BINKLEY, Wm. WALKER, Andrew McKILLIP, Obediah MARTIN, Zachariah RAY, Thomas ANTHONY, Henry KERBY, John SNEED, Richard COX, John HARVEY, Senr., Patrick HELSABECK, William JEAN, Jurors next County Court. Signed by: Jo. WILLIAMS, Clerk of Court; Mark ARMSTRONG, Robert LANIER and Matthew MOORE.

Second Monday February 1783
Richmond

Present: Martin ARMSTRONG, Esqr.

11th February 1783

Present: Martin ARMSTRONG, Matthew MOORE, Robert WALKER, George HOUZAR, William COOK, Esqrs.

Last Will and Testament, Thomas HOWELL, deceased; oath James HOWELL and Henry SPEER; Also HOWELL and David HOWELL, Execrs. qualified.

Last Will and Testament, Joseph SMITH, deceased; oath Joseph GINURARY (?), Marth SMITH, Execrs. qualified.

Last Will and Testament, Christian BAKER, deceased, proved oath Edwin HICKMAN and Wm. HICKMAN; Henry BAKER, Execr. qualified.

Last Will and Testament, James BURK, deceased; oath Andrew SPEER and John T. LONGINO.

Inventory Estate, Noble LADD, deceased, returned by Noble LADD (Jr.), Execr.

Inventory Estate, Edward SHELTON, deceased, returned John APPLE-TON, Execr.

Inventory Estate, John FARGESON, deceased, returned by Rebekah FARGISON, Admrx.

Grand Jury: John HARVEY, foreman; Samuel MOSBY, Phil HOWARD, Phil ROTHROCK, Henry SMITH, Fredrick HELSEBECK, Wm. LAIN, Michael FRY, George HOUZAR, William WALKER, James DOAK, Jacob SHEPPERD, Adam WOOLF, Malcum CURRY.

Deed from John GRANT to Thos. WOOTEN; oath James and John SANDERS.

Deed from Stephen OSBORNE to Wm. HALL; oath John McKINNEY.

Deed from Levy SPEER to Levin SAVAGE; oath said SPEER and Henry SPEER pay fee.

Deed from David GREEN to Sam'l GENTRY; oath Wm. RATCLIFF and Levy SPEER.

Deed from Samuel MOSBY to John JOHNSON; oath said MOSBY.

Deed from Joseph PATTERSON to Noble LADD; oath Constant. LADD.

Deed from Alexander JOHNSON to Jos. WILLIAMS, 212 acres; oath John ALLEN.

Deed from Alexander JOHNSON to Jos. WILLIAMS, 8 acres; oath John ALLEN.

Deed from Robert LANIER to Edward YOUNG; oath John ALLEN.

Deed from Robert LANIER to Wyatt GARNER; oath said LANIER.

Bill of Sale from Zeanos BALDWIN to Wm. SHORES; oath Gilbert KEEN.

Bill of Sale from John PIPES, Junr. to Silvanus PIPES; oath Thos. HIGHSMITH.

Ordered Edward SMITH have leave keep Tevern at his now Dwelling place in Surry County; Amos FREEMAN and Chris. LAY, securities.

Ordered John Thomas LONGINO have leave keep Tevern in this County; Abraham WINSCOTT and Jos. WINSCOTT, securities.

12 February 1783

Present: Joseph WINSTON, William COOK, George HOUZAR, Esqrs.

Ordered John RANDLEMAN have Licence keep Tavern at his now Dwelling house; Martin ARMSTRONG, security.

Indenture binding Meshack GREEN by his Mother (not named) to Samuel HUMPHRIES presented to Court.

Power of Attorney from John COOK to William COOK; oath Benj. BURCH, William Nichols COOK and John COMBS.

Last Will and Testament, Michael GERBER, deceased; oath Joseph BULITSHECK and Mrs. Elizabeth LOBLIN; Anna Magdalin GERBER, Execrx. qualified.

Inventory Estate, James MARTIN, deceased, returned by John MARTIN, Admr. Ordered sale perishable part of Estate.

Account Sale of Estate, William RIDINS, deceased, returned Admr.; LONGINO to pay fee.

John Thomas LONGINO admitted as Deputy Sheriff and quallified.

13 February 1783

Present: Martin ARMSTRONG, Charles McANALLY, Joseph WINSTON, William SHEPPERD, William COOK, Esqrs.

Deed from John HARVEY to John HARVEY, Junr.; oath John Senr.

Deed from David LAWSON to Adonijah HARBOUR; oath James GAINS.

Ordered new cut road from Salem to Bethabra; thence to Bethany (Bethania); thence to Richmond deemed public road; overseer that formerly worked on old road, work on new.

LANIER and WILLIAMS vs Joseph CARMICHAEL; Jury: John BINKLEY, Peter BINKLEY (also spelled Pinkley), Laughlin FLYNN, Zachariah RAY, John FLEMING, Edward LOVILL, Richard HAZELWOOD, Barna ROWARK, David ALLEN, John BRUCE, David HUDSPETH, and Thomas HUGHES.

Matthew WARNOCK vs Williamson MAYO; same jury.

John HUDSPETH'S Executors vs Francis BAKER and others; same jury.

Henry AIRS vs Robert SPEERS; same jury.

James HOWARD vs George DEATHERAGE; same jury.

William COOK, Esq. vs Olive ROBERTS; assault and battery; same jury.

Ordered Gibson WOOLDRIDGE be fined 24 pounds for contempt court for not serving as Juror; fine paid to Charles McANALLY, County Trastee; WOOLDRIDGE released.

Inventory Estate, Moses WILBURN, deceased, returned Admr. Ordered Sheriff sell perishable part estate.

14 February 1783

Present: Joseph WINSTON, William COOK, Charles McANALLY, Esqrs.

David OWEN vs Thomas McCARREL; slander; Jury: John BRINKLEY, Peter PINKLEY (this name spelled over 33 ways, but accepted spelling in this area is Binkley), Laughlin FLINN, Zachariah RAY, Job MARTIN, Joseph BANNER, Wm. QUILLEN, David ALLIN, Druary GOOLESBY, Carlton LINDSAY, and Thomas HUGHES.

Barbara BEALS vs Jacob SUTTON; same jury.

Abraham CRESON vs Solomon OWEN; same jury except Boswell RIDDLE in place Job MARTIN.

Seth COFFIN vs John COOK and Jesse GREEN; same jury.

Inventory Estate, Abraham HOWARD, deceased, returned by Admr.

Inventory Estate, Gideon WRIGHT, deceased, returned by Elizabeth WRIGHT, Admr.

Deed from Matthew MOORE, Esq. former Sheriff, to Henry SPEER, 500 acres; oath William HUGHLETT.

Ordered Philip WILSON overseer road in room John CAMMERON.

Ordered John LYNCH overseer road in room George GROCE.

Ordered John FLEMING be fined 40 pounds contempt court in going off without leave after he served one day as Juror.

Ordered following persons be fined 20 pounds each Ni Si: George EBERT, James BADGET, James FREEMAN, Obediah MARTIN, Thomas ANTHONY, Henry KERBY, Richard COX for not appearing as Jurors.

Ordered Amos LADD, Thomas POINDEXTER, Martin ARMSTRONG, Fredrick MILLER, Esq., Richard LAWRENCE, Robert FORBIS, Robert WARNOCK appointed Jurors to serve next Superior Court at Salisbury for District of Salisbury 15th March next.

Ordered following attend next county Court as Jurors: Joseph WAGGONEER, Jacob BLUME, Joseph EASON, Hardy REDDICK, James DAVIS, Michael ROUARK, Charles SMITH, Thomas DUNNINGAN, Anthony DEARING, Jesse BUMPS, Henry SPEER, Thomas GALLION, Reuben SHORES, Abiel COBB, Robert AIRS, Thomas ADDIMAN, Thomas BRIGGS, William WOOL-DRIDGE, William BURRIS, Philip SHOUSE, David HUDSPETH, John DEATHERAGE, Thomas EAST, Michel HENDERSON, Lewis CONNER, James EASON, John DUNLAP, Thomas GOODE, Junr., William CAMPBELL and Gibson WOOLDRIDGE.

12 May 1783
Richmond

Present: Robert WALKER, Esq.

13 May 1783

Present: Joseph WINSTON, George HOUZAR, Robert WALKER, Esqrs.

Presented to Court copy Last Will and Testament, Jacob LEASH, deceased; Northampton County in Commonwealth of Penna.; George

LASH and Jacob BLUME, Execrs. qualified.

Samuel PEPPER, Execr. Last Will and Testament James BURK, deceased, qualified.

Inventory Estate, Moses WILBURN, deceased, returned by John TEAGUE and Moses WILBURN, Admrs.

Last Will and Testament, Henry WALLER, deceased; oath Elkanah LEWIS, James SHORT; Sarah WALLER, wife and relict said deceased, claimed her right of Admrx. which was granted; Elkanah LEWIS and James SHORT, securities.

Ordered John TATE overseer road in room Philip SHOUSE.

Indenture from John SHADWICK binding himself to John ALLIN; oath Jos. WILLIAMS.

Deed of Gift from Andrew ROTH (?) to Nancy HUITT: oath Samuel FREEMAN, Stokes YEOMANS to pay cost.

Deed from William BOYLES and Eve, his wife, to Wm. EAST; oath said BOYLES.

Deed from Robert WALKER, Junr. and wife (not named) to Wm. SNOW; oath said WALKER.

Deed from Benjamin ISBELL to Thomas SHIP; oath James GAINS.

Ordered Philip SHOUSE excused from serving as Juror this term.

Inventory Estate, Moses WILBURN, deceased, returned by John TEAGUE and Moses WILBURN, Admrs.

Agreeable to order for notifying sundrie persons to appear and show cause why fine 20 shillings for not appearing as Jurors not be made absolute, following persons appeared: Henry KERBY, James BADGET, James FREEMAN, Richard COX, George EBERT, Thomas ANTHONY; after hearing excuses, ordered fines be remitted; Obediah MARTIN made absolute; KERBY and COX paid no fee.

Grand Jury: Charles SMITH, foreman; Joseph EASON, James DAVIS, John DUNNIGAN, Reuben SHORES, Abial COBB, John DUNLAP, Thomas GOODE, Junr., William CAMBELL, Michael RANK, Thomas GALLION, Thomas ADDIMAN, David HUDSPETH, William BURRIS.

John HINE records his mark.

14 May 1783

Court summoned by Sheriff for Tryal of a Negroe named Bartlet, property of Joel LEWIS, charged with burning House and Mill of David ALLIN.

Present: Robert LANIER, Joseph WINSTON, Hugh ARMSTRONG, Justices of Peace; Job MARTIN, Robert HARRIS, Absalom BOSTICK, David HUDSPETH, Free Holders.

BARTLET being charged, pleads Not Guilty; The Justices and Free Holders, having heard witnesses for State and for Prisoner, are of opinion he is Not Guilty and that he be discharged.

14 May 1783

Present: Joseph WINSTON, Benjamin WATSON, Traugott BAGGE, Esqrs.

Deed from Philip ROTHROCK, Senr. to Philip ROTHROCK, Junr.,; oath Traugott BAGGE, Esq.

Deed from Noble LADD, Executor Noble LADD, deceased, to Wm. LADD and Judith LADD; oath Joseph LADD.

Deed from Littleberry STONE to Henry FRANCE; oath said John CHILDRESS.

Deed from Robert LANIER to John LANCHESTER: oath said Robert.

Deed from James COFFEE to Job MARTIN; oath said COFFEE.

Deed from James MATTHEWS and Mary, his wife, to John FLEMING: oath Hugh ARMSTRONG.

William MEREDITH, Esq., elected Sheriff.

The Governor vs Traugott BAGGE; Debt; Jury: Benjamin ANDERSON, Joseph WAGGONER, Jacob BLUME, Thomas EAST, Michael HENDERSON, James CARSON, John LANKFORD, Arthur TATE, Gabriel JONES, William PATRICK, John BLACKWELL and Constant LADD.

The Governor vs Frederick MILLER: same jury.

Robert LANIER vs John BLACKWELL; Debt; same jury except John MARTIN in place of John BLACKWELL.

Robert LANIER vs John COX; Debt; Jury find defendent guilty; Court ordered defendent not pay penalty; Pltf. prayed appeal, John BRUCE, security; Jury: Benjamin ALDERSON, Joseph WAGGONER, Thomas EAST, Michael HENDERSON, James CARSON, John LANKFORD, Arthur TATE, Gabriel JONES, William PATRICK, Constant LADD, John MARTIN and David ALLIN.

State vs Francis HOLT; Principal bound 50 pounds his good behavior six months; Wm. MEREDITH and Edward LOVILL, securities.

State vs John MERRYMAN; Principal bound 50 pounds for his good behavior; John BRUCE, security.

Ordered County Treasurer store up sundrie articles received from several collectors for year 1782 in Town of Richmond.

Ordered John MERRYMAN be fined 5 pounds for contempt; above fine remitted.

Ordered James RINGOLD, Richard LINVILL, Barnabas FARR, Senr., Michael FARR, John DAVIS, William QUILLIN, John DOLEN, William BOSTICK, Henry COOK, Hugh McKILLIP, Andrew McKILLIP, John CUMMINS, William DOBSON, Michael FULP view road from Salem leading near Barna FARRS into Dan River road leading to Valentine ALLINS.

Ordered Sheriff expose to sale perishable part estate Gideon WRIGHT, deceased.

15 May 1783

Present: Joseph WINSTON, George HAUZAR, Benjamin WATSON, Esqrs.

Ordered John HORN, Senr., Henry KERBY, Martin HOUZAR, John HOUZAR, Valentine FRY, Matthew BROOKS, Alexander MOORE, Joseph CARMICHAEL, Noble LADD, John MORGAN, John CHILDRESS, William MARTIN, (C.C.) Isaac GARRISON, William BOSTICK, John HUTHINS, Daniel MOSBY, John B. COLVARD, James SANDERS, John ELLSBERRY, Robert AYRES, John BLACKWELL, Peter SALLY, William McBRIDE, Samuel HUMPHRIES, Robert HARRISON, John SNEED, Joshua COX, John BURCH, Joseph WOODROUGH, Joseph PHILIPS, serve as Jurors next county court.

Ordered citation issued against Jane BALDRIDGE, wife and relict, Wm. BALDRIDGE, deceased, to bring Orphans of said deceased, show cause why said orphans should not be bound out.

Amount Insolvants property returned by several collectors for 1782: Rexia JARVIS in SHEPPERD District, 33 pounds; John COOLEY in HILLS District, 100 pounds; Geo. HOUZAR in BINKLEYS District, 1 poll tax, 190 pounds; property 290 pounds.

(blurred) BRONE (?) overseer road in room William BURRIS.

Ordered Thomas WILSON overseer road in room Robert WARNOCK.

Christopher STANTON vs David GORDON; Jury: Jacob BLUME, James
CARSON, William SHORES, Robert BRIGGS, John COMBS, Phil HOLCOMB,
George HOLCOMB, William BURCH, Carlton LINDSAY, Nathaniel WATSON,
John COE and Leonard BRADLEY.

Richard PHILIPS vs Thomas FLOYD; same jury.

Richard PHILIPS vs Laughlin FLYNN; same jury.

Thomas ISBELL vs William COLLINS; same jury; mistrial.

Peter MYERS and wife vs Peter IRONS; Slander; Jury: Henry SHORE,
Samuel GENTRY, Job MARTIN, John HARKWELL, Jacob BLUME, James
CARSON, William SHORES, Robert BRIGGS, John COMBS, William BURCH,
Nathaniel WATSON, and John COE; Jane WILLIAMS, witness, 3 days, 17
miles; John WILLIAMS, 8 days, 17 miles twice travelling; Hannah
MYERS, 6 days, 16 miles twice travelling.

The State vs Peter MYERS; Petty Larceney; not guilty; Jury: James
CARSON, Jacob BLUME, William BURCH, William SHORES, Robert BRIGGS,
John COMBS, John COE, David ALLIN, James GITTINS, Leonard BRADLEY,
Daniel WRIGHT, Matthew BROOKS; Francis HAYNES witness for defend-
ant 6 days, 40 miles, Hannah MYARS witness, 6 days, 32 miles.

Ordered Job DEAN, orphan John DEAN, deceased, aged 16 years be
bound to Zadock RIGGS until he arrives 21 years to learn Art and
Mistrey Blacksmith.

Ordered Laurance ANGLE appointed Constable in room Mark HARDIN
who has moved out of the county.

Deed from James LANKFORD to John DEATHERAGE: oath Thomas ISBELL.

Ordered Absalom BOSTICK, Terry BRADLEY, Amos LADD, Joshua TILLERY,
John MORGAN, Robert WARNOCK, Moses HAZLET, John DUNLAP, Charles
McANALLY, Noble LADD, James DAVIS, Edward THOMPSON, Adam THOMP-
SON, James WHITE, William DAVIS, George RAY view road from Reubin
GEORGE to Carmichaels Ford.

16 May 1783

Present: Joseph WINSTON, Richard GOODE, George HOUZAR, Esqrs.

Jacob MYERS vs John WAGGNON; Jury: Jacob BLUME, James CARSON,
Michael HENDERSON, John BRUCE, Olive ROBERTS, Stephen CROWDER,
George HOLCOMB, Carlton LINDSAY, Leonard BRADLEY, Constantine
LADD, David ALLIN, John BLACKWELL.

Joseph WINSTON vs John WAGGNON; same jury. (The surname WAGGNON
was consistently spelled NON throughout the record.)

William HALL, having been committed to Jail on susspicion of
Horse Stealing is discharged by proclamation.

Ordered Abraham ENYERT produce next Court David ENGRAM; orphan
boy in his possession to answer complaint against him for illegal
using said orphan; William BERNEY (?) and John SKIDMORE to appear
on behalf orphan.

Ordered Sheriff take into his custody Colo. Joseph PHILIPS and
keep him until he delivers up to the Court certain judgement Bill
he detains from said Court.

Bill of Sale from John SMITH to Patience GLEN; oath Thompson GLEN.

Reuben MATTHEWS vs Moses PRITCHETT; Jury: Jacob BLUME, John BRUCE,
Stephen CROWDER, George HOLCOMB, Carlton LINDSAY, Leonard BRADLEY,
Constantine LADD, David ALLIN, John BLACKWELL, Thompson GLENN,

Airs HUDSPETH and Joseph WINSCOTT.

Reuben MATTHEWS vs John BULLOCK; same jury.

Ordered County Trustee pay Mrs. Rachel TATE 8 pounds to enable her to maintain her same child til next Court.

Ordered County Trustee pay Alexander MOORE 8 pounds for maintance of Henry HENDRICK til next Court.

Nathan DILLEN vs John WAGGNON; Jury: Matthew BROOKS, Benjamin PETTIT, John FRANKLIN, Thomas HUGHES, John CONNELL, John COOMBS, Becket NICHOLS, John SUTTON, Arthur TATE, Wm. HUGHLETT, Jesse KNIGHTEN, John MARTIN.

Samuel CUMMINS vs Thomas CLARKE; same jury; George SMILEY witness for pltf., 3 days, 39 miles.

John HARPER vs Orman MORGAN; same jury.

Matthew BROOKS vs Francis BAKER; same jury.

Leander HUGHES vs Philip CULCLEASURE: same jury.

Matthew BASS vs George PARRIS; same jury except Samuel GENTRY in place John FRANKLIN.

Thomas SMITH vs John REAVIS: same jury.

Adam FISHER vs Godfrey MILLER; same jury.

Henry SMITH vs John KETCHAM; same jury.

James TODD vs Etheldred SUTTON; same jury.

Jacob WINSCOTT vs Thomas NORMAN; Pltf. granted appeal; George HAUZAR and Spruce MACAY, securities; Jury: Jacob BLUME, John BLACKWELL, David ALLIN, John REAVIS, Benjamin PETTIT, Samuel GENTRY, Thomas HUGHES, John CONNELL, John COMBS, Arthur TATE, Jesse KNIGHTEN and John MARTIN; Samuel GENTRY witness for Pltd. 8 days, 10 miles.

Ordered Jacob BLUME have leave keep Tavern in Bethabra; William MERREDITH and Joseph WILLIAMS, securities.

Ordered Jacob MYERS have leave keep Tavern in Salem, same securities.

Old Grist Mill already built on Deep Creek by John WILLIAMS be deemed public mill.

Ordered Joseph MILLER overseer road from John MERRYMANS to Bethany (Bethenia) road and hands that worked under George LASH and those that live within compass of LASHS District work thereon.

Ordered Anthony DEARING be fined 25 shillings for contempt in not serving as Juror.

Ordered citation issued against (blank) MOSER to bring to next Court Orphans of Leonard MOSER, deceased, show cause why they not be bound out.

Assessors not having entered some property 1782, Ordered Joseph WILLIAMS, Clerk, enter same.

Ordered list assessment Quakers property in Capt. COOKS District be collected by said clerk.

Ordered Robert WALKER have leave keep Tavern at his house in Richmond; Jos. WILLIAMS, security.

Ordered Samuel CUMMINS has leave keep Tavern at his house in Richmond; Robert LANIER, security.

Ordered Peter HAUZAR have leave keep Tavern in Bethany; Robert

WALKER, security.

Special session Court summoned by Sheriff for appointment of
Justices, Assessors and Constables in various Districts, 1783.

Present: Martin ARMSTRONG, Robert WALKER, George HOUZAR, Henry
SPEER, Esqrs.

Capt. MOSBYS: Henry SPEER, Samuel MOSBY, James TODD; Capt. BOS-
TICKS: Richard GOODE, Constant LADD, Lawrence ANGLE; Capt. LINVILLS:
Mark ARMSTRONG, Malcum CURRY, Roger GIDDINS; Capt. HILLS: Ben
WATSON, Gray BYNUM, John COOLEY; Capt. HICKMANS: Matthew MOORE,
James MARTIN, Reubin GEORGE; Capt. HUMPHRIS: Hugh ARMSTRONG, John
FLEMINS, Collins HAMPTON; Capt. GAINS: Micajah CLARK, Joseph
CLOUD, David GRAVES; Capt. WRIGHTS: Gibson WOOLDRIDGE, John WRIGHT,
John WILLIAMS; Capt. COOKS: William DOBSON, David MORROW, Augus-
tine BLACKBURN; Capt. BLACKBURNS: Joseph WINSTON, Ambrous BLACK-
BURN, John SMITH; Capt. KROUSE: Traugott BAGGE, John RIGHTS, Phil
GREEN; Capt. ATKINS: William COOK, William ATKINS, John MOORE;
Capt. LEWIS: William T. LEWIS, Reuben SHORES, William N. COOK;
Capt. CARSONS: Thomas SMITH, Job MARTIN, John Thomas LONGINO.

Ordered above Justices deliver lists before 30th July and every
Assessor meet at Richmond on 2nd August in order to put themselves
into classes, etc.

(End of first book Minutes on film from which these abstracts
have been taken. There are no Minutes for remainder of 1783, no
Minutes at all for 1784 although film states second book begins
with 1784 and ends with 1788. The second book begins with 1784
and ends with 1789.)

14 February 1785
Richmond

Present: Charles McANALLY, Robert WALKER, William Terril LEWIS,
Henry SPEER, Esqrs.

Deed from Joseph BURKE to Thomas ELLIOTT: oath said Joseph BURKE.

Deed from William MERRIDETH and Ann , his wife, to Andrew MOORE;
oath said William MERRIDETH.

Deed from Thomas EVANS and Ann, his wife, to Samuel CLARKE: oath
John HALL.

Mary HUDSPETH, a widow charged with Poll Tax, she has not one;
Ordered she be released from paying same.

Ordered Elizabeth LAKEY be released from paying Poll Tax 1784.

Ordered Ann WHITEHEAD be released paying Poll Tax 1784.

Ordered Winniford RIDGE has but two Poll Tax and charged with
three for 1784; ordered she be released from one.

Present: Charles McANALLY, George HOUZAR, William T. LEWIS,
Henry SPEER, Jacob BLUME, Esqrs.

William SHARPE, Esq. produced proper Licence to practice as
Attorney; ordered he be admitted to the Bar.

Deed from William HEAD to Leavin SAVAGE; oath Thomas ADDIMON.

Deed from John Thomas LONGINO to Thomas ADDIMON; oath said
LONGINO.

Deed from Joseph FRANCIS and Lucee, his wife, to Thomas LOVIN; oath William MERRIDETH.

Deed from Thomas SKIDMORE to Henry SPEER; oath John SKIDMORE.

Deed from Thomas SKIDMORE to John SKIDMORE; oath Henry SPEER.

Deed from William WHITTON to Charles PARKER; oath Thomas SMITH.

Deed from Joseph PHILIPS and wife to John MERRIMAN; oath William LANCASTER and William DOUGLAS.

Deed from William SOUTHERLAND and wife to Lemuel SMITH; oath Absalom BOSTICK.

Deed from (blank) JOHNSON to Moses LINVILLE: oath said JOHNSON.

Deed from George CARTER by his Attorney William CARTER; oath Wm. FORKNER.

Power of Attorney from George CARTER to William CARTER; oath Benj. HUMPHRIS.

Deed from James DOAK and wife to Richard LAURENCE; oath Benj. HUMPHRIS.

Deed from Richard GOODE and wife to John STONE; oath said GOODE.

Deed from William RUTLEDGE to Matthew McHAND; oath James DOYLE.

Deed from Andrew HANNAH and wife to John DURGINS (?); oath James GAMMEL.

Deed from John QUILLEN and wife to John VANNOY and James PERRY; oath John QUILLIN.

Deed from George DEATHERAGE and wife to Arkillis DEATHERAGE; oath James GAINES.

Last Will and Testament, Elias TURNER, deceased, proved; oath Evan and Sarah ELLIS; Andrew SPEER appointed Administrator; Moses BAKER and Robert AYRES, securities.

Appraisement Estate, Stephen CLAYTON, deceased, returned by Stephen CLAYTON, Admr.

Account sale Estate, Heziah WRIGHT, deceased, returned by Deputy Sheriff.

Grand Jury: Fredick MILLER, Foreman; John HURT, Amos LONDON, John HUTHENS, Joshua FREEMAN, Jesse GEORGE, Joel HALBERT, William CAMBELL, John ALLIN, Henry AIRS, Thompson GLEN, John LYNCH, William FREEMAN, James DAVIS, Joseph HAMM, and Henry COOK.

Samuel BROWN and Hardy CONANT brought before Court for Breeding a Riot; ordered BROWN fined 40 shillings and CONANT ordered into custody until fine and fees paid; ordered CONANTS fine be remitted and he be released.

Docter RANDLEMAN has but one Poll; charted with two 1784; ordered released from one.

Ordered Elizabeth WRIGHT be released from one Poll.

Alexander MOORE satisfied court his son, John MOORE, is under age and not liable to poll tax.

Joseph AYRES made oath he has no taxable person but himself, ordered charge only one poll.

Lewis ELLIOTT made oath it was out of his power to give in his list taxable property for year 1784; is excused from penalities and admits to 670 acres land, 1 negro and himself; ordered this be inserted in list.

Ordered William HILL be exempted from paying Poll Tax from this
time on.

Nicholas HORN overseer, road in room William FREEMAN.

Ordered Colo. James MARTIN, Henry WADKINS, Philip WILSON, John
SMITH, John McANALLY, Ambrose BLACKBURN, Robert HILL, Joseph
WINSTON, William JAMES, Gray BYNUM, Jos. BANNER, Ephraim BANNER,
Benjamin BANNER, James McKOIN, William CAMBELL, Alexander MOORE,
James MARTIN, George HAUSER, Michael HOUSER, Abraham MARTIN,
William WAGGONER, Henry SHORE, Charles McANALLY, Jacob BLOOM,
Samuel CLARK, John HALL, Samuel WAGGONER view road from Reuben
GEORGES' to Salem Road near where it leaves Walkers old road.

Benjamin ALDERSON vs --dim-- PATRICK; same jury as below.

----uel CROSS vs --dim--- HOL--- and Matthew SHAR; Jury: Wm.
FORKNER, ----ck RAMEY, ----- KEEN, -----ih COX, Joseph PORTER,
Daniel SCOTT, Airs HUDSPETH, George HOLCOMB, David BRAY, David
RIGGS, John ELLSBERRY, and William JOHNSON.

Reubin GEORGE vs William VANCE; same jury.

Ordered William TUCKER keep in his possession a child he now has
til next Court.

16 February 1785

Present: Charles McANALLY, Joseph WINSTON, George HAUSER, Henry
SPEER.

Ordered William THORNTON and John BRUCE appointed Commissioners
to mark out a line of tract land commonly known by name Shallowford Tract.

Ordered John CHILDRESS qualified as Justice.

Deed from Timothy COE and wife to Patience GLEN; oath said COE.

Deed from Bennedick ALDERSON to George WADKINS: oath James GIBSON
(2).

Deed from James GRAHAM to John RIDENS; oath Thompson GLEN.

Deed from Daniel HOOF (Huff) and wife to Mordicai MENDEHALL.

Deed from Mordicai MENDENHALL to Joseph MANDENHALL.

Deed of Gift from James SANDERS to John SANDERS.

Ordered all monies heretofore paid by County Trustee in favor of
poor, now be paid by Wardens of Poor.

Ordered County Trustee pay to Matthew BROOKS, 4 pounds, six shillings, four pence for his attendance as Juror at Salisbury March
Term.

Ordered William ADKINS appointed Constable in room Rezia JARVIS,
resigned.

Last Will and Testament, Terry BRADLEY, deceased, proved; oath
Absalom BOSTICK; John BRADLEY, Execr. qualified.

Ordered Daniel COCKRAM be released from paying Poll Tax 1784; he
proved he was under age.

Ordered Timothy WILLIAMS be released from paying Poll Tax; he
being poor, aged and infirm.

Ordered Catharine GIBSON, orphan John GIBSON, deceased, aged 7
years be bound Ashley JOHNSON to learn Mistry of Spinster til
18 years.

Ordered Phebe GIBSON, orphan John GIBSON, aged 9 years be bound to Daniel HUFF to learm Mistry of Spinster til 18 years.

Ordered John SMITH (powder) be fined 10 shillings for contempt; ordered into custody til fine and fees paid.

Last Will and Testament, Samuel GUIN, deceased; oath Jabez JARVIS; Deborah GUIN and Volentine REESE, Execrs. qualified.

Ordered Letters granted John APPLETON last term, be continued til next term.

Clerk bring record of Probate of SHELTONS Will next Court and James HAMPTON appear and prove said Will next term.

Last Will and Testament, William SHELTON, deceased; oath James GAINS; James GAINS and Benj. SMITH, Execrs. qualified.

Ordered Thomas DAY overseer, in room (blurred) WAGGONER.

Ordered John RIDONS overseer, road from Forbis Creek to Glens Tavern.

Winnifred RIDGE vs William T. LEWIS; discontinued; John ALLEN, witness for Defendent proved, 44 miles, 1 day; Keziah MURPHY for Pltf., 70 miles, 3 days.

17 February 1785

Present: Joseph WINSTON, Absalom BOSTICK, James MARTIN, Esqrs.

Deed from John LANIUS and wife to Fredrick MILLER; oath Tragott BAGGE.

Deed from Seth GORDON to George LASH; oath Jacob BLUM and Geo. BEVIGHOUSER.

Power of Attorney from Robert POAGE to Joseph CLOUD; oath Joseph WILLIAMS.

State vs Frank HOLT; ordered HOLT be released.

State vs Traugott BAGGE; find guilty in manner and form; Jury: William FORKNER, David MORROW, Thomas HAMPTON, Robert HARRIS, William THORNTON, Jacob SHEPPERD, John BURCH, Matthew BROOKS, George HOLCOMB, Jabez JARVIS, James GAINS, John MARTIN. John MARTIN, witness for State, 150 miles, 3 days; Richard OLDHAM, witness for State, 150 miles, 3 days.

State vs Jonathan HAINS; Abner PHILIPS witness for Deft. 60 miles, 3 days; Mason COMBS, Junr., witness for Deft., 60 miles, 3 days.

John JARVIS vs William UNDERWOOD; Abner ROSE witness for Pltf., 176 miles; John TALLIFERRO proves 240 miles.

Richard THOMASON vs TATES Admrs. not tried; John WORD, witness for Pltf., 80 miles, 4 days.

Justice REYNOLDS vs William SHEPPERD; James GRAHAM witness for Pltf., 20 miles, 4 days.

Ordered Collins HAMPTON suspended from acting Constable for misdeameanor in office.

Joseph WINSTON entered 200 acres land on waters Town fork adjacent Samuel CLARK, Thomas GOODE, Senr. and himself.

Matthew BROOKS overseer, road in room John LYNCH.

Ordered John COE overseer, road from Matt. BROOK'S Ferry to Creek at Patrick LOGANS.

Ordered Matthew BROOKS shall not receive more than following rates for Ferriage: Loaded waggon 5 shillings; empty waggon 3 shillings, 9 pence; loaded Cart 2 shillings, 6 pence; empty Cart

1 shilling, 6 pence; man and horse, 6 pence; single horse or
footman 4 pence; <u>Neat</u> cattle per head 4 pence; hogs and sheep
per head 2 pence.

18 February 1785

Present: Joseph WINSTON, William COOK, Matthew MOORE, Henry SPEER,
John CHILDRESS, Esqrs.

Ordered Mary GIBSON, orphan of (blank) GIBSON, aged 4 years last
Christmas Day be bound to John LOVE until 18 years to learn Art
and Mistry Spinster. LOVE to give spinning wheel and feather bed
at her freedom.

Deed from Amos LADD to Peter HAIRSTON; oath Constantine LADD.

Deed from Wm. GIBSON and wife to Patrick McGIBONEY; oath Andrew
ROBERSON.

Ordered Sheriff be fined 40 shillings for neglect of duties attending on Court.

Ordered Joseph RAMEY be fined 30 shillings contempt Court in ab-
senting Court without leave, he being Juror.

Ordered William WILSON have leave keep Tavern at his own Dwelling
House; William CAMBELL, security.

Ordered John COLVARD have leave keep Tavern; Joseph WILLIAMS,
security.

Mary FRETWELL vs Charles SNEED; find Defendent guilty; Jury:
William FORKNER, Sylvanus PIPES, Abner GREENWOOD, Nathan ALLEN,
David HUMPHRES, Benjamin HUMPHRES, John MARTIN, Thomas ISBELL,
Zeanos BALDWIN, Joseph GOING, Joshua COX, and Justice REYNOLDS.

James ROBERTS vs Philemon HOLCOMB; same jury; Wm. T. LEWIS, witness Deft., 250 miles, 18 days; nonsuit.

John WAGGNON vs Joseph PRICE; same jury.

Henry SMITH vs Thomas SMITH; same jury.

Barney and Chris. ROWARK vs Samuel KING; same jury.

Sterling McLIMORE vs Dread SUTTON; same jury.

Catherine HUDSPETH vs David HOWELL; same jury.

William BONER vs Joseph PHILIPS,, Wm. SHEPPERD, James SHEPPERD.
Jury: Moses WOODRUFF, Ben. BURCH, Thomas CLARK, Michael BACON,
John LANCASTER, George SPRINKLE, William FORKNER, Joshua COX,
Justice REYNOLDS, John BURCH, John KROUSE, and James GAINS.

Ordered William MEREDITH appointed Sheriff and County Treasurer;
James MARTIN, Constantine LADD, John ARMSTRONG, securities.

Ordered Richard GOODE overseer, road from Townfork to BURRIS'
Mill.

Ordered John HALL overseer, road from Dan River to cross roads at
Winstons Tavern.

Ordered Keziah MURPHY released paying Poll Tax, she having proved
she has only two Polls.

Ordered James REAVIS pay only on 175 acres he being taxed with
775 acres.

Henry SPEER, Esq. records his mark.

19 February 1785

Present: Joseph WINSTON, Matthew MOORE, Absalom BOSTICK, John CHILDRESS.

Reubin DODSON vs George JOICE; Jury: George HOLCOMB, Abijah ELMORE, Edward CLATON, Willis BRADLEY, Peter SHERMON, Jesse KNIGHTEN, Richard HORN, Isariah CAMERON, Philemon HOLCOMB, Gideon WOODRUFF, William RUTLEDGE, and John REAVIS.

William CONNER vs James COFFEE; same jury.

William Terril LEWIS vs Jacob CARTER: same jury.

Parris CHIPMAN vs John WAGGNON; same jury.

Reubin SMITH, Junr., vs William PEDYCORD; same jury.

William Terril LEWIS vs John COMBS; same jury.

Fredrick ALBERTY vs Richard PHILIPS; same jury.

Michael HENDERSON vs Robert OBARR; same jury.

James WARNOCK and wife vs Moses HAZLETT; same jury.

James TODD vs William IRONS; Rich. CHILDRESS witness for Pltf., 16 miles, 5 days.

John FAGIN vs Etheldred SUTTON; same jury.

John CHILDRESS vs Daniel CARDWELL; same jury.

Fredrick MILLER vs Godfrey MILLER; same jury.

Malcom CURRY vs Francis FORKNER; same jury.

Mordicai MENDENHALL vs Jonathan HARROLD; same jury.

Airs HUDSPETH vs John and Ann MILLER; Wills BRADLEY, witness for Deft., 72 miles, 7 days; John REAVIS, 120 miles, 11 days; Gibson WOOLRIDGE, 240 miles, 16 days.

William HUGHLET vs Abraham WOOD, Junr.; Matthew BROOKS, witness 64 miles, 17 days; William PHILIPS, witness Deft., 18 miles, 13 days; appeal prayed and granted; Spruce McCAY, security.

George REED vs John ALLIN; same jury.

William MEREDITH, Esq. vs Edward COOLEY; Thomas NEIL witness Pltf., 180 miles, 9 days; David SMITH, 112 miles, 6 days.

Airs HUDSPETH vs John and Ann MILLER; Philamen HOLCOMB witness for Pltf., 38 miles, 6 days; Abner GREENWOOD, 200 miles, 25 days; George HOLCOMB, 32 miles, 6 days; Airs HUDSPETH, Junr., 45 miles, 9 days.

William COOK, Esqr. resigned as Corner; Absalom BOSTICK, Esq. appointed Corner; Henry SPEER, William COOK and Wm. T. LEWIS, Esqrs., securities.

Robert SMITH surrendered Thomas SMITH to court; ordered in custody of Sheriff in following suits: Samuel CUMMINS vs Thomas SMITH; Benjamin HERNDON vs Thomas SMITH; Roger GIDDENS vs Thomas SMITH; John WILLIAMS vs Thomas SMITH; David OWEN vs Thomas SMITH; John Thomas LOGINO vs Thomas SMITH.

Ordered Prison Bounds from henceforth be limits of this Town.

Deed from William MEREDITH, Sheriff, to John RING.

Deed from William MEREDITH, Sheriff, to Richard WOOD.

Deed from Edward MOORE to John McGIMSEY; oath Henry SPEER.

Nathan DILLION vs George HYDE and Michael HENDERSON; bails for Edward RIGGS (?).

John ARMSTRONG vs Richard MURPHEY and George WATKINS; bails for

Edward RIGGS (?).

The Office vs Reubin GEORGE.

Benjamin HERNDON vs Etheldred SUTTON; summon bail surrendered Gibson WOOLDRIDGE into custody of Sheriff.

Benjamin HERNDON vs Etheldred SUTTON; WOOLRIDGE surrendered John SUTTON into custody of Sheriff.

Major SLATTON vs John NEIL; appearance Wm. NEIL, his Attorney and claims property in a mare; jury said property is William NEILS; ordered officer deliver said mare up.

Martin ARMSTRONG vs Collins HAMPTON.

Simon GROCE vs Basdel RIDDLE; Sarah GORMAN, witness for Pltf., 120 miles, 11 days; Elizabeth McCOLLUM, 120 miles, 11 days.

James M. LEWIS vs Jonathan HAINS; Sylvanus PIPES, witness for Pltf., 120 miles, 10 days; John PIPES, 120 miles, 19 days.

The State vs Jonathan (no other name written); No true Bill; Ezeriah CAMRON, witness for State, 50 miles, 4 days.

Abner GREENWOOD vs William JOHNSON; Philemon HOLCOMB, witness for Pltf., 76 miles, 11 days; Charlton LINDSAY, 72 miles, 10 days.

Richard HORN vs Thomas BARNETT; Philm. HOLCOMB, witness for Pltf., 38 miles, 6 days.

Valentine REASE vs Gibson WOOLRIDGE; George HOLCOMB, witness for Deft., 96 miles, 16 days.

Ordered William MEREDITH, James MARTIN, Charles McANALLY, Absalom BOSTICK, William HAWKINS, Joseph EASON, Thomas EVANS (Mill Creek), Joseph WINSTON, John COOLEY, Samuel CLARK, Jesse GEORGE, John HALL, Thomas EVANS (cooper), John MORGAN, Joel HALBERT, Joseph REED, John HALBERT, Robert HALL, John DUNLAP and Reuben GEORGE view road from what is called McANALLYS road to best way to road leading to Salem.

Ordered John BRANSOM, William GIBSON, John WELLS, Stephen FOUNTAIN, Thomas REAPER, Isaac GARRISON, John COOLEY, William DAVIS, William WAGGONER, William JAMES, Edward COOLEY, Ezekiel YOUNG, Thomas DAVIS, David DAVIS, and Joseph WINSTON view road from School House Branch to Cape Fear Road.

Ordered John THOMPSON overseer, road from Shallowford to Edward MOORES old place; also road from John McCOLLUMS leading into same and that he clear road to cross Deep Creek near his Plantation.

Ordered John THOMPSON (of Muddy Creek) overseer, road from Muddy Creek to Wachovia Tract.

Ordered Thomas GILLION overseer, ----(?) road out of Iron Works road crossing NICHOLS ford near Chestnutt Hill as far as John PETTYJOHNS.

Ordered Thomas CLANTON overseer, road from Edward MOORES old place to Christian MILLERS.

Ordered Jacob ROMINGER overseer, road in room Michael SITES.

Ordered Thomas HUGHS overseer, road in room Fredrick HELSABECK.

Ordered following attend next County Court as Jurors: Charles CLAYTON, Thomas BRIGGS, Matthew BROOKS, Moonijah HARBOUR, William HAWKINS, Alexander JOICE, John BRINKLEY, Martin HAUSER, John HALBERT, Michael FRY, George HAUSER, Senr., Henry SHORE, John MILLER, William KINMAN, David HOWEL, Robert FORBIS, Joseph REED (Reed Creek), Abraham REACE, William BOSTICK, Daniel DAVIS, Younger BLACKBURN, John BURCH, Benjamin BURCH, Thomas SHIP, David

HARCILLE, James DOAK, Seth COFFIN, James SANDERS, William ELLIOTT, and Valentine MARTIN.

Ordered Joseph WINSTON, William Terril LEWIS, Joel LEWIS, Job MARTIN, Henry SPEER, Thomas POINDEXTER and Thompson GLEN appointed Jurors attend Superior Court at Salisbury for District of Salisbury 15th March next.

Ordered following to be appointed to explore Yadkin River from Wilkes County line to Rowan County line and mark best navigation for same, take notice several Shoals and Obstructions and expense of deepening the channel to 18 inches at low water, for canoes or batteaux of sixty feet long and six or eight feet wide: Joel KERBY, Edmond KERBY, Job MARTIN, Thomas SMITH, Esq., Moses COCKRAM, Wyatt GARNER and John BURCH.

Ordered Gideon EDWARDS overseer, Fishes River road from Wilkes County line to an old School house on said road.

Ordered Darby IRON overseer, from old Schoolhouse to Howards on Fishes River (Fishers River).

9 May 1785
Richmond

Present: Richard GOODE, Micajah CLARK, Henry SPEER, Robert WALKER, Ben WATSON, Esq.

Ordered Tavern Rates be ammended as follows: Good cider 6 per quart till 1st February annually; afterward at 8; corn at 2 per quart.

10 May 1785

Present: Richard GOODE, Charles McANALLY, Ben WATSON, Henry SPEER, Esqrs.

Last Will and Testament, Robert SUMNERS, proved, Stangeman STANDLEY; Boawater SUMNERS, Execr. qualified.

Inventory Estate, Terry BRADLEY, deceased, returned by John BRADLEY, Execr.

Ordered William MEEKS be exempt from paying Poll Tax for future.

Ordered James COFFEE be exempt from paying Poll Tax for future.

Ordered William STEEL be exempt from paying Poll Tax for future.

Ordered Thomas HEATH be exempt from paying Poll Tax for future.

Michael HAUSER has leave build Water Grist Mill on Stewarts Branch on his own land; deemed publick Mill.

Richard THOMERSON vs John TATES Admrs. Jury: William BOSTICK, George HAUSER, Martin HAUSER, John MILLER, William ELLIOTT, Henry SHORE, Thos. BARNETT, Andrew SPEER, Moses BAKER, Moses COCKRAN, James MATTHIS, John BLALOCK; John THOMERSON, witness for Pltf., 260 miles, 7 days.

Elizabeth and Mary RIDGE, orphans William RIDGE, deceased, chose Nathan ALLIN, their guardian; Court appointed Nathan ALLIN guardian to Seth RIDGE, Wm. RIDGE, Thomas RIDGE, and Winnefred RIDGE, orphans of the deceased; ALLIN accepted; William T. LEWIS, Mason COMBS, John PIPES, Silvanus PIPES, Zeanos BALDWIN, Isham THOMPSON, and William N. COOK, securities.

Ordered Drury WILLIAMS appointed Constable in Capt. BOSTICK District in room James COFFE resigned.

Ordered Thomas BOONE appointed Constable in Capt. HUMPHRIES Dist.

Joseph EASON overseer, road in room Philip WILSON.

Ordered James LOVE overseer, road leading from Bethabra to Town-fork; hands work from where the Bethabra line crosses said road to Mosers old place.

Major Richard GOODE, resigned his office as Ranger.

Court elected Richard GOODE, Esq., Sheriff; Henry SPEER, Esq., Surveyor in room Robert LANIER, deceased; Joseph WILLIAMS, Joseph WINSTON and William COOK, securities.

William DOBSON elected Ranger in room Major GOODE, resigned.

Charles McANALLY, William THORNTON and Joseph CLOUD qualified as Deputy Surveyors under Henry SPEER, Esq.

Deed from Wm. MEREDITH, Sheriff, to Wm. T. LEWIS; oath said MERE-DITH.

Deed from Wm. MEREDITH, Sheriff, to Thomas GRYMES; oath said MEREDITH.

Deed from William BOSTICK to Wm. JEAN, Junr.; oath said BOSTICK.

Deed from Barnabas FARE to William HOLBROOK; oath Wm. BOSTICK.

Deed from Spencer ALTUM and Ann, his wife, to Zebedci BILLATOR: oath Nath. LASH.

Deed from John CARMICHAEL, Ruth CARMICHAEL, Rebekah CARMICHAEL and Amos LADD to Joseph CARMICHAEL; oath John BRADLEY.

Deed from John GOODE to Morgan DAVIS; oath John COOLEY.

Deed from Stephen CLAYTON to Hugh DENNUM; oath John COOLEY.

Deed from Thomas DOVE to Leonard DAVIS; oath Chichester BENSON.

Deed from William WOOLRIDGE and Martha, his wife, to Abraham WINSCOTT; oath Airs HUDSPETH and Wm. WOOLRIDGE.

Deed from Thomas TINSLEY and Tabitha, his wife, to Constantine LADD; oath Lem SMITH.

Deed from John HUTCHINGS and Libby, his wife, to Andrew ROBERSON; oath John LOVE.

Deed from Alex. HAWKINS to Moses AYRES: oath Isham THOMPSON and Aaron MOORE.

Deed from Micajah CLARKE to James McKINNY; oath said CLARKE.

Deed from Richard CHILDRESS and Ann, his wife, to Wm. MARTIN; oath James MATTHIS.

Deed from Jacob LOWRY to John SANDERS; oath William SWIM.

Deed from Jacob LOWRY and Eve, his wife, to Jonathan SELL; oath John SANDERS.

Deed from John TEAGUE and Martha, his wife, to Wm. SWIM; oath John SANDERS.

Deed from William MEREDITH, Sheriff, to Charles DAVIS; oath said MEREDITH.

11 May 1785

Present: Joseph WINSTON, William COOK, Henry SPEER, John CHILD-RESS, Esqrs.

Ordered John BRANDON, orphan William BRANDON, deceased, age 4 years be bound unto Joseph WALDROON until 21 years to learn Art and Mistery of Cooper and Shoemaker.

Thomas FROHOCK has leave build Water Grist Mill on Forbis Creek on his own land; deemed publick mill.

Ordered three pounds fine inflicted on Collins HAMPTON last term, be remitted.

Ordered Charles CARTER be exempt paying Poll Tax for future, being aged and inform.

Ordered Joshua CASH and Joseph HILL be exempt from paying Poll Tax for future.

Ordered Toliver DAVIS be released from paying more than two polls 1784.

State vs William UNDERWOOD; find Deft. guilty; Jury: Matthew BROOKS, Martin HAUSER, George HAUSER, Henry SHORE, John MILLER, David HOWELL, Abraham REASE, James SANDERS, Valentine MARTIN, John CUMMINS, Robert FORBIS, William ELLIOTT. Witnesses: John TOLIVER, 240 miles, 15 days; Sarah TAYLOR, 240 miles, 12 days; John BLEDSOE, 60 miles, 2 days; David RIGGS, 360 miles, 24 days; Aaron WRIGHT, 120 miles, 5 days.

Simond GROSE vs Brasseell RIDDLE; Elizabeth McCOLLUM witness for Pltf., 32 miles, 3 days; William HUGLETT, witness for Deft., 20 days.

Deed from John DOUGLAS to John BRISON, Senr.; oath said DOUGLAS.

Deed from John BRISON, Junr. to John BRISON; oath John BRISON, Jr.

Deed from James BROWN to Wm. and Jacob McCRAW; oath John McNAIRY.

Deed from Roger TURNER to Toliver DAVID; oath Daniel BRYAN.

Bill of Sale from Toliver DAVIS to Daniel BRYAN, acknowledged.

Articles Agreement between Toliver DAVIS and Daniel BRYAN; acknowledged.

Samuel FRETWELL chose Mary FRETWELL, his guardian; John WILLIAM, L.T., security.

Thomas BOONE appointed Constable in HUMPHRIES District, qualified.

John FLEMING appointed Collector in HUMPHRIS District, returned list Insolvants.

12 May 1785

Present: Joseph WINSTON, William DOBSON, William CASH, Esqrs.

Zeanos BALDWIN, Collector in LEWIS District 1784: Ordered John WILLIAMS, Constable fined 5 shillings, neglecting his attendance; John WRIGHT, Collector in KROUSES District, returned Insolvants.

Bill of Sale and Power of Attorney jointly 12 August 1784 to Jonathan HAINS; oath Rezia JARVIS.

Deed from William MEREDITH, Sheriff, to William HUGHLETT; oath said MEREDITH.

Inventory Estate, Samuel GUINN, deceased, returned Valentine Reese and D. GUINN, Execrs.

Case APPLETON and HALL respecting Edward SHELTONS Will; after hearing both sides, Court of opinion they have no right to make void any of preceeding Court.

Ordered James GITTENS be exempt from paying Poll Tax for 1784, he proved he is not 21 years of age.

Ordered John GUILBERT be exempt from paying Poll Tax in future.

William THORNTON and John BROWN appointed last term mark lines Shallowford Tract, gave report.

Ordered County Treasurer pay Colo. Wm. SHEPPERD 140 pounds for exoficio service for year 1779.

John BLAKE vs Joseph PHILIPS; Jury: James SANDERS, Matthew BROOKS, Martin HOUSER, John MILLER, David HOWELL, William ELLIOTT, Abraham REESE, Thomas CODY, Thompson GLEN, William BURRIS, John DEATHER-AGE, David REAVIS.

Matthew BASS vs Peter SIMMONS, Junr.; Jury: Robert FORBIS, Valentine MARTIN, George HAUSER, Joshua COX, Joseph MURPHY, Moses BAKER, Moses COCKRAM, Airs HUDSPETH, Henry SHORE, Henry SMITH, James REAVIS, Wm. READ.

William BONER vs William SHEPPERD and others; Jury find Deft. guilty; Jury: George HAUSER, Joseph MURPHY, Moses COCKRAM, Airs HUDSPETH, Henry SMITH, Henry SHORE, Samuel GENTRY, Thomas EVANS, Matthew WARNOCK, John COE, Charles DUDLEY, John PIPES; Adam ELROD, witness for Pltf., 150 miles, 20 days.

Mordicai MENDENHALL vs Jonathan HARROLD; John STONE, a Garnishee, says he has nothing.

Thomas GREEN vs James GITTENS; find Deft. guilty; Jury: Henry SHORE, Robert FORBIS, Valentine MARTIN, Joshua COX, William RAMEY, Henry COGGBURN, Samuel GENTRY, John REAVIS, John PARKER, Justice REYNOLDS, John BLALOCK, Richard HORN; John HARRIS, witness for GITTENS, 200 miles, 11 days.

Edward BRUMGER vs Edmond BALL; same jury.

John PENN, Esq. vs David ALLIN; same jury.

13 May 1785

Present: Joseph WINSTON, William COOK, Wm. T. LEWIS, John CHILD-RESS, Esqrs.

Ordered Mary KING, orphan Richard KING, deceased, aged six years be bound unto John BURCH to learn Mistery Spinster until age 18 years.

Ordered Sarah BRANDON, orphan of Wm. BRANDON, deceased, aged seven years be bound unto Robert WALKER and his wife, Mary, learn Mistery Spinster until 18 years and at her freedom be given feather bed, furniture, cow and calf.

Ordered Nathan ALLIN, Admr. in right of his wife, Winneford, appear next Court and render account of Admr. Estate William RIDGE, deceased.

Ordered Samuel MOSBY and Job MARTIN returned valuation of Negro, part Estate James CLEN, deceased.

The Court vs Joseph RAMEY; ordered fine laid last Court be remitted.

Thomas CODY vs James SHEPPERD; land docket; Moses COCKRAM, witness for CODY, 150 miles, 12 days; John JARVIS for same, 100 miles, 11 days.

John ARMSTRONG vs Abraham CRESON and Edward RIGGS; bails for John SIMPSON. Jury: James SANDERS, Junr., Valentine MARTIN, Martin HAUSER, George HAUSER, Henry SHORE, James SANDERS, William ELLIOTT, John MILLER, Matt. BROOKS, Abraham REESE, David HOWELL, Joseph RAMEY.

William SHEPPERD vs MORGAN and BASS; same jury.

Christopher ROLES vs Matthew BASS: same jury.

Matthew WARNOCK vs Thomas WALKER; same jury.

Michael NULL vs William NULL; same jury.

William SHEPPERD vs Matthew BASS; same jury.

Joseph WINSTON vs Joseph CARMICHAEL; same jury.

John Thomas LONGINO vs Thomas SMITH (jockey); same jury.

Samuel CUMMINS vs Thomas MOORE; same jury.

Christopher STANDLEY vs David COLBERSON; same jury.

Lemuel HARVEY vs Hezekiah ROBERTS; same jury.

Ordered John GIBSON, orphan John GIBSON, deceased, be bound Wm. DOBSON, Esq. to learn Art and Mistry Spinning Wheel Maker until 21 years old.

William N. COOK, Constable in LEWIS District, resigns his office; Zachariah RAY appointed in his room.

Deed from Thomas NORMAN to John GITTINS; oath Robert HARRIS.

Deed from Wm. BURRIS to John McKINNEY; oath Robert HARRIS.

Deed from Thos. HUGHES and wife, to Thos. McCARRELL; oath James COFFEE.

14 May 1785

Present: Joseph WINSTON, Henry SPEER, Wm. T. LEWIS, Esqrs.

Ordered Tavern licence granted Jacob MIRES of Salem; Wm. THORNTON, security.

An affidavit of Winneford ALLIN, taken before John CHILDRES; proved by Joel LEWIS.

Ordered Nicholas GENTRY, an aged and infirm person, be exempt from paying Poll Tax for future.

Ordered John RIDDLE be released from paying Poll Tax for 1784, he being under age.

Ordered John McCOLLUM be exempt from a Poll Tax for future.

The jury impannelled and sworn: James SANDERS, William ELLIOTT, David HOWELL, Matthew BROOKS, Martin HAUSER, Valentine MARTIN, John MILLER, Henry SHORE, George HAUSER, Abraham REESE, Joseph RAMEY, and William N. COOK.

Samuel CUMMINS vs Richard HAZELWOOD.

Francis McNAIRY vs William BOSTICK.

Joseph WILLIAMS vs Peter IRONS, John DYALL and Abner GREENWOOD.

John GRANT vs Henry SMITH.

John ROBERTSON vs Thomas GALLION; Christopher STANTON witness for Pltf., 140 miles, 11 days.

Roger GIDDEONS vs David VAUGHN.

Valentine REESE vs Gibson WOOLRIDGE; Matthew BROOKS, witness for Pltf., 3 miles, 8 days; Willis BRADLEY, 72 miles, 8 days; George HOLCOMB, 32 miles, 6 days.

James RAMEY vs Justice REYNOLDS; John LAKEY witness for RAMEY, 16 miles, 5 days; Henry COGGBURN, 18 miles, 5 days; Thomas ORMAN, 18 miles, 5 days.

Jane HOWARD vs Matthew BASS; Anna MEDDLEN, witness for Pltf.,

120 miles, 13 days.

John RANDLEMAN vs John SUTTON; Carlton LINDSEY, witness for Pltf., 36 miles, 4 days.

James M. LEWIS vs Jonathan HAINES; John PIPES, witness LEWIS, 60 miles, 5 days; Silvanius PIPES, witness for LEWIS, 60 miles, 5 days.

Ordered Jacob MOSELEY, son of Jacob MOSELEY, orphan, 15 years old 15th March last be bound to Job COLE til 21 years, learn Mill Wright trade.

Ordered William HUGHLETT be exempt from paying Taxes on four lotts in town Richmond 1784; proved Samuel CUMMINS gave in same in his own name.

Ordered Jacob SHEPPERD be exempt from Poll Tax for future.

Ordered James PILCHER be exempt from Poll Tax for future.

Ordered Peter BINKLEY be exempt from paying his Poll Tax for future.

Ordered Mary BEALS, Admrx. Estate, Matthias BEALS, deceased, render account her Admr. Estate.

Ordered Jacob ROMINGER, appointed Constable in room John HINE.

Ordered Moses MARTIN, Senr., Robert WALKER, Junr., Thomas GRYMES, Andrew MILLER, William DOBSON, James RINGGOLD, Seth COFFIN, John FARE, James GAMEL, David MORROW, Jacob BLOOM, John MICKEY, Henry STARR, Charles DAVIS, George BEVEHOUSE view road from David MORROWS to Bethabra Town.

Ordered Abraham REESE, Justice REYNOLDS, James JONES, Junr., Laurance HOLCOMB, Nathaniel WOODRUFF, John WILLIAMS L.T., Henry SPEER, Thos. WILLIAMS, John JOHNSON, Wyatt GARNER, Benjamin BURCH, John DURHAM, William COOK, John BRUCE and Jonas REYNOLDS view road from Critchfields ford to Shallowford on Yadkin River.

Ordered Samuel RIGGS, Benjamin SCOTT, Joseph LASSFIELD, Thomas CODY, William McFEE, Edmund HODGES, Edward TAYLOR, Gideon EDWARDS, Zadoc RIGGS, John SCOTT, Eliphalet JARVIS, Samuel DAVIS, John JARVIS, Bartholemew HODGES, John McCARTER view road from where Wilkes line crosses Mitchels River to Critchfields ford on Yadkin River.

Ordered Thomas SMITH, Esq. overseer, road from Shallowford to William HOLMONS.

Ordered Robert FORBIS overseer, road called Brooks's road from Patrick LOGANS, Senr. to Chesnutt Hill.

Ordered John MICKEY overseer, road in room Peter ROSE.

Ordered Joel KERBY, Edmund KERBY, Job MARTIN, Wyatt GARNER, Thomas SMITH, Esq., Moses COCKRAM, John BURCH, Nathaniel WOODRUFF, Junr., Valentine MARTIN and Slathiel MARTIN appointed to explore Yadkin River from Wilkes to Rowan County line; mark best navigation through same, taking note several Shoals and Obstructions and expense of deepening Channel to at least eighteen inches at low water for Canoes or Batteaux of 60 feet long and 8 feet wide; make report same.

Ordered following be appointed Jurors attend County Court, Richmond August next: John HURT, Peter DOWNY, Joseph PORTER, Isaac SOUTHARD, David HUMPHRIS, Robert HARRIS, John DEATHERAGE, Randal MILLER, William WEBB, John FARMER, John DUNLAP, Matthew WARNOCK, Gray BYNUM, William JAMES, Senr., Hardy REDDICK, Younger BLACKBURN, Richard LINVILL, William GIBSON, Senr., Malcum CURRY,

Edward LOVELL, Windle KROUSE, Charles CLAYTON, John ALLIN (Honey John), Samuel GREENWOOD, John B. COLVARD, John THOMPSON (Deep Creek), John RIDINS, John COE, and John JOHNSON (Forbis Creek).

Court proceeded laying out county into Districts, appointed Justices and Constables for 1785: Capt. WRIGHTS and ATKINS: William COOK, Wm. ADKINS, John WILLIAMS; Capt. WILLIS'S: John Talliafero, Elijah SMALLWOOD, Capt. HUMPHREYS: Hugh ARMSTRONG, Thomas BOONE; Capt. LEWIS: Salathiel MARTIN, Zachs. WRAY; Capt. CARSONS: Thomas SMITH, John Thomas LONGINO; Capt. MOSBYS: Henry SPEER, James TODD; Capt. KROUSE'S: Jacob BLOOM, Jacob ROMINGER; Capt. CASH'S: Benj. WATSON, Augustine BLACKBURN; Capt. BOSTICKS: Absalom BOSTICK, Drerey WILLIAMS; Capt. BLACKBURNS: Chas. Mc-ANALLY, John SMITH; Capt. HICKMANS: John CHILDRESS, Reuben GEORGE; Capt. GAINS: Matt. MOORE (no Constable); Capt. LOVELLS: Robert WALKER, Bazel RIDDLE; Capt. HILLS: Joseph WINSTON, John COOLEY. Assessors for town of Richmond: Samuel CUMMINS, William HUGHLETT, and John RANDLEMAN.

Ordered Clerk furnish Representatives of County with lists of acting Justices to enable them to git a Dedimus from General Assembly, so they may know who have right to act as aforesaid.

2nd Monday August 8th day, 1785
Richmond

Present: Robert WALKER, John TALLIFERRO, Henry SPEER, Esqrs.

Admr. Estate, Mason COMBS, deceased, granted John COMBS; John HURT and Joseph PORTER, securities.

Bill of Sale from Wm. CHANDLER to Reubin DODSON; oath Thomas HICKMAN.

Mortgage from Wm. CHANDLER to Reuben DODSON; oath Thomas HICKMAN.

Samuel PATRICK brought before Court accused Horse Stealing; committed to jail for further examination.

Ordered Wm. WHITE be bound in Recogninance in sum of 100 pounds to give testimony in behalf State vs Samuel PATRICK.

9 August 1785

Present: William T. LEWIS, John TALLIAFERRO, Henry SPEER, Esqrs.

Deed from Joseph WOODRUFF to Wm. MOORE, Senr.; oath Wm. MOORE, Junr.

Deed from John Doak HANNA and wife to Thomas BURRIS; oath Stephen K. SMITH.

Deed from Mark PHILIPS to Thomas SMITH; oath David STEWARD.

Deed from John SPURLOCK to (blank) RENNONGER; oath Zepheniah DOWDIN.

Deed from Matthias STEELMAN and wife to Zephaniah DOWDEN; oath Henry SPEER.

Deed from Michael SPEANHOUR to Joseph HAUSER; oath Michael HAUSER, Junr.

Deed from William LANE and wife to Adonijah HARBOUR; oath said LANE.

Deed from Matthew BASS and wife to Edward LOVELL; oath Jesse BUMPS; Samuel CUMMINS to pay 11 shillings.

Deed from Ambrouse BLACKBOURN to Anthony COLLINS; acknowledged.

Deed from Frederick Wm. MARSHALL to John BADGETT; oath John RIGHTS.

Deed from Frederick Wm. MARSHALL to John FREY; oath John RIGHTS.

Deed from Thomas EVANS to Stephen JAYNE; oath Joseph WINSTON.

Deed from Stephen JAYNE to John BURRIS; acknowledged.

Deed from the Sheriff to Matthew MATTHIS; acknowledged.

Deed from William BOSTICK to David LINVILL; oath James KNIGHT.

Deed from John DEATHERAGE to Phillip DEATHERAGE; oath James GAINES.

Deed from Frederick ALBERTY to John HUNTER: oath Laughlin FLINN.

Grand Jury: Gray BYNUM, foreman; Richard LINVILL, William GIBSON, Charles CLAYTON, Samuel GREENWOOD, John HURT, John COE, Joseph PORTER, Isaac SOUTHARD, William WEBB, John FARMER, David HUMP- HREYS, John JOHNSON and William JONES, Senr.

Ordered following be exempt from paying a Poll Tax for the future: George BRUCE, Thomas WOOTEN, Peter EDDLEMAN, John SPEER, Jacob SPEER, John KELL, James PILCHER, and Frederick SHORE.

Jacob ROMINGER qualified as Constable.

Ordered Jesse BUMPS and John TALLIAFERRO, Esqrs. appointed to Committee of Claims.

Ordered Joseph EASON have leave build Water Grist Mill on his own land.

Ordered James EVANS be exempt from paying Poll Tax for future; Gray BYNUM to pay fee.

Ordered George FULP be exempt paying Poll Tax for future.

Ordered Thomas BALKIUM be exempt from paying Poll Tax for future.

Ordered Nathaniel JAYNE be exempt from paying Poll Tax for future.

Last Will and Testament, George ROBERSON, deceased, proved oaths Benjamin PAGOTT and Robert ELROD; ordered Letters of Administra- tion be granted Christopher STANTON and Judith STANTON, Execrs.

Admr. Estate, Joseph COLEMAN, deceased, granted Joseph ASHLEY: Edward LOVELL and Charles DUDLEY, securities.

William WALKER, Collector Capt. COOKS District for 1784, returns insolvants; Samuel JOHNSON, John WATSON, Philip JONES, George BLACK who were allowed off by Court.

Richard GOODE, Esq. appointed Sheriff; Joseph WINSTON, Lemuel SMITH, John ARMSTRONG, Absalom BOSTICK, Matthew MOORE, securities.

Also, John Thos. LONGINO, Charles TALLIAFERRO and John GOODE, appointed Deputies.

Richard GOODE, Esq., Sheriff, objects to sufficience Jail.

Ordered Hugh MORRIS overseer, road in room Thomas ADDIMON.

Thomas SMITH, Job MARTIN, Edmund KERBY, Joel KERBY, Wiatt GARNER, Valentine MARTIN, John BURCH, Nathaniel WOODRUFF, Thomas WOODRUFF appointed last court explore Yadkin River from Wilkes to Rowan line, report that it may be made navigatable for 100 pounds.

Airs HUDSPETH vs Daniel BAILEY; Jury: Robert HARRIS, Moses BAKER, Thomas GALLION, Adonijah HARBOUR, Robert FORBIS, John WILLIAMS, John ALLEN, George WOOTON, Younger COLEMAN, John DEATHERAGE, John DUNLAP and Thomas WILLIAMS; Gibson WOOLRIDGE, witness for Pltf., 250 miles, 15 days; Joel LEWIS, 90 miles, 3 days; George HOLCOMB, 96 miles, 14 days; Carlton LINDSEY, 144 miles, 30 days.

Thomas CARLIN vs William WHORTON; same jury.

Peter MYARS vs Robert WILLIS; Henry SMITH, witness for Pltf., 10 miles, 6 days.

State vs Samuel PATRICK; charged of Horse Stealing by Manor. John Johnson ROWAN; ordered Sheriff convey him, the said PATRICK, safely into jail of Salisbury District to be further dealt with.

State vs John JOHNSON, William WHITE and William ADKINS; Recognizance; JOHNSON bound 50 pounds; prosecute PATRICK at next Superior Court; WHITE and ADKINS bound 50 pounds, appear as witnesses.

Following allowed off as Insolvants: James CHAPMAN, James LANKFORD, Timothy CHANDLER, Cesar AUGUSTUS, Richard CHEEK, Senr., Foil MARS (Myers ?) (not found), William EDMUNDS, Abraham HORTON, Senr., Edwin SMITH, Daniel SHIP, Abraham HORTON, Junr., John FISHER, John CHANDLER and Micajah PRUET.

10 August 1785

Present: Joseph WINSTON, Jesse BUMPS, John CHILDRESS, Esqrs.

Deed from Francis BARNARD to Abraham OSBURN; oath said BARNARD.

Deed from Samuel CUMMINS to Francis BERNARD; oath Wm. CRAWFORD.

Deed from John BLALOCK to Thomas EVERTON; acknowledged.

Deed from Lewis CONNER and wife to Jacob JACKSON; oath Lewis CONNER.

Power of Attorney from Glass CASTON to John WELLS; oath Wm. WAGGONER.

Deed of Gift from George WATERS to John WATERS; oath Jacob SHEPPERD.

Ordered Abraham WOOD be exempt from paying Poll Tax for future.

Ordered Samuel RIGGS be exempt from paying Poll Tax for future.

Ordered William BILES, Senr. be exempt from paying Poll Tax in future.

Matthew BROOKS vs Thomas ROSS; Jury: John CARTEY, James YORK, Eliphalet JARVIS, James TUCKER, James MATTHIS, John RING, James RAINWATER, Joel MACKEY, John DYER, Valentine FULP, Jonathan HAINS, and David OWENS.

Peter EDDLEMAN vs Isham WESTMORELAND; same jury.

Thomas CARLIN vs James QUILLEN; Thos. ROSS, witness, 240 miles, 12 days.

Phebe SUMNER vs David ROWARK; Jury: John DUNLAP, Phil. HOLCOMB, John RIDENS, John DEATHERAGE, Malcomb CURRY, John COMBS, John MARTIN, Daniel BAILS, James GIBSON, Jason ISBELL, John DAVIS and James GAINS.

David ALLIN vs Salathiel MARTIN; same jury.

Joseph THOMPSON vs Andrew MARTIN; same jury.

Francis HOLT vs John HARPER (little); same jury.

John TAYLOR vs John SUTTON; same jury.

John GILBERT vs Jacob MILLER; Jury: John CARTEY, James YORK, Eliphalet JARVIS, James TUCKER, James MATTHIS, John RING, James RAINWATER, Joel MACKEY, John DYER, John COX, Jonathan HAYNES, and David OWENS.

Francis HOLT vs George JOICE; same jury.

Joseph MASTERS Execrs. vs John Etheldred SUTTON; same jury.

Thomas WOOLDRIDGE vs Etheldred SUTTON (2 cases); same jury.

Thomas BURNETT vs Richard HORN; Eleanor AYRES, witness, 100 miles, 4 days.

Richard SAYERS vs John and Matthew COX; same jury.

William BURRIS vs Richard VARNALS Execrs.; same jury.

Ordered Henry SPEER, William COOK, James JONES, Junr., Abraham REESE, John JOHNSON, Jonas REYNOLDS, Thomas WILLIAMS, Ben. BURCH, John DURROM, John WILLIAMS, John BURCH, and Laurence HOLCOMB view road from Scritchfields ford to Shallowford on Yadkin River at last Term, report road marked from said ford passing by John SUTTONS old House; thence by Aaron SPEERS House into the Richmond Road at John ALLINS and down same to Thomas COMBES'S; thence along Ridge Road leading to MURPHEYS old Meeting House; thence crossing Deep Creek below Henry SPEERS House and through his field and into Mulberry field road and down same at the Battle Ground; thence down same to Shallowford.

Ordered Abraham REESE overseer, road from Scritchfields ford to Round Hill.

Ordered John JOHNSON overseer, new road from Round Hill to James PILCHERS.

Ordered John BRUCE, overseer, road from James PILCHERS to Shallowford on Yadkin River.

Ordered Jacob BLUM, Seth COFFIN, George BEIWZHAUS, John MICKEY, Henry STARR, Moses MARTIN, James GAMIL, James RINGGOLD, Andrew MILLER, Robert WALKER, Jr., William DOBSON and Thos. GRAHAM view road leading from Bethabara to David MORROWS, report they find new road best.

11 August 1785

Present: Charles McANALLY, John TALLIAFERRO, Jacob BLUM, John CHILDRESS, Henry SPEER, Esqrs.

Deed from William GIBSON and wife to Wm. LEWIS; oath Andrew ROBERTSON.

Deed from Peter FULP to Michael FULP; oath Andrew ROBERTSON.

Deed from Michael EBERT and wife to Cornelius SCHNIDER; oath Tragott BAGGE; BAGGE to credit Wm. THORNTON for 11 shillings.

Deed from Sheriff to Michael NULL; acknowledged.

Deed from Sheriff to James SANDERS; oath Wm. COOK; LONGINO to pay fee.

Bill of Sale from Thomas SPEER to Henry SPEER; acknowledged.

Deed from Laurence SMITH to John BOUREN; oath Airs HUDSPETH.

Deed from Wm. LEWIS to Elijah KIRKMAN; acknowledged.

Deed from Gamaliel BALEY and wife to Matthew MOORE; oath Thomas ISBELL.

John LANKFORD qualified as Constable in GAINS District.

Ordered James DAVIS, Constable in Capt. BLACKBURNS District in room John SMITH.

Ordered Philip VOGLER and Henry SLATER appointed Constables in Capt. KROUSES District.

Ordered Thomas RING be exempt from paying Poll Tax in future.

Ordered John ADAMS, Senr. be exempt paying Poll Tax in future.

Ordered Charles McANALLY and Wm. DOBSON, Esqrs. appointed to committee settle with Excrs. Marmaduke KIMBROUGH, deceased.

List Insolvents Capt. BOSTICKS District 1784: John CARMICHAEL, moved to Georgia, 3 polls; Moses SPENCER moved to South Carolina, 200 acres land, 1 poll; William WATSON in Guilford County, 1 poll. List Insolvants Capt. ATKINS District 1784: William BRANNON, 1 poll; Peter IRONS, 1 poll.

The State vs Philemon HOLCOMB. Jury: John DUNLAP, John RIDENS, John DEATHERAGE, Andrew MARTIN, Edward LOVELL, Wm. N. COOK, John BLALOCK, James GAINS, Thomas TUTTLE, Isaac CLOUD, Matthew WOMACK, and John PIPES. Witnesses for State: Laurance HOLCOMB, 108 miles, 8 days; Pricilla BRADLEY, 72 miles, 8 days; William COOK, 100 miles, 8 days.

State vs Richard HOOPER; same jury; find Deft. not guilty.

State vs Lindsay CHARLTON; witnesses for State: Laurence HOLCOMB, 108 miles, 8 days; Priscilla BRADLEY, 72 miles, 8 days; William COOK, 100 miles, 8 days.

John FAGIN vs Thomas and John SMITH; same jury.

Joseph PORTER vs William UNDERWOOD; same jury except Moses WOOD-RUFF in room John PIPES. Witnesses for Pltf.: Joel LEWIS, 90 miles, 5 days; David HUMPHREYS, 162 miles; Larkin STRAWN, 240 miles, 18 days; James HOWARD, 288 miles, 25 days; James GUNSTON, 128 miles, 14 days; Jane HOWARD, 384 miles, 24 days; John TALLIA-FERRO, 720 miles, 29 days.

Ordered John RIGHTS overseer, road in Salem in room Martin SNIDER.

Ordered James SANDERS, Junr., John WRIGHT, Airs HUDSPETH, John WILLIAMS (L.T.), Valentine REESE, Peter SPRINKLE, Thomas CALLION, little John WILLIAMS, Thomas WILLIAMS, Nicholas HUTCHINS view road from James SANDERS on Hunting Creek to Yellow Bank Ford on Yadkin River near Richmond.

Ordered Richard KERBY overseer, road from Ford of little Yadkin to the Black Mountain.

Ordered Edward LOVELL overseer, road from Black Mountain to Ford of Toms Creek.

Ordered Joseph ASHLEY overseer, road from Ford of Toms Creek to upper Ford Flat Shoal Creek.

Ordered Ratliff BOON, Junr. overseer, road from Flat Shoal Creek to Rutledges Creek.

Ordered Richard LAURANCE overseer, road from Rutledges Creek to Ozburns Creek.

Ordered Matthew DAVIS overseer, road from Ozburns Creek to Burris Creek.

Ordered Nathaniel STEWARD overseer, road from Burris Creek to the Virginia line.

Ordered following attend as Jurors Superior Court of Law and Equity for District of Salisbury: Henry SPEER, Esq., William T. LEWIS, Esq., John PIPES, Silvanus PIPES, Joel LEWIS, Gray BYNUM, and Henry HAMPTON.

The Committee appointed to receive claims for 1785 report: Capt. Samuel MOSBY as Juror at Salisbury March 1785; Job MARTIN, same; Samuel FREEMAN, Juror Salisbury September 1777; Michael Brown ROBERTS for himself and guard taking Prisoner to Salisbury Jail; Wm. T. LEWIS, Juror Salisbury 1785; Joel LEWIS, same; Thomas POINDEXTER, same; Thompson GLEN, same; Henry HAMPTON, same;

Wm. MEREDITH, repairing Prison and his Exoficio service as Sheriff; Matthew MOORE made oath he had never received anything for Exoficio Services for one of years he served as Sheriff, is now allowed; Joseph WILLIAMS, Clerk, for Exoficio Service 1784; Salathiel MARTIN Juror Salisbury 1784 (given by John Thomas LONGINO); John Thomas LONGINO for finding sundry articles for benefit of Court; James TODD for himself and two men as guards convey Prisoner to Salisbury Jail 1784; James TODD for warning Inhabitants to give taxable property 1784-85; James TODD for himself and three men as guard convey Prisoner Salisbury Jail 3 April 1785; Robert WALKER for committing, releasing and dieting several prisoners in Jail; John HAINS for conveying William BATES to Prison; Henry SPEER, Juror at Salisbury 1785.

Ordered County Tax for year 1785 be one shilling on every poll; one shilling on every 300 acres.

12 August 1785

Present: William T. LEWIS, James M. LEWIS, Henry SPEER, William DOBSON, Charles McANALLY, Esqrs.

Ordered Robert KEEL, overseer road leading from Shallowford to Mulberry field in room John BLALOCK.

Ordered David RIGGS, overseer, road from Wilkes line to Brushy Ridge.

Ordered John SHOUSE, overseer, road from Brushy Ridge to Critchfields ford.

In obediance Order directed, We, Samuel RIGGS, Benjamin SCOTT, Joseph LASSFIELD, Thomas CODY, William McAFEE, Edmund HODGES, Edward TAYLOR, Gideon EDWARDS, Zadock RIGGS, John SCOTT, Eliphalet JARVIS, Samuel DAVIS, Barthomew HODGES, and John CARTEY have viewed road beginning Wilkes County line; running upon Ridge to Joseph GENTRYS road; thence to Iron Works Road; then on Ridge to Critchfields ford.

Ordered James MARTIN overseer, road from Thomas GRAYHAMS to MOSERS old place.

Ordered Adam WOOLF overseer, road from Hollow Road from Maravian line to Arthur TATES.

Ordered Francis HOLT to be committed to Jail till tomorrow morning for insulting Sheriff in his office.

Ordered Daniel CHANDLER be committed to Jail til tomorrow morning.

Joseph RAMEY, with Wm. T. LEWIS and Isaac UPTIGROVE, securities, bound in Recognization for RAMEYS behavior for one year as a good member for civil Society, especially toward Jordan MANNERING.

Ordered George HAUSER, Esq. and John RANDLEMAN appointed Commissioners to employ workman to erect Pair Stocks and Whipping Post at Court House in Richmond and apply to County Traustee for money to defray expence.

Ordered following be exempt from paying Poll Tax in future: Richard GIDDENS, Roger GIDDENS, Senr., John JOHNSON, William MASH.

Ordered William GILL be exempt paying Poll Tax in future.

Isaac UPTIGROVE, having paid Poll Tax in Rowan County 1784, is excused in this County.

Ordered Benjamin HEARNDON and Richard MURPHEY and other persons chosen by them determine suit James HOWARD vs Robert WILLIS.

Ordered Wm. N. COOK be allowed 4 pounds keeping Negro and Horse, property James BELL, taken by attachment at suit Wm. T. LEWIS.

Deed from Wm. T. LEWIS, Heir of Micajah LEWIS, deceased to Nathan ALLIN'; oath James M. LEWIS.

Deed from James SANDERS to John Thos. LONGINO; oath John WILLIAMS.

Mary SHELTON, widdow Edward SHELTON, deceased, relinquishes her right Administrator of Estate provided no Will should be established, to John APPLETON, said APPLETON, her Attorney.

Committee appointed to settle with Exectors, Marmaduke KIMBROUGH, deceased; Estate made following report: Account paid Michael DOUGHORDY; Matthew HAY; Levies paid for 1767; Ballance Bond paid Abraham WILSON, James DOUGHORDY; Doctor bill paid Jacob BONN; Execution YANCY vs KIMBROUGH; to William WILLIAMS for burying deceased; Paid Francis WHITNEY, John WILLIAMS, John POTTER; Paid Thomas TURNER as per bond; Paid Balance note Abraham CRESON; Account paid William PRUET, Adam LASH, Abraham POTTER: Allowed Roger and Elias TURNER for their services as Executors; Goods bought at sale by Widow KIMBROUGH sworn to by Roger TURNER.

Thomas SMITH vs Benjamin HERNDON; Jury: John DUNLAP, John RIDENS, Edward LOVILL, Malcum CURRY, John DEATHERAGE, Jesse COUNCIL, David HOWELL, John BURCH, James GAINS, Silvanus PIPES, Samuel GENTRY, and David MORROS; Evan DAVIS, witness for Deft., 280 miles, 12 days.

Traugotte BAGGE vs John HAIXT (?); same jury.

Rudolph NECT vs Robert SMITH, Junr.; same jury except Wm. RUTLEDGE in room Edward LOVELL.

William T. LEWIS vs James BELL; John BURCH, witness for Pltf., 250 miles, 22 days; Benjamin BURCH same 250 miles, 23 days.

Robert WALKER, Esq. vs William SHEPPERD and Martin ARMSTRONG; same jury.

Thomas CODY vs James SHEPPERD; Caveat; Jury: John DUNLAP, John RIDENS, John DEATHERAGE, Samuel GENTRY, David MORROW, John BLALOCK, George SPRINKLE, John Adam WOOLF, Henry WORD, George HOLCOMB, John LYNCH, John KROUSE; Griffith REATHERFORD, witness for Deft., 100 miles, 12 days; David BRAY, witness for Deft., 44 miles, 3 days; CODYS Attorney filed for New Trial.

Ordered Malcum CURRY, Collector Capt. LOVELLE District 1784 allowed following Insolvents: John SMITH, 200 acres land, 3 polls; John MURRAY, 1 poll; Thos. FLINN, 1 poll; John FRANKLIN, 100 acres, 1 poll; Richard LEE, 1 poll; Wm. PENDLETON, not to be found. Capt. HILLS District: Thomas WAGGONER, 100 acres, 1 poll.

Ordered following attend next Court as Jurors: Joseph RAMEY, John HARVEY, Junr., Thomas GALLION, George HOLCOMB, William ELLIOTT, Airs HUDSPETH, Moses WOODRUFF, Samuel GENTRY, Wm. N. COOK, Silvanus PIPES, John PIPES, Nathan ALLIN, Joseph PORTER, Henry SOUTHARD, James FIELDER, Robert HARRIS, James BRYSON, Christopher SMITH, Benjamin HUMPHRES, James BADGETT, Job MARTIN, Roger GIDDENS, Lazarus TILLEY, James GAINS, Thomas ISBELL, Godfrey FIDLER, and Jacob NULL.

Ordered William THORNTON appointed to superintend Election for Senate Box and Olive ROBERTS for Commons Box on 19th and 20th instant.

13 August 1785

Present: Wm. T. LEWIS, William COOK, Henry SPEER, James M. LEWIS, Esqrs.

Ordered Francis HOLT and Daniel CHANDLER, who were committed to Jail yesterday be discharged on paying fines.

Roger TURNER, Executor Last Will and Testament, Marmaduke KIMBROUGH, deceased, made final settlement. Ordered he have discharge for same. "This order entered on a Script of Paper signed by Jo. WILLIAMS, I suppose by William THORNTON who acted for Clerk, but as it was not then entered on record (By some omission I suppose) I've now entered it from said Script showed me by Roger TURNER this 20 September 1785." Signed JWCC.

On motion William MEREDITH, late County Treasurer, the following Jury appointed to try following case against Tax Gatherers for 1783: The Governor vs John FLEMING, Micajah CLARK, John MOORE (James BADGET his security), William ADKINS, Henry SPEER, Esq., John WILLIAMS LT., George DEATHERAGE and John B. COLVARD.

Phil. HOLCOMB vs Edmund REAVIS; Jury: James GAINS, George HOLCOMB, Phil HOLCOMB, Thomas GALLION, Jesse KNIGHTEN, David OWENS, Matthew BROOKS, Robert WILLIS, Job MARTIN, William WOOLDRIDGE, Airs HUDSPETH and Wyatt GARNER.

Burket NICHOLS vs James PILCHER; Geo. HOLCOMB, witness for Pltf., 96 miles, 18 days.

Richard HORN vs Thomas BURNET; Henry REAVIS, witness Pltf., 172 miles, 18 days.

Benjamin HEARNDON vs Thomas SMITH; John SUTON, witness for Pltf., 480 miles, 13 days.

The State vs Jonathan HAINES; John PIPES, witness for State, 60 miles, 6 days; Silvanus PIPES, 60 miles, 6 days.

Joel LEWIS vs Jonathan HAINES; John and Silvanus PIPES, witnesses for Pltf., 60 miles, 6 days.

Jane HOWARD vs Robert WILLIS; James HOWARD, witness for Pltf., 240 miles, 24 days; Sarah HOWARD, witness for Pltf., 192 miles, 17 days; Keziah MURPHY, 70 miles, 4 days.

Mary RUTLEDGE vs Henry WORD; Buckner RUSSEL, witness for both proves 50 miles, 6 days.

Justice REYNOLDS vs William SHEPPERD; Geo. SPRINKLE, witness for Pltf., 18 miles, 15 days; Laughlin FLINN, 16 miles, 18 days; James GRAHAM, 40 miles, 7 days.

Valentine REESE vs Gibson WOOLDRIDGE; Matthew BROOKS, witness for Pltf., 60 miles, 17 days; George HOLCOMB, witness Deft., 32 miles, 6 days.

Peter LUDWICK vs William HOWELL; Michael FARR, witness for Pltf., 168 miles, 7 days; Augustine BLACKBURN, 160 miles, 6 days.

Philemon HOLCOMB vs Edmund REAVIS; James SANDERS, Junr., witness for Deft., 180 miles, 9 days.

State vs John YORK; Laurence HOLCOMB, witness for State, 108 miles, 8 days; Priscilla BRADLEY, 72 miles, 8 days; William COOK, 100 miles, 18 days.

Philemon HOLCOMB vs Thomas BURNET; Robert EPPERSON, witness for Deft., 600 miles, 11 days.

State vs Joseph RAMEY; James DOWNEY, witness for State, 100 miles, 8 days; Geo. MOORE, 80 miles, 8 days; Jordan MANNING, 100 miles, 8 days.

Jesse FRANKLIN vs Robert WILLIS; not tried; John TALLIAFERRO, witness for Pltf., 60 miles, 7 days; Joseph PORTER, 6 miles, 7 days.

John RANDLEMAN vs John SUTTON; not tried; Wm. COLVARD, witness, 90 miles, 5 days.

Jonas LAWSON vs Joshua COX; Jury: John RIDENS, Edward LOVELL, Moses WOODRUFF, Joseph RAMEY, Jonathan HAINS, Samuel GENTRY, John BLALOCK, John PIPES, Silvanue PIPES, Thompson GLENN, Zeanos BAL-WIN, and William RUDLEDGE.

Peter EDDLEMAN vs Robert WALKER, Esq.; Appeal; Peter EDLEMAN pay costs.

John APPLETON who had Letters Ad Coligendum granted him on Estate Edward SHELTON, deceased, made return.

Nathan ALLEN ordered to make true return property of Estate Wm. RIDGE, deceased, at or since his intermarriage with Winneford RIDGE, widdow of said William RIDGE; which he did. Signed by Order: William THORNTON, Assistant Clerk; William COOK, Henry SPEER and J. M. LEWIS.

14 November 1785
Richmond

Present: Martin ARMSTRONG, Wm. MERREDITH, Robert WALKER, Esqrs.

15 November 1785

Present: William MERREDITH, Micajah CLARKE, Henry SPEER, Esqrs.

Deed from John ALLIN and Mary, his wife, to Thos. KELL; oath Robert KELL.

Deed from Wm. PORTER and Jane PORTER to John HARROLD; oath Edward NORTH.

Deed from David OWEN to George HOUZAR; oath Michael HOUZAR.

Deed from Valentine FRY to Valentine FRY, Junr.; oath Valentine FRY.

Deed from Valentine FRY to Michael FRY; oath Valentine FRY.

Deed from John LANCHESTER to William HOLIMAN; oath David STEWART.

Deed from John NULL and Christina, his wife, to Andrew BLACK; oath Christian CARVER.

Deed from Richard WOOD and wife to Delaney HERRIN; oath John RING.

Grand Jury: Joseph RAMEY, foreman; Thomas GALLION, George HOLCOMB, William ELLIOTT, Airs HUDSPETH, William N. COOK, Silbanus PIPES, John PIPES, Nathan ALLEN, Joseph PORTER, Benjamin HUMPHRIES, James BADGET, Roger GIDDINS, Lazarous TILLEY, and Moses WOODRUFF.

Appraisement Estate, Robert SUMNER, deceased, returned Boater SUMNER, Executor.

Christopher STENTON, Executor, Last Will and Testament, George ROBERSON, deceased, quallified.

Ordered Justices take list to assertain number White and Black inhabitants and citizens of every age, sex and condition as required by Act of Assembly.

Ordered Crispen HUNT, an aged man who has but one hand, be released from paying a Poll Tax and doing Public Work.

Ordered William SOUTHERN, aged and infirm person be exempt from a Poll Tax for future.

Ordered Benjamin YOUNG be exempt paying Poll Tax for future.

Ordered William FULK overseer road in room Joseph HOLDER.

Ordered Dann HILL overseer, road in room John SHAMBLE.

Ordered Amos LONDON overseer, road in room Richard HORN.

Ordered Isaac MIZE overseer, road in room Robert KELL.

Ordered Peter HOUZAR overseer, road in room Michael HAUZAR.

Ordered John FARR, overseer, road in room James HOLBROOK of Capt. Fear road from Guilford line to Lick Creek.

Ordered Charles ANGLE, continue overseer Cross Creek road from Absalom BOSTICKS ford on Dan River to top of Ridge on South side of North fork Blews Creek.

Ordered Joseph NELSON overseer, Cross Creek road from Top Ridge on South side North fork Blews Creek into old road near James HOLBROOKS.

Ordered Samuel WARNOCK overseer, road in room Amos LADD.

LANIER and WILLIAMS vs Amos LADD; not tried; Richard GALLIWAY, witness for Pltf., 200 miles, 2 days.

Daniel SHIP vs John ROGERS. Jury: Samuel GENTRY, Joseph PHILLIPS, Thos. ADDIMAN, Charles WADDLE, Wm. FREEMAN, Jonathan HAINES, James SANDFORD, Samuel HUMPHRIS, Joshua COX, Robert WALKER, Stephen HYDE, and David BRAY.

Charles DUDLEY vs Benedic ALDERSON; non-suit.

David HUMPHRIES vs Richard GITTENS and wife; slander; New trial prayed and granted. Following jury find the woman guilty: Samuel GENTRY, Joseph PHILIPS, Chas. WADDLE, Jonathan HAINES, James SANFORD, Joshua COX, Stephen HYDE, Joel LEWIS, Richard HORN, Carlton LINDSAY, William YORK, Philip HOLCOMB; Rich. LAWRENCE, witness for Deft., 150 miles, 3 days; Ratliff BOONE, 100 miles, 2 days; Jonathan VERNON, witness for Pltf., 100 miles, 3 days; Benjamin GRIFFETH, 100 miles, 4 days; Samuel HUMPHRIES, 104 miles, 9 days.

16 November 1785

Present: Benjamin WATSON, Thomas SMITH, Henry SPEER, Absalom BOSTICK, Esqrs.

Ordered citation issued against Reason WILLIAMS and wife, Mary, to appear next term and produce John and Ann DOUTHIT, orphans of James DOUTHIT, deceased, to be dealt with according to law.

Ordered Nathan ALLIN, Admr. in right his wife Winneford, be notified to appear next Court and render Account of their Admr. Estate Wm. RIDGE, deceased.

Inventory Estate, Mason COMBS, deceased, returned by John COMBS, Admr.

Power of Attorney from Benj. FARMER to Joseph CLOUD; oath Wm. HALBERT.

Deed from Isaac CLOUD to Thomas SMITH; oath Thomas KIRKMAN.

Deed from Reuben MATTHEWS to Benjamin HUMPHRIES; oath Boling CLARKE.

Deed from Richard COX to John HARROLD; oath Andrew ROBINSON.

Deed from Fredrick Wm. MARSHALL to Fredr. MILLER: oath Traugott BAGGE.

Deed from Philip ROTHROCK and Eve Elizabeth, his wife, to Martin EBERT, Senr. and Mark HONS (Hanes); oath Traugott BAGGE.

Bill of Sale from John JAMES to John REAVIS; oath Henry REAVIS.

Robert SMITH vs Thomas SMITH (jockey); Martin ARMSTRONG, Garnishee, being sworn says he did owe 75 pounds, 5 shillings on a bond, said bond assigned to Wm. SMITH and further that Capt. Anthony CROUCHER of Davidson County owes 75 pounds, 5 shillings to Thomas SMITH. Joseph PHILIPS sworn, sayed he owes 6 pounds on condition a Horse is returned him by said Thomas SMITH. Samuel HARVEY sworn sayd he had 5 small Books in his possession.

John KROUSE vs Thomas SMITH (jockey), (same Garnishees; same questions and answers).

Ordered Toliver DAVIS be released from paying any Poll Taxes for 1784, he had not any Polls in State and he paid tax on 337 acres land only.

17 November 1785

Present: Martin ARMSTRONG, Robert WALKER, Henry SPEER, Thomas SMITH.

Deed from Thomas WOOTEN to Thomas GLOVER; oath Samuel HAGGARD.

Power of Attorney from John GARRET to William FREEMAN; oath John SIGILL.

Deed from James SANDERS and wife to Isaac JOHNSON; oath said SANDERS.

Deed from John WRIGHT to Jeremiah RILEY; oath James SANDERS, Senr. and Junr.

Inventory Estate, Joseph COLEMAN, deceased, returned Joseph ASHLEY, Admr.

On affirmation, Samuel JACKSON; Ordered Letters Ad Collijendum Bona Defuncti issue to said JACKSON to collect goods, etc. James FISHER, deceased, Estate.

Fredrick COLEMAN, orphan Wm. COLEMAN, deceased, chose Joseph ASHLEY his guardian; Edward LOVILL and Charles DUDLEY, securities.

York, a slave of William LATHANS, Esq. charged with abuseing Mrs. Sarah VEST, ordered said York confined in Stocks for two hours.

The State vs Jonathan HAINES; Indictment; John PEPES, witness for State, 60 miles, 3 days; Joel LEWIS, 60 miles, 3 days; Silvanue PEPES, 60 miles, 3 days; Nathan ALLEN, 120 miles, 7 days.

The State vs Jonathan HAINES; Indictment; (same witness as above, etc.).

Robert HAMMET vs Edmund HOLT; Jury; Verdict for Deft.; Samuel GENTRY, Robert HARRIS, Joseph PHILIPS, James GAINES, Abner GREENWOOD, John ALLIN, Thomas CLARKE, David REAVIS, Lewis CONNER, John SHORES, Benjamin BURCH, and Justice REYNOLDS.

Philemon HOLECOMB vs Edmund REAVIS; Non-suit; Jury: Samuel GENTRY, Robert HARRIS, Joseph PHILIPS, James GAINES, John ALLIN, Benjamin BURCH, Lewis CONNER, John SHORES, Justice REYNOLDS, David MORROW, Jonathan HAINES, and John CUMMINS; George HOLCOMB, witness for Pltf., 192 miles, 36 days; John DOYL, witness for Deft., 90 miles, 12 days; John WILLIAMS, 300 miles, 54 days; John REAVIS, 80 miles, 6 days; Henry REAVIS, 72 miles, 8 days; James SANDERS, Junr., 60 miles, 9 days; Abner GREENWOOD, witness for Pltf., did not serve; Henry SPEER, 160 miles, 30 days.

William SHARPE, Attorney for John RIDINS respecting remainder land claimed by said RIDING; warrant ought to be issued in favor

RIDING agreeable to his Ancient entry August 1777.

Richard HORN vs Thomas BENNET; not tried; Grimes HOLCOMB, witness for Pltf., 120 miles, 17 days.

David MORROW vs John WAGGNON; same jury except Charles DUDLEY in room David MORROW.

Samuel CUMMINS vs Hezekiah ROBERTS; same jury.

Jacabud BLACKLEDGE overseer, road in room Silvanue PIPES.

Ordered Drurey WATSON, overseer, road from Guilford line to Cross Roads at David MORROWS.

Ordered Joseph PATTERSON overseer, Guilford road to Cross Roads.

Ordered John TEAGUE overseer, Salisbury road from Rowan line to Cross Roads.

Ordered James SANDERS overseer, road in room John SANDERS.

Ordered Thomas GOODE, Junr. overseer, road in room Richard GOODE, Esq.

18 November 1785

Present: Martin ARMSTRONG, Thomas SMITH, Henry SPEER, Esqrs.

Deed from John NULL and wife to Fredrick MILLER: oath Wm. THORNTON.

Deed from John FORKNER and wife to Thomas TLOVIRD (?); oath Wm. MERREDITH.

Ordered John Thomas LONGINO has leave keep Tavern at this House in this county; Thompson GLEN and John KROUSE, securities.

John COX vs Benjamin ALDERSON; Jury: John KROUSE, Samuel GENTRY, Joseph PHILIPS, Thompson GLEN, James GAINES, Thomas ISBELL, James TODD, Robert WILLIS, James DOYLE, John APPLETON, Abial COBB, and Andrew ROBINSON.

Charles McANNALLEY, County Trustee vs John COLVARD; Citation; Jury: Malcom CURREY, Joshua COX, Matthew BROOKS, James REAVIS, Michael FRY, William PRATHER, Matthew WARNOCK, Richard HORN, John CUMMINS, Jacob SHEPPERD, Justice REYNOLDS, and Richard BLALOCK.

Fredrick MILLER vs Godfrey MILLER; tried some time ago; ordered Scire Facias issue against all Garnishees that failed to appear.

Henry SPEER, Esq. vs Airs HUDSPETH; same jury.

Wm. Terril LEWIS vs John RANDLEMAN; same jury.

Mary RUTLEDGE vs Henry WORD; not tried; Gibson WOOLDRIDGE witness for Deft. proves 200 miles, 23 days.

State vs Thomas BURNET; not tried; Richard HORNE, witness for State, 252 miles, 34 days.

James Martin LEWIS vs Jonathan HAINES; not tried; Silvanus PIPES, witness for Deft., 70 miles, 6 days; John PIPES, witness for Pltf., 70 miles, 6 days; Zeanous BALDWIN, 180 miles, 13 days.

Benjamin HEARNDON vs Thomas SMITH (jockey); not tried; John SUTTON, witness for Pltf., 160 miles, 4 days.

William Terrel LEWIS vs Gibson WOOLDRIDGE; not tried; John SUTTON, witness for Deft., 640 miles, 17 days.

Ordered John SLATTEN overseer, road in room Lazarus TILLEY.

Ordered James WILLIAMS released from paying Poll Tax for future.

Receipt from Wm. WHITE, Clerk to Comptroller, to Joseph PHILIPS,

Commissioner Confiscated Property for sundry receipts given by Colo. Robert LANIER, recorded.

19 November 1785

Present: Martin ARMSTRONG, Charles McANALLY, William DOBSON, Robert WALKER, Esqrs.

Obligation from Joel LEWIS to Salathiel MARTIN for deliquent Bill of Sale; acknowledged.

Deed from Peter ELDER and wife to William FLYNN; oath Wm. ROBERSON.

Affadavits of Henry SPEER and Joseph GENTRY; acknowledged by Henry SPEER.

On hearing prayer of Littisha DAVIS, widow and Admrs. Phillip DAVIS, deceased, Ordered James HAMPTON, Joseph WINSTON, Joseph BANNER, Abraham MARTIN, Thos. EVANS, and Gray BYNUM be appointed Jury to direct Surveyor lay off one third part land belonging to Estate said DAVIS, deceased, and Charles McANALLY shall lay off same. (Charles McANALLY was surveyor at this time.)

It is opinion of Court there is none of Estate Thomas SMITH in hands of Martin ARMSTRONG nor Anthony CROUCHER.

Inventory and Account Sales Estate, John MARLATT, deceased, returned Admr. Rebekah MARLATT, Admrx. of Estate.

Account Settlement part Estate, Benj. BURK, returned by Admrx.

Ordered Adam MITCHELL appointed Constable in Capt. BLACKBURNS District.

Court appointed Collectors for 1785 in following: Capt. GAINS: James GAINES; Capt. BLACKBURNS: John McANALLY; Capt. MOSBYS: Philip HOWARD; Capt. SANDERS: John WILLIAMS; Capt. CARSONS: John Thomas LONGINO; Capt. BOSTICKS: Druary WILLIAMS; Capt. KROUSES: Michael HAUZAR; Capt. HICKMANS; Reuben GEORGE; Capt. HILLS: John COOLEY; Capt. COOKS: William WALKER; Capt. LOVILLS: Malcum CURRY; Capt. HUMPHRIES: Robert HARRIS; Capt. ATKINS: William ADKINS; Capt. WILLIS: Thomas BACON; Capt. LEWIS: Zachariah RAY.

Ordered John COLVARD collect arrears Taxes in his District 1784.

Ordered William CRAWFORD, Esq. fined 5 shillings for profane swearing and speaking in contempt of Court after he was order to Silence; fine paid and delivered to Robert WALKER, Esq.

Ordered Nathan PIKE overseer, road in room John LOVE.

Ordered James HAMPTON overseer, road in room Samuel CLARKE.

Ordered Zephiniah DOWDEN overseer, road in room John THOMPSON, deceased.

Ordered Robt. BRIGGS overseer, Streets Town Richmond and road leading to Yellow Bank Ford on Yadkin River in room John ARMSTRONG.

Ordered David BALLARD, Thomas BALLARD, Moreman BALLARD, Boater SUMNER, Joshua SUMNER, Wm. REYNOLDS, Nathaniel REYNOLDS, Wm. HIATT, John BURROUS, Daniel BAILES, Jonathan HARROLD, Richard PINSON, Abraham McMILLON, Joseph JESSOP, John HIATT, Isaac JONES view road from upper and Quaker road near Jonathan HARROLDS Shop to road crossing Mountain Wards Gap.

Ordered James SANDERS, Jr. overseer, road from Williams Mill to Vanderfords Mill.

Ordered Charles VANDERFORD overseer, road from Wm. PHILIPS to Yellow Bank Ford.

Ordered Andrew ROBINSON, Wm. GIBSON, Isaac GARRISON, Augustine BLACKBURN, John COOLERY, Patrick McGIBBONEY, Lemuel SMITH, Richard GOODE, John MARTIN, Edward COOLEY, Samuel CLARKE, Mordical HAMM, Thomas RAPER, John BRUNSON view road called Cape Fear Road from above Lick Creek near Wells Meeting House.

Ordered Wm. PETTY, Wm. OWEN, James ELLROD, Daniel HOPPAS, Edward CLANTON, Thomas CLANTON, John BLALOCK, John HUMPHRIS, Joseph RAMEY, David HOWELL, Henry SPEER, John MOORE, James HOWELL, Jacob HOOTS view Mulberry Field road from Wm. PETTYS to shun the hill at HOPPAS, thence into Shallowford road again.

Thomas CODY vs James SHEPPERD: Caveat; CODY to shew cause within first 3 days next Superior Court why writ Certionare not be issued.

Nathaniel McCARREL vs John COOLEY; Caveat; John COOLEY, same above.

The State vs Joseph RAMEY; On motion John WILLIAMS, Attorney; ordered Jordan MANNING prosecutor last term bind Joseph RAMEY good behavior, pay witnesses.

Ordered following attend next Court as Jurors: John HARVEY, Jr., Joseph GENTRY, Henry SOUTHARD, James FIELDER, James BRYSON, Christopher SMITH, Jacob NULL, John TEAGUE, John CUMMINS, Wm. WALKER, Patrick McGIBBONY, John BOLES, Robert HILL, Isaac GARRISON, Anthony DEARING, William HUTCHERSON, Thomas LOVORN, Andrew MOORE, Joshua COX, Thomas GAINS, Arkilus DEATHERAGE, John STATEN, John HORN, Sr., Adonijah HARBOUR, Wm. FREEMAN, Andrew SPEER, Wm. ROBERSON, Jacob SHEPPERD, Henry WAGGONER, and John ELLSBERRY.

Arthur TATE charged insulting Colo. Martin ARMSTRONG during setting of Court fined and bound to his good behavior for three months, especially toward Colo. ARMSTRONG; Ordered into custody til give security; Colo. ARMSTRONG made motion his name be struck out in above order and said TATE be released from same. Opinion of Court, Colo. ARMSTRONGS situation as an Officer both Civil and Milatory requires particular attention and order stands as is.

Ordered Richard GOODE, Esq. appointed repair Breaches in Public Jail; same paid for by County Trustee.

Ordered an Arbitration Bond jointly signed by Matthew BROOKS, George LASH and George HOUZAR admitted to record.

An award under hands of Henry SPEER, John ARMSTRONG, Joseph GENTRY proved; oath Martin ARMSTRONG.

Ordered Martin ARMSTRONG, Esq. appointed committee procure County Seal, County Trustee defray Expense.

Ordered Wm. MERREDITH, Esq. procure Book Keeping County Records.

COURT MINUTES
(1786-1789)

VOL. II

13 February 1786
Richmond

Present: Robert WALKER, William MERREDITH, Esqrs.

14 February 1786

Present: William T. LEWIS, Henry SPEER, Absalom BOSTICK, Esqrs.

Grand Jury: Patrick McGIBBONY, Foreman; John HARVEY, Junr., Joseph GENTRY, Henry SOUTHARD, Jacob NULL, John TEAGUE, William WALKER, John BOLES, Robert HILL, William HUTCHERSON, Thomas LOVEN, Andrew MOORE, Joshua COX, Jacob SHEPPERD, Henry WAGGONER, and John ELLSBURY.

Deed from William BOSTICK to Henry COOK; oath Lawrence ANGLE.

Deed from Matthew WARNOCK to Lemuel SMITH; oath Maj. Richard GOODE.

Deed from Jacob SPEER to Benjamin SPEER; oath Henry SPEER.

Deed from David CLARKE to David BALLARD; oath Moreman BALLARD.

Deed from Robert WALKER to Mordicai MENDENHALL; oath said WALKER. (2)

Ordered Richard GOODE, Charles ANGLE, Druary WILLIAMS, Noble LADD, Edward THOMPSON, Almon GUINN, Harry TERREL, William KINMAN, John COOLEY, Wm. BOSTICK, Andrew ROBINSON, John HOLBROOK, John BRANSON, Absalom BOSTICK, and Joseph NELSON view road from Richard GOODES to John THOMPSONS.

Ordered Anthony BITTING has leave to keep Tavern at his house; John ADDAMS and John Adam WOOLF, securities.

Ordered Philip HOWARD, guardian of Ann DOUTHIT and John DOUTHIT, orphans of James DOUTHIT, deceased; John and Issac DOUTHIT, securities.

15 February 1786

Present: Martin ARMSTRONG, Absalom BOSTICK, Wm. Terrel LEWIS, Henry SPEER, Esqrs.

John BOSTICK qualified as Deputy Sheriff.

Ordered John GILES appointed Constable in KROUSES District in room of Henry SLATER.

Ordered John ADAMS appointed same in HILLS District in room of Adam WOOLF.

Ordered Charles SMITH overseer, Hollow road from Old Store at McCraws to Virginia line.

Ordered John LAW be exempt from paying Poll Tax for Ellerd MELVIN who lives with him for year 1785. (Possibly John LOW.)

Inventory Estate, George ROBERTSON, deceased, returned by Christopher and Judith STENTON, Executors.

Last Will and Testament, Thomas PETTIT, deceased; oath Wm. COOK; Judith PETTIT and Thomas PETTIT, Executors, qualified.

Last Will and Testament, Benjamin PETTIT, deceased; proved George
PETIT and Job MARTIN, Executors, who qualified.

David OWEN vs Robert WALKER: slander; Jury find for Deft.: John
CUMMINS, Thomas GAINES, John STATTEN, John HORN, William FREEMAN,
William ROBINSON, Anthony DEARING, James BRYSON, Olive ROBERTS,
Peter FULTZ, Peter ROTHROCK, and John HALBERT.

Robert WALKER vs David OWENS; same jury except Thomas EVANS in
place of Olive ROBERTS; find for Deft.; Daniel SHOUSE, witness
for Pltf., 50 miles, 9 days.

Bill of Sale from Andrew SWATZ to Mary and Elizabeth FISHER; oath
Christian REASOR.

Deed from Richard WOOD to Thomas RING; oath of John RING.

Deed from Richard WOOD to Thomas RING; oath John RING.

Deed from Thomas POINDEXTER to William PHILIPS; oath said
POINDEXTER.

Deed from Richard GOODE, Sheriff, to Jos. VAUGHN; oath Andrew
ROBINSON.

Deed from Mark HARDIN to Robert DEARING; oath William M. COOLEY.

Deed from Elizabeth WOOLF to John Adam WOOLF; oath George HAUZAR.

Deed from Samuel RIGGS to Benjamin SCOTT; oath John TALIAFERRO.

Mortgage from Peter SALLE to Richard MURPHY, 386 acres; oath
Elihu AYERS.

Ordered Mary CRITZWITCHER, orphan of Philip CRITZWITCHER, deceased, be bound to Philip SNIDER for three years and four months
to learn mysterry of a Spinster.

                    16 February 1786

Present: Martin ARMSTRONG, William Terrel LEWIS, Henry SPEER,
Esqrs.

Bill of Sale from Benjamin BINGE to Archelus HUGHES; oath James
GAINES.

Deed from John TALIAFERRO to Micajah OGLESBY; oath said TALIAFERRO.

Ordered John DAVIS appointed Constable in Capt. COOKS District
in room Augustine BLACKBURN.

Ordered Adam MITCHELL, qualified as Constable.

Ordered William COOK, Charles McANNALLY and William DOBSON, Esqrs.
committee to receive, etc. lists of Inhabitants in Surry County.

Ordered Edward YOUNG have leave to keep Tavern at his house;
Joseph WILLIAMS and Joseph RAMEY, securities.

John BOWLES acknowledged he had done Major Richard GOODE injury
by speaking Slanderous words to his prejudice in charging said
GOODE of having robbed him of a gunn, is groundless.

Ordered William HOLLBROOK in COOKS District be hereafter exempt
from paying a Poll Tax because of advanced age and infirmith.

Additional Inventory, Fredrick COX'S Estate returned by Milly
COX, Admrs.

Verdict of Jury summoned by Coroner to assign Lutisha DAVIS her
dower, returned by Charles McANALLY.

Ordered Charles DUDLEY be fined 20 shillings for failing to
attend as Juror; fine remitted.

Ordered Adam ELRODE overseer, of road from Douthits Bridge to
Enochs Ferry for one year.

Ordered John BLAKE be appointed overseer road from Douthits Bridge
to Stoners Mill for one year.

Ordered road leading from end Quaker road to Virginia line lately
laid out by Jury and John BYREHAM, overseer of same.

Ordered Thomas CLANTON overseer, road laid off from William PETTYS
in old road leading to Shallowford.

The State vs Thomas BURNET; Indictment, assault and battery; jury
find BURNET guilty and fined 5 pounds. Ordered BURNET committed
until same be paid. Jury: Thomas GAINS, John SLATTEN, William
FREEMAN, Anthony DEARING, James BRYSON, John DEATHERAGE, John
CUMMINS, Thomas PETTIT, James YORK, James McKOIN, David MORROW,
and John WELLS; Henry REAVIS, witness for State, 72 miles, 5
days; Richard HORN, 34 miles, 3 days; John AYERS, 180 miles, 13
days.

The State vs Arthur TATE; Indictment assault and battery; same
jury; find Deft. guilty, fined 10 shillings.

Hannah TOMERSON by her next friend vs John LYNCH, Junr.; slander;
same jury except Thompson GLEN in place of John CUMMINS; Thompson
GLEN, witness for Pltf., 36 miles, 8 days.

Christopher ELLIS vs Henry BURCH.

Thomas SMITH vs Orman MORGAN.

Samuel CUMMINS vs Thomas SMITH. Jury: John CUMMINS, John SHORES,
James BALDWIN, John APPLETON, Gabriel WAGGONER, Charles DUDLEY,
John BURCH, Moses WOODROUGH, Samuel GENTRY, Thomas McCARREL,
James TODD, and Collins HAMPTON.

William Terrel LEWIS vs Joseph THOMPSON.

Robert HARRIS vs Ormon MORGAN.

Thomas HAMM vs William MORELAND.

George AUST vs John DROUSE.

William Terrel LEWIS vs Thomas STENTON; Thomas BINGHAMAN, witness
for Pltf., 240 miles, 10 days; Wm. HAMM, 300 miles, 14 days;
Zachariah RAY, 360 miles, 16 days.

Ordered following appointed as Jurors to serve May Term: Noble
LADD, Harry TERREL, Robert CRUMP, Henry COOK, Drewry WATSON, Seth
COFFIN, Alex. MOORE, John BOWLES, Gray BYNUM, John HALBERT, Joseph
EAST, Joseph REID (B.I.), William HICKMAN, Joseph CLOUS, Joshua
COX, David HUMPHRIS, James DOAK, James BADGETT, Joshua FREEMAN,
Malcum CURRY, Thomas BRIDGES, Fredrick MILLER, Samuel MOSBY, Junr.,
Philip HOWARD, Ayres HUDSPETH, David HOWELL, John BRUCE, John
COOK, Nathaniel MORRIS, Gideon EDWARDS, Job MARTIN, Jacob SHEPPERD,
Thomas SPENCE, and Stephen SMITH.

17 February 1786

Present: Henry SPEER, Absalom BOSTICK, Matthew MOORE, Esqrs.

Ordered John CUMMINS, Thomas GAINES, John STATTEN, John HORN,
Senr., Wm. ROBERSON, Anthony DEARING, James BRYSON fined 20 shillings each for failing to appear as Jurors. Ordered fine for
GAINES, DEARING, CUMMINGS, ROBERSON and STATTON be remitted after
hearing excuses.

Ordered Letters of Administration, Estate of Joshua COOK, deceased,
granted Thomas COOK; James REAVIS and Wm. RUTLEDGE, securities.

Ordered perishable part of Estate be sold.

Ordered Matthew BROOKS overseer, road in room of John COE.

Ordered William HOLLIMAN overseer, road in room of Matthew MOORE which formerly was under care of John LYNCH.

Ordered Edward COOLEY overseer, road lately marked out from Wells Meeting house to Lick Creek.

Ordered John HORN be exempt from payment Tax on Negro Jenny for 1785 who was inlisted by John WATTERS for same year.

Deed from James SANDERS and Sarah, his wife, to John N. ANDERSON; oath of said SANDERS.

Deed from Pepter EDDLEMAN to George PRIDDY; oath Toliver DAVIS.

Ordered following appointed a Venire to Superior Court at Salisbury March Term, 1786: Henry SPEER, Henry HAMPTON, Joel LEWIS, John PIPES, Matthew BROOKS, Silvanus PIPES, and Thomas EVANS.

Ordered Charles VEST appointed Constable in Town of Richmond.

John RING vs John WAGGONON. Jury: William WAGGONER, Justice REYNOLDS, Robert HARRIS, John WELLS, Olive ROBERTS, Reuben DODSON, Jonathan HAYNES, Richard THOMERSON, Thomas EVANS, Joseph BANNER, Michael FRY, and Jesse KNIGHTON.

James QUILLEN vs John WAGGNON; same jury.

Phileman HOLCOMB vs Thomas BURNET; same jury except Wm. VENABLE in place Reuben DODSON; Wm. T. LEWIS, witness for Pltf., 540 miles, 30 days; Robert EPPERSON, witness for Deft., 200 miles, 4 days; Edward REAVIS, 90 miles, 4 days; Carlton LINDSAY, witness for Pltf., 240 miles, 30 days.

William Terrel LEWIS vs William SHEPPERD. Jury: William FREEMAN, Job MARTIN, Wyatt GARNER, Thomas McCARREL, Anthony DEARING, Thomas GAINS, Abraham WOOD, John LYNCH, John BRUCE, Isaac JOICE, Wm. N. COOK, and Jason ISBELL; Job MARTIN, witness for Pltf., 30 miles, 24 days; Olive ROBERTS, 200 miles, 17 days.

David ALLIN vs William BIRNEY.

Jane HOWARD vs Matthew BASS; John MARTIN, witness for Deft., 120 miles, 9 days; Lucy HOWARD, witness for Pltf., 360 miles, 29 days; James HOWARD, 360 miles, 33 days; Anne MIDLEN, 140 miles, 12 days; Katey McCLOUD, witness for Deft., 264 miles, 31 days.

James TUCKER vs William RAMSEY; Trover; same jury except Adonjah HARBOUR in place of Jonathan HAYNES; James HOWARD, witness for Deft., 432 miles, 29 days; John ALLIN, 200 miles, 23 days; Branch TUCKER, witness for Pltf., 120 miles, 7 days; John BRANCH, 120 miles, 7 days.

Henry SPEER vs Airs HUDSPETH; John WILLIAMS, witness for Pltf., 40 miles, 7 days.

William BELL vs John COLVARD; John WILLIAMS, witness for Deft., 20 miles, 4 days.

William T. LEWIS vs John RANDLEMAN; same jury except Thompson GLEN and Zeanos T. BALDWIN in room of Abraham WOOD and Jason ISBELL; John DOYLE, witness for Pltf., 90 miles, 13 days.

Jane SCOTT vs Abraham CRESON; David HALL, witness for Pltf., 200 miles, 4 days.

Thomas BURNET vs Richard HORN; Thomas AYRES, witness for Pltf., 144 miles, 6 days; John DIER, 192 miles, 21 days.

Justice REYNOLDS vs William SHEPPERD; same jury except Jonathan

HAYNES in place of Wm. N. COOK; James GRAYHAM, witness for Pltf., 40 miles, 10 days; George SPRINKLE, 12 miles, 9 days; Laughlin FLYN, 8 miles, 9 days.

18 February 1786

Present: Martin ARMSTRONG, Henry SPEER, William MERREDITH, Matthew MOORE, Esqrs.

Ordered taxable property of William Terrel LEWIS, Esqr., on the Eastern Waters be returned under oath.

Ordered William HUGHLETT have leave to keep Tavern in Town of Richmond.

Ordered John ARMSTRONG, Samuel CUMMINS, William HUGHLETT lay off Prison Bounds.

On motion of Mr. SHARPE, ordered Survivours of Commissioners appointed to superintend building Court House, Prison and Stocks by act of Assembly in 1770 or 1771, appear next court May in order to settle respective accounts relating to said public buildings.

Ordered John HALBERT, John McANNALLY, Joel HALBERT, John DANIEL, Samuel CLARKE, John DUNLAP, Richard GOODE, Lawrence ANGLE, John MORGAN, Charles ANGLE, Adam MITCHELL, Andrew ROBINSON, Edmund PETERS, Harry TERREL, Moses HAZLETT, Edward THOMPSON view road from John HALLS to John THOMPSONS shop.

Ordered William BOSTICK, Moses MARTIN, Junr., William JAMES, John MARTIN, Thomas GOODE, Junr., Patrick McGIBBONY, Andrew ROBINSON, Benj. YOUNG, John BRANSON, William WAGGONER, Thomas FLINT, John COOLEY, Martin BURRIS, Thos. GOODE, Senr., John HALBERT, Isaac GARRISON and Edward COOLEY view road from Townfork where Major GOODES road crosses into Cross Creek road.

Report of committee to examine lists of Inhabitants of County as follows: Capt. CARSONS District: Thomas SMITH; HILLS District: Jo. WINSTON; LOVILLES District: Robert WALKER; HICKMANS District: John CHILDRESS; GAINES District: M. MOORE; MOSBYS District: Henry SPEER; BLACKBURNS District: Chas. McANALLY; WRIGHTS District: Wm. COOK; ADKINS District: Wm. COOK; HUMPHRIS District: Hugh ARMSTRONG; WILLIS District: John TALIAFERRO; BOSTICKS District: Absalom BOSTICK; KROUSES District: Jacob BLUMO; LEWIS and COOKS Districts: not come in.

William T. LEWIS vs Gibson WOOLDRIDGE; Zeanos BALDWIN, witness for Pltf., 300 miles, 24 days.

James Martin LEWIS vs Jonathan HAINES; Zeanos BALDWIN, witness for Pltf., 60 miles, 5 days; Silvanus PIPES, 60 miles, 4 days; John PIPES, 60 miles, 4 days.

Benjamin HEARNDON vs Thomas SMITH; John SUTTON, witness for Pltf., 160 miles, 3 days.

Moses WOODROUGH vs Michael HENDERSON. Jury: John KEER, Thompson GLEN, Wm. N. COOK, Thomas GAINES, John PIPES, Wm. FREEMAN, Anthony DEARING, Adonijah HARBOUR, Olive ROBERTS, Phil HOLECOME, Thomas McCARRELL, and Jonathan HANES; Gideon WOODROUGH, witness for Pltf., 360 miles, 25 days; Samuel GENTRY, 300 miles, 21 days.

Joshua FREEMAN vs Godfrey MILLER.

Mordicai MENDENALL vs Samuel JACKSON.

James ARMSTRONG vs James ROBERTS.

Traugott BAGGE vs Thomas SMITH.

Matthew BASS vs Orman MORGAN.

William Terrel LEWIS vs John WILKERSON.

Matthew BROOKS vs Francis BAKER.

William MERREDITH, Esq. in behalf of County vs John HARPER.

Robert HAMMET vs William BURRIS.

John WELLS vs Joseph GARRISON.

Jonathan HANBY vs George CARRELL.

John NULL vs Wm. NULL.

William HAMM vs William BROWN.

David BRAY vw William NULL.

James GLENS Executors vs Philip STULTZ; same jury except Roger GIDDENS in place of Thompson GLEN.

Samuel CUMMINS vs Edmund FRANKLIN.

Thomas SMITH, whealwright vs William COOK.

Godffey CODY vs David BRAY; Hannah ROSE, witness for Pltf., 280 miles, 21 days.

Gray BYNUM, James HAMPTON, Thomas EVANS, Committee to lay off third part of Philip DAVIS land as dower for widow and divide 264 acres on South bank of Town Fork above upper fence, etc. with consent of widow and David DAVIS, heirs at law to said land; 29 November 1785 reported; ordered recorded.

8 May 1786

Present: Martin ARMSTRONG, Esqr. (Adjourned till tomorrow).

9 May 1786

Present: Joseph WINSTON, Hugh ARMSTRONG, Henry SPEER, Absalom BOSTICK.

Grand Jury: Samuel MOSBY, Junr., Foreman; Noble LADD, Gray BYNUM, John HALBERT, Joseph EAST, Thomas SPENCE, David HUMPHRIS, James BADGETT, Malcum CURRY, Fredrick MILLER, Philip HOWARD, Airs HUDSPETH, Gideon EDWARDS, Stephen I. SMITH and William HICKMAN.

James BRYSON and John HORN failing to attend as Jurors, make known reasons, ordered be excused.

Ordered notice against Wm. PUKET, Esq., Sheriff of Randolph County appear next court to show cause why he shall not pay 50 pounds returning an execution Sarah BUTNER, Admr. vs John COLYER, Esq.

Ordered John HALL overseer, new marked road from his house to ford of Dan River above Absalom BOSTICKS.

Ordered Edward THOMPSON overseer, new road from ford of Dan River above BOSTICKS into old road at THOMPSONS Old Shop.

Ordered Samuel PAFFORD, orphan of John PAFFORD, deceased, aged 20 years 14 March last, bound to James DAVIS until 21 years old, said DAVIS agrees to give him 3 months schooling.

Inventory Estate of Benjamin PETTIE, deceased, returned by Job MARTIN and George PETTIT, Executors.

Admr. Estate of Henry TILLEY, deceased, granted Jane TILLEY, widow and relict; Thomas ADDIMAN and Thomas PETTIT, securities.

Deed from Nathaniel WOODROUGH to Samuel WOODROUGH; oath Abner GREENWOOD.

Deed from John BOOTH to Jonas REYNOLDS; oath Henry SPEER.

Deed from Benjamin YOUNG to Benjamin YOUNG, Junr.; oath Richard GOODE.

Deed from Adam SWARTZ to Baswell PINKSTON; oath Nicholass DULL.

Deed from John DOUG and Marthy, his wife, to John BRYSON, Junr.; oath of Wm. BURRIS.

Deed from Daniel HUMPHRIS to David HUMPHRIS; oath Benjamin HUMPHRIS.

Deed from George WADKINS to Warham EASLEY; oath Jason ISBELL.

Quit Claim Deed from Francis BARNARD to Trustam BARNARD; oath Wm. THORNTON.

Deed from Fredrick Wm. MARSHALL to Jacob NOLL; oath Traugott BAGGE.

Deed from John HORN to Thomas EAST; oath said HORN.

Thomas BARNET vs Richard HORN; Jury: Seth COFFIN, Jacob McGRAW, Richard KERBY (or Kerley), James BRYSON, Abraham STOE, Joel KERBY (or Kerley), Alexander MOORE, John BOWLS, Wm. BOYLES, John BRANSON, James DAVIS, and Ephraim McLEMORE: Nathaniel AIRS, witness for Pltf., 120 miles, 7 days; John DYAR, 32 miles, 1 day; Elenor AIRS, 102 miles, 4 days.

Ordered John WELLS be exempted paying Poll Tax in future; also Thomas WHITTICOR.

Ordered Charles McANALLY, Henry SPEER, Traugott BAGGE, Esqrs., appointed to settle with Commissioners; appointed to superintend public buildings in Surry County, etc.

10 May 1786

Present: Joseph WINSTON, William MERREDITH, Absalom BOSTICK, Esqrs.

Deed from Robert WALKER and wife, Mary, to Archibald CAMBELL; oath of William WALKER.

Deed from Joseph GIBSON and wife to John VAWTER: oath Reuben GEORGE.

John RIDING produced order from Governor to suspend signing two grants for lands to James GLEN til matter is tried according to law.

Deed from Toliver DAVIS to Jacob SPEER; oath Henry SPEER.

Ordered following in COOKS District be admitted to give in tax-ables 1785: Chas. CLASBY, 222 acres, 1 poll; Trustum BARNARD, 212 acres, 1 poll; Lathan FOLGER, 333 acres, 2 polls; Gwyn MACY, 133 acres, 1 poll.

James SHEPPERD vs Samuel and Jacob McCRAW. Jury find Pltf. against Samuel McCRAW and find for other Deft. Jacob McCRAW: Seth COFFIN, Job MARTIN, Alexander MOORE, James GRINES, Abner GREENWOOD, Wm. N. COOK, Richard HORN, John BURCH, John PIPES, Silvanus PIPES, Jesse KNIGHTON and Zeanos BALDWIN.

The State vs Jonathan HAINES; jury find Deft. guilty: Seth COFFIN, Job MARTIN, John BRUCE, Alexander MOORE, Michael FRY, Johnson HEATH, James GAINES, Richard HORN, David MORROW, James MARTIN, Thomas HUGHES, and John SHORES; Zachariah WRAY, witness for State, 210 miles, 11 days; Wm. T. LEWIS, 150 miles, 12 days. On motion ordered Wm. T. LEWIS, Zeanos BALDWIN and Zachariah WRAY only be allowed for attendancy in case State vs Jonathan HAINES for Assault and Battery.

Absalom BOSTICK vs Lemuel SMITH; Peter PERKINS and Wm. LANKFORD, witnesses for Pltf. failed to appear.

State vs William T. LEWIS; Jury find Deft. guilty and finded him 20 pounds; James READ, witness for State, 30 miles, 2 days; Jonathan HAINES, 180 miles, 8 days.

Jury appointed to view road from Richard GOODES to John THOMPSONS leaving old road at Townfork, taking ridge to Dan River near Lemuel SMITHS Fish Trap; thence up River to ford above Absalom BOSTICKS plantation; thence crossing Evans Creek upper side Edward THOMPSONS plantation; into road at John THOMPSONS.

Ordered Martin BURRIS be overseer said road.

Ordered old Shop be continued as public road and Harry TERRIL overseer from Halls to River and hands of John DANIEL, Gibson SUTHERN, Amos LADD, James EASON, William LEWIS and hands under him; Joshua DODSON and Kreel, his son-in-law, work under said overseer.

Ordered Joseph VAUGHN overseer, road from Carmichals ford to Thompsons Shop and hands of William SUTHER, Richard WEBSTER, George RAY, Moses HAZLET, Edmund PETERS, Samuel WARNOCK, Joshua YOUNG, and Peter HARSTON (Hairston) work thereon.

Last Will and Testament of John THOMPSON, deceased, proved by James HOWELL, Matthias STEELMAN, and David HOUSE; Catharine THOMPSON, Exectx. quallified.

Ordered Edward THOMPSON appointed Constable in place Drury WILLIAMS.

Richard GOODE, Esqr., chosen Sheriff for ensuing year.

John GILES and John ADAMS quallified as Constable.

Ordered Adam JACOBI be exempted from paying Poll Tax for future.

Committee appointed to settle with Commissioners superintend public buildings report buildings not finished according to Undertakers obligation; opinion of Commissioners take speedest steps to have work finished. Signed: Charles McANALLY, Henry SPEER, and Traugott BAGGE.

Peter HOUZAR has leave to keep Tavern in Bethany (Bethania); Martin ARMSTRONG and Jo. WILLIAMS, securities.

John HALL has leave to keep Tavern at his now dwelling house; Joseph WINSTON and Joseph WILLIAMS, securities.

Jacob BLUME has leave to keep Tavern in Bethabra; Martin ARMSTRONG and William MERREDITH, securities.

Jacob MYARS have leave to keep tavern in Salem; Frederick MILLER and Traugott BAGGE, securities.

Fredrick MILLER has leave to keep Tavern at his now dwelling house; Traugott BAGGE, security.

11 May 1786

Present: Joseph WINSTON, Traugott BAGGE, Wm. T. LEWIS, Esqrs.

Deed from John DEATHERAGE and wife to Wm. DEATHERAGE; oath James GAINES.

Deed from Samuel RIGGS and wife to Zadock RIGGS; oath Elephelet JARVIS.

Deed from John REED to Elijah GILLISBY; oath Robert WILLIS.

Deed from Elijah THOMPSON to Charles WADDLE, acknowledged.

Deed from Elijah THOMPSON to Isham THOMPSON, acknowledged.

Deed from John BOHANNAN to Airs HUDSPETH; oath Carlton LINESAY.

Deed from George HOUZAR to Adam FULK; oath Henry SPOONHOUR.

Inventory Estate of Thomas PETTIT, deceased, returned by Thomas PETTIT and Judith PETTIT, Executors.

Adam WOOLF, an Executor, Estate, Leonard MOSSER, deceased, returned account said Estate.

Ordered Last Will and Testament, Edward SHELTON, deceased, be admitted to record, having been proved by James HAMPTON, who declares he saw same signed, etc. by said Edward SHELTON in presence of said James HAMPTON and John APPLETON; also by oath of Mary WILSON; Ordered Letters Testament be issued to John APPLETON, Executor.

Mary RIDGE and Elizabeth RIDGE, orphans of Wm. RIDGE, deceased, choose Wm. COOK and Jonathan HAINES their guardians; same time Court assigned COOK and HAINES guardians to Sythe RIDGE, William RIDGE, Thomas RIDGE and Winneford RIDGE, orphans said deceased; Joseph WINSTON, John BURCH and Henry SPEER, secretary for COOK; John BRUCE, Salathiel MARTIN securities for HAINES.

Zeanos BALDWIN vs Solomon Sparks; Jury: Seth COFFIN, John BRUCE, Job MARTIN, Alex. MOORE, James DOAK, David MORROW, John BURCH, John ALLEN, James GAINES, Michael FRY, Michael HAUZER, and Robert HILL.

Richard PHILIPS vs Robert WALKER; Joel LEWIS, witness for Pltf., 360 miles, 25 days.

Traugott BAGGE vs Matthew MARKLAND.

Salathiel MARTIN vs Richard JACKS.

Elijah STINSON vs John BRYAN.

Thomas HAMM vs William MORELAND; William CALLIHAN, witness for Pltf., 160 miles, 6 days.

Abraham WOOD and wife vs Edwards YOUNG; Micahel Brown ROBERTS, witness for Deft., 30 miles, 7 days.

John CLEAVLAND vs Robert WALKER; Wm. ELLIOTT, witness for WALKER, 130 miles, 11 days.

Michael HAUZER, collector of KROUSES District, returned list Insolvants 1785.

William MARTIN, overseer road from Moravian Line down to Cross roads.

Thos. FLINT, overseer road from his Mill to Cross Roads at Frys.

Ordered Clerk tax only 25 shillings for an attorney fee hereafter on Caveat causes of land and 3 shillings each Jurors attendance on Jury view Caveat Trials til April 1783, agreeable to Act of Assembly passed in 1762; from 1783 tax 8 shillings for such service to present time and hereafter til otherwise directed by law.

12 May 1786

Present: Joseph WINSTON, Matthew MOORE, Henry SPEER, Wm. COOK, Esqrs.

Deed from Matthew MOORE, Sheriff, to Joseph PHILIPS; oath said MOORE.

Deed from Joseph PHILIPS to Charles VANDEFORD: oath said PHILIPS.

Bond from Matthew BROOKS to Joseph PHILIPS; acknowledged by said Matt BROOKS.

Bond from Wm. RUTLEDGE to James, John, Isaac and Joel RUTLEDGE, minors of William RUTLEDGE, deceased; acknowledged by said William.

Bill of Sale from THOMAS heirs to Wm. T. LEWIS; oath Zeanos BALDWIN.

On motion of John McNAIRY, attorney in behalf of Thomas LINDSAYS Admrx. ordered Scire Facias issued against Thomas DUNAHOE, former Sheriff of Guilford County, appear and show cause why two executions not be received against him for judgments against him by Thomas LINDSAY in 1775.

Ordered citation issued against Nathan ALLEN, guardian of orphan children of Wm. RIDGE, deceased, and securities of said ALLEN as guardian; that he and they render account of Estate come into his hands during his guardianship; also citation against Nathan ALLEN and Winneford, his wife, Admrs. Wm. RIDGE, deceased, to render account.

John KIMBROUGH vs Thomas WHITWORTH; Wm. WHITWORTH, witness for Deft., 600 miles, 13 days; Samuel WHITWORTH, 460 miles, 13 days.

John SHELTON vs Reuben DODSON; William CHANDLER, witness for Pltf., 240 miles, 16 days.

Ordered Clerk issue writ to bring up proceedings in case of George CLIFTON vs Richard TOMERSON from Justice who tried same; said Richard THOMERSON give security Wyatt GARNER.

James Martin LEWIS vs Jonathan HAINES; Wm. T. LEWIS, witness for Pltf., 60 miles, 5 days; Zeanos BALDWIN, 60 miles, 4 days; John PIPES, 60 miles, 4 days; Silvanus PIPES, 60 miles, 4 days.

William T. LEWIS vs Gilbert WOOLDRIDGE; Zeanos BALDWIN, witness for Pltf., 60 miles, 4 days.

Mary RUTLEDGE vs Henry WARD; Gibson WOOLDRIDGE, witness for Deft., 230 miles, 4 days.

Joseph WILLIAMS vs Samuel CUNNINGHAM; Caveat; Jury in favor WILLIAMS. Appeal prayed and granted; Abraham CRESON, guardian to CUNNINGHAMS orphans entered into bond with David REAVIS and Justice REYNOLDS.

Ordered Joseph WILLIAMS, Clerk of Court, be empowered to give Mr. BAGGE list of blank boos for use in Clerks office and ask County Treasurer for money to pay Mr. BAGGE.

Ordered Zeanos BALDWIN, Thomas SPENCE, Michael BACON, David HERRYMAN, Richard PARSONS, John PARSONS, Moses SWAIM, Airs HUDS-PETH, Thomas JACKS, David SPENCE, Joel LEWIS, James PARSONS, Abraham DOWNEY, Jordin MANNERING and Isaac AUSTIN view road leaving Shallowford road near Thomas SPENCES to Salisbury road near YOUNGS.

Henry SPEER maketh oath he surveyed tract of land for Michael HENDERSON, 400 acres head Deep Creek, agreed line of Samuel GENTRY, top Fox Knob, agreed line Moses WOODROUGH; said SPEER surveyed for said HENDERSON without warrant, including 600 acres, but warrant called for 400 acres; land which Michael HENDERSON had sold to Fredrick MILLER for 600 acres 26 January 1784.

Court proceeded to lay off county Districts, Justices and Constables: KROUSES; Traugott BAGGE, (blank); MOSBYS: Henry SPEER, John WILLIAMS; HILLS: Joseph WINSTON, John COOLEY; COOKS: Wm. DOBSON, John DAVIS; BOSTICKS: Absalom BOSTICK, (blank), BLACK-BURNS: Charles McANALLY, Adam MITCHELL; HICKMANS: John CHILDRESS, Reuben GEORGE; GAINES: Micajah CLARK, (blank); ADKINS: William COOK, (blank); LOVILLES: George HAUZAR, (blank); LEWIS: Henry SPEER, Zachariah RAY; SANDERS: Henry SPEER, John WILLIAMS; HUMPHRIS: Hugh ARMSTRONG, (blank); CARSONS: Thomas SMITH, John Thomas LONGINO; WILLIS: John TALIAFERRO, (blank).

Ordered following appear as Jurors next term County Court in
August: Moses BAKER, James HOWELL, Stephen WOOD, William ELLIOT,
Salathiel MARTIN, Reuben SHORES, Senr., John SHORES, John BURCH,
William CRITCHFIELD, John PARKER, Robert HARRIS, Benjamin HUMPHRIS,
James GAINES, Joseph CLOUD, Reubin DODSON, John FARMER, Philip
WILSON, John DAVIS, Amos LADD, Henry TERREL, Joseph NELSON, Edward
LOVILL, Thomas BRIGGS, Samuel CLARK, Matthew BROOKS, Henry SMITH,
John KROUSE, Joseph EASON, and Joseph BANNER.

At County Court at Richmond Court House 9 May 1786. Present the
Worshipfull Martin ARMSTRONG, Joseph WINSTON, William COOK,
Matthew MOORE, Sm. MERREDITH, William DOBSON, Henry SPEER, William
T. LEWIS and James MARTIN, Esqrs. On motion of Joseph WILLIAMS,
Esqr., Clerk of Court, appears said Clerk did not collect public
Tax on Original Process: Deeds of Conveyance, Marriage Licence
and Ordinary License previous to August Court 1785 due by a delay
of publishing Act of Assembly directing tax be collected; it is
therefore opinion of this court that Mr. WILLIAMS cannot be charg-
ed with or compeled to pay those taxes before August Session.
(Signed by Justices named above).

Jonathan HAINES vs Wm. T. LEWIS; Assault and Battery; James READ,
witness for Pltf., 30 miles, 3 days.

Wm. T. LEWIS vs Jonathan HAINES; Assault and Battery; same
witnesses.

Benjamin HEARNDON vs Thomas SMITH (Jockey); John SUTTON, witness
for Pltf., 160 miles, 3 days.

William T. LEWIS vs Gibson WOOLDRIDGE; John SUTTON, witness for
Deft., 320 miles, 6 days.

John DOYLE vs William BURRIS; same witness, 160 miles, 4 days.

David CONNELLY vs Roger GIDDINS; John BOWLS, witness for CONNELLY,
48 miles, 4 days.

Bickel NICHOLS vs James PILCHER; George HOLCOMB, witness for Pltf.,
189 miles, 34 days.

Justice REYNOLDS vs William SHEPPERD; George SPRINKLE, 6 miles,
4 days; James GRAHAM, 20 miles, 4 days.

John RANDLEMAN vs John SUTTEN; Wm. COLVARD, witness for Deft.,
360 miles, 16 days.

14 August 1786
Richmond

Present: Martin ARMSTRONG, Esqr. (Adjourned til tommorow 10 o'clock).

15 August 1786

Present: Martin ARMSTRONG, Joseph WINSTON, George HAUSER, Absalom
BOSTICK, Henry SPEER, Esqrs.

Deed from Micajah CLARK to Joseph HIATT: oath Joseph JESSUP.

Deed from Michael REYNOLDS to Isaac COPELAND; oath James FREEMAN.

Deed from Jesse MAUPIN and wife to John SHELTON; oath David SHELTON.

Deed from Elijah SMALLWOOD to Sarah SMALLWOOD; oath Thomas ROSS.

Power of Attorney from Jacob Van VLECK and Henry Van VLECK to
Jacob BLUME; oath of Godfried BREAZEL and Fredrick STREALE.

Deed from Peter Myars to Wm. HUGHLETT: oath Martin ARMSTRONG.

Deed from Robert MARTIN to Alexander MARTIN; oath John BRADLEY.

Deed from Jesse MAUPIN and wife to Robert GAINS; oath David SHELTON.

Deed from John HARROLD and wife to Thomas BURRIS; oath James MATTHEWS. (2).

Deed from Lewis CONNER to Boater SUMNERS: oath James HAMPTON.

Deed from John FORKNER and wife to James DILLARD; oath Wm. MERREDITH.

Deed from William MEREDITH and wife to John WILKINS: oath said MERREDITH.

Deed from Solomon NELSON to John McKINNEY; oath Matthew COX.

Deed from Thomas NORMAN to John McKINNEY; oath Matthew COX.

Deed from Fredr. Wm. MARSHALL to Christian CUNROD; oath Traugott BAGGE.

Deed from Fredr. Wm. MARSHALL to Abraham LINEBECK; oath Traugott BAGGE.

Deed from Wm. SHEPPERD to John ARMSTRONG; oath Constant LADD.

Deed from Charles VANDEVER to Robert AYRES; oath Henry SPEER.

Deed from John LANKASTER and wife to William HARVEY; oath John LANKASTER.

Grand Jury: Matthew BROOKS, Foreman; Reuben SHORES, John SHORES, John BURCH, Wm. CRITCHFIELD, Robert HARRIS, Reuben DODSON, Phil WILSON, Henry TERRIL, Thomas BRIGGS, Henry SMITH, Samuel CLARKE, and Salathiel MARTIN.

Last Will and Testament, Solomon NELSON, deceased; oath Elijah SMALLWOOD; Margaret NELSON, Exectx., qualified.

Inventory Estate, Henry TILLEY, deceased, returned by Jane TILLEY, Admrx.

Ordered Joshua DODSON, Samuel WARNOCK, Michael ROMINGER, George HOLDER, Thomas LOYD, aged and infirm men, be exempt from paying Poll Tax in future. Also, Christian TRUBEL, James HURST, Henry ZILLMAN, John Fredr. PRIEM, Jeremiah SHOAF, Christopher MERKLY, George JEPFERT, Christopher SMITH, Samuel FOCKLE, Melchour SNIDER, Andrew VOLK, Jacob BLACK, and Michael NULL.

Jury appointed to lay out road from near Thomas SPENCES into Salisbury road near Youngs give in report; road must begin on ridge between Michael BACONS and Thos. SPENCES running on Ridge to David HEREMANS; thence between Gideon WOODRUFFS fields leaving his house to right; thence to Airs HUDSPETHS and through his field by his consent and by his Mill; thence by John WARDS; thence into Shallowford road below PETTYS; thence into Salisbury road between Moses MITCHELS and Thomas YOUNGS.

William DOBSON vs David EVANS; Jury: Moses BAKER, Wm. ELLIOTT, Edward LOVELL, John KROUSE, Joseph EASON, Joseph BANNER, Matthew WARNOCK, John APPLETON, Wm. WALKER, Rezia JARVIS, James DAVIS, and Charles LAY.

Matthew BROOKS vs William BIRNEY.

John DEATHERAGE vs William BINGHAM; same jury except Job MARTIN in room of Rezia JARVIS; James GAINS, witness for Pltf., 700 miles, 61 days.

Commissioners of Town of Richmond report they have elected Doctor John RANDLEMAN a Commissioner in room of Robert WALKER, Esqr., deceased.

Ordered William MEREDITH, Wm. T. LEWIS, Henry SPEER, George HAUSER appointed Committee of Claims to take list of taxables and settle accounts with Executors and Administrators.

Ordered Mary WALKER has leave to keep Tavern at her now dwelling; John and Martin ARMSTRONG, securities.

16 August 1786

Present: Martin ARMSTRONG, Joseph WINSTON, Henry SPEER, Jacob BLUM, Esqrs.

Ordered Nathaniel WOODRUFF, Issact MANUEL, John ALLIN (Honey), and Daniel HUFF be exempt from paying Poll Tax for future.

It appears Almond GUIN inlisted William COTTERAL as a Poll Tax and proved COTTERAL not of age; ordered GWIN be released from paying.

Ordered John MARTIN overseer, road in room James FREEMAN.

Ordered Constant LADD overseer, of Volentine ALLINS road from Guilford line to David MORROWS.

Ordered John JOHNSON, Junr. overseer, road in room of John SHORES.

Deed from Robert WALKER, Job MARTIN and Martin ARMSTRONG, Commissioners Town of Richmond to Mary BRANDON, wife of John BRANDON; oath Wm. HUGHLETT.

Deed from Edmund WOOD and wife to Robert FORBIS; oath Richard MURPHY.

Deed from William BOSTICK to Constantine LADD; oath John BOSTICK.

Bill of Sale from Henry WARD to James SANDERS; oath said WARD.

Deed from Benjamin SAMPSON to Henry HOLDER: oath Windle KROUSE.

Deed from William JOHNSON to Robert LANIER; oath Johnson SUMMERS.

Robert BRIGGS has leave to keep Tavern; Reuben DODSON and Jos. PHILIPS, securities.

State vs Philemon HOLCOMB; Tresspass; Jury find Deft. not guilty; Jury: William ELLIOTT, James GAINES, Edward LOVELL, Joseph EASON, Joseph BANNER, Zeanos BALDWIN, Ayres HUDSPETH, John REAVIS, John DEATHERAGE, Benjamin BURCH, Wm. N. COOK, and Abner GREENWOOD.

John RAMEY vs John GRANT; on motion to take deposition of John READ who is about to leave the State; Ordered take deposition this day at 5 o'clock before Charles McANALLY and James MARTIN on giving Spruce McCAY, Esqr. Attorney for Deft. notice of same.

Last Will and Testament of Edward WHELTON, deceased, at last term confirmed, John APPLETON surviving Executor qualified.

Last Will and Testament of Robert WALKER, Esqr., deceased, proved by comparision of hands by oaths of Joseph WILLIAMS, John RANDLE-MAN, Malcum CURRY, William HUGHLETT, John ARMSTRONG, John Thomas LONGINO, and James GAINS; ordered will be admitted to record; Letters Testimony issued to Mary WALKER, Robert WALKER, and Martin ARMSTRONG, Executors.

17 August 1786

Present: Joseph WINSTON, Matthew MOORE, William DOBSON, Esqrs.

Ordered Rachel PARFORD, orphan of John PARFORD, deceased, aged 9 years, bound to Jesse McANALLY until 17 years old and learn Art and Mistry of Spinster.

Joseph WILLIAMS appointed guardian to Thomas LANIER, orphan of

Robert LANIER, deceased; Henry SPEER and Samuel MOSBY, Junr., securities.

David MORROW has leave to keep Tavern at his house; Fredr. MILLER, security.

John LYNCH has leave to keep Tavern in this county; Joseph WILLIAMS and Francis POINDEXTER, securities.

Ordered William SWIM overseer, road which leads to Cross Creek from Wachovia line near Fredr. MILLERS to line of Rowan County.

Ordered Peter ROTHROCK overseer, road in room of Adam FISHEL at south fork of Muddy Creek in Capt. KROUSES District.

Ordered Frederick MILLER, overseer, road in room Jacob ROMINGER.

Ordered Stephen CLAYTON, Henry WADKINS, Philip WILSON, John SMITH, Richard HEATH, Alexander MOORE, William CAMBELL, Joseph EASON, James COFFEY, Moses MARTIN, Thomas EVANS, Hardy REDDICK, Robert HILL, Daniel DAVIS, Younger BLACKBURN, and Samuel FITZPATRICK view best way from McANALLYS Ford on Dan River to Jacob PETREES Ford on Townfork.

Ordered John HINE overseer, road in room of Jacob ROMINGER.

James TUCKER vs William RAMSEY.

The State vs Henry HOUSER; submitted and fined and bound to peace and good behavior for 12 months to Citizens in general; John ARMSTRONG and Malcum CURRY securities; Joseph SANDERS, witness for State, 34 miles, 2 days; Adam GARNAND (?), 34 miles, 3 days; Michael SIDES, 34 miles, 2 days; Joseph DIXON, 34 miles, 2 days.

LANIER and WILLIAMS vs Amos LADD; continued by consent on condition that Defts Attorney and Constant LADD agree to take deposition of Richard CALLOWAY, a witness in behalf Pltf. any day this week; is agreed; Richard CALLOWAY, witness, 200 miles, 2 days.

State vs Jonathan HAINES; Zachariah RAY, witness for State, 60 miles, 2 days.

Edward REAVIS vs Joshua BROWN; Caveat.

Joseph SPARPOINT vs Henry SPEER; Jury: Moses BAKER, William ELLIOTT, James GAINES, Edward LOVELL, Joseph EASON, Stephen K. SMITH, Samuel HUMPHRIS, James DOAK, Silvanus PIPES, James MARTIN, Thomas GRIMES, Philip EVANS.

John RANDLEMAN, M.D., vs Phil HOLCOMB and Abner GREENWOOD; John DOYLE, witness for Pltf., 108 miles, 9 days.

Last Will and Testament of Robert LANIER, deceased; oath John LYNCH; Jane POINDEXTER, late widow and relict of said Robert LANIER, deceased, and Joseph WILLIAMS, Executors, quallified.

Last Will and Testament of Adam SHOEMAKER, deceased, proved by oath of Henry SPANHOWER and Michael HAUZER; George HAUSER, Junr. and Samuel STOLTZ, Executors, quallified.

Deed from Samuel CALLOWAY to Samuel DAVIS acknowledged by said CALLOWAY.

Ordered ten shillings be allowed for every grown woolf, 2 shillings and 6 pence every young woolf, 20 shillings every Panther, 1 shilling every Wild Cat killed and scalp produced according to law; and not one thing allowed for bears, as the value of the Bacon and Hide will be inducement sufficient.

18 August 1786

Present: Martin ARMSTRONG, Charles McANALLY, Matthew MOORE,

Wm. T. LEWIS, Jesse BUMPS, Esqrs.

Account settlement estate of James BURK, Junr., deceased, returned by Samuel TATE, Admr. in right of his wife.

Account settlement estate of Martin ROMINGER, returned by Henry SPENHOWER.

Ordered Jacob ROMINGER be appointed guardian Jacob ROMINGER, orphan of Martin ROMINGER, deceased, entered into bond with Fredrick MILLER and David MORROW.

Ordered William THORNTON and William ARMSTRONG appointed superintend Senate Box in this present Election and Joseph CLOUD and Malcum CURRY the Box for Commons.

Ordered Absalom BOSTICK, Henry SPEER, Andrew ROBINSON, Constantine LADD, Henry HAMPTON, Michael FREY and John ARMSTRONG appointed Jurors serve next Superior Court held at Salisbury 15 September next.

Ordered the order establishing new road from John HALLS to John THOMPSONS be recinded.

Ordered present road leading from John HALLS to CARMICHAELS ford be continued.

Ordered John BRADLEY, Drury WILLIAMS, Robert MAJORS, Joshua DODSON, Senr., Matthew WARNOCK, Thomas STAMPS, William LEWIS, Martin BURRIS, James EASON, Amos LADD, John DANIEL, Elijah OLIVER, Samuel WARNOCK, and Thomas KREEL view road from CARMICHAELS Road to Townfork towards Salem.

The State vs John VAUGHN; Indenture Misdeameanor; Guilty and bond for his good behavior for 12 months. Jury: Moses BAKER, William ELLIOTT, Thomas GAINS, Joseph CLOUD, Henry BANNER, Philip EVANS, David BRAY, John SMITH, Matthew WARNOCK, John HUGHES, John HARPER, and Frederick MILLER.

William T. LEWIS vs Jonathan HAINS; James REED, witness for Deft., 90 miles, 4 days.

Jonathan HAINS vs Wm. T. LEWIS; same witness.

Wm. T. LEWIS vs Gibson WOOLDRIDGE; Benj. BURCH, witness for Deft., 400 miles, 34 days.

Matthew BASS vs Orman MORGAN; Robt. HARRIS proves he has absolutely nothing in hand.

The Orphans of H. WRIGHT vs Thomas POINDEXTER.

Ordered citation issued against William SHEPPERD, Esqr., former Sheriff to show cause why he shall not be subject to payment of an execution John and Samuel HENDERSON vs Robert BOWMAN.

Ordered Robert BRENON and Nicholas LEDFORD be exempt from paying Poll Tax for future.

Indenture signed by Delilah ALDRIDGE and Henry SPEER for binding Daniel ALDRIDGE and Elizabeth ALDRIDGE to said SPEER, ordered recorded.

Deed from John DANIEL to Major WILKERSON; oath of Edmund PETERS.

Deed from John PIPES and Pricilla PIPES to Peter DOWNEY; oath of Abraham DOWNEY and Daniel COCKRAM.

19 August 1786

Present: Charles McANALLY, Matthew MOORE, Wm. COOK, Henry SPEER, Esqrs.

Deed from John GIBSON and wife to James LANGHAM; oath Wm. MEREDITH.

Article of Agreement between Jane LANIER and John COLVARD; oath Henry PETTITT, Jr.

Deed from James and Martha TILLEY to James GAINES: oath Joseph CLOUD.

Deed from Gabriel JONES and wife to Aaron COFFIN; oath of Wm. DOBSON.

Deed from Andrew HANNAH to James GAMBLE; oath of Wm. GAMEL.

Ordered John COLVARD have leave to keep Tavern at his house; Henry SPEER and John ALLIN, securities.

Ordered Thomas SUMMERS be exempt from paying Poll Tax in future.

Account and Settlement of Estate of Thomas HOWELL, deceased, returned.

Committee appointed to receive Claims 1786 report as follows: Salathiel MARTON, John PIPES, Silvanus PIPES, Henry SPEER, Wm. T. LEWIS, Joel LEWIS, Jos. WINSTON, and Thomas EVANS for attending as Juror in Salisbury.

Zachariah RAY as Constable Capt. LEWIS District and guarding Gaol (?).

Joel KERBY, Edmund KERBY, Job MARTIN, Wiatt GARNER, Thomas SMITH, Esq., John BURCK, Nathaniel WOODRUFF, Junr., Valentine MARTIN (in lieu Salathial MARTIN), for exploring Yadkin River.

Charles TALIAFERRO, Deputy Sheriff for carrying Samuel PATRICK to Salisbury Gaol in August 1785.

John SMITH, Constable in Capt. BLACKBURNS District and attending court 8 days.

Matthew BROOKS, Juror in Salisbury and carrying Robert SMITH to Jail.

Samuel KERBY for carrying Robert SMITH to Jail.

Jacob ROMINGER, Constable and carrying Wm. BOOTH (charged of Horse Stealing) to next Constable.

Thomas BOON, Constable.

Richard GOODE, Esq., Sheriff, his extra office Services.

James TODD, Constable.

Michael HAUZER, Constable and carrying John YOUNG (a Felon) to Goal.

George HAUZER for making irons for John YOUNG (a Felon).

Reuben GEORGE, Constable and attending court.

Jacob ROMINGER for taking Clabourne GENTRY, Bazel PINKSTON and John HARVEY, Junr. and bringing them to justice.

Gray BYNUM, Esq., Juror Salisbury.

Chas. VEST repairing Goal and other public Services, keeping Goal with Samuel PATRICK, keeping Robert SMITH (charged with Horse Stealing) til he broke Goal.

James TODD, warning Inhabitants Capt. MOSBYS District.

John WILLIAMS, Constable and attending court.

Joseph WILLIAMS, Esq., Clerk, for extra officio services.

Hardy REDDICK, 1 grown woolf.

Anthony COLLINS, 1 young woolf.

John EVANS, 1 wild cat.

Edward EVANS, 1 grown woolf, 2 wild cats.

Committee appointed to examine estate of Wm. RIDGE, deceased, returned and ordered recorded.

State vs Thomas BURNETT; ordered in Sheriffs Custody; bonds Richard GOODE, Esq. and afterwards broke bonds; Robert SMITH and John CARLTON securities. Major GOODE brought said BURNET and surrendered him in custody of Sheriff.

Richard GOODE, Esq., quallified as Sheriff.

John GOODE and John BOSTICK quallified as Deputy Sherrifs.

Ordered list taxable property 1786 returned by John CHILDRESS, Esq. sent back to him to make out according to law; also ordered Hugh ARMSTRONG, Esq. be privileged to make his list and return to Clerk.

Ordered John BRUCE, Joseph GENTRY, Frederick LONG, John HUMPHRIS, John McMICKLE, Peter DOWNY, John SWIM, Edward WILBURN, David BRAY, Moses AYERS, Reuben SHORES, Junr., John WILLIAMS (little), Thomas ELLIOTT, John FLEMING, Wm. McCRAW, Thomas EAST, Jesse HORN, Jacob SPOONHOUR, George HAUSER, Senr., John SLAUGHTER, Robert MAAB (Mabe), John FARMER, Joseph NELSON, Thomas COOK, Patrick McGIBBONY, and Ephraim BANNER attend County Court 2nd Monday in November as Jurors.

13 November 1786
Richmond Court House

Present: Martin ARMSTRONG, Hugh ARMSTRONG, Joseph WINSTON, Esqs.

Grand Jury: John BRUCE, Foreman; Thomas ELLIOTT, Henry SHORES, Joseph NELSON, Patrick McGIBBONY, John HUMPHRIS, John WILLIAMS, Ephraim BANNER, Jesse HORN, John FLEMING, Thomas EAST, Joseph READ (B.I.), Joseph REED, Thomas COOK, and John SLATTON (or Statton).

Ordered Roger GIDDENS, the elder, and Richard GIDDENS be exempt from paying Poll Tax 1786.

Bill of Sale from John WELLS to Henry FRY; oath of Joseph WINSTON.

Deed from Peter SMITH to Peter PAFF; oath Christian SMITH.

Deed from Peter SMITH to John KROUSE; oath Peter PAFF.

Deed from Benjamin WHELES to Lewis WHEALES; oath James DURHAM.

Deed from Matthias STEELMAN to James SANDERS; oath Henry SPEER.

Deed from Richard GOODE, Sheriff, to John WELLS; oath A. ROBINSON.

Deed from Micajah CLARK to Joseph JESSOP; oath Mereman BALLARD. (2)

Admr. Estate of John THOMPSON, deceased, granted Mary THOMPSON, widow and relict said deceased; John HILL and Samuel SEWARD, securities.

Last Will and Testament of George FULPS, deceased; oath Andrew ROBINSON; Patrick McGIBBONY and John LOWE, Executors, qualified.

Ordered Philip SHOUSE, Daniel SHOUSE, Adam FULK, Jacob SPOONHOUR, Andrew FISHER, Jacob HELSEBECK, Roger GIDDENS, Thomas BRIGGS, Ezekiel OLIVER, Frederick HELSEBECK, Bazzell RIDDLE, Anthony BITTINS, John CONNEL, Henry BANNISTER and Thomas EAST view road from Ford of Little Yadkin to Anthony BRITTENS.

James DAVIS has leave to keep Tavern at his house; Joseph READ and Joseph REED securities.

Henry SPEER vs Silas ENYART; Jury: William FREEMAN, Charles LAY, David LINVELL, John LOWE, William WILSON, Zeanos BALDWIN, William BURRIS, James DAVIS, David SCOTT, Samuel CALLOWAY, John BOLLIJACK, and Boeter SUMNERS.

15 November 1786

Present: Martin ARMSTRONG, Joseph WINSTON, Henry SPEER, Esqrs.

Deed from Frederick Wm. MARSHALL to Christopher KLEIN; oath Traugott BAGGE.

Deed from Thomas EVANS to Peter SMITH; oath Richard GOODE, Esq.

Deed from Constant LADD to Absalom BOSTICK; acknowledged.

Deed from Richard GOODE, Sheriff, to Gottlieb SHOBER; oath Michael HAUZER.

Deed from Adam WOOLF and Adam PINKLEY to Anthony BITTING.

Deed from Peter MOSSER to Anthony BITTING; ordered Dedimus issue take relinquishment Catharine MOSSERS, Dower.

Deed from Joseph AYRES to Laurence HOLCOMB; acknowledged.

Deed from Moses BAKER and wife to Henry SPEER: oath John WILLIAMS.

Joseph JESSOP vs William CHEEK; Jury: David BRAY, Jacob SPOONHOUR, Jonathan HAINS, William WILSON, Phil HOLCOMB, Roger GIDDENS, Airs HUDSPETH, William ELLIOTT, Andrew ROBINSON, David STEWART, Isaac JOICE (Joyce), and Constant LADD.

William T. LEWIS vs John FORRISTER: same jury.

State vs John BRADLEY; Indenture, Tresspass; find Deft. guilty.

State vs Joseph REAVIS; Indenture, Trespass; same jury except John LOWE in place of Phil HOLCOMB.

The State vs Bazwell RIDDLE; Indenture, Tresspass; find Deft. guilty. Ordered Bazwell RIDDLE be removed from his office as Constable for misbehavior; ordered to be reinstated.

Jesse KINGHTON failing to give his list of taxables 1786 now gives in 940 acres, 2 black polls, and 1 white poll and a stud horse; Capt. GAINS District.

Ordered Alexander MOORE overseer, road from Town Fork leading to Capt. Charles McANALLYS where said road intersects the Quaker Road.

Ordered Matthew EASTERLINE overseer, road in place of John MICKEY.

Ordered Absalom BOSTICK, overseer road in room of Martin BURRIS.

Ordered George SMITH, George AUST, Thomas EVANS, and Henry HOLS-CLAW be exempt from paying Poll Tax after 1786.

Ordered Catharine ARNEY, an orphan aged 12 years February last, be bound to John DAUB til 18 years old.

Admr. Estate of John LOVE, deceased, granted to Ruth LOVE, widow and relict of said deceased; James MIDDLETON security; James LOVE and Wm. CAMPBELL securities.

Inventory part of estate of Joseph COLEMAN, deceased, returned by Joseph ASHLEY, Administrator.

Ordered John WILLIAMS have leave to keep Tavern at his house; Henry SPEER security.

16 November 1786

Present: Martin ARMSTRONG, Joseph WINSTON, Absalom BOSTICK, Esqrs.

Ordered John DUNLAP be exempt from paying Poll Tax after 1786.

Ordered William COOK and William MEREDITH, Esqrs., committee to settle with Executors and Administrators.

The State vs Davis BRAY; Indenture, Trespass; find Deft. guilty; Godfrey CODY, witness for State, 120 miles, 12 days; Joshua CRITCH-FIELD, 120 miles, 13 days; Hannah ROSE, 120 miles, 9 days. Jury: Jacob SPOONHOUR, Joseph GENTRY, Andrew ROBINSON, Jonathan HAINS, David LINVILLE, Charles VEST, James TODD, James McCOIN, Justice REYNOLDS, Thomas GALLION, John LYNCH, and John DUNLAP.

The State vs Thomas and Alex DOUTHIT and Phil HILL; Indenture, Riot and Assault; same jury except Matthew DAVIS and John BURCH in room of John DUNLAP and David LINVILLE; find Defts. guilty; Reason WILLIAMS, witness for State, 36 miles, 3 days; Mary WILLIAMS, 36 miles, 2 days; Nancy ROBINSON, 36 miles, 2 days.

Deed from Amos LADD to Noble LADD; acknowledged.

Deed from Ambrose BLACKBURN to James COFFEE; oath Wm. HEATH.

Francis POINDEXTER has leave to keep Tavern at the Cane Brake; Wm. T. LEWIS and Henry PETTITT, securities.

Ordered Henry BAKER Constable in room of Reuben GEORGE, resigned.

17 November 1786

Present: Martin ARMSTRONG, Joseph WINSTON, Absalom BOSTICK, Esqrs.

LANIER and WILLIAMS vs Amos LADD; Deft. LADD came into court and confessed judgment for all costs including whatever McDANIEL paid in taking depositions whereupon Pltf. Jo. WILLIAMS discontinued suit; James HOLLAND, witness for Pltf., 4 days; John ALLIN, 15 miles, 4 days; John COLVARD, 15 miles, 4 days.

Admr. Estate of William REYNARD, deceased, granted Sophia RAYNARD, widow and relict of said deceased; Henry SPEER and John WILLIAMS (LT) securities.

Ordered perishable part of estate of Henry TILLEY, deceased, be sold.

John CUNROD overseer, road in room of Peter HAUSER.

Ordered James COFFEE, overseer, open and keep in repair new road lately laid off from BLACKBURNS old field on Richmond road to Jacob PETREES Ford on Townfork; allow Phil SUTHERLIN 16 shillings damage for removing one corner of his fence.

Ordered John HUTCHINGS overseer, Cross Creek road from top of Ridge to South side North fork Blews Creek in old road near James HOLBROOKS in room of Joseph NELSON.

Ordered Henry FRY overseer, road from Townfork to Anthony BITTINGS clear path that now made use of by Travellers.

Ordered Peter HARSTON (Hairston), Thomas GOODE, Isaac GARRISON, Wm. DOBSON, Patrick McGIBBONY, Andrew ROBINSON, Constant LADD, Barnabas FARE, Barnabus FARE, Junr., Henry HAMPTON, James HAMPTON, Peter FULP, Seth COFFIN, David MORROW, Henry TERRILL, and Michael FARE view road from David MORROWS to Richard GOODES.

Ordered Daniel HUFF, Alexander THOMPSON, James JONES, Absalom REESE, Thomas HADLEY, John MARTIN, Greenberry PATTERSON, Justice REYNOLDS, Samuel CALLOWAY, Rezia JARVIS, David CRAFFORD, Palmer

SCRITCHFIELD, Simon HADLEY, Thomas BURCH view road from Hills Iron Works on Elkins to begin near Hendersons old place; road leads from SCRITCHFIELD Ford to Shallowford above John MARTINS near Chesnut Hill.

Ordered John CUMMINS overseer, road from John CUMMINS to David MORROWS.

Deed from Richard GOODE, Sheriff, to Michael NULL; oath Wm. THORNTON.

Deed from Benj. GRIFFITH to John COX; oath Robert HARRIS.

Deed from Christian SHOUSE and Madalene SHOUSE to John CUNROD; oath of Jacob MILLER.

Deed from John LANKASTER to Joseph WILLIAMS, 640 acres; oath Wm. THORNTON.

Deed from Baswell PINKSTON to John McBRIDE; oath Jos. WILLIAMS.

Deed from William MEREDITH to Ebenezer SNOW; acknowledged.

Job MARTIN appointed guardian Jesse BASKET who accepted as such; Wm. T. LEWIS, security.

Charles McANALLY, County Trustee, vs John COLVARD; Citation.

Ordered Justice REYNOLDS be fined 20 shillings for contempt of Court.

Thompson GLEN has leave to keep Tavern at his house; Job MARTIN and Roger GIDDENS, securities.

Court appointed Collectors for 1786 as follows: Capt. LEWIS; Zachariah RAY; LOVELLS: John RANDLEMAN; HILLS: John COOLEY; COOKS: Andrew ROBINSON; BOSTICKS: John BOSTICK; ADKINS: Wm. ADKINS; GAINS: James GAINS; HICKMANS: John HUGHES; KROUSES: Michael HAUSER; HUMPHRIES: John HUMPHRES; CARSONS: John Thos. LONGINO; MOSBYS: John BRUCE; BLACKBURNS: Joseph EASON; SANDERS: John WILLIAMS (LT); WILLIS: Rezia JARVIS.

Ordered John HALBERT, Robert HILL, Gray BYNUM, John CUMMINS, John HUTCHINS, James GAMMEL, William KINMAN, Drury WILLIAMS, Charles ANGLE, John HUGHES, Joshua COX, James GAINES, Joseph CLOUD, David HUMPHRES, John FLEMING, James DOAK, John BRYSON, Gideon EDWARDS, James SANDERS, James SANDERS, Jr., James CARSON, Job MARTIN, Malcum CURRY attend County Court 2nd Monday in February as Jurors.

Whereas Traugott BAGGE, Esq., one of the Justices of Peace, hath committed Peter CORBIN of Worchester and Samuel BLEDSWORTH of Somerset Counties in Maryland to County Jail for not having no pass and on suspicion that fice Negroes: Nora Bird (a wench), Stephen and Abner (boys), and Titus and Cudger (fellows) which they had with them and offered for sale, were bad property and conveyed away from Maryland to loss of proper owners or liberty which some of these Negroes pretend to have obtained by Court of Princess Anne County, Maryland; Whereas CORBIN and BLEDSOE have since broke jail and made their escape confirming their stealing said negroes; Ordered Sheriff advertise them in Virginia and Maryland newspapers and hire out said Negroes with reliable House Holders, etc. so that Adam ELROD and others against those who brought them here be satisfied.

18 November 1786

Present: Charles McANALLY, William MEREDITH, William COOK, Absalom BOSTICK, Henry SPEER, Esqrs.

Deed from Commissioners of Town of Richmond to John Thomas LONGINO;

oath of William HUGHLETT. (2)

Deed from John Thomas LONGINO to Thomas POINDEXTER: oath said LONGINO.

Deed from John Thomas LONGINO to Hugh MORRIS; acknowledged.

Inventory personal estate of Robert LANIER, deceased, returned by Joseph WILLIAMS.

Inventory and appraisement estate of Robert WALKER, deceased, returned.

Ordered Robert BRIGGS be allowed three pounds, 12 shillings for finding sundry Criminals in Jail, etc.

Wm. T. LEWIS vs Abner PHILIPS; Zenas BALDWIN, witness for Pltf., 120 miles, 28 days.

Henry SPEER vs Aires HUDSPETH; Gibson WOOLDRIDGE, witness for Deft., 460 miles, 7 days; Rebekah CRITCHFIELD, 21 miles, 7 days.

Mary RUTLEDGE vs Henry WARD; Gibson WOOLDRIDGE, witness for Deft., 460 miles, 7 days.

Samuel SHINN vs Carter HUDSPETH; Gibson WOOLDRIDGE, witness for Deft., 345 miles, 7 days.

Abner GREENWOOD vs John DOYLE; same witness.

Wm. T. LEWIS vs Jonathan HAINES; Zachariah RAY, witness.

James M. LEWIS vs Jonathan HAINS; Wm. T. LEWIS, witness for Pltf., 120 miles, 10 days; Zenas BALDWIN, witness for Pltf., 120 miles, 8 days.

Wm. T. LEWIS vs Gibson WOOLDRIDGE; Zenas BALDWIN, witness for Pltf., 120 miles, 9 days; Wm. COOK, 800 miles, 20 days.

Henry SPEER vs Airs HUDSPETH; Drury HOLCOMB, witness for Deft., 160 miles, 21 days; John WILLIAMS, witness for Pltf., 240 miles, 46 days.

Becket NICHOLS vs James PILCHER: John WILLIAMS, witness for Pltf., 240 miles, 40 days.

Henry SPEER vs Airs HUDSPETH; John WILLIAMS, witness for Pltf., 240 miles, 41 days; Geo. HOLCOMB, witness for Deft., 240 miles, 39 days.

State vs Thomas and Abram DOUTHIT and Phil HILL; Judgement Traversed; fined DOUTHIT 10 pounds each.

12 February 1787
Richmond Court House

Present: Martin ARMSTRONG, Esqr. (Adjourned til tomorrow.)

13 February 1787

Present: Martin ARMSTRONG, Joseph WINSTON, Hugh ARMSTRONG, Esqrs.

Thomas POINDEXTER has leave to keep Tavern at his House in Richmond; James GAINES, security.

John DOOLING exempted paying any more taxes 1786 in CARSONS District than 3 polls and 500 acres.

Wm. MORRIS exempted paying tax on 100 acres, Capt. HILLS District.

Also Jacob PETREE, Wm. RUTLEDGE and Richard MELTON exempt in future.

Deed from Christian Fredrick COSSART by Fredr. Wm. MARSHALL to

Peter PAFF; oath of John KROUSE.

Deed from William RUTLEDGE to Mary RUTLEDGE; acknowledged by said Wm. RUTLEDGE.

Deed from James READ to Joseph PIKES; oath Boeter SUMNER.

Deed from John PETTYJOHN to Thomas HADLEY; oath John MARTIN.

Deed from Richard LAWRENCE to Claiborne LAWRENCE: oath James LAWRENCE.

Deed of Gift from Richard GITTINS to Margarett GITTENS; oath of Hugh ARMSTRONG.

Deed from Marget NELSON to Zachariah SENTER; oath Elijah SMALLWOOD.

Deed of Gift from James SANDERS to Daniel HOLEMAN and wife; oath of James SANDERS, Junr.

Adonijah HARBOUR overseer, road in room Joseph EAST.

Henry FRY submitted on presentment against him as overseer road and fined 2 shillings, 6 pence.

John HUMPHRIS appointed Collector Capt. HUMPHRIES District; refuses to act; Ordered James LAURANCE be appointed in his place.

Grand Jury: Malcum CURRY, Foreman; Robert HILL, John CUMMINS, James GAINES, Wm. KINMAN, Charles ANGLE, John HUGHES, Joshua COX, David HUMPHRIS, John BRYSON, Job MARTIN, James GAMBLE, John HALBERT, and James SANDERS, Junr.

Jesse HILL appointed guardian to William FOWLER, orphan of William FOWLER, deceased; Adam WOOLF and Robert HILL, securities.

Ordered Hugh ARMSTRONG, William MERREDITH, William COOK and Henry SPEER, Esqrs. be committee to settle with Executors, Administrators and Guardians.

14 February 1787

Present: Matthew MOORE, Joseph WINSTON, Henry SPEER, William T. LEWIS, Hugh ARMSTRONG, Esqrs.

Philip SHOUSE records his mark.

Ordered William ROSEBERRY of HICKMANS District was no inhabitant of the State at time of giving in Taxes; he therefore be exempted.

Deed from Edmund REAVIS to Henry SPEER; oath Edward REAVES.

Deed from Henry SPEER to Carlton LINDSAY; oath said SPEER.

Deed from Silas ENYERT to Henry SPEER; oath John WILLIAMS.

Deed from Henry SPEER to John SKIDMORE: oath said SPEER.

Deed from John HENDERSON to William WEBB; oath James GAINES.

Deed from Jacob MILLER to John MILLER: oath Wm. THORNTON.

Deed from Jacob MILLER to Frederick MILLER; oath Wm. THORNTON.

Deed from Michael HOOPER, Senr. to John KAYSER: oath Jacob SHORE.

Deed from John GILBERT and wife to Matthew BROOKS; oath said GILBERT.

Deed from Thomas SKIDMORE to Abraham SKIDMORE; oath Henry SPEER.

Bill of Sale from Michael PRUIT to William SOUTHERN; oath Henry BAKER.

William DILLON vs David EVANS; Jury: Patrick McGIBBONY, Wm. SOUTHERN, Jonathan HAINES, David REAVIS, Charles DUDLEY, Jesse

KNIGHTON, Jason ISBEL, Wm. BURRIS, Wm. WILSON, Silvanus PIPES, Ephraim BANNER, and John PIPES.

William BERNEY vs Matthew BROOKS; same jury; non suit.

Moses BAKER vs Daniel CHANDLER: same jury; Robert FORBIS, witness for Pltf., 264 miles, 30 days.

Michael FRY vs Matthew WARNOCK.

Last Will and Testament of David LINVILL, deceased, proved by oath Constant LADD, Richard LINVILL, Executor, quallified.

Deed from William MERREDITH, late Sheriff, to Jonathan VERNON: acknowledged.

Ordered Henry MAINS, Benjamin BRANNUM, Richard BOYES, Andrew MACKMILLION, Samuel CLARKE and John HEATH be exempt from paying Poll Tax after 1786.

Ordered Thomas SPENCE overseer, new road from near his house to Gideon WOODRUFFS.

Ordered John PARSONS overseer, new road from Gideon WOODRUFFS to Airs HUDSPETHS field.

Ordered Airs HUDSPETH overseer, new road from his plantation into Shallowford road below Wm. PETTYS.

Ordered Ephraim McLEMORE overseer, new road from where it comes into Shallowford road below Wm. PETTYS to Rowan County line.

Anthony BITTING has leave to keep Tavern at his now Dwelling House; Michael FRY and Ephram BANNER, securities.

15 February 1787

Present: Martin ARMSTRONG, Joseph WINSTON, William COOK, Henry SPEER, Absalom BOSTICK, Esqrs.

Deed from Richard GOODE, Esq., Sheriff, to Wm. Terrel LEWIS, oath John CHILDRESS.

Deed from Barnabus FARR to John LOWE; oath Andrew ROBINSON.

Deed from James McKOIN to David JAMES; oath Andrew ROBINSON.

Deed from Hugh ARMSTRONG to Wm. BURRIS; oath said ARMSTRONG.

Deed from Joseph HOBBS and Anna HOBBS to John SATER; oath Joshua HOWARD.

Power of Attorney from Joseph HOBBS to Robert LANIER and Philip HOWARD: oath of Joshua HOWARD.

Deed from Benjamin STEWARD, Joseph STEWARD, Elizabeth STEWARD and Sarah STEWART to Matthew BROOKS; oath Wm. THORNTON.

Deed from Henry TILLY to James DUNCAN: oath said TILLEY.

Deed from Wm. DAVIS and Mary, his wife, to James DAVIS; oath John DAVIS.

Deed from James WHITE to John DAVIS: oath James DAVIS.

Deed from William ARMSTRONG to Samuel WOOD; oath said William ARMSTRONG.

Deed from Joseph ALLEN to Daniel ALLEN; oath Thomas RCBINSON.

William HAWKS, Constable, in room of Elijah SMALLWOOD.

Inventory Estate, George FULP, deceased, returned by Executor.

Last Will and Testament of William HILL, deceased; oaths Abraham MARTIN and William FOLLIS; Robert HILL and Daniel HILL, two Execrs.

qualified; 5 shillings paid to Robert WILLIAMS.

Inventory Estate of John THOMPSON, deceased, returned by Admr.; ordered part of estate be sold.

William BELL vs John COLVARD.

John SHELTON vs Reuben DODSON; Reuben GEORGE, witness for Pltf., 900 miles, 54 days.

William SHEPPERD vs Orman MORGAN and Matthew BASS; Jury: John FLEMING, Justice REYNOLDS, Thomas GRAYHAM, James MATTHEWS, David BRAY, Andrew ROBINSON, Benjamin BURCH, Zeanos BALDWIN, Philip WILSON, Lewis CONNER, James REAVIS, and Daniel SHOUSE.

Mary RUTHLEDGE vs Henry WARD; Deft. not guilty; Buckner RUSSELL, witness for Deft., 250 miles, 11 days.

Peter RIFFE vs John LANKESTER; Jury: Peter FULPS, Isaac JOICE, Matthew WARNOCK, James DOYLE, John HARPER, James BADGET, Henry BANNISTER, David REAVIS, Wm. N. COOK, William ELLIOTT, Nicholas HORN, and Joseph MANAKEY.

Philemon HOLCOMB vs William RUTLEDGE and Joseph BRADLEY; same jury except William BOYLES, Anthony BITTING and Michael HOOPER vice James DOYLE, David REAVIS, and Wm. N. COOK; George HOLME, witness for Pltf., 1280 miles, 36 days; Elizabeth HULMO, 640 miles, 16 days; George HOLCOMB, 274 miles, 45 days; Carlton LINDSAY, 274 miles, 45 days.

Francis HOLT vs George JOICE; Daniel CHANDLER, witness for Deft., 300 miles, 14 days.

Daniel SHIP vs John ROGERS; Daniel CHANDLER, 600 miles, 34 days.

Ordered William BURRIS overseer, road in room of Matthew DAVIS.

Ordered Thomas BALLARD overseer, in room Nathaniel STEWART.

Ordered Zeanos BALDWIN overseer, road in room Michael BACON.

Ordered Fredrick THOMPSON overseer, road from Beant Shoal Creek up fork road below COARSES.

Ordered Wm. COOK, Jr. overseer, road in room Nathaniel MORRIS.

Ordered George HUSK overseer, road from Mitchells River to BLACKBURNS.

William HOLLEMAN has leave to keep Tavern at his Dwelling House; John ALLEN, security.

Ordered Fredrick MILLER, David MORROW, Ashley JOHNSON, James JOHNSON, Phil GREEN, Mordicai MENDENHALL, Fredrick KINSELL, David WALKER, Cornelius SCHINIDER, John HAINES, George LOCKENOUR, Jacob HINE, Samuel VOGLER, Michael SIDES, William WALKER, Phil ROTHROCK, Peter ROTHROCK, Robert WALKER, James RINGGOLD, Jonathan SILLS, John SANDERS, William SWAIM, Aaron MILLS, and Jacob SHUTT view road from David MORROWS towards Salisbury as fare as Rowan County line.

Ordered Jacob FLYN be exempt from payment one Poll Tax 1786.

Ordered Benajah KING be exempt from payment of Poll Tax.

Ordered Thomas ROWE, an orphan aged 17 years next August, be bound to Argee GARNER until 21 years old to learn Art and Mistry of a Blacksmith.

Ordered Fload CARLTON, orphan of Blake CARLTON, deceased, be bound to Wm. COOK, Jr. for term of 22 months from date to learn Art and Mistry of Saddler.

William THORNTON, John RANDLEMAN, Zachariah WRAY, Harry TERRELL,

William F. HUGHLETT, and Stephen WOOD quallified as Justices of Peace.

Ordered Absalom BOSTICK, William Terrel LEWIS, Henry SPEER, Constantine LADD, Andrew ROBINSON, John ARMSTRONG, and Michael FRY serve as Jurors at next Superior Court held at Salisbury 15 March next.

Ordered Robert FORBIS, Samuel MOSBY, Jr., Joseph CLOUD, James DOAK, James SANDERS, Sr., Drury WILLIAMS, John HUTCHINGS, James CARSON, Wm. COOK, Jr., Wm. COCKRAM, James BADGET, John RIDINS, Adonijah HARBOUR, Samuel WOODRUFF, Edward LOVILL, John LYNCH, Daniel JARVIS, James BRYSON, Giddeon EDWARDS, Robert WILLIS, Daniel HOWELL, John MORGAN, Anthony DEARING, Peter HOOSER, Jacob NULL, Fredrick MILLER, Henry SMITH, and John PINKLEY to serve as Jurors next County Court.

16 February 1787

Present: Martin ARMSTRONG, Joseph WINSTON, Charles McANALLY, William Terrel LEWIS, Esqrs.

Deed from John Thomas LONGINO to Fredrick MILLER; acknowledged.

Deed from Robert AYRES to James MATTHEW; oath John VEVENDER.

Bill of Sale from Grizilla SMITH to Philip SMITH; oath Thomas GAINES; James GAINES to pay 2 shillings.

Deed from Matthew BROOKS and wife to Acquilla MATTHEWS; acknowledged.

Ordered Jesse SCOTT, a baseborn Mullatto child aged two months, bound to Wm. Terrel LEWIS, Esq. til 21 years old.

Ordered James COLLINS, a baseborn child age 13 years be bound to Jesse KNIGHTEN to learn Art and Mistry of farmer.

Ordered Mima SCOTT, a baseborn Mulatto girl bound to Joseph WILLIAMS and wife, Rebekah from age 18 years to 21 years.

Ordered Pricilla and Happy SCOTT, two baseborn Mulatto girls bound to Wm. Terrel LEWIS and wife, Mary, from ages of 18 to 21 years.

Ordered Jesse SCOTT (son of Sarah), a baseborn Mulatto child aged now 6 months bound to Henry SPEER, Esq. til 21 years.

Joseph GIDDIN appointed Constable in room of John ADAMS, resigned, KROUSES District.

Matthew WARNOCK vs Richard GOODE, Caveat; John MARTIN, witness for WARNOCK, 80 miles, 5 days.

Christopher ROWLES vs Matthew BASS; Execution Docket August 1786.

Jonathan HAINES vs Wm. T. LEWIS; John JONES, witness for Pltf., 20 miles, 1 day.

State vs John HARRIS; James COFFEE, witness for State, 45 miles, 15 days; Robert BRIGGS, 15 days.

Thomas EVANS vs Matthew WARNOCK; not tried; Constant LADD, witness for Pltf., 100 miles, 9 days.

Ordered notice issued against Collins HAMPTON, a late Constable, to appear and show cause why he shall be subject to pay off said judgment.

Court proceeded appointed place for a Tobacco Inspection and also Inspectors agreeable Act of Assembly when Town of Richmond was chosen the place for the Warehouse to be errected; Job MARTIN and Edmund KERBY appointed Inspectors.

Court proceeded to set rate for Taverns: Good proof Wiskey per half pint, 11 shillings; good proof Brandy, same; Common Rum, 1 shilling, 6 pence; West India Rum, 2 shillings; A Horse Stabled and fodder, 12 hours, 1 shilling; Pasturage for horse 12 hours, 1 shilling; Breakfast with tea or coffey, 2 shillings; Dinner: hot roast and boiled, 2 shillings; ordered former rules be abolished.

Ordered William COOLEY, Jacob PFAW (Faw), and Rudolph HIRE be exempt from paying Poll Tax for themselves after 1786.

Ordered following persons collectors for 1785: John COOLEY, HILLS District; John T. LONGINO, CARSONS District; Elihu AYRES, ADKINS District, make returns.

Ordered Matthew ESTERLINE overseer, roads near Bethabara in room John MICKEY.

Ordered Joshua CRESON overseer, road from Forbis Creek to Rowan County line in room of Henry SPEER.

Ordered Isham EAST, William SIZEMORE, Arthur TATE, Peter MYARS, Benajmin BENNETT, William BOYLES, Matthew CHILDRESS, Samuel FOX, John FITZPATRICK, Adam FULK, Adam FISKET, Jacob SPOONHOUR, Henry SPOONHOUR, Thomas EVANS, and Peter MOSSER view road from Quaker road where Adam FULKS path comes into it, the nearest way to Richmond.

Ordered John WRIGHT overseer, road from Salem to Moravian line near Robert WALKERS old habitation.

Ordered John CUMMINS overseer, road from Moravian line near Robert WALKERS old habitation to Guilford County line.

Ordered Seth COFFIN overseer, new road leading from Major GOODES to Daniel MORROWS from said MORROWS to Wm. DOBSONS, Esq.

Ordered Mordicai HANOM (?) overseer, new marked road leading from MORROWS to GOODES, from Wm. DOBSONS to John WELLS old plantation.

Ordered John ANGLE overseer, new marked road from MORROWS to GOODES and from John WELLS old plantation to Major GOODES.

Ordered Peter HARSTON (Hairston), Lemuel SMITH, Drury WILLIAMS, Joseph EASON, William LEWIS, John DANIEL, Benjamin YOUNG, Jr., Moses MARTIN, Thomas GOODE, Sr., Thomas GOODE, Jr., James HAMPTON, John HALBERT, Samuel CLARKE, Robert HILL, Johnson HEATH, Constantine LADD, and Absalom BOSTICK view road from CARMICHAELS Ford to Townfork leading towards Salem.

Committee appointed to settle estates of Orphans this term have examined Vouchers of Joseph BARRET, Admr. for James REYNOLDS, deceased; also report of Patrick MCGIBBONY, Executor estate of George FULPS, deceased, has paid several legatees.

Sundry certificates, with letter from His Excellency, the Governor, respecting CORBINS Negroes, etc. filed at this term at request of Major Richard GOODE, Sheriff.

17 February 1787

(No Esquires listed)

James McKOIN permitted to give in his tax: 349 acres, 1 poll.

Ordered Lemuel SMITH list taxables returned by him for 1786.

Ordered Col. Martin ARMSTRONG pay tax for only 1,000 acres land for 1786.

Ambrouse GAINS quallified as Deputy Surveyor.

Ordered notice issue against Sheriff Rockingham County show cause why he failed to serve Scire Facilas William T. LEWIS vs Nathaniel WILLIAMS, bail for James BELL issued from this Court to him sometime ago.

Ordered writ Certierari issue Jacob BLUM, Esq. bring proceedings in case of Adam PINKLEY vs Samuel CUMMINS, Constable John T. LONGINO and Adam PINKLEY be given notice.

Ordered Carlton LINDSAY have leave to build water Grist Mill on Swishers Creek to be deemed public mill.

John CLEAVELAND vs Robert WALKER; Wm. ELLIOTT, witness for WALKER 136 miles, 16 days.

Philemon HOLCOMB vs Edmond REAVES; discontinued; Henry SPEER came 20th February 1787 proving his attendance as witness.

Ordered attendance proved by Gibson WOOLDRIDGE for 2200 miles, 23 days in suit RUTLEDGE vs WARD; be not allowed; also his attendance same distance and days in suit of Wm. T. LEWIS vs John RANDLEMAN be not allowed.

Ordered Thomas BRIGGS overseer, road in room of Thomas HUGHES, runaway.

14 May 1787
Richmond Court House

Present: Martin ARMSTRONG, Henry SPEER, William HUGHLETT, Esqrs.

Deed from Philip BRITTAIN and wife to John BROWN; oath David RHOTEN.

Deed from Thomas KELL and Esebella KELL to David RHOTEN; oath John BROWN.

Deed from Phillip BRITTAIN and wife to Thoushuway TALBOT: oath John BROWN.

15 May 1787

Present: Joseph WINSTON, Absalom BOSTICK, Jacob BLOOM (Blum), Henry TERRIL, Esqrs.

Thomas BURRIS and Edward SMITH, members original pannel of Jurors, are excused from serving.

Deed from James DOAK to Thomas BALLARD; oath Stephen SMITH.

Deed from Wm. Fredr. MARSHALL to Gottlieb SPACH; oath Peter YARNEL.

Deed from Gottlieb SPACH and Martha, his wife, to Gottfried PRAEZEL; oath of Peter YARNAL.

Deed from Henry SMITH to George HAUSER, Junr.; oath Michael HAUSER.

Deed from Frederick Wm. MARSHALL to Isaac DOUTHIT: oath John BLAKE.

Deed from Frederick Wm. MARSHALL to John BLAKE; oath Isaac DOUTHIT.

Deed from Edward THOMPSON to Wm. Justice THOMPSON; oath Jos. LADD.

Deed from Robert FORBIS and wife to John CARTER: oath Matt. BROOKS.

Deed from Peter ELRODE and wife to Adam WAGGONER; oath Barney FARR.

Deed from Margret NELSON to John FLETCHER; oath Robert SAXTON.

Deed from John Christian LASH to John BINKLEY; oath Jacob BLUM.

Deed from John ALLEN to Isaac ALLEN; acknowledged.

Deed from John ALLEN to John ALLEN, Junr.; acknowledged.

110

Deed from John ALLEN to William ALLEN; acknowledged.

Deed from Wm. GRUDGE to James YOUNG; oath Wm. MEREDITH.

Deed from William MEREDITH to Thomas GRAHAM; acknowledged.

Deed from Andrew MOORE to Robert CRUMP; oath Anthony DEARING.

Deed from Matthias RICHARDSON to Abel SHIELDS; oath Wm. DOBSON.

LANIER and WILLIAMS vs John DAMMERSON. Jury: Robert FORBIS, James DOAK, Joseph CLOUD, John HUTCHINGS, John RIDENS, Adonijah HARBOUR, John PINKLEY, Gideon EDWARDS, Stephen SMITH, Wm. FORKNER, Drury WILLIAMS, and David HOWELL.

The Governor vs William SOUTHERLAND and wife; Wm. WILSON, witness for Pltf., 224 miles, 29 days.

Becket NICHOLD vs John REAVIS. Jury: John WILLIAMS, John KROUSE, John LOW, Frederick LONG, Wm. WAGGONER, Henry SHORES, Thomas BRIGGS, Richard LINVILL, Henry HAMPTON, Constant LADD, James GAINES, and David BRAY.

Matthew WARNOCK vs John CUMMINS; James COFFEE, witness for Pltf., 240 miles, 27 days.

Thomas EVANS vs Matthew WARNOCK; Samuel FITZPATRICK, witness for Deft., 78 miles, 5 days; James COFFEE, 210 miles, 23 days; Lewis CONNER, 120 miles, 10 days; Constantine LADD, witness for Pltf., 125 miles, 11 days.

Deed from Elihu AYRES to Wm. T. LEWIS; oath of Jeffrey JOHNSON.

Grand Jury: Samuel MOSBY, Foreman; Robert FORBIS, Drury WILLIAMS, Joseph CLOUD, James DOAK, John HUTCHINGS, William COOK, Junr., Wm. COCHRAM, James BADGET, John RIDINS, Gideion EDWARDS, David HOWELL, Adonijah HARBOUR, Anthony DEARING, and John PINKLEY.

Ordered William WAGGONER overseer, road in room of James HAMPTON.

Last Will and Testament of David MELTON, deceased; oath William LONDON that he signed MELTONS name to said will by said MELTONS Special Directions; Thomas EAST, Executor, qualified.

Settlement Estate of William HILL, Senr., deceased, returned by Executors.

Inventory Estate of David LINVILL, deceased, returned by Richard LINVILL and Aaron LINVILL, Executors.

Administration of Estate of James ROBERTS, deceased, granted Wm. ROBINSON; James DOAK and John ARMSTRONG, securities.

Ordered Matthias STEELMAN exempt from paying Poll Tax 1786 and in future.

Ordered Sarah BRABBIN, aged 15 years be bound to John CLAYTON til 18 years and learn Art and Mistry of a Spinster.

Ordered James BRABBIN, aged 3 years (orphan of Wm. BRABBIN, deceased) bound to John CLAYTON til age 21.

Ordered John Marquiss BRABBIN, aged 7 years (orphan of Wm. BRABBIN, deceased) bound to Joseph EASON til age 21 years and learn Art and Mistery of a Hatter.

Ordered Martha JACKSON, a baseborn child aged two years 21 October last, bound to John JACKSON til 18 years.

Ordered Anna MOORE (daughter of James MOORE) aged 14 years bound to Peter FULPS to learn Art and Mistry of Spinster.

Ordered Edmund DAVIS aged 15 years (orphan of Philip DAVIS, deceased) bound to Daniel DAVIS and learn Art and Mistery of Blacksmith and learn him to read, write and cypher as far as the Rule of Three.

Ordered Strangeman HUTCHINGS, George HOPPAS, Senr., Matthew TAYLOR Senr., Edward YOUNG, Stephen JARVIS and Thomas MEERS be exempt from paying Poll Tax after year of 1786.

Michael HOOSER, collector for FROUSES District returned following Insolvants: John SKRIMSHAW and Daniel SMITY, 2 polls only for 1786.

John DUNLAP, Junr. is inserted in two lists Taxables 1786. Ordered his father, James DUNLAP be released from payment on one in BOSTICKS District.

(The following list with words "Examined and Qualified" after each, appears next in the court minutes; no Court Order or Heading.)

Joseph WINSTON and Absalom BOSTICK; John T. LONGINO and James GAINES; John GILES and Isaac HILL; John WILLIAMS and Wm. T. LEWIS; William THOMPSON and Harry TERRIL; Joseph BRITTEN and Thomas Mc-CAREL; John DAVIS and John CUMMINS; George KIMBROUGH, John ALLEN and Samuel MOSBY, securities.

Boswell RIDDLE, William GAMBLE and John BOLES, securities; Reuben GEORGE, James MARTIN, securities; Isaac SOUTHARD, Jonathan HAINES and John PIPES, securities; Joseph PORTER, John TALIAFERRO, securities; John LANKFORD, James Gaines, security; Reuben DODSON, John CHILDRESS, security; John LANKFORD, James GAINES, security; John McANALLY, Charles McANALLY, security; Richard KERBY, Jacob SHEPPERD, security; Zenos BALDWIN, Wm. T. LEWIS, security; Jeffery JOHNSON, Wm. FREEMAN, security; Charles VEST, John RANDLE-MAN, security.

16 May 1787

Present: Henry SPEER, Jacob BLUME, John CHILDRESS, Absalom BOS-TICK, William THORNTON, Zac. RAY, Esqrs.

John HOWARD vs John and Robert SMITH. Jury: Stephen SMITH, John McANALLY, Jonathan HAINES, Wm. WAGGONER, Reziah JARVIS, John LOW, Charles DUDLEY, James FREEMAN, Barnabas FAIR, Richard LINVILL, Richard HORN and John FLEMING: John ALLEN, witness for Pltf., 150 miles, 13 days.

John SCHAUB vs Michael HENDERSON.

Wm. T. LEWIS vs Abner PHILLIPS; Joel LEWIS, witness for Pltf., 140 miles, 7 days.

Alexander SCAMERON vs Salathiel MARTIN. Jury: Edward THOMPSON, John REAVIS, John WILLIAMS, Peter FULPS, John KROUSE, Michael FULPS, Zenos BALDWIN, George HOOSER, Thomas GALLION, Ben BURCH, John BURCH, and Zephaniah DOWDEN.

James BELL vs W. T. LEWIS; same jury except Silvanus PIPES and John FLEMING in room of Ben. BURCH and John BURCH; Benjamin BURCH, witness for Pltf., 450 miles, 30 days; John BURCH, 450 miles, 25 days (also same case, same witnesses).

Moses BAKER vs Daniel CHANDLER: Joseph MURPHY, witness for Pltf., 100 miles, 17 days; Robert FORBIS, 20 miles, 3 days.

John SHELTON vs Reubin DODSON; Wm. CHANDLER, witness for Pltf., 240 miles, 16 days; David SHELTON, 1088 miles, 62 days.

William N. COOK vs James TODD.

John MARR vs Robert WARNOCK; same jury except Joshua FREEMAN in room of John FLEMING.

112

Becket NICHOLS vs James PILCHER.

William T. LEWIS vs Gibson WOOLDRIDGE: Ben HEARNDON, witness for Pltf., 222 miles, 6 days.

Arthur TATE vs Arthur SCOTT; Jesse SCOTT, witness for Deft., 10 days (no miles).

Becket NICHOLS vs James PILCHER: James CURD, witness for Deft., 144 miles, 42 days; Bennet SMITH, 340 miles, 39 days; Sarah BOHAN-NON, 320 miles, 35 days; James McKOIN, 240 miles, 34 days; George HOLCOMB, 120 miles, 18 days; Abijah ELMORE, witness for Deft., 192 miles, 24 days; David REAVIS, 200 miles, 39 days; James REAVIS, 400 miles, 27 days.

Henry SPEER vs Airs HUDSPETH; John WILLIAMS, witness for Pltf., 100 miles, 14 days; Rebekah CRITCHFIELD, witness for Deft., 252 miles, 19 days.

Ordered Elizabeth WRIGHT be exempt from paying tax on 500 acres of land 1785.

Ordered Peter NORMAN be released from paying Poll Tax 1787 being under age.

Last Will and Testament of Samuel MOSBY, deceased; oath of Joseph WILLIAMS; Susannah MOSBY, Samuel MOSBY and Joseph WILLIAMS, Executors, quallified.

Richard GOODE, Esq. chosen Sheriff by Large Majority.

Deed from George HIDE to Moses WRIGHT: oath of Joshua FREEMAN.

Deed from Richard LAWRENCE and Isobell, his wife, to James LAW-RENCE; oath of John BRYSON, Senr.

Deed from Micajah CLARKE and Luranny, his wife, to John MARTIN; oath of Boater SUMNER.

Deed from Commissioners of Town of Richmond to Charles VEST; oath of John ARMSTRONG.

Ordered Jacob BLUM have leave to keep Tavern at Town of Salem; Peter HOOSER security.

Ordered Peter HOOSER have leave to keep Tavern at his house in Bethany; Jacob BLUM, security.

Ordered Christian LASH have leave to keep Tavern at Town of Bet-habra; Jacob BLOOM, security.

Ordered Wm. HUGHLETT have leave to keep Tavern at his house in Richmond; John ARMSTRONG, security.

James CURD by his friend, Jesse COUNCIL vs Becket NICHOLS; David REAVIS, witness for Pltf., 200 miles, 39 days; James PILCHER, 240 miles, 35 days.

Ordered Daniel SHORES overseer, new road from BITTINS to Little Yadkin.

Ordered Isham EAST overseer, road from Adam FULKS path to Richmond.

Ordered Isaac SOUTHARD overseer, road in room of Icabud BLACKLEDGE.

Ordered John WILLIAMS overseer, road from little fork Mitchells River to David RIGGS.

Ordered Joseph SPARKS overseer, in room of Wm. SPARKS.

Ordered William MEREDITH overseer, road from Critchfields Ford to where GENTRYS road leaves Oar Road.

17 May 1787

Present: Martin ARMSTRONG, Joseph WINSTON, William COOK, James MARTIN, Harry TERRIL, Esqrs.

Wm. T. LEWIS vs Gibson WOOLDRIDGE. Jury: Henry SMITH, George PETTIT, John BRUCE, Francis POINDEXTER, John FLEMING, Joseph BANNER, Jesse KNIGHTON, Silvanus PIPES, John PIPES, John SATER, James MARTIN, Constantine LADD; Witness for Deft.; Ben BURCH, 440 miles, 45 days; John SUTTON, 320 miles, 5 days; Witnesses for Pltf., Joel LEWIS, 140 miles, 7 days; Zenos BALDWIN (no miles) 3 days.

Thomas McCARREL vs Matthew BASS. Jury: George DEATHERAGE, Adam MITCHELL, Joshua COX, Eliphalet JARVIS, Job MARTIN, Thompson GLEN, Salathiel MARTIN, Abner PHILIPS, John ROBERTS, Thomas GALLION, Matt. BROOKS, and Thomas PETTIT.

John Allen WATERS vs Stephen CROWDER.

Moses LINSTER (?) vs James SHEPPERD.

James Martin LEWIS vs Jonathan HAINES. Jury: George DEATHERAGE, Adam MITCHELL, Joshua COX, Job MARTIN, Thompson GLEN, John ROBERTS, Thos. GALLION, Matthew BROOKS, Thomas PETTIE, Henry SMITH, James GAINES, Ben. BURCK. Ordered Deft. be not subjected to paying more witnesses of Pltf. than the two PIPES; John PIPES, witness for Pltf., 180 miles, 13 days; Silvanus PIPES, 180 miles, 13 days.

Alexander JOICE vs George BREWER. Jury: Salathiel MARTIN, John PIPES, Silvanus PIPES, Elephalet JARVIS, Jesse KNIGHTON, Jo. BANNER, George PETTIT, Abner PHILIPS, Frank POINDEXTER, Joshua COX, Zenas BALDWIN, and Jonathan HAINES.

Ordered John SWAIM and Thomas CHURCH exempt from paying Poll Tax for themselves 1786.

John CONNEL of LOVILLS Old District had but 200 acres 1785 but charged with 800; ordered he be released from paying on 600 acres.

Deed from David DUGLASS to John HUNT; acknowledged.

Deed from George DEATHERAGE to John DEATHERAGE; oath Phil DEATHERAGE.

Deed from Ralph SHELTON and Susannah, his wife, to Alexander BURGE; oath of Phil DEATHERAGE.

Bill of Sale from Thomas HANDLAN to Gideon EDWARDS; oath Micajah OGLESBY.

Ordered George PHILIPS overseer, road from Wilkes line down to Polebranch.

Ordered Ephraim McLEMORE overseer, road from Polebranch to where Clanton leaves off.

Ordered William FOLLIS overseer, road in room of Henry FRY.

Ordered Lewis ELLIOTT overseer, road in room of James SANDERS, Junr.

Ordered Samuel HAMPTON overseer, road in room of Philip EVANS.

Ordered Harry TERRILL overseer, road leading from Winstons Tavern to Carmichaels Ford and from Townfork into said road on next side said TERRELLS and hands of Major HARSTONS on South side Dan River viz William DANIEL, James EASON, Gibson SOUTHERN, and Thos. CRELL work under said overseer.

Jacob SHEPPARD, Esq. qualified as Justice of Peace.

David JOHNSON vs William CHANDLER.

Francis KIDNER vs Abner GREENWOOD and John RANDLEMAN; same jury except Thomas McCARREL in room of Frank POINDEXTER.

Wm. T. LEWIS vs Robert WALKERS Executors; Zenos BALDWIN, witness for Pltf., 60 miles, 3 days.

John KIMBROUGH vs Thomas WHITWORTH; Samuel WHITWORTH, witness for Deft., 360 miles, 11 days; Wm. WHITWORTH, 600 miles, 10 days.

18 May 1787

(No Esquires listed)

The State vs Patience GLEN; find Deft. not guilty; Jury: Matthew BROOKS, Henry PATTILLO, John PIPES, Silvanus PIPES, Frank POINDEXTER, John FLEMING, Wm. BURRIS, Joel LEWIS, John DEATHERAGE, Charles DUDLEY, Abner GREENWOOD, Justice REYNOLDS; Thompson GLENN, witness for Deft., 12 miles, 1 day; Andrew PHILIPS, 10 miles 1 day.

The State vs William HUGHLETT; find Deft. not guilty; Jury: Matthew BROOKS, John PIPES, Silvanus PIPES, John FLEMING, William BURRIS, Joel LEWIS, Charles DUDLEY, Abner GREENWOOD, Justice REYNOLDS, Airs HUDSPETH, Wm. FOLLIS, John BOLES; David POINDEXTER, witness for Deft., 14 miles, 1 day.

Benjamin HEARNDON vs Thomas SMITH (Jockey); not tried; John SUTTON, witness for Pltf., 320 miles, 4 days.

David BRAY vs William HOWARD; not tried; Anna MIDDLEN, witness for Deft., 240 miles, 10 days.

William BURCH and wife vs Samuel CALLOWAY; not tried; Winna DUNCAN witness for Pltf., 74 miles, 4 days.

Ordered Milley BRABBIN, orphan of William BRABBIN, aged 15 years, be bound to William FOLLIS until 18 years old.

19 May 1787

Present: Joseph WINSTON, Henry SPEER, William COOK, Esqrs.

Deed from Edward WILBURN to John MEREDITH: oath William COOK.

Deed from George STEELMAN to Stephen DAVIS; acknowledged.

Deed from John LANKFORD and wife to Woody BURGH; oath James GAINES.

Deed from Matthew MOORE to William Hargus GRAY; acknowledged.

Deed from John KIMBROUGH to John BRUCE; oath Arge GARNER.

Ordered John SATER overseer, road from Shallowford to Mark PHILLIPS.

Ordered John CARTER overseer, road from Brooks Ferry to Logans Creek in room of Matthew BROOKS.

Ordered Matthew BROOKS overseer, road from his Ferry to Moravian line in place of Christian CUNROD.

Jury appointed to view road from David MORROWS to Salisbury report have laid off said road.

Ordered Thomas KNIGHT exempt from paying one Poll Tax 1786 in HUGHLETTS District as is mistake, he being in ADKINS District.

RANDLEMAN to pay 2 shillings.

Ordered Elizabeth BLACKBURN be admitted now to give her taxable propery 1786, 60 acres and 1 Poll.

Ordered Peter MIER (Deep Creek) be exempt from paying Poll Tax for himself 1786 and in future.

James GAINES appointed Corner in room Absalom BOSTICK, resigned; Matthew MOORE and Nathaniel WILLIAM, securities.

David BRAY vs Wm. and James HOWARD; not tried; John PADGET, witness for Pltf., 240 miles, 16 days; Robert SAXTON, witness for Deft., 180 miles 11 days.

William LATHAM, Esq. vs Charles VEST; Jane HOWARD, witness for Pltf., 125 miles, 15 days.

Simeon SHORES vs William COOK, Senr.; Zenos BALDWIN, witness for Pltf., 90 miles, 5 days.

Edward LOVELL vs John HUNT. Jury: Abner GREENWOOD, Thompson GLEN, Jesse KNIGHTEN, Charles CLAYTON, Godfrey FIDLER, Fredr. HELSEBECK, Thomas PETTIT, David BRAY, John FLEMING, Reuben SHORES, James MATTHEWS, and William BURRIS.

William RAMEY vs Justice REYNOLDS; not tried; John CARLTON, witness for Deft., 230 miles, 5 days.

William WATT vs Robert LANIERS Executors.

Abner GREENWOOD vs John DOYLE; not tried; Gibson WOOLDRIDGE, witness for Deft., 230 miles, 5 days.

Henry SPEER vs Airs HUDSPETH; discontinued; Gibson WOOLDRIDGE, witness for Deft., 230 miles, 2 days.

Samuel SHINN vs Carter HUDSPETH; not tried; Airs HUDSPETH, witness for Deft., 200 miles, 19 days.

John DOYLE vs William BURRIS: not tried; Airs HUDSPETH (same).

Henry SPEER vs John ALLEN; James TODD, witness for Pltf., 220 miles, 11 days.

Joseph RAMEY vs Henry SPEER; James TODD, witness for Deft., 216 miles, 26 days.

Joseph WILLIAMS, Clerk of Surry County Court, entered into bond with John WILLIAM, William MEREDITH, and John RANDLEMAN, securities.

Ordered Sheriff summons Jury, make known Letters of Administration proving Wills, Deed, dtc. will be on Monday each term. Trials on State Docket begin on Friday, etc.

Ordered the following Justices appointed to take lists Taxable property in 1787: MOSBYS: Henry SPEER; KROUSES: Jacob BLUME: HILLS: Joseph WINSTON; LADDS: William DOBSON; BOSTICKS: Absalom BOSTICK; HICKMANS: James MARTIN; GAINES; Matthew MOORE: McANALLYS: Charles McANNALLY; HUMPHRIS: Hugh ARMSTRONG: ADKINS: William COOK; LOVILLS: Jesse BUMPS; HUGHLETTS: John RANDLEMAN; LEWIS: William T. LEWIS; WILLIS: William MERREDITH: SANDERS: Stephen WOOD; GLENS: William HUGHLETT.

Ordered John ARMSTRONG, William HUGHLETT, and John RANDLEMAN, Esqrs. appointed Assessors for Town of Richmond.

Following appointed to serve as Jurors next County Court 2nd Monday August next: Charles DODSON, John MORGAN, Hardy REDICK, William CAMBELL, John ROBINSON, William WEBB, Alexander JOICE, Daniel JARVIS, Samuel WOODROUGH, Henry KERBY, William LAIN, Edward LOVILL, Joseph ASHLEY, Wm. BURCH, John SHORES, Michael RANK, Daniel SHOUSE, John HARVEY, Wm. HOLLIMAN, William ELLIOTT, Lewis ELLIOTT, James SANDERS, Junr., Valentine FREY, Daniel HILL, Obediah MARTIN, Thomas SPENCE, Henry SOUTHERS, Thomas ALLEN, Silvanus PIPES, Abraham DOWNEY, and Fredrick MILLER.

On petition of George HUDSPETH and others, ordered George HUDSPETH have leave to keep Ferry at his own plantation on Yadkin River and rates of said ferry be same as Matthew BROOKS Ferry.

Ordered Giles HUDSPETH, Ben. HUDSPETH, Robert FORBIS, John JOINER, Joshua CRESON, Abraham SKIDMORE, George HUDSPETH, Robert MATTHEWS,

Francis POINDEXTER, Joseph HUDSPETH, Phil HOWARD, Samuel MOSBY, John HARVEY, John HARVEY, Junr., Alexander DOUGLASS, John COLVARD, John SATER, Leander HUGHES view road from Henry SPEERS Bridge on Deep Creek to cross at HUDSPETH Ferry; thence to Shallowford Road leading toward Salem.

Committee appointed to examine Collectors of Insolvants report returns as follows:

HILLS District: John COOLEY, Collector 1785: David CONNELY, 1 poll, 50 acres; James FOSTER, 2 polls, 100 acres; William CLAYTON, 1 poll, 150 acres; James MERRIT, 1 poll. For year 1786: David CONNELY, 1 poll, 50 acres; Wm. CLAYTON, 1 poll, 150 acres; James FOSTER, 2 polls, 100 acres; James MERRIT, 1 poll; Robert BYRD, 1 poll and Robert GAMMIL, 1 poll.

HUMPHRIS District: James LAWRENCE Collector 1786: William CHANDLER and Charles STEWARD, 1 poll each.

McANALLYS District: John McANALLY Collector 1785: Ambrose BLACKBURN, 1 poll, 450 acres; John REACH, Robert BRASHEARS, Moses MOTT, John WILSON, Christian STANDLEY, Thomas WILSON, and Thomas WILSON, Junr., 1 poll each; Thomas COLLINS, 1 poll, 400 acres; Anthony COLLINS, 1 poll, 100 acres; Christian STANDLEY, 1 poll, 150 acres; For 1786: Martin BRANNUM, 1 poll, 200 acres; Anthony COLLINS, 1 poll, 377 acres.

COOKS District: Andrew ROBINSON Collector 1786: William BOSTICK, 4 polls; Hezekiah COCKRAM, Jesse DEES, William LOVE, Andrew MILLER, and Peter CLEMMINS, 1 poll each; John LOVE, 1 poll, 400 acres; Wm. POGE, 1 poll, 200 acres.

LEWIS District: Zeanus BALDWIN, Collector 1786: Job HAMBLIN and Henry MULL, 1 poll each; James NELEY, 1 poll, 100 acres; Wm. FRAZER, 1 poll, 200 acres; Phil HOLCOMB, 0 polls, 740 acres.

CARSONS District: John Thomas LONGINO Collector 1785: David BAKER, Thos. COOPER, Thomas DICKERSON, Charles GUTTERY, William JONES, Richard TOMERSON, 1 poll each; Evan JONES, 1 poll, 199 acres; For 1786: Randal BROWN, 1 poll; Evan JONES, 1 poll, 142 acres; James OLIVER, 1 poll, 100 acres.

SANDERS District: (No collector) 1786: Willis BRADLEY, John CURRY, Wm. JEFFERY, Amos PILGRIM, William PILGRAM, and Amos PILGRIM, Junr., 1 poll each; John DOYLE, 1 poll, 400 acres; Thomas JINKINS, 1 poll, 125 acres; Isaac MIZE, 1 poll, 200 acres; John GAME, 1 poll, 260 acres; James JAMES, 1 poll, 340 acres; Bazwell PINKSTON, 1 poll, 180 acres.

MOSBYS District: John BRUCE, collector 1786: George BILLS, 1 poll, 400 acres; John LANKESTER, 1 poll, 640 acres; John RAMEY, 1 poll, 78 acres; John LANKASTER, 3 polls; William LANKESTER, James STEPHENS, and Richard THOMERSON, 1 poll each.

BOSTICKS District: John BOSTICK Collector 1786: John BOSTICK, 5 polls; David HENDERSON, Valentine MORGAN, Thomas POWERS, and Elisha PARKER, 1 poll each; Amos LADD, 2 polls, 100 acres.

GAINES District: James GAINES Collector 1786: Boling CLARKE, Thomas DAVIS, John OWENS, and William SPENCER, 1 poll each; John GARRET, 1 poll, 50 acres; Daniel SMITHERLAND, 1 poll, 150 acres; Josiah YOUNG, 1 poll, 150 acres.

ADKINS District: Elihu AIRES (Ayres, Ayers), Collector 1786: Thomas BURNET, 1 poll, 150 acres; John HAYBURN, Wm. ROBINSON, James SUMMERS, Thomas SAMPFORD, Isaac WILLIAMS, and William OVERBY 1 poll each; Nathaniel AYRES (blank); Reuben MATTHEWS, 1 poll, 100 acres; John PATRICK, 1 poll, 100 acres; Isham THOMPSON, 1 poll, 350 acres; John YORK, 1 poll, 100 acres.

117

KROUSES District: Michael HOOSER, Collector 1786: John KRIMSHAW and Daniel SMITH, Jr., 1 poll each.

Following inserted in BRUCES and SANDERS lists though they live in MOSBYS District: 1786: Wiatt GARNER, 2 polls, 400 acres; Simon GROCE, Devall GROCE and James TODD, 1 poll each; Simon GROCE, Senr., 1 poll, 230 acres; Alse HOWELL 0 polls, 183 acres.

George HIDE, 1 poll, 350 acres in ADKINS District twice on same list.

Following given in LEWIS and SANDERS Districts but live in LEWIS District: Abraham BUTTERY, 1 poll, 50 acres; Obediah COLLINS, 1 poll, 200 acres; David HARVILL, 1 poll, 600 acres; John SPARKS, 1 poll, 200 acres.

Following given in ADKINS and HUGHLETTS District but live in ADKINS District: Thos. KNIGHT, 1 poll.

Following appear to be taxed with too much: COOKS District: John HALE, 1 stud horse, has none; HILLS District: Joseph BANNER, 300 acres too much; LEWIS District: Wm. T. LEWIS, 1 poll too much; SANDERS District: Philiman HOLCOMB, 600 acres too much.

Following in HILLS District failed to give in 1786: Thomas TUTTLE, 1 poll, 200 acres and Wm. COOK, 1 poll only, but as they neglected not through Contempt; ordered to be excused by paying single tax.

(Committee reports above persons who have moved out of county after they gave in their lists are allowed as insolvants.)

Thomas BURNET vs Phileman HOLCOMB; Jury: Wm. ELLIOTT, Lewis ELLIOTT, Thomas ADDIMAN, William CAMBELL, Teague QUILLEN, Joseph LAWRENCE, Matthew DOSS, John PARKER, John HUGHES, James CARR, Samuel HARVEY, and Wm. N. COOK.

Benjamin HEARNDON vs Thomas SMITH (Jockey); same jury except Justice REYNOLDS in room of Lemuel HARVEY; Evan DAVIS, witness for Pltf., 210 miles, 4 days; John SUTTON, 160 miles, 1 day.

Arthur TATE vs Arthur SCOTT; same jury except Airs HUDSPETH and Justice REYNOLDS in room of James CARR and Lem HARVEY; Jesse SCOTT, witness for Pltf., be not taxed in bill of cost.

Joseph PHILIPS vs Abner GREENWOOD; same jury.

William CONNER vs Daniel CHANDLER: non-suit.

Mary DOUTHIT, Admr. vs Jo. PHILIPS and Jno. L. JONES; non suit.

William SHEPPERD, assignee vs Becket NICHOLS and Phil HOLCOMB; find for Deft.; Wm N. COOK, witness proves 330 miles, 34 days; Carlton LINDSAY, witness for Deft., 100 miles, 20 days.

Harry TERRIL, Henry SPEER and Stephen WOOD, Esqrs. appointed committee of Claims to lay County Tax.

15 August 1787

Present: Matthew MOORE, Absalom BOSTICK, Harry TERRILL, Esqrs.

Inventory Estate of David MELTON, deceased, returned by Thomas EAST, Executor.

Admr. estate of Thomas ELLIOTT, deceased, granted Mary ELLIOTT, widow and relict; John Thomas LONGINO, security on bond.

Nathaniel WILLIAM, Esq. vs Gibson WOOLDRIDGE and David HUDSPETH. Jury: Wm. ELLIOTT, Lewis ELLIOTT, Matthew WARNOCK, Abner GREEN-WOOD, Charles DUDLEY, Jonathan HAINES, Thomas PETTIT, Alex. BOLES, Edward CLANTON, Jos. LAWRENCE, Thompson GLEN, Samuel CROCKET;

find for Pltf.

Nathaniel HARRISON vs Lewis HUFFMAN, Adam KIGER and Peter FISLER; same jury except Airs HUDSPETH in room of Joseph LAWRENCE; David STEWART, witness for Pltf., 200 miles, 39 days; Abraham POTTER, witness for Pltf., 180 miles, 29 days.

John and William INGRAM vs Thomas HANLIN; Gideon EDWARDS, Garnishee, says he bought 17 Negroes (16 and 40 pounds, Virginia money each), paid 110 pounds Virginia money in horses. One Negro by certificate under hand of Col. Martin ARMSTRONG and a girl of the 17 were never delivered to said Garnishee, but has been taken from about Dickeys Iron Works by one ARMSTRONG to said INGRAM.

Sarah MILLS vs John BLALOCK, recovered to use of John HOWARD. Jury: James TODD, James DOYLE, James TUCKER, Thompson GLEN, Justice REYNOLDS, Eliphalet JARVIS, John JARVIS, Thomas PETTIT, Samuel CROCKET, John SIDE, John LOGEN, and John ADAMS.

James TODD vs John DOYLE: same jury except Wm. and Lewis ELLIOTT in room of James TODD and James DOYLE; non suit.

John CLAYTON registered up his Indentures who had been bound to him last term: Sarah BRABBIN, aged 15 years and James BRABBIN, aged 3 years.

Ordered Abraham LAST overseer, road in room of John RIGHT.

Ordered Cornelious SNIDER overseer, road in place of Jacob ROMINGER.

Deed from Peter SALLE to Elihue AIRS; oath of Richard MURPHY.

Deed from Fredr. Wm. MARSHALL to Robert MARKLAND: oath Jacob BLUME.

Deed from Benjamin SAMPSON to John CROUSE: oath Windel KROUSE.

Mrs. PINKSTON, wife of Baswell PINKSTON privately examined by Jos. WINSTON, Esq. relinquishes her right of Dower land, 180 acres on Blacks Branch adjacent Joseph WILLIAMS, Daniel HUFFINES, WAGGONERS tract and tract belonging to BLACKS orphans, meaning all lands conveyed by Baswell PINKSTON to John McBRIDE, November 1786 probate.

Ordered Harry TERRILL, Henry SPEER and Stephen WOOD appointed committee to receive claims County Tax; also allow Insolvants years 1785 and 1786.

Justice REYNOLDS vs William RAMEY; same jury except James DOYLE in room of Justice REYNOLDS; non suit; tax paid; John RAMEY, witness for Deft., 280 miles, 11 days; Elijah ELMORE, 144 miles, 23 days; Lindsay CARLTON, 230 miles, 24 days.

Benjamin KENSLEY vs James BROWN; same jury.

Thomas GLEN vs Thomas SMITH (Jockey). Jury: William ELLIOTT, Lewis ELLIOTT, James DOYLE, James TICKER, Justice REYNOLDS, Eliphalet JARVIS, John JARVIS, Thomas PETTIT, Samuel CROCKET, John SCOTT, John LOGANS, and John ADAMS.

Robert WALKER vs James SHEPPERD; same jury.

16 August 1787

Present: Joseph WINSTON, Absalom BOSTICK, Wm. COOK, Jacob BLUM, Esqrs.

Deed from David DOAK and wife to John HANNA; oath James MATTHEWS.

Deed from John BLEDSOE and wife to Michael A. HART; oath Wm. LAFFOON.

Deed from John BLEDSOE and wife, Susannah, to FROST & SNOW; oath

James MATTHEWS.

Deed from Wm. HARDEN and wife to Wm. LAFFOON; oath FROST & SNOW.

Deed from Hall HUSTON and wife to Nathaniel CHAMBERS: oath Joseph PORTER.

Deed from Martin ARMSTRONG, John RANDLEMAN and Samuel CUMMINS, 3 committees for Town of Richmond to Adlai OSBOURN; oath Wm. HUGH-LETT; McCAY to pay to Trustees.

Bill of Sale from Jesse MOBBS to Mary MOBBS; oath Frederick DESERN.

Deed from James DOAK to Jacob McCRAW; acknowledged.

Lees (lease) from Lawrence ANGEL to Sebella ANGEL; oath James ANGEL.

Deed from Ephraim McLIMORE and wife to Jacob JONES; oath Sterling McLIMORE and Nicholas MASTERS.

Deed from Isaac GARRISON and wife to Stephen FOUNTAIN; acknowledged.

Warrant from Bench signed by Matthew MOORE, Esq. handed down; ordered delivered by Sheriff.

Ordered Philip GREEN and Wm. MEREDITH appointed Judges of Senate.

Ordered Harry TERRILL and Fredr. MILLER appointed Inspectors for future elections.

Ordered in future Court proceed to State Docket on Thursday every Court.

Ordered John PENROY be exempt paying Poll Tax for future; he is infirm.

Ordered Joseph KING be exempt paying Poll Tax for future; he is infirm by wounds received when a soldier.

Ordered James BROWN, orphan of (blank) BROWN, deceased, aged 7 years 6 months, bound to Jesse McANALLY til 21 years to learn Art and Mistery of Blacksmith, read, write, cypher and have a good suit of clothes at his freedom.

Ordered John BROWN, orphan of (blank) BROWN, deceased, aged 5 years, bound to Charles McANALLY, Esq. til 21 years, learn Art of Planter, read, write, cypher and receive horse, saddle and bridle at his freedom.

Ann MOORE, orphan of James MOORE, deceased, bound last term to Peter FULP by age 14 years, it appears she is but 13 years.

Thomas GOINES vs John HARPER; Jury: Wm. ELLIOTT, Lewis ELLIOTT, David HOWELL, Frederick MILLER, John EVANS, Jesse McANALLY, John JINKINS, Jonathan HAINES, John BLALOCK, Wm. STEELMAN, James DOYLE, and Wm. ADKINS.

Thomas RAPER vs James MOORE: same jury.

Mary ROBERTS vs Joshua COX, bondsman JOHN NIEL; same jury; find that John NEAL is dead.

William BELL vs John COLVERT; motion Spruce McCAY; ordered Richard GOODE, Esq. appear next court shew cause why he shall not pay the money.

Parris CHIPMAN vs Daniel CHANDLER and Nathaniel WATSON for John WAGGNON; same jury; debt is not paid.

William SHEPPERD vs Becket NICHOLS and Phil HOLCOMB: same jury; find for Deft., Carlton LINDSAY, witness for Deft., 100 miles, 21 days; Wm. N. COOK, 220 miles, 35 days.

John ANTHONY vs Joseph PORTER: Zachariah RAY, witness for Pltf.,

120 miles, 9 days.

Francis POINDEXTER and wife vs Lewis LANIER. Jury: James DAVIS, Isaac GARRISON, Andrew ROBERTSON, Thompson GLEN, Wm. PRATHER, Wm. ELLIOTT, Lewis ELLIOTT, Frederick MILLER, John EVANS, Jesse Mc-ANALLY, John JINKINS, and Jonathan HAINES: John ALLEN, witness for Deft., 30 miles, 1 day; Goldman KIMBROUGH, 15 miles, 1 day.

Andrew SPEER vs John JOHNSON; John BREVARD, former Sheriff of Rowan to appear and shew excuse why he shall not pay money.

Inventory Estate of Wm. REYNOLD, deceased, returned by Suffiah REYNOLD, Administrator.

Last Will and Testament of Ratliff BOON, deceased, proved by Richard HAZLEWOOD, Ratliff BOON, Junr., Executor quallified.

Power of Attorney from Joshua K. SPEER to John BURCH; oath Wm. KEELINGS.

Ordered following appointed Juriors to serve next Superior Court held at Salisbury 15 September next: Absalom BOSTICK, Wm. T. LEWIS, Zachariah RAY, Constant LADD, William COOK, Esq., Zenos BALDWIN, and Henry SPEER.

Ordered following appear as Jurors next County Court: John LYNCH, James CAMBELL, Joseph GENTRY, John N. ANDERSON, John WRIGHT, Thomas SPENCE, Henry SOUTHARD, Carby RYAN, David RIGGS, Richard LAWRENCE, James BRYSON, John COX, Wm. HICKMAN, Wm. MARTIN, Lemuel SMITH, Matthew WARNOCK, Jos. BANNER, Gabriel WAGGONER, Patrick McGIBBONY, John CUMMINS, Philip GREEN, John KINE, Thomas EAST, Thomas BRIGGS, Wm. CRITCHFIELD, Reuben SHORE, Wm. FREEMAN, John MOORE, Hugh MORRIS, and Lawrence HOLCOMB.

Joseph WINSTON, Esq. resigned as Entry Taker.; William THORNTON, Esq. appointed Entry Taker and also to take charge of Old Entry Books; Henry SPEER and Joseph WILLIAMS, securities.

Ordered James BURNSIDES appointed overseer road in room of John SANDERS.

Ordered Joshua FREEMAN overseer road in room of John DYER, deceased.

Ordered William CHILDRESS overseer road in room of Isham EAST.

Ordered County Trustee pay Joseph WILLIAMS, Clerk of Court to pay for binding Acts of Assembly and repairing Clerks Table.

Ordered Stephen SMITH be released from one Poll Tax for year 1785.

17 August 1787

Present: Jesse BUMPS, Stephen WOOD, Hugh ARMSTRONG, Esqrs.

Deed from Augustine BLACKBURN to Thomas EKMORE: oath Robert JOHNSON.

Deed from David BROOKS to Thomas ELMORE: oath Robert JOHNSON.

Deed from Christian MILLER to George LONG; oath William DAVIS.

Power of Attorney from Thomas BEALS to Joseph JESSUP; oath Daniel BEALS.

Ordered Michael HOOSER, collector KROUSES District 1786 be empowered to collect from Jacob MAYER tax on 200 gallons of Rum.

Ordered Randolph MILLER be released paying One Poll Tax.

Last Will and Testament of Thomas WHITTICOR, deceased, proved by oath Jo. WILLIAMS, Mary and Johnson WHITTICOR, Executors quallified.

Court adjourned for 3 hours to House of Charles VEST; Court met according to Adjournment.

Present: William COOK, Henry SPEER, Stephen WOOD, Esqrs.

Deed from Robert FORBIS to Henry SPEER; acknowledged.

Deed from James GIMET to Leven WARD: acknowledged.

Deed from Daniel SWINEY and wife to Wm. SWEAT: oath Wm. THORNTON.

Deed from John ALLEN to Amos CRITCHFIELD; acknowledged.

Deed from Obediah ROBERTS to Daniel LIBERTINE; oath Henry SPEER.

Deed from Elijah KIRKMAN to Aaron MOORE: oath Davis SPENCE.

Ordered William MARTIN overseer, road in room of James MEREDITH.

Ordered Peter FULPS overseer, road in room of James HOLBROOK.

Ordered Airs HUDSPETH be released from tax on 640 acres, 1786.

Ordered Daniel HUFFINES be exempt from paying Poll Tax in future.

James THOMPSON vs John LAW; not tried; Almon GUIN, witness for
Deft., 12 days, 270 miles.

Ordered Writ of Certeoiare, etc. case of Moses HAZLET against
Edmund PETERS, lately tried before Absalom BOSTICK, Esq.

Ordered said Writ issue to Absalom BOSTICK, a Supersideas to Wm.
THOMPSON and a Sci Fa to Moses HAZELET.

18 August 1787

Present: Matthew MOORE, George HOOSER, John RANDLEMAN, Esqrs.

Deed from John LINEBACK to Philip SNIDER: oath George HOOSER.

Deed from James TILLEY and wife to Enoch KONLE; oath John BULLOCK.

Deed from Enoch CONLEY and wife to Richard BEASLEY; oath Joseph
CLOUD.

Deed from William CLATON to Joel LABERRT: oath John HALBERT.

Deed from Peter PERKINS to Peter HAIRSTON; oath Lemuel SMITH.

Deed from James THOMPSON to Peter HAIRSTON; oath Reubin LINDSAY.

Power of Attorney from John VANHOY to John VANHOY, Junr.; acknowledged.

Deed from Barnabas FARE, Senr. and wife to Michael FARE; oath
Andrew ROBINSON.

Joseph JOHNSON vs David BRAY; John HARRIS, witness for Pltf., 180
miles, 10 days.

John DOYLE vs Wm. BURRIS; not tried; John SUTTON, witness for
Pltf., 480 miles 10 days.

The Governor vs John BRUCE; Tax; Richard GOODE, County Treasurer.

The Governor vs James GAINES; Tax Gatherer 1786; Richard GOODE,
County Treasurer.

James GAINES resigned his office as Coroner; Andrew ROBINSON
appointed to that office with Joseph WINSTON, Charles McANALLY
and Richard GOODE, securities.

Ordered John FAIR be released from payment 10 shillings in price
of Stud Horse for 1786.

Ordered Robert MAJORS be released payment 10 shillings price of
Stud Horse year 1786.

Ordered Joshua CRESON be released payment two Poll Tax 1786.

Ordered Jacob SHEPPARD, Senr. be released payment tax on 150 acres 1785-1786, having proved to court by oath of Wm. SHEPPERD that land belongs to William SHEPPERD and not Jacob.

Ordered John WALTERS be released from paying 5 Polls 1785.

Jesse LESTER has leave to keep Tavern at his now Dwelling house; John ARMSTRONG, security.

Richard GOODE, Esq. appointed Sheriff by Richard CASWELL, Esq., Governor; Jos. WINSTON, Charles McANALLY and Samuel CUMMINS, securities.

John GOODE and John BOSTICK quallified as Deputy Sheriffs; Richard GOODE objects to Sufficientey of the Jail.

Following appointed Collectors for 1787: HUMPHRIS District: James LAWRENCE; LOVELLS: Jo. ASHBY; BOSTICKS: John MORGAN; MOSBYS: George KIMBROUGH; KROUSES: Michael HAUSER; SANDERS: James SANDERS; HUGHLETTS: Thomas GORDON; HILLS: John COOLEY; GLENS: John Thomas LONGINO; GAINES: Joseph CLOUD; BUSLEYS: Charles BUSLEY; ADKINS: Jeffrey JOHNSON; WILLIS: Reziah JARVIS; LADDS: Andrew ROBINSON; LEWIS: Isaac SOUTHARD; McANALLYS: James DAVIS.

Account of Sale Estate of John LOVE, deceased, returned by Richard GOODE, Sheriff.

Account of Sale part Estate of Robert WALKER, Esq., deceased, returned by R. GOODE.

Account of Sale Estate of John THOMPSON, deceased, returned by Rich. GOODE, Sheriff.

Ordered Phil HOWARD, Edward SWEAT, Wm. SWEAT, Thos. MOSBY, Samuel MOSBY, John ALLEN, Geo. KIMBROUGH, Mannering SUMMERS, Johnson WHITTICOR, Wm. THORNTON, Battaly BRYAN, Chas. BERRYMAN, John COLVARD, Adam SPOON, Henry PATTILLO and John McBRIDE view and mark road leaving old Cross Creek road at Double Creek near Leon HARVEYS, crossing Panter Creek near COLVARDS old cabbin, near school house leaving Pinckle of high hill into old road again; Jos. WILLIAMS, overseer.

Committee appointed to receive Claims and Lay County Tax for this year report as follows: Constant LADD, serving Juror Salisbury Superior Court September 1786 and March 1787; Wm. SPARKS, Junr., destroying two wild cats; Wm. SPARKS, Senr., destroying 7 young wolves; Henry HAMPTON for Juror Salisbury Superior Court September 1786 and March 1787; Michial FRY for Juror Salisbury Superior Court September 1786 and March 1787; Thomas RAPER, destroying 1 wild cat; William FOLLIS, one woolf; Henry SPEER, Esq., Juror Salisbury Superior Court September 1786 and March 1787; Hardy REDDICK, two old wolves and 3 young ones; Elijah SMALLWOOD, 7 young wolves; John CARTER, 2 wolves; Joseph HART, 1 woolf, 2 wild cats; Pinson WILSES, 3 wolves; Wm. WEBB, 1 wild catt; Hardy REDDICK, 3 wolves; Elijah SMALL, Constable Capt. WILLIS District 1784-85-86; John COOLEY, Constable Capt. HILLS District; John DAVIS, Constable Capt. COOKS District; Esaiah GAMMON, six wild cats; Col. John ARMSTRONG Juror Salisbury Superior Court September 1786; Zachariah RAY for services done as Constable; Richard GOODE, Sheriff for Exoficious Services 1786; John ADAMS, Constable service done at Surry Court 1786-1787; John ADAMS, Constable carrying Nathan PARMER to County Jail; Capt. William ADLOMS, Constable in his district; John GOODE, Deputy Sheriff, carrying Georard GLADDEN (Prisoner) from Richmond to Salisbury Jail; Godfrey MILLER, Jailor; John GILES, Constable CROUSES District; Joseph BITTIN, Constable CROUSES District; Baswell RIDDLE, Constable; Jeffrey JOHNSON, Constable ADKINS District; Stephen R. SMITH, Constable HUMPHRIS District; Absalom BOSTICK, Juror Salisbury; Andrew ROBINSON, Juror at Salisbury; John Thomas LONGINO, Constable CARSONS District and for service Surry County and candles, etc. for 2 years; Gray BYNUM, furnishing Matthew PEGGS with provisions when carrying Judd ROADH to Salisbury Jail; Wm. T. LEWIS, Esq. Juror Salisbury; Joseph PORTER, Constable WILLIS District; John McANALLY, Constable McANALLYS District; James MARTIN and Jacob BOYER destroying old wolves; Jacob SHEPPERD, two wild cats; Joel CARBY, one wolf and one wild cat; Shadrack MOONAHAN, one wolf; Jabez JARVIS, one wild cat; John Thos. LONGINO warning inhabitants Capt. SCOTTS District and Riding Express 6 days; Barlet HILL, killing wolf; Henry SOUTHARD, one woolf scalp; John MORGAN, Assessor 8 days; John WILLIAMS, Constable Capt. SANDERS District; Thomas POINDEXTER, putting John LINCH, Junr. in Jail, keeping Aaron SPEER 14 hours and Bennedict WHITE 24 hours; Andrew ROBINSON, Juror Salisbury; Azael CROSS, one wolf, certificate to be issued to Michael HOOSER; John STANLEY, two wolves, certificate to Michael HOOSER; Michael HOOSER, carrying the body of John YOUNG to Salisbury Jail; Samuel STRUPE carrying Francis HOLT; Joseph WILLIAMS for Exoficio Services; Zachariah RAY for services as Constable.

12 November 1787

Present: William HUGHLETT, Esq.

13 November 1787

Present: George HAUZAR, William HUGHLETT, John RANDLEMAN, Esqrs.

Grand Jury: Patrick McGIBBONY, Foreman; William MARTIN, John LYNCH, Joseph GENTRY, John RIGHT, David RIGGS, Wm. HICKMAN, Lemuel SMITH, Gabriel WAGGONER, Joseph BANNER, Thomas BRIGGS, William CRITCHFIELD, Hugh MORRIS, and Reuben SHORES.

Deed from Thomas FROHOCK to Benjamin HUTCHINGS: oath John JOHNSTON and Jonas REYNOLDS.

Deed from Joseph HAUZAR to William CHILDRISS: oath Joseph CHILDRESS.

Deed from James McKINNE to John JACKSON; oath Boarter SUMNER.

Deed from Stephen JAYNE to James McKINNE; oath Boeter SUMNER.

Deed from Boeter SUMNER to Garrot GIBSON; acknowledged.

Deed from John NULL to John HAIET: oath Geo. HOLDER; Manning SUMNERS to pay.

Deed from Carlton LINDSAY to James LINDSAY; acknowledged.

Deed from Gideon BROWN and wife to Abraham WOOD; oath John WILLIAMS.

William CUPPLES (?) and Andrew JACKSON, Esqrs. produced license from Hon. Samuel ASHE and John WILLIAMS, Esqrs. authorizing them as Attorneys.

Ordered Mary BURKE, widow of Josiah BURKE, deceased, cited to court to shew cause why her son, William, should not be bound out; Daniel HILL, Informer.

Sheba HAWLEY by Dice HAWLEY, her next Friend vs Frederick MILLER. Jury: John HINE, Lemul HARVEY, Wm. FREEMAN, Abraham JAMES, Adonijah HARBOUR, Thomas EAST, Charles DUDLEY, Michael FREY, Thomas McCARRELL, Jesse HORN, Thompson GLENN, and John BOWLES.

Matthew WARNOCK vs Sarah CARMICHAEL; same jury; non suit.

Thomas COOK vs James COFFEE and John MARTIN; same jury except Alex. MOORE in room of Jesse HORN; John MOORE, witness for Pltf., 14 days, 70 miles; John BOWLES, 12 days, 144 miles.

Elizabeth WRIGHT, Admrx. vs James BADGET: same jury except Dan HILL, Frederick MILLER and Godfrey CODY in room of Lemuel HARVEY, Wm. FREEMAN and Alex MOORE: Wm. FREEMAN and Mathew BROOKS, witness 90 miles, 22 days and 80 miles, 20 days.

Inventory Estate of Werner SPOONOUR, deceased, returned by Execrs.

Edward GOODE has leave to build Grist Mill on Lick Creek.

Ordered Frederick MILLER overseer, new marked road from David MORROWS by said MILLERS; thence to county line towards Longs Ferry.

Ordered John LYNCH, Frederick MILLER, John MILLER, Jacob NULL, Phil HOWARD, Christian SMITH, Zebulan BILLITER, Samuel MOSBY, John HARVY, Wm. HOLLOMAN, Henry SPUNHOUR, Junr., George HAUZAR, Junr., Frank KIDNER, David STEWART and Reubin STEWART serve as road jury to view part of road leading from Shallowford to Betha-bra; leading by CONRODS and FOTHS old place.

14 November 1787

Present: Henry SPEER, Jacob BLUM, John RANDLEMAN, Esqrs.

Ordered Joseph VAUGHN appointed Constable in BOSTICKS District in room of William THOMPSON, removed.

Inventory Estate of Ratliff BOON, deceased, returned by Ratliff BOON, Junr., Executor.

Inventory Estate of Samuel GUINN, deceased, returned by Deborah GUINN, one of Executors.

List Taxable property ordered inserted in Collectors lists of MOSBYS District: Maj. Samuel MOSBY, 823 acres, Surry County, 2880 acres Cumberland, 4 negroes and himself; Thomas MOSBY, 350 acres, 5 negroes and self.

John KIMBROUGH vs Thomas WHITWORTH; Jury: John HINE, Thomas HOL-COMB, George HOLCOMB, Ephraim McLEMORE, Joseph ASHLEY, Jesse HORN, James DOYLE, George PETTIT, John HALL, Wm. WAGGONER, John DEATHER-AGE, Jesse SCOTT; non suit; Samuel WHITWORTH, witness for Deft., 120 miles, 3 days; William WHITWORTH, 200 miles, 2 days.

John WILLIAMS vs William and James SHEPPERD; same jury; Aaron SPEER, witness for Pltf., 160 miles, 14 days; to be applied to John WILLIAMS use.

Roger GIDDENS vs Thomas SMITH; same jury.

John ARNOLD vs George HUDSPETH; same jury; non suit.

Hanes GLENS Executors vs Joseph HARRISON; same jury; John LYNCH, witness for Pltf., 18 miles, 3 days.

Moses LINSTOR vs Nicholas HAWKINS; same jury.

Henry BANNER vs Matthew WARNOCK; same jury; Moses MARTIN, witness for Deft., 112 miles, 4 days; Joseph BANNER, 192 miles, 16 days; John COOLEY, 520 miles, 53 days.

Daniel LIBERTINE vs Joseph POWERS; John SHEPPERD, Garnishee, swears he owes nothing and has sold his claim 100 acres adjacent Nicholas HORNS land on a creek of the Yadkin River.

Joshua H. SPEER vs John CARLTON; same jury; non suit.

Thomas MORRIS vs Jno. L. JONES; same jury; non suit; Matthew DAVIS, witness for Pltf., 300 miles, 9 days.

Deed from Mathew BROOKS and wife to George LASH; oath Wm. THORNTON.

Deed from Joseph WINSTON to John HALL; oath Wm. THORNTON.

Deed from Ashley JOHNSON to James JOHNSON; oath William SWAIM.

Deed from Philip ROTHROCK to Matthias NORTING (Noeding ?); oath of George HAUZER, Junr.; William THORNTON to pay.

Deed from James MARTIN and wife, Mary, to Moses MARTIN; acknowledged by said JAMES.

Deed from Spencer BALL to Joel GURLEY; oath of David HUMPHRIS by Power of Attorney.

Deed from David HUDSPETH to Joseph HUDSPETH; oath Airs HUDSPETH, Junr.

Deed from David BRAY to William T. LEWIS; acknowledged.

Deed from Aquilla MATTHEWS and wife to Wm. ALFORD: oath Wm. THORNTON.

Deed from Samuel WAGONER to Executors of Robert LANIER; deceased; oath of Wm. THORNTON.

Deed from Abraham LINEBACK and wife to Christian SMITH; oath Wm. THORNTON.

15 November 1787

Present: Absalom BOSTICK, James MARTIN, Henry SPEER, Esqrs.

Last Will and Testament of Barnabas FAIR, deceased; proved by Andrew ROBINSON, Barnabas and Michael FAIR, Executors, quallified.

Last Will and Testament of Keziah DEAN, deceased, proved by Richard MURPHY who swears he seen Godfrey ISAACKS, a witness sign same.

Inventory Estate of Thomas ELLIOTT, deceased; returned by J. T. LONGINO; ordered Sheriff sell perishable part thereof.

Ordered William PICHET, Esq. of Richmond County appear next court and shew why he shall not pay money in execution Sarah BURNER vs John COLVERISS of Randolph County.

Ordered Absalom BOSTICK, Esq. overseer, road in room of Edward THOMPSON.

Ordered John COOK overseer, road in room of George HURST and following hands work thereon: Francis KERBY, Michael GILBERT, Jacob SANDERS, FROST & SNOW, Abner PHILLIPS and son, Cornelius PHILLIPS, and Elias PHILLIPS.

Ordered words "to read and write and also" be deleated from certain Indenture binding Jesse SCOTT to Wm. T. LEWIS, Esq.

Prisscle and Happy SCOTT to Wm. T. LEWIS, Esq. and wife Mary.

Jeremiah SCOTT is bound to Jos. WILLIAMS, Esq. and Rebecca, his wife and Jesse SCOTT is bound to Henry SPEER, Esq; they being Base Born Children and of mixed blood.

Thomas LINDSAYS Admr. vs Thomas DONOHO. Jury: John HINE, David HOWELL, Zepheriah DOWDEN, Thos. McCARRELL, Garner TUCKER, William FORTNER, Richard MURPHY, John BOLES, Ephraim McLIMORE, Zachariah MARTIN, Thos. PETTIT, Jonathan HAINES; Wm. DONOHO, witness for Deft., 180 miles, 4 days; find Judgement paid as former Francis NcNAIRYS receipt; verdict for Deft. Also, SAME vs SAME; jury find money was paid to John TATE and balance to Francis McNAIRY.

State vs Carlton LINDSAY; same jury except John BRYSON in room of John BOLES; find Deft. not guilty.

State vs Philamon HOLCOMB: same jury; Deft. not guilty.

State vs Carlton LINDSAY; same jury; Deft. guilty; Arthur SCOTT, witness for Pltf., 18 miles, 6 days.

State vs James BREEDON; same jury except George PETTIT in room of David HOWELL; Deft. not guilty; Catharine CLOUD, witness for Deft., 40 miles, 4 days.

State vs Henry SPEER; Noll Pross; Abraham WOOD, witness for Deft., 15 miles, 3 days; William HEAD, 6 miles, 3 days; Thomas PETTIT, 5 miles, 6 days; James DOYLE, (no miles), 3 days.

William WAGGONER and wife vs Absalom BOSTICK; also Wm. WAGGONER and wife vs William JAMES. It is agreed William JAMES, Senr. surrender negro girl named Phebee to William WAGGONER and said JAMES retains boy named Bob and the Negro wench Nan to be sold and equally divided between said Wm. JAMES and Wm. WAGGONER.

State vs Henry HOLTSCLAW. Jury: John HINE, George PETTIT, Zephaniah DOWDEN, Thomas McCARRELL, Garner TUCKER, John DEATHERAGE, John BOLES, Ephraim McLIMORE, Zachariah MARTIN, Thomas PETTIT, John KROUSE, and Matthew BROOKS; find Deft. guilty; Catharine CLOUD, witness for Deft., 120 miles, 12 days.

16 November 1787

Present: Charles McANALLY, William COOK, Henry SPEER, Esqrs.

Charles BEASLEY has leave to keep Tavern; James GAINES, security.

Ordered Commissioners examine Mrs. Mary COX whether she relinquishes her Dower in land sold by her husband to Richard ADAMS.

Deed from Edmund PETERS to Peter HAIRSTON; oath John BOSTICK.

Deed from Barnabas FARE and wife to Barnabas FARE, Jr.; oath Andrew ROBINSON.

Deed from Wm. HOLBROOK and wife, Susannah, to Moses LINVILL: oath said ROBINSON.

Deed from James LEFOY to Henry PATTILLO; oath William THORNTON.

Ordered Reziah JARVIS Constable in MEREDITHS District; Wm. MEREDITH and William COOK, securities.

State vs Aaron SPEER. Jury: Jesse KNIGHTON, Matthew BROOKS, Thomas PETTIT, Jno. DEATHERAGE, Jonathan HAINES, James TUCKER, Joseph PHILLIPS, Malcum CURRY, Airs HUDSPETH, Charles WADDLE, Charles DUDLEY, and John BRUCE; find Deft. guilty; Saml. CALLIWAY, witness for Pltf., 120 miles, 7 days; Bennet SMITH, 180 miles, 8 days; John STEPHENS, 22 miles, 7 days.

The Governor vs William SOUTHERLAND and wife; not determined; Chas. McANALLY, witness for Pltf., 480 miles, 32 days.

Christopher BOLES vs Matthew BASS.

Ordered a citation issued vs Collins HAMPTON to appear to shew cause why he shall not pay off above execution.

Ordered Thomas EAST overseer, Hollow Road from Stony Ridge to Moravian line and following work thereon: Edward EDWARDS, Thomas EVANS, Jr., Elijah EVANS, John EVANS, Mary BANNISTER, Joshua JONES, Arthur TATE, Joseph MILLER, George KRUGER, Henry KRUGER, Jacob KRUGER, Frederick SHOUSE, John STANDLEY and Edward OWENS.

Ordered Philip SHOUSE overseer, MaCANALLYS Rode from Quaker road to forks road between Col. Martin ARMSTRONGS, Richmond and following work thereon: Jacob SPUNHOUR, Adam FULK, Peter MOSER, Daniel SHOUSE, Col. Martin ARMSTRONGS hands, Henry SHOUSE, Daniel BOATRIGHT, Jacob HESABECK and Ahijah OLIVER.

Ordered Richard BEASON overseer, road in room of Nathan PIKE.

17 November 1787

Present: Matthew MOORE, William HUGHLETT, Zach. RAY, Esqrs.

Ordered Wm. N. COOK come in and prove his attendance in suits Wm. T. LEWIS; Admr. James BELL for Assault and Battery; Wm. T. LEWIS, Admrs.; James BELL for Tresspass.

James BELL vs Wm. T. LEWIS; Assault and Battery; Wm. N. COOK, witness for Deft., 475 miles, 34 days to be delivered to Wm. T. LEWIS.

James BELL vs Wm. T. LEWIS; Trespass; Wm. N. COOK, witness for Deft., 475 miles, 34 days to be delivered to Wm. T. LEWIS.

Robert WALKER vs Peter EDDLEMON; Js. RAMEY, witness for Deft., 160 miles, 7 days.

Henry SPEER vs Carlton LINDSAY; Deft. came into court and acknowledged if he said disrespectful things of Capt. SPEERS character, he does not remember for he had no cause to say such; discontinued suit.

George PETTIT vs Justice REYNOLDS; Jury: Charles DUDLEY, Matthew BROOKS, Airs HUDSPETH, Thompson GLENN, Wm. FORTNER, Samuel HUMPHRISS, Zach MARTIN, Wm. ROBERTSON, James MARTIN, Arthur SCOTT, Jesse KNIGHTON, and Thomas GALLION; George HEAD, witness for Pltf., 22 miles, 5 days; Michael B. ROBERTS, witness for Deft., 15 miles, 2 days.

Godfrey CODY vs David BRAY; Reuben MATTHEWS, witness for Deft., 10 miles, 3 days.

State vs Zach RAY; Wm. T. LEWIS, witness for Deft., 120 miles, 3 days.

State vs Zach RAY; same witness.

Henry SPEER vs Phil HOLCOMB; Peter SHEARMON, witness for Pltf., 75 miles, 8 days; Frederick DANNER, 75 miles, 8 days.

Ordered Robert MARKLAND appointed Guardian to John and Ann DOUTHIT, orphans of James DOUTHIT, deceased; Jacob and Thomas DOUTHIT, securities.

Ordered Zenos BALDWIN, David SPENCE and Samuel DOWNEY appointed Patrollers Capt. James Martin LEWIS old district.

Ordered George PRIDDY, Geo. KIMBROUGH and Goldman KIMBROUGH appointed Patrollers, COLVARDS district.

Ordered citation against Susannah WORD, widow and relict of Wm. WORD, deceased, why her three children not be provided for according to law.

Ordered John PERSONS overseer, road in room of Thomas SPENCE.

Ordered Jesse LESTER overseer, road in room of Robert BRIGGS as overseer Streets of Town of Richmond.

Ordered Goldman KIMBROUGH, William DUGLASS, John SATER, Frank POINDEXTER, William HOWARD, and Thomas MARTIN be added to road jury to mark road leaving old Cross Creek Road at Double Creek near Lemuel HARVEYS; thence into old road again.

Ordered Jesse LESTER overseer, road in room of Robert BRIGGS, (an overseer of Streets of Richmond).

Ordered Jeffery JOHNSON overseer, road in room Thomas JOHNSON.

Ordered road leading from Town of Richmond to Wm. BOYLES be deemed

128

public road.

Ordered Richard MORPHISS, John DEAN, Isam RIGGS, David RIGGS, Moses WILLIAMS, Moses BAKER, Joseph MURPHY, Benjamin SCOTT, Zadock RIGGS, Joseph LASSWELL, Samuel RIGGS and Silas RIGGS road jury from Little fork of Mitchells River to David RIGGS, thence Fishers River Gap.

Ordered Sheriff summons jury to lay out road best way from Ford Little Yadkin where Hollow Road crosses, thence best way to Moravian Town.

Ordered County Treasurer not demand tax of Jacob MYER of Salem on 200 gallons Rum and 2 slaves for 1786.

Ordered for future, Jesse LESTER take keys of Court House and keep same clean and in good order, find candles for court from time to time, etc.

Ordered following appointed as Juriors serve next County Court: David HOWELL, George PRIDDY, John HUMPHRISS, John BLALOCK, Silvanus PIPES, James SANDERS, Jonathan HAINES, Joshua FREEMAN, William ADKINS, Gideon EDWARDS, Matthew DAVIS, James BRISON, David HUMPHRISS, John MARTIN, Jesse KNIGHTON, George DEATHERAGE, Charles DUDLEY, Joseph ASHLEY, Job MARTIN, Windle CROUSE, Anthony BITTEN, Constantine LADD, Charles BEAZLEY, Joseph NELSON, Druary WILLIAMS, Anthony DEARING, Jesse McANALLY, Younger BLACKBURN and John HUGHES.

11 February 1788

Present: William HUGHLETT, Esquire.

12 February 1788

Present: George HAUZER, William HUGHLETT, John RANDLEMAN, Esqrs.

Grand Jury: David HUMPHRISS, Foreman; George PRIDDY, Jon. HAINES, John MARTIN, Joseph ASHLEY, Jesse McANALLY, John HUMPHRISS, Joshua FREEMAN, Jesse KNIGHTON, Joseph NELSON, John BLALOCK, Matthew DAVIS, George DEATHERAGE, and Drury WILLIAMS.

Deed from Cornelious HEITH to James STEWART: oath Wm. STEWART.

Deed from Eli NORMAN to Cornelious HEITH; oath James STEWART.

Deed from Francis DONALSON and wife, Ann, to Benj. BENSON; oath Matthew DAVIS.

Deed from Boarter SUMNER to Thomas GIBSON; acknowledged.

Deed from David CRAFFORD to Joseph HINSHAW: oath Abraham REESE.

Deed from George HOLCOMB and wife to Grimes HOLCOMB: oath John WILLIAMS.

Deed from John HARVEY, Junr. to John HARVEY; acknowledged.

Deed from Daniel ALLEN to Ezekiel REYNOLDS; oath George HEAD.

Deed from Christian Fredr. COSSART by Fredr. Wm. MARSHALL to John KROUSE; oath of Peter PFAFF.

Deed from Thomas CAIN and wife to George BROOKS; oath Henry SPEER.

Last Will and Testament of Griffith DICKERSON, deceased; proved by oath of James GAINES; James GAINES and Ann DICKERSON, Executors, quallified.

Appraisement Estate of James GLENN, deceased; signed by Robert LANIER, Job MARTIN and Samuel MOSBY, Junr., returned by Job MARTIN.

Giddeon EDWARDS, James GAINES, Constantine LADD and James BRISON produced as Justices of Peace; all quallified except Giddeon EDWARDS.

Ordered Gideon EDWARDS and Anthony DEARING, who were appointed Jurior attend court; be fined for failing to attend and appear and give cause why.

Leroy SPEER exempted from paying Poll Tax in future.

Phebe SUMNER vs David HOWARD; Jury: Charles DUDLEY, Windle KROUSE, Matthew WARNOCK, Thomas ISBELL, Thomas EAST, James WRIGHT, Jesse HORN, Airs HUDSPETH, Charles WADDLE, William FREEMAN, Malcum CURRY, Thompson GLENN; verdict for Pltf.; John FIELD, witness for Pltf., 240 miles, 25 days.

Frederick DANNER vs Michael ROOPE; same jury except William WAG-GONER in room of Jesse HORN.

Samuel CUMMINS vs Thomas GALLION; same jury except Jesse HORN in room of Thompson GLENN.

John KROUSE vs Thomas SMITH (Jockey); same jury except Thompson GLENN in room of Windle KROUSE.

13 February 1788

Present: Martin ARMSTRONG, Joseph WINSTON, Constantine LADD, Esqrs.

Deed from George ZEIGLER, Adam BLACK and Anna M. CARVER to Christine CARVER; oath John BOSTICK.

Deed from Adam BLACK, George ZEIGLER and Anna M. CARVER to George CARVER; oath of John BOSTICK.

Bill of Sale from William HOWARD to James HOWARD; oaths of James and John HOWARD.

Deed from Thomas WOOTEN to James DUNTHER; oath of Jesse BUMPS.

Deed from Richard GOODE to Samuel FREEMAN; oath Andrew ROBINSON.

Deed from Philip CULCLASURE to William HOLIMAN: oath Francis FORTNER.

Deed from Nathaniel WOODROUGH to William COOK; oath William MEREDITH.

Inventory Estate of Barnabas FARE, deceased; returned by Barnabas and Michael FARE, Executors.

Account of Settlement Estate of James DOUTHIT, deceased; returned by Administrator.

Account of Settlement Estate of Zach CASH (?), deceased; returned by Matthew WARNOCK, Administrator.

William MERIDETH and James GAINES, Esqrs. appointed Committee to settle with all Executors, Administrators, and Guardians that apply for said settlement.

Ordered Robert ELRODE overseer, road in room of John THOMPSON, deceased.

Ordered John RANCK and Lewis LINEBACK be exempt paying Poll Tax in future.

Ordered Clerk draw up copies for each Justice Resolve of General Assembly respecting Inhabitants giving in Western Lands; were produced.

Thomas McCARREL vs David CLARKE; Jury: Charles BEAZLEY, Windle KROUSE, Charles DUDLEY, William ATKINS, John LOW, Michael FAIR,

Barnabas FAIR, Justice REYNOLDS, John DEATHERAGE, Frederick MILLER, David HOWELL, and Gabriel JONES.

John HILL, Trustee, vs Jason ISBELL; same jury; non suit; Thomas ISBELL, witness for Pltf., 160 miles, 20 days.

Benjamin HERNDON vs Daniel WRIGHT and others (bond) for Etheldred SUTTON.

James THOMPSON vs John LOW; same jury except Thomas POINDEXTER in room of John LOW; Almon GUINN, witness for Deft., 56 miles, 1 day; Peter SCALES, witness for Pltf., 180 miles, 4 days; Peter FARE, witness for Pltf., 240 miles, 6 days.

Matthew BROOKS vs Robert SMITH; Jury: William CAMBELL, Michael FRY, David BRAY, George PETTIT, Matthew DOSS, Thomas GAINES, Henry BANNISTER, Airs HUDSPETH, Samuel FREEMAN, Wm. JOHNSTON, Matthew MARKLAND and James DAVIS.

Ordered Wm. SHEPPERDS attendance be not taxed in bill lost (?).

14 February 1788

Present: Joseph WINSTON, Absalom BOSTICK, Jacob BLUM, Hugh ARMSTRONG, Stephen WOOD, Esqrs.

Deed from Mark HARDIN to John WEBSTER: oath John HAMPTON, Senr.

Deed from John HAIET to Samuel FOGLER: oath Francis KIDNER.

Deed from John LYNCH and wife to Mark PHILLIPS: acknowledged by said LYNCH.

Deed from Greenberry PATTERSON to John BOHANNON; oath John SUMNERS.

Ordered Archibald CAMBELL appointed Constable in LADDS District in room of John DAVIS, resigned; William DOBSON, security.

Maj. Peter HAIRSTON, having omited to return part of amount of his taxable property for 1787 is priviledged now to do so; Sterling Currency, Rum, 324 gallons Continent Rum, Sugar, bottles wine, salt, 84 bottles Port, molasses.

Ordered Enoch STONE appointed Constable LOVILLS District; Jesse BUMPS, security.

Ordered following persons take following children into their possession and keep until next court: Jon. HAINES, Thomas RIDGE; Wm. COOK, Jr., Wm. RIDGE; and William COOK, Esq., Winneford RIDGE;.

Ordered Winniford ALLEN appear next court to shew why above children should not be bound out according to law.

Elizabeth GLENN, Sarah GLENN and Nancy GLENN chose Thompson GLENN their guardian; Henry SPEER and Wm. T. LEWIS, securities.

John LYNCH appointed guardian to Martha and Patience GLENN; Samuel MOSBY and Jo. WILLIAMS, securities.

Jesse LESTER appointed guardian to (blank and blank), orphans of Robert WALKER, deceased; John ARMSTRONG, Constant LADD and George HOOSER, securities.

Inventory Estate of Samuel MOSBY, deceased; returned by Samuel and Susannah MOSBY, Executors.

Ordered Gotlieb CRAMMER appointed overseer, road in room of John CONROD.

Ordered jury view road leading near Christian CONRODES be resinded.

George STEELMAN vs Stephen DAVIS. Jury: Richard HORN, John WEBSTER,

John HAMPTON, Christian CUNRODE, Francis KIDNER, James DOAK, William ATKINS, Charles BEAZLEY, Charles DUDLEY, Windle KROUSE, Adonijah HARBOUR, and James TODD.

Elizabeth HEATH vs Oliver CHARLES; James COFFEE, witness for Pltf., 150 miles, 15 days; John EVANS, witness for Pltf., 40 miles, 3 days.

Robert SIMINGTON vs James KELL. Jury: Richard HORN, John WEBSTER, Christian CUNRODE, Francis KIDNER, Charles BEAZLEY, Charles DUDLEY, Windle KROUSE, Adonijah HARBOUR, James TODD, David HOWELL, Justice REYNOLDS, and William ATKINS.

James TODD vs Isaac UPTHOGROVE: same jury except Samuel CROCKETT in room of James TODD; Henry SPEER, witness for Pltf., 168 miles, 35 days.

Matthew MOORE, Esq. vs MILLER & CUMMINS; same jury except Samuel CROCKET in room of John WEBSTER.

Joshua H. SPEER vs James YORK; same jury; non suit.

Frederick DESERN vs Jesse POWERS: same jury except John BOHANNON and Saml. HUMPHRISS in room of Windle KROUSE and John WEBSTER.

15 February 1788

Present: William MEREDITH, William COOK, James MARTIN, Esqrs.

Power of Attorney from George HOLDER and Elizabeth, his wife, to Christian REICH; oath of George HOOSER, Esq.

Bill of Sale from Henry TILLEY, Senr. to Charles BEAZLEY; oath of John CHILDRESS.

Deed from John WELLS (or Wills) to John DAVIS: oath Andrew ROBINSON.

Deed from Evan THOMAS and Deborah THOMAS to Isaac GARRISON; oath of Andrew ROBINSON.

Deed from Arthur TATE to John VENABLE: acknowledged.

Deed from William VENABLE to William STEEL; acknowledged.

Patrick McGIBBONY has leave to build Water Grist Mill on Belews Creek.

Ordered William GIBSON overseer, road in room of John ANGLE.

John RAMEY vs John GRANT. Jury: Charles DUDLEY, Charles BEAZLEY, Geo. HOLCOMB, James TODD, Joseph LOUFIELD, William JOHNSTON, William ATKINS, Augustine SAMUEL, W. N. COOK, William FREEMAN, Frederick MILLER, and Roger GIDDENS.

William T. LEWIS vs Nathaniel WILLIAMS (bond) for James BELL; same jury except William RAMEY in room of Roger GIDDINS.

William DOBBINS vs William SHEPPERD; same jury.

Airs HUDSPETH vs Jno. DOYLE; not tried; Milly HUDSPETH, witness for Pltf., 92 miles, 6 days.

Matthew MARKLAND, Junr. vs John COLVARD; same jury.

William MORRISON vs John ALLEN; same jury.

Jacob BALLINGER vs Phil HOLCOMB and Carlton LINDSAY; same jury except Wm. and George PETTIT in room of Geo. HOLCOMB and Augustine SAMUEL.

Thomas ADDIMAN vs Ben and Thos. ELLIOTT: George HEAD, witness for Pltf., 77 miles, 23 days.

Edward NUNNELY vs William ROSEBERRY; same jury except Joseph RAMEY,

Wm. BURRIS and Geo. PETTIT in room of Augustine SAMUEL, Fredr. MILLER and Roger GIDDINS.

Ordered John WILLIAMS (L.T.) and Joseph BITTEN, Constables, be fined for neglecting duty.

16 February 1788

Present: Joseph WINSTON, Charles McANALLY, William THORNTON, Esqrs.

Account Sale of Estate of Thomas ELLIOTT, deceased; returned by Richard GOODE, Sheriff.

Joseph WILLIAMS vs Phil HOLCOMB, Henry SPEER, Jno. BRUCE and Geo. HOLCOMB. Jury: Charles DUDLEY, Wm. ATKINS, Windle KROUSE, Blont GARROT, Caleb GRAMMER, Jno. ROBERTS, James DOYLE, Thomas POTTIT, Zach. MARTIN, David BRAY, Thomas ISBELL, and Justice REYNOLDS.

Charles BARNETT vs Jo. PHILLIPS and Henry SPEER; same jury.

(Dim film) ISBELL vs Francis HOLT and Jason ISBELL; same jury except Roger GIDDENS in room of Thos. ISBELL; find Thos. ISBELL did not assume verdict vs HOLT.

William and James HOWARD vs David BRAY; not tried; Elijah SMALL-WOOD, witness for Deft., 400 miles, 19 days.

James TUCKER vs Jo. HENFIELD and others; not tried; Elijah SMALL-WOOD, witness for Deft., 150 miles, 9 days.

George HOLCOMB vs John RANDLEMAN; appeal; same jury; James DOYLE, witness for Pltf., 255 miles, 3 days.

Phil HOLCOMB vs John WILLIAMS; appeal; same jury except Obediah BENGE and Abijah OLIVER in room of Windle KROUSE and Justice REYNOLDS.

Obediah BAKER vs Charles DUDLEY; discontinued; Bazzlo RIDDLE, witness for Deft., 180 miles, 30 days; Wm. ATKINS, 80 miles, 7 days.

William RAMSEY vs Justice REYNOLDS; not tried; John CARLTON, witness for Pltf., 144 miles, 15 days.

At a court called for Trial of Negro Jim, the slave of James DOAK, charged with stealing saddle baggs, the following qualified; Esqrs. Hugh ARMSTRONG, Absalom BOSTICK, Con. LADD; Freeholder, John ARMSTRONG, Frederick MILLER, William FORKNER, Peter HAIRSTON. Upon examination of witnesses, court adjudged Jim is not guilty of stealing saddle baggs of John TATE as charged.

Deed from Thomas PETTIT to Zach MARTIN; oath of William HUGHLETT.

Deed from Mark PHILLIPS to John HARVEY, Junr.; oath William HARVEY.

Deed from Mark PHILLIPS to John RAMEY, Junr.; oath William HARVEY.

Ordered Joseph NELSON, Henry HAMPTON, Constant LADD, Esq., John HUTCHINGS, Aaron LINVILL, William GIBSON, Patrick McGIBBONY, John COOLEY, William WAGGONER, William HINMAN, William JAMES, Andrew ROBINSON, Charles ANGLE, Charles DAVIS, Isaac GARRISON, Richard LINVILL and Joseph WINSTON, Esqr. appointed road jury from Joseph WINSTONS Mill to Rockingham County Court House and Joseph NELSON appointed overseer.

Ordered Isaac GARRETT, John BRANSON, Thomas RAPER, John COOLEY, Henry HAMPTON, Wm. DOBSON, Constantine LADD, Andrew ROBINSON, Patrick McGIBBONY, Peter Fulps, Barnabas FARR, Seth COFFIN, John WELLS, John HOLBROOK, Jos. HAMM, Thomas GOODE and Thomas GOODE, Junr., jury to view road leading from Richard GOODES to David MORRORS and it be public road if Wm. GIBSON will clear out same at his own expense.

Ordered David HOWELL, James HOWELL, Zepheniah DOWDEN, Samuel CROCKET, Thos. HORN, Peter EDDLEMAN, John SKIDMORE, John GARNER, John HUMPHRISS, Joshua CRESON, Abraham SKIDMORE, John DEPORTER, Henry SPEER, Ben SPEER, Thos. WELLS and John GROCE jury to view road from Surry County line where Island Ford road through Rowan County entersects said Surry line to Shallowford; James HOWELL, overseer to clear road.

Ordered Charles McANALLY overseer, road from McANALLYS Ford to Reuben GEORGES old place in room of Thomas NEIL.

Ordered Thomas HADLY overseer, Brooks road from Chestnut Ridge to Iron Works road in place of Jacob FERREE.

Ordered Richard MURPHY, John WILLIAMS, Moses WILLIAMS, Joseph LASWELL, Ben SCOTT, Zadock RIGGS, Iram RIGGS, William STEWART, Samuel RIGGS, Silas RIGGS, Peter MURPHY, Jno. BEAN road jury to view road from Jno. BRYSONS on Little fork Mitchells River nearest way into Fishers Gap Road.

Ordered John FARMER, James YOUNG, William WEBB, Charles BEAZLEY, John HUGHES, Wm. HICKMAN, Thomas LOVING, James VERNON, Alexander JOICE, Robert GAINES, James WALKER, Ben HAWKINS, Randol RIDDLE and John RIDDLE jury to mark road if necessary from Virginia line near William WEBBS to Rockingham County line near Abraham MARTINS.

Ordered Phil WILSON, Jno. SMITH, Morgan DAVIS, Stephen CLAYTON, Junr., Richard HEATH, John McANALLY, Adam MITCHEL, Hardy REDDICK, Joseph EASON, Henry WATKINS, Thomas NEIL, Charles DODSON and Charles McANALLY road jury to review Richmond road from McANALLYS Ford on Dan River to Mill Creek; Jesse McANALLY appointed overseer.

Ordered following appointed as Jurors next County Court at Court House in Richmond: Charles DODSON, Samuel WARNOCK, Alexander BOLES, Samuel GREENWOOD, Reuben SHORES, Junr., Thomas MOSBY, John CARTER, James SANDERS, Junr., Thomas HADLEY, Micajah OGILSBY, David RIGGS, James MATTHEWS (surveyor), John FLEMMING, Samuel STOLTS, John MACKEY, Henry SHORE, Wm. KINMAN, Henry HAMPTON, Samuel HAMPTON, Younger BLACKBURN, Silvanus PIPES, Wm. COOK, Junr., Richard COX, Thomas SHIP, Adonijah HARBOUR, Matthew DAUSE (Doss), Edward SEWEL, John ARMSTRONG, James BADGET, and James MATTHEWS.

Ordered following appointed Jurors next Superior Court, District of Salisbury: John Thomas LONGINO, Henry SPEER, Joseph PHILLIPS, Salathial MARTIN, Joshua COX, Anthony DEARING and John BURCH.

Ordered Sheriff not demand payment of John (dim film) as said John paid Jo. WILLIAMS, Clerk of Court that sum.

Ordered Wm. MEREDITH former Trustee and Chas. McANALLY, present Trustee, etc. etc.

Ordered Clerk strike off from Lists of Taxable property returned for 1787 all returns lands entered in late Office of Jno ARMSTRONG, Esq., it appearing that grants cannot be obtained for same: All that said land has been mostly ceded to the Indians by a Treaty held at Hopewell on Kewee, so that the claimants may probably never possess same.

12 May 1788

Present: Charles McANALLY, John CHILDRESS, William HUGHLETT, Esqrs.

Deed from Wm. Justice THOMPSON and Edmond THOMPSON to Absalom BOSTICK; by oath of Noble LADD.

Deed from Edmond THOMPSON and Pegge, his wife, to Absalom BOSTICK; oath of Noble LADD.

Deed from Matthew CREED and wife, Margit, to Bennett CREED: oath John CREED.

Deed from Matthew COX to Henry HERRING: oath Bennett CREED.

Deed from Matthew CREED and wife to John DAVIS; oath of Bennett CREED.

Deed from Matthew CREED to Henry HERRING; oath of John CREED.

Deed from Jos. JANNAWAY to Archelaus HUGHES and Geo. HAIRSTON; oath of John CHILDRESS.

Deed from James MEREDITH to William MARTIN; oath John CHILDRESS.

Deed from John WALKER and wife to Edward BOMAN; oath Samuel CLAMPET.

Deed from Henry HOLDER and wife to Daniel SMITH: oath Nicholas DULL.

Deed from Moses MARTIN and wife to John FLINT: oath Charles Mc-ANALLY.

Deed from Henry BAKER, Senr. to Henry BAKER, Jr.; oath John HUGHES.

Deed from William BLEDSOE and wife to Thomas RABURN; oath Silkend RABUN.

Deed from William BLEDSOE and wife to Silkend RABURN; oath Thos. RABURN.

COURT ADJOURNED FOR TWO HOURS.

Present: James MARTIN, Absalom BOSTICK, Constantine LADD, Esqrs.

Ordered Thomas MOSBY, a Juror, be excused for non-attendance, he being infirm.

Ordered Anthony DEARING and Gideon EDWARDS who were fined last court be remitted.

John Luis TAYLOR, Esq. produced License from Honorable Samuel SPENCER and John WILLIAMS, two Judges, authorizing him to practice as an Attorney in several County Courts.

Ordered Johnston CREWS be exempted from payment Poll Tax for future.

Ordered James WRIGHT be released from paying tax on 500 acres in 1787, it being given in by James HUNTER in Orange County.

Jury appointed last court to view road where it parts with old course report road to keep along ridge William GIBSONS outside fence, crossing small branch; Wm. GIBSON engages to open and support such piece or road.

13 May 1788

Present: Charles McANALLY, Absalom BOSTICK, John CHILDRESS, John RANDLEMAN, Esqrs.

Grand Jury: John ARMSTRONG, foreman; Charles DODSON, Samuel GREENWOOD, John CARTER, Micajah OGLESBY, Edward LOVILL, Samuel HAMPTON, William COOK, Junr., Henry HAMPTON, Richard COX, James BADGET, Thomas SHIP, Adonijah HARBOUR and Matthew DAUSE.

Ordered George HUFFMAN, Junr. exempt paying Poll Tax because of infirmity.

Ordered Moses HAZLETT and James TANNER exempt paying Poll Tax for future.

Ordered John BADGET be exempt from paying Poll Tax in future.

Ordered Joseph MANAHA, Nicholas TULL, Henry ARNOLD exempt paying Poll Tax in future.

Ordered Nathaniel BOYE be exempt paying Poll Tax in future, he being Cripple.

Ordered John WELLS exempt paying Poll Tax for future.

Ordered Randol MILLER released payment two Polls 1787.

Ordered Daniel DAVIS of McANALLYS District failed to give in taxables 1787 is now privledged to do so; 209 acres, 1 Poll.

Ordered John LYNCH and wife, Patience, Executors Last Will and Testament of James GLENN, deceased, appear and account for same.

Sheriff returned amount of sale of perishable part estate of James GLENN, deceased.

John HARVEY has leave to keep Tavern at his dwelling house; John HARVEY, Senr., security.

Ordered Sheriff be impowered to contact immediately to repair Jail, windows and doors.

Ordered following Justices appointed to receive taxable property 1788: BEAZLEYS: John CHILDRESS; BOSTICKS: Absalom BOSTICK; GAINES: James GAINES; McANALLYS: Charles McANALLY; HILLS: Joseph WINSTON; LADDS: Constant LADD; CROUSE: George HAUZER; COLVERTS: William THORNTON; HUGHLETTS: William T. HUGHLETT; GLENS: John RANDLEMAN; LOVELLS: Jacob SHEPPERD; ATKINS: William MEREDITH; WILLIS: Giddeon EDWARDS; SANDERS: Stephen WOOD; LEWIS: Zachariah RAY.

Charles BARNITZ vs Jo. PHILIPS and Henry SPEER, Esq. Jury: Younger BLACKBURN, Alex BOLES, James MATTHEWS, Henry SHORES, John DEATHERAGE, James JONES, Godfrey CODY, Francis POINDEXTER, John STONE, Roger GIDDENS, Wm. JOHNSTON, and Daniel DAVIS.

John Allen WATERS vs Stephen CROWDER· same jury; non suit.

James LEFOY vs Augustine BLACKBURN; same jury; non suit.

William GRAHAM, Assignee vs William and James SHEPPERD; same jury.

William BURRIS vs Robert HARRIS; same jury.

Gabrial ENOCHS vs William SYSEMORE: same jury except Amos LONDON in room of Roger GIDDENS.

Thomas ADDIMAN vs Ben and Thomas ELLIOTT: same jury.

William T. LEWIS vs Mason COMBS; William SILVA, Garnishee, has nothing except 16 pounds made by Jon. HAINES and Obediah MARTIN. .

Appears by returned jury to view road leading near Christian CUNRODES that some of said jury was left out and others not appointed by Court; ordered on motion of Matthew BROOKS that new Jury be appointed as follows: Christian LASH, Jno. MARKEY, George HOUZAR, Esq., Thompson GLENN, Andrew SPEER, John T. LONGINO, Jno. COE, Jno. CARTER, Jno. STEPHENS, Robert MATTHEWS, Joseph PHILLIPS, Henry SHORE, Samuel KERBY, William WOLDRIDGE, Jno. RIDENS and Abraham WAINSCOTT.

Ordered John FARMER, John HUGHES, William HICKMAN, James MARTIN, William MARTIN, William WEBB, James WALKER, Charles BEAZLEY, William SOUTHERN, Ambrose HOLT, John CHILDRESS, Robert GAINES, James DUNCAN, and Reuben DOBSON appointed to view road nearest way from place in Old Virginia road by name Chandlers Burnt Cabbin to the Virginia line where it crosses and old road between John CHILDRESS and Archelois HUGHES.

136

Ordered Jacob McCRAW appointed overseer road in room William BURRIS.

Ordered Anthony BITTIN overseer, Quaker road from his own house to where Dan River road crosses.

Ordered Samuel ARNOLD appointed overseer, road in room of Ephraim McLIMORE.

Ordered James SANDERS, John ANDERSON, Thomas CLANTON, Edward CLANTON, John WILLIAMS, Thomas GALLION, Jr., George HOPPAS, John HOPPIS, Daniel HOPPIS, Matthew MARKHAM, Gabrial FENDER, Elijah CARLTON, Jacob MILLER, John BLAYLOCK, James REAVIS, and Richard WOOTEN jury to view new road from ridge near Christian WEATHERMANS to next ridge North side Deep Creek.

Deed from Frederick Wm. MARSHALL to Geo. FARNER: oath Jno. RITES (Right).

Deed from Richard GOODE, Sheriff, to Thos. RAPER; oath Stephen FOUNTAIN.

Deed from John CONNELL to William LONDON; acknowledged.

Deed from James SANDERS, Senr., and wife to James SANDERS, Junr.; acknowledged.

Certificate of John AYRES proved by oath of William MEREDITH.

Ordered James COFEE, Constable in McANALLYS District in room of John McANALLY, resigned; William HEATH and Dan DAVIS, securities.

Ordered Thomas LOW, Constable LADDS District; Henry HAMPTON and Peter FULPS, securities.

14 May 1788

Present: Matthew MOORE, Gideon EDWARDS, John CHILDRESS, Wm. COOK, Esqrs.

Lease from Samuel DAVIS to William DAVIS; oath of Jesse FRANKLIN.

Deed from George HAUZER; oath Matthew BROOKS.

Deed from David WALKER and wife to Nathan PIKE; oath Joseph McPHARSON.

Deed from Salathial MARTIN to Isaac AUSLETT: oath Jonathan HAINES.

Deed from Salethiel MARTIN to Nathan HAINES; oath Jonathan HAINES.

Deed from Martin ARMSTRONG to John SMITH; acknowledged.

Deed from Francis HALE, Senr. and wife to James BOHANNON; oath James GAINES.

Bill of Sale from Godfrey CODY to Sarah ROSE; acknowledged.

Deed from John COX to Richard ADAMS; oath Hugh ARMSTRONG; also Mary COX relinquishes dower in tract.

Deed from Edward HUGHES to Eliphalet JARVIS; oath Andrew ROBINSON.

Jacob BLUM has leave to keep Tavern at his now dwelling house in Salem, Christian LASH, security.

Christian LASH has leave to keep Tavern at his house in Bethania; Jacob BLUM, security.

Peter HOOSER has leave to keep Tavern at his house in Bethania, Christian LASH, security.

Wm. DOBSON has leave to keep Tavern at his house; Andrew ROBINSON, security.

Gibson WOOLRIDGE vs Henry WORD; James SANDERS, Garnishee, states
he owes nothing.

Joseph RAMEY vs Henry SPEER; Wm. COOK, witness for Deft., 100
miles, 4 days; Samuel HAGGOOD, witness for Pltf., 24 miles, 4
days; James TODD, witness for Deft., 96 miles, 16 days. Jury:
Alexander BOLES, Samuel HAGGARD, Airs HUDSPETH, William ADKINS,
Ephraim McLIMORE, John LYNCH, Charles WADDILL, Ambrose GAINES,
James MATTHEWS, James BOHANNON, Isaac AUSTON, and Henry SHORES.

Godfrey CODY vs David BRAY. Jury: Ephraim McLIMORE, James
MATTHEWS, Henry SHORES, Michael HOOSER, Matthew WARNOCK, Peter
HOOSER, John CUNRODE, David HOWELL, James HAMPTON, James HOWARD,
John HUMPHRISS, Mathew BROOKS; John ALLEN, witness for Pltf., 180
miles, 10 days; Hannah ROSE, 120 miles, 18 days; Joshua CRITCH-
FIELD, 250 miles, 50 days; George HENDERSON and William BRAY,
witnesses for Deft. failed to appear.

James BOLES vs John WINSTON; same jury except William JOHNSON in
place of Matthew WARNOCK; find Deft. not guilty; James FREEMAN,
Sorry TOWN, witnesses for Pltf. failed to appear; John COOLEY,
witness for Deft., 440 miles, 53 days; Samuel HAMPTON, 200 miles,
23 days.

Ordered Amos LONDON, William ALLEN, John MARSH, Charles WADDILL,
Joseph CLOUD, Phillip GREEN, John KROUSE, Thomas GRYMES, Malcum
CURRY, Thomas GAINES, William COCKERAM, James JONES, James BOLES,
Alexander MOORE, Greenbury PATTERSON, Ambrouse BRAMBLET, John
HURT, Gabrial WAGGONER, Henry FRY, Job MARTIN, Robert GAINES,
William HAWKINS, John ROBERTSON, Zadock RIGGS, Leonard DAVIS,
Gray BYNUM, William KINMAN, John DWIGGINS, John CUMMINS, and
William LEWIS appointed Juriors next County Court.

Richard GOODE, Esq. elected Sheriff for ensuing year.

Ordered Capt. Wm. MEREDITH, William COOK and Giddion EDWARDS,
Esqrs. appointed committee to settle with Collectors.

Ordered Michael FRY, Valentine FRY, John PETREE, Gray BYNUM,
Ephraim BANNER, Joseph BANNER, William DAVIS, John APPLETON,
Daniel HILL, Moses MARTIN, William CROOK, Thomas GRAHAM, Jacob
BLUME, Martin LICK, John RIGHTS and Samuel STOLTZ view and lay out
nearest way from where Old Moravian Road crosses the Townfork
near Jacob PETREES to Salem and make return.

Ordered John APPLETON overseer, road from Townfork to Muddy Creek.

Ordered Martin LICK overseer, road from Muddy Creek to Salem.

Ordered John WATSON overseer, road from Widow HOWARDS down to
MORRISSES.

15 May 1788

Present: Con(stantine) LADD, James GAINES, William MEREDITH, Esqrs.

Deed from Joshua BROWN to James PILCHER, Junr.; acknowledged oath
said BROWN.

Anthony BITTEN has leave to keep Tavern at his house; Michael FRY
and Jesse KNIGHTEN, securities.

Thomas POINDEXTER has leave to keep Tavern in Richmond; Jesse
LESTER, security.

Court ammended Tavern Rates: Good proof Whiskey, half pint 1
shilling, 6 pence; Breakfast or Dinner with tea or coffee or with
hott roast or boiled, 2 shillings, 6 pence; Brandy, 1 shilling,
6 pence; Malt Beer or Cyder per quart, 4 pence; Oats, 3 pence;
Tineriff (?) wine, half pint, 2 shillings.

Ordered John HESTER overseer, road room William DOBSONS, Esqr. old place to place of his present residence at the Cross Roads.

Ordered Phil SOUTHERLAND overseer, road in room of James COFFEE.

Ordered George WATKINS, Thomas DUNNAGAN, George WOOTEN, Samuel DENNY, Isaac DUNNAGAN, Isaac COPELAND, Thomas HUGHES, Jo----ASHLEY, John BURCHAM, Capt. Edward LOVELL, John TILLEY, Charles DUDLEY, Jesse BUMPS, Christopher ELLIS, Joshua CRITCHFIELD and (too dim) HUMPHRESS mark nearest way from CRITCHFIELDS Ford near Quaker Settlement on Toms Creek and mark road crossing Dan River.

Ordered Jury appointed to view road from Virginia line near William WEBBS to Rockingham County line near Abraham MARTINS, make report.

Ordered James WALKER overseer, road from Virginia line to George JOINS Cabbins.

Ordered Thomas LOVING overseer, road from JONES Cabbins to Rickingham County line.

Ordered Reuben SAMUEL overseer, road in room of Phil EVANS.

Ordered John VENABLE overseer, road in room of Richard KERBY.

Ordered Edmund KERBY, Arthur SCOTT and David WALKER appointed Pattrollers Capt. HUGHLETTS District.

Francis POINDEXTER came into Court and took following oath: "as Executor in right of my wife, I will return just and true Inventory of all goods, etc. of Robert LANIER, deceased."

Ordered James MILLWOOD be exempt paying Poll Tax in future.

Ordered Sheriff sell 100 acres lands of Benjamin BANNER in LADDS District for his publick taxes.

The State vs William UNDERWOOD. Jury: Alexander BOLES, Henry SHORE, James MATTHEWS, Justice REYNOLDS, Samuel CROCKET, Airs HUDSPETH, Greenberry PATTERSON, Jesse KNIGHTON, John WEATHERFORD, Airs HUDSPETH, Junr., Daniel LIBERTINE, and Jordan MANNING: find Deft. guilty; John JARVIS, witness for Pltf., 180 miles, 14 days.

State vs George WATKINS; same jury; Deft. not guilty.

Jobe COLE vs Jonathan HAINES; not tried; Zach RAY, witness for Pltf., 240 miles, 11 days. Ordered Jobe COLE cited to appear next Court to answer questions as may be objected against him by complaint of Jacob MOSBY.

Ordered Con. LADD take into his possession said apprentice, Jacob MOSBY, and keep him til next Court.

Wardens of County (by motion) vs John COLVARD, Collector in MOSBYS District for poor tax.

Samuel SPIRGIN vs Matthew WARNOCK and James COFFEE: same jury; verdict for Defts.; Frederick MILLER, witness for Deft., 290 miles, 14 days; Gabrial JONES, 160 miles, 8 days; William SWAIM, 320 miles, 16 days; William SPIRGIN, witness for Pltf., 450 miles, 27 days.

William BURCH and wife vs Samuel CALLEWAY; Abraham JAMES, witness for Pltf., 300 miles, 11 days.

Ordered the order of last Court appointed jury to lay out road from Rowan line to Shallowford be renewed.

Ordered Certorire issued against Zachariah RAY, Esq. to bring up proceedings in suit of David POINDEXTER vs William HARRISON.

Petition Inhabitants residing North fork Belews Creek.

Ordered former order Court authorizing Patrick McGIBBONY to build Grist Mill on said Creek be resinded, it being within distance prohibited by Law of Henry HAMPTONS Mill, which from now on will be deemed a publick mill.

Ordered Nancy BURRIS appear next Court to shew cause why her son Jesse BURRIS shall not be bound out by Court agreeable to law.

16 May 1788

Present: Martin ARMSTRONG, Matthew MOORE, James GAINES, Esqrs.

William RAMEY vs Justice REYNOLDS: find Deft. not guilty. Jury: Daniel LIBERTINE, George HOLCOMB, Samuel CROCKET, John GARNER, James MATTHEWS, Airs HUDSPETH, Airs HUDSPETH, Junr., David HOWELL, Alexander BOLES, Jesse SCOTT, Godfrey CODY, and William BURRIS.

Joseph RAMEY vs Jordan MANNING; same jury; non suit; John HUMPH-RISS, witness for Deft., 96 miles, 10 days; Tobias FURCHASE, witness for Deft., 208 miles, 18 days.

Joseph RAMEY vs David HOWELL and Jordan MANNING; same jury except Matthew BROOKS and John BRYSON in room of David HOWELL and Samuel CROCKET: Jordan MANNING not guilty and David HOWELL not guilty; Henry SPEER, witness for Deft., 66 miles, 12 days; Charles STEEL-MAN, 196 miles, 19 days; Benj. SPEER, 60 miles, 6 days; John STEELMAN, witness for Pltf., 192 miles, 16 days.

Obed BAKER vs Charles DUDLEY; Jesse KNIGHTON now privledged to come in and prove his attendance, 136 miles, 16 days.

John THOMPSON vs John LOW; John DEARING, witness for Pltf., 180 miles, 7 days.

David BRAY vs William and James HOWARD; Jane HOWARD, witness for Deft., 550 miles, 43 days; John PADGET, witness for Pltf., 150 miles, 6 days; Elijah SMALLWOOD, witness for Deft., 50 miles, 6 days.

Airs HUDSPETH vs John DOYLE; not tried; Milly HUDSPETH, formerly VAUGHN, 46 miles, 1 day.

John RANDLEMAN vs Joseph REAVIS to use James REDIN; John DOYLE, witness for Pltf., 390 miles, 37 days.

James TUCKER vs Jo. LANFIELD and others; not tried; Elijah SMALL-WOOD, witness for Deft., 50 miles, 5 days.

Lewis JARVIS vs John ALLEN and A. ELMORE: same jury except Henry SHORE and Elijah OLIVER in place of Jesse SCOTT and James MATTHEWS.

Gibson WOOLDRIDGE vs Henry WARD (or Word); same jury except Henry SHORE and Elijah OLIVER in room of Jesse SCOTT and Airs HUDSPETH; John DOYLE, witness for Pltf., 105 miles, 4 days; Airs HUDSPETH, witness for Pltf., 125 miles, 10 days.

Jacob ROGER (?) vs Airs HUDSPETH, Executor for John HUDSPETH, deceased; same jury except Arthur SCOTT in room of Airs HUDSPETH, Junr.

Robert SMITH vs Michael B. ROBERTS; John PRICE, witness for Pltf., 48 miles, 15 days.

Samuel VEST appointed Jailer by Sheriff.

Deed from Thomas and Richard CHILDRESS to Wm. MARTIN; oath John BARWONGER.

Ordered Nicholas TULL be released paying tax on 400 acres 1787 as it appears Jacob BLACK gave in said land.

Return Insolvants May 1788: Capt. KROUSES District; Michael HOOSER, Collector: Adam BINKLEY, 112 acres, 1 poll; Asail CROSS, 112 acres, 1 poll; John FISHEL, 112 acres, 1 poll; John FULERMAN, 1 poll; Samuel GOSLIN, 200 acres, 1 poll; Adam GINNAND (?), 200 acres, 1 poll; George GRACE, 200 acres, 1 poll; Adam HANISH, 200 acres, 1 poll; John MILLER, 440 acres, 1 poll; Matthew COX, 100 acres, 1 poll; Francis MOSSER, 1 poll; James MOORE, 1 poll; Charles PARKER, 230 acres (dim); Michael FEREE (too dim); Daniel WOOLF, 100 acres, 1 poll; Benjamin CHITTY, 150 acres, 1 poll; John HAYNE, 251 acres, 1 poll; Jacob HINE, 150 acres, 1 poll; Peter SNIDER, 300 acres, 1 poll; John BAZEL (?), 1 poll; John JOBS living in Rowan, 150 acres, 1 poll; Capt. WILLIS District: Reziah JARVIS, Collector: John BRYSON, 200 acres, 1 poll; Matthew CHAMBERS, 1 poll; Charles ROSS, 1 poll; Robert SEXTON, 1 poll; William WORD, 1 poll. Capt. LADDS District, Andrew ROBERSON, Collector: Enos ADDAMSON, 1 poll; Amaziah BEASON, 100 acres, 1 poll; Jonathan CREWS, 1 poll; John McCONNEL, 1 poll; William PERRY, 200 acres, 1 poll; John STEPHENS, 1 poll; Thos. THORNBERRY, 1 poll; Charles JONES, 1 poll; Jo. THORNBERRY, 1 poll. Capt. LADDS District 1787, Andrew ROBESON, Collector: Enias ADAMSON, 1 poll; Amaziah BEESON, 1 poll, 100 acres; Jonathan CREWS, 1 poll; John McCONNEL, 1 poll; William PERRY, 200 acres, 1 poll; John STEPHENS, 1 poll; Thomas and Joseph THORNBERRY, 1 poll each; Charles JONES, 1 poll.

17 May 1788

Present: Matthew MOORE, Hugh ARMSTRONG, John RANDLEMAN, Esqrs.

Deed from Samuel KERBY to Henry ARNOLD; acknowledged.

Ordered William HUGHLETT overseer, road in room of Philip (too dim) on McANALLYS road to forks road between Col. Martin ARMSTRONG and Richmond and following work thereon: Jowde SPEENHOUR, Adam FULK, Col. Martin ARMSTRONG, John SHOUSE, Daniel BOATRIGHT, James BOATWRIGHT, Jacob HELSABECK and Ahijah OLIVER.

John BRISON, Assignee vs Jacob McCRAW. Jury: Henry SHORE, Hugh MORRIS, William ROBINSON, William N. COOK, George HOLCOMB, Blunt GARROTT, Arthur SCOTT, William HEAD, George PETIT, Justice REYNOLDS, Malcum CURRY, James MATTHEWS; John BRISON, Junr., witness for Pltf., 180 miles, 7 days.

Phil HOLCOMB vs John WILLIAMS; same jury.

George HOLCOMB vs Crispen HUNT: same jury except Thomas EAST in room of George HOLCOMB; Jeffery JOHNSTON, witness for Pltf., 100 miles, 8 days; John JERVIS, witness (- - - blank).

Roger GIDDENS vs Jacob MILLER: same jury; Ahijah OLIVER, witness for Pltf., 20 miles, 6 days, Ezekiel OLIVER, witness for Pltf., 20 miles, 5 days.

Elizabeth HEATH vs Oliver CHARLES; not tried; James COFFEE, witness for Pltf. (too dim) miles, 5 days.

Caleb CRAMMER vs Wyatt GARNER; appeal; same jury except Ahijah OLIVER and Robert MARKLAND in room of Malcum CURRY and Jesse SCOTT; Thomas GALLION, witness for Pltf., 170 miles, 6 days; John RANDLEMAN, witness for Pltf., 7 days.

Arthur SCOTT vs Samuel CUMMINS; not tried; Jesse SCOTT, witness for Pltf., 9 miles, 15 days; Blunt GARROTT, witness for Pltf., 60 miles, 10 days.

(Next entry follows on next page of file). Last Court held in Richmond November Term 1789. February Term 1790 at Richard HORNS House. May Term 1790 at Richard HORNS house. August Term 1790 at Richard HORNS house. November Term 1790 at Elihue AYERS house near White Rock Ford. First Court held in Rockford May Term 1791. November Term 1790 held at the house of Elihue AYERS. February Term 1791 held at house of Elihue AYERS near White Rock Ford, afterwards called Rockford. Archibald HENDERSON qualified as Attorney February Term 1791, First day of the Term.

11 August 1788
Court House in Richmond

Present: John RANDLEMAN, Esq.

12 August 1788

Present: George HAUZER, William HUGHLETT, Gideon EDWARDS, Esqrs.

Deed from James LINDSAY to Thomas WILES: oath of John BLALOCK.

Deed from James JONES to James JONES, Junr.; oath Greenbury PATTERSON.

Deed from Josiah FREEMAN to James FORRESTER: oath Edward SMITH.

Deed from Thomas HOLCOMB to Abraham REESE; oath Greenbury PATTERSON.

Deed from Henry SPEER to Leonard RICHARDS: acknowledged.

Deed from Henry SPEER to Delilah ALDRIDGE: acknowledged.

Deed from William DEVENPORT to John DOYLIN; acknowledged.

Deed from John BRUCE to Robert ADAM; oath Edward YOUNG.

Deed from William HEAD to John STEPHENS: acknowledged by said Wm. HEAD.

Deed from William FLYNN to Thomas CHILDRESS; oath James MATTHEWS and George FLYNN.

Deed from William HOWARD and wife to John PADGET; oath Joel MACKEY.

Deed from James LINDSAY and wife to John BITTICK; oath John DURHAM and John CARTER.

Deed from James LINESAY to John DURHAM; oath John BITTICK.

Bill of Sale from Robert SMITH to Isaiah COE; acknowledged.

Deed from John JOHNSON to Abraham VANDEPOOLE: oath Charles DUDLEY.

Deed from Phillemon HOLECOMB to Elijah CARLTON; oath Edward CLANTON.

Deed from John Thomas LONGINO to Christopher MONDAY; acknowledged.

Power of Attorney from Abraham WOOD to Airs HUDSPETH; acknowledged.

Grand Jury: Gray BYNUM, Foreman; Charles WADDLE, Malcum CURRY, Wm. KINMAN, Alexander MOORE, Leonard DAVIS, John ROBINSON, Zadock RIGGS, Amos LONDON, John MARSH, John KROUSE, Thomas GRAHAM, William COCKRAM, and James JONES.

Ordered Abraham CHILDRESS exempt paying Poll Tax in future.

Ordered Thomas HOLCOMB exempt paying Poll Tax for future.

Ordered Jonathan PARKER exempt paying Poll Tax for future.

Alexander DOBBINS vs William McAFEE; execution docket November 1779; returned satisfied by Sheriff; ordered S.F. issue against Executors John HUDSPECK, deceased, former Sheriff.

Daniel HOUSTIN vs John KIMBROUGH. Jury: Greenburry PATTERSON,

John HURT, Job MARTIN, Gabrial WAGGONER, James FREEMAN, James MATTHEWS, John MEALE, Meredith SMITH, Bartlett CREED, James BROWN, Isaiah COE, and Godfrey CODY.

Sarah KIRKPATRICK vs Jo. SPEAPOINT, Peter MYERS and George HOLCOMB; same jury; John Thos. LONGINO, witness for Pltf., 50 miles, 29 days.

Traugott BAGGE vs William BEATS; same jury.

Robert SMITH vs Michael B. ROBERTS; same jury.

Joseph PHILLIPS vs Alexander HAWKINS; John ALLEN, witness for Deft., 360 miles, 19 days; Thompson GLENN, witness for Pltf., 144 miles, 65 days; Wm. Terril LEWIS, witness, 540 miles, 34 days.

James GLENS Executors vs John SPEER; same jury.

John KROUSE vs Thomas SMITH (Jockey); same jury.

Joseph WILLIAMS, guardian to Thomas LANIER vs James and William BEATS; Frank POINDEXTER, garnishee, says he owes Wm. BEATS something for work.

Joseph WINSTON vs Joseph CARMICHAEL. Jury: Greenbury PATTERSON, Job MARTIN, Gabriel WAGGONER, John CUMMINS, Richard LINVILL, John BLALOCK, John FAIR, Wm. FREEMAN, Thomas PETTIT, Wm. N. COOK, John SATER, and John BRYSON.

William GRAGG vs James KNIGHT: same jury; non suit; Thomas KNIGHT, witness for Deft., 160 miles, 20 days; Caty McCLOUD, witness for Deft., 320 miles, 32 days.

Moses LINSTER vs Nicholas HAWKINS, Heir of James HAWKINS, deceased, same jury.

Terry BRADLEYS Executors vs James COFFEE; same jury.

Joel LEWIS vs John COMBS, Senr.; same jury; Wm. N. COOK, witness for Pltf., 660 miles, 34 days; Wm. T. LEWIS, 480 miles, 28 days.

Thomas EASTOP vs Abraham WOOD; Thomas PETTIT, witness for Deft., 54 miles, 18 days; Wm. PHILLIPS, 40 miles, 16 days.

Gibson WOOLDRIDGE vs Henry WORD; ordered S.F. issued vs Jeremiah RILEY as Garnishee, to appear.

Gibson WOOLDRIGE vs Henry WORD; Ninian RILEY sworn as Garnishee says he owes nothing.

Ordered Jacob BOROTH overseer, road in room of Peter ROTHROCK.

Ordered Richard HORN overseer, Iron Works road from Fish River to Double Creek.

Ordered Joseph LADD overseer, road in room of David LINVILL.

A Marriage Contract from George KIRKMAN to Mary THOMPSON in behalf of Orphans of John THOMPSON, deceased; acknowledged by said George KIRKMAN; also endorsed on back acknowledged by said Mary THOMPSON.

Ordered Wm. TUCKER released payment tax on 200 acres as appears his Father, James TUCKER, paid for same.

Ordered Wm. CHILDRESS be released payment tax on 300 acres 1787 as Jo. HAUZAR give in said land.

Ordered Henry SPEER appointed Guardian to Ben and Joel REYNARD, orphans of Wm. REYNARD, deceased; Thompson GLEN and Joseph WILLIAMS, securities.

Ordered Charles SCOTT, son of Sarah SCOTT, a mullattoe child aged 3 months, 5 days be bound unto Henry SPEER until age 21 years to learn art and mistery of a Planter.

Ordered following serve as Jurors next Superior Court District Salisbury: John Thomas LONGINO, Zach RAY, Job MARTIN, William COOK, Wm. T. LEWIS, William MEREDITH and Joseph PHILLIPS.

Ordered John LYNCH be excused payment Poll Tax for negro lad named Charles in his possession.

Ordered Matthew MOORE, Jacob SHEPPERD and Gideon EDWARDS, Esqrs. appointed committee of Claims to receive and inspect lists tax-ables 1788; also settle with Executors, Administrators of deceas-ed Estates and also receive Insolvants.

14 August 1788

Present: Joseph WINSTON, Charles McANALLY, Absalom BOSTICK, Stephen WOOD, Esqrs.

Deed from Frederick MILLER to Gabrial JONES; oath Andrew ROBINSON.

Deed from Wm. T. LEWIS to John MARSH; acknowledged.

Deed from George HAWN and Barbary, his wife, to Phillip SNIDER and Elizabeth SNIDER: oath of Fredr. MILLER.

Deed from Frederick Wm. MARSHALL to Daniel HUFF: oath John RITES (Rights).

Deed from George WATKINS to John SHELTON; oath Jesse BUMPS.

Deed from Barnaba FAIR to William KNOTT: oath William JEAN.

Deed from Benjamin PARKS to Nathaniel MORRIS: oath Isaac SOUTHARD.

Power of Attorney from Abejah and Thos. ELMORE, Joel SANDERS and Ashley JOHNSON to Robert JOHNSON; oath John CUMMINS.

Deed from Jason ISBELL and wife to Timothy JESSOP; oath Isaiah MADHIFF (?).

Ordered Jonathan PARKER, overseer, road instead of Lewis ELLIOTT.

Ordered Wm. FORKNER overseer, road in room of Richard LAWRENCE.

Ordered Matthew DOSS overseer, road in room of Ado. HARBOUR.

Ordered Michael FULPS overseer, road in room of Mordicai HAMM.

Ordered Claibourn WATSON overseer, road from John CUMMINS to Will-iams DOBSONS in room of said CUMMINS.

Ordered Benjamin YOUNG, Junr. overseer, road in room of Thomas GOODE, Junr.

The State vs John BOHANNON; Alexander TOMMERLIN, witness for Pltf., 12 miles, 10 days; David POINDEXTER, 40 miles, 10 days.

William T. LEWIS vs Benjamin CLEVELAND: Joel LEWIS, Garnishee saith he will owe 12 pounds and 4,000 pounds tobacco on 1st January 1789 and more on condition.

Matthew WARNOCK vs Richard GOODE; Caveat Land Docket. Jury: Airs HUDSPETH, John BLALOCK, Ephraim McLIMORE, Richard LINVILL, Jesse KNIGHTON, James DOWNEY, Obed BAKER, Matthew BROOKS, Frede-rick MILLER, William SWAIM, Abner PHILLIPS, John BOWLES. In favor GOODE, the Caveatee; James COFFEE, witness for Deft., 90 miles, 13 days; John COOLEY, 120 miles, 10 days; Joshua TILLEY, witness for Pltf., 300 miles, 12 days; Leonard BRADLEY, witness for Deft., 26 miles, 1 day; Michael FRY, 72 miles, 5 days.

State vs Epps LITTLEPAGE. Jury: Gabrial WAGGONER, Job MARTIN, John CUMMINS, Obediah BAKER, Richard LINVILL, Abner PHILLIPS, Elias PHILLIPS, Richard HORN, Edward CLANTON, Isaac SOUTHARD, John BRYSON, Joel APLING; find Deft. guilty; Mary CHURCH, witness for State, 30 miles, 2 days.

State vs John MARTIN; same jury except Aaron LISBY in room of Job MARTIN.

State vs John DEATHERAGE; Recognization bound to his good Behaviour; Eve DUNCAN, witness for State, 60 miles, 3 days.

State vs Jacob McCRAW; John TUCKER, witness for State, 60 miles, 2 days; Branch TUCKER, 60 miles, 2 days; Bartlett CREEK (CHEEK, CREED ?), 60 miles, 2 days.

John DOYLE vs William BURRIS; not tried; Roger GIDDINS, witness for Deft., 8 miles, 4 days.

Ordered Elisha WIGGINS, a Criple Man, be exempt payment Poll Tax in future.

Ordered Executors of John HUDSPETH, deceased, expose to sale such part personal estate can spare to satisfy Executors vs said Estate.

Isaac SOUTHARD resignes his office as Constable.

15 August 1788

Present: William COOK, Absalom BOSTICK, Jesse BUMPS, John CHILD-RESS, Esqrs.

Deed from Mary EASON to Wm. T. LEWIS; oath of Peter HAIRSTON.

Deed from James DUNLAP to Peter HAIRSTON; oath Reuben LINDSAY.

Deed from John MILLER and wife to Adam SHEEKS (Skeeks); oath John PERSONS.

Deed from John Thomas LONGINO to John RIGHTS; acknowledged.

Deed from LANIERS Executors to Alexander DOUGLASS; oath William THORNTON.

Deed from John ALLEN to John GOODE: oath William THORNTON.

Deed from Joe LINEBACK to Jacob KRUGER: oath William THORNTON.

Deed from Jacob KRUGER and wife to Henry KRUGER; oath William THORNTON.

Deed from William Terril LEWIS to William MEREDITH; acknowledged.

Ordered James FOSTER and Robert HAZLETT be exempt paying Poll Tax in future.

State vs James DOWNEY; Jonathan HAINES, witness for Pltf., 120 miles, 3 days; Abner PHILLIPS, 60 miles, 1 day.

State vs James DOWNEY; same witnesses; same payment attendance.

Edward REAVIS vs Joshua BROWN; Caviat on Land Docket; not yet determined; Frederick TANNER, witness for Pltf., 150 miles, 9 days.

Ordered John LYNCH, Executor, in right of his wife of James GLENNS Estate, appear and render account of estate.

Ordered Francis BARNARD overseer, road leading from Salem to Iron Works from Guilford County line into Toms Creek Road.

Ordered Sheriff summon only three Constables attend courts, etc. (no names).

16 August 1788

Present: James MARTIN, John CHILDRESS, Gideon EDWARDS, Jacob

SHEPPERD, Constant LADD, Esqrs.

Richard GOODE appointed Sheriff and John GOODE admitted as Deputy; William MEREDITH, Constantine LADD, William THORNTON, Gideon EDWARDS and Zachariah RAY, securities.

Ordered Henry SPEER, Esq. allowed 15 pounds out of tax 1788 for building bridge across Deep Creek and Joseph WILLIAMS appointed Commissioner to see bond executed.

Ordered James DOWNEY appointed Constable in LEWIS District in room of Isaac SOUTHARD; Wm. T. LEWIS and Zach. RAY, securities.

Ordered Clerk make correction on following: Michael HOOSER, Collector in KROUSES District, paid tax 1786 on 200 gallons Rum too much; also mistake made in KROUSES list of Taxables 1787.

Ordered Wm. T. LEWIS and Jonathan HAINES appointed Commissioners to let lowest bidder on Bridge across the Elkin at the Iron Works.

Deed from Frederick ALBERTY to Henry KRUGER: oath William THORNTON.

Court appointed Collectors 1788: GLENS District: John Thomas LONGINO; LADDS: Andrew ROBINSON; SHOUSES: Michael HOUZAR; BEASLEYS: Charles BEASLEY; HILLS: John COOLEY; GAINES: Reubin GEORGE; BOSTICKS: John MORGAN; HUMPHRIS: Stephen K. SMITH; EDWARDS: Joseph PORTER: McANALLYS: John EVANS; SANDERS: Thomas WRIGHT; LEWIS: Zeanos BALDWIN; MEREDITHS: Reziah JARVIS; ATKINS: Jeffery JOHNSON; LOVILLS: Joseph ASHLEY; HUGHLETTS & COLVARDS: Thomas GORDON.

Report of Committee appointed to receive Claims: 1788 Henry SPEER, Juror Salisbury March Term 1787, September Term 1787: James BOWLES, 2 woof scalps; Jeffrey JOHNSON, attendance Court, warning ATKINS District, keeping guard with 3 men over C. LINDSAY; Richard JACKS, 5 woolf scalps; West MOSBY, 4 wild catt scalps; John COOLEY, 20 days attendance Court, warning HILLS District; John BURCH, Juror Salisbury March 1788; Stephen SMITH, 1 old woolf and 6 young woolf scalps and 1 wild catt scalp; Wm. T. LEWIS, Juror Salisbury September 1787; Salathiel MARTIN, same but money to be delivered to Wm. T. LEWIS; Zenos BALDWIN, Juror Salisbury 1787 to be delivered to WM. T. LEWIS, warning LEWIS District 1787 and 1788; Reziah JARVIS, warning MEREDITHS District; Joseph PORTER, warning EDWARDS District; Stephen SMITH, attending court 4 days, warning HUMPHRIS District; Constantine LADD, Juror Salisbury September 1787; William GIBSON, damages laying off road from GOODES to MORROWS; John BRANSON, same as GIBSON; Isaac RULPP, one woolf scalp; Jacob DRAM, one woolf scalp, 4 wild catt scalps; Ashley JOHNSON, one wolf scalp (money due GIBSON, BRANSON, RULPP, DRAM & Ashley JOHNSON to be issued to A. ROBINSON); Andrew ROBINSON, Corners fees on inquest held over Thomas MARTIN; Wm. N. COOK, Constable 4 days attending court; Richard COOMES (Coomer ?), one wild catt scalp; Anthony DEARING, Juror Salisbury March 1788; Alexander MOORE, 6 young woolf scalps; John MERRET, 8 young woolf scalps 1787; Charles McANALLY, damages laying out road; Jacob ROMINGER, carrying prisoners to Salisbury; Benjamin BENSON, 2 wild cat scalps; Absalom BOSTICK, Jury Salisbury September 1787; Reubin GEORGE, services carrying prisoners to Salisbury; John COOLEY, on behalf Amb. BLACKBURN, assessor 1781; Joseph BITTING, carrying sundry prisoners to Salisbury; George JOICE, guarding prisoners and delivering them to Sheriff; Jesse LESTER, 2 horses, 3 days carrying prisoners to Salisbury; George KIMBROUGH, warning COLVARDS District; Reubin DODSON, carrying prisoners to Salisbury as Constable; Samuel VEST, putting barrs in Jail windows, putting Gibson WOOLDRIDGE in Jail and find him 3 days; Thomas LOW, warning LADDS District and one wild cat scalp behalf Richard BROCK; Isaac SOUTHARD, 7 days attendance court August 1787; Benjamin BENNIT, 1 woolf scalp; Wm. BALES, 2 woolf scalps;

Richard GOODE, Sheriff holding election for delegates to convention, carrying Samuel SMITH to Salisbury, repairing Jail and extra services; James VERNON, 6 young woolves scalps; Zachariah RAY, Juror Salisbury 1787; John Thomas LONGINO, Juror Salisbury and warning in GLENS District; Samuel STROOPE, one woolf scalp; John WILLIAMS, claims of attending Court, Prisoners Expenses, etc.; Joseph WILLIAMS, Clerk Exoficio services last year; Thomas SPARKS, 3 catt scalps; Jordan MANNING, 3 catt scalps; Caleb CRAMMER, 3 days carrying prisoners to Salisbury; Ambrouse GAINES, 4 days carrying prisoners to Salisbury; Philemon BUCHANNON, carrying prisoners 4 days to Salisbury. Committee also Lay County Tax of 1 shilling each poll and four pence each 100 acres of land.

Ordered following attend next County Court as Jurors: Thomas WRIGHT, Lewis ELLIOTT, James SANDERS, Senr., Airs HUDSPETH, John PIPES, Richard WILSON, James DOWNEY, Wm. N. COOK, Abraham DOWNEY, Richard MURPHY, John FARMER, Wm. HAWKINS, David HUMPHRESS, Jacob McCRAW, Wm. ARMSTRONG, Wm. LEWIS, Drury WILLIAMS, Joseph EASON, Jesse McANALLY, John HALBERT, Thomas GOODE, Junr., Joseph BANNER, Joseph NELSON, John HUTCHINGS (Hutchens), Daniel HUTCHISON (Hutcherson), Frederick MILLER, Robert MARKLEN, Michael HOOSER, Junr., and Patrick McGIBBONY.

Jury appointed to view road from Chandlors Burnt Cabbin to Virginia line reports it will be good road; ordered William MARTIN, overseer.

Jury appointed to view road from Scritchfields ford on the Yadkin to Morrows Ford on Dan river have done so.

Ordered John MARSH overseer, new marked road from Critchfields Ford to Fishers River.

Ordered Isaac COPELAND overseer, new marked road from Fishers River to Bull Run.

Ordered Charles DUDLEY overseer, new marked road from Bullrun to Tarrarat River.

Ordered John TILLEY overseer, new marked road from Tarrarat River to Hollowroad.

Ordered Henry BURCHAM overseer, new marked road from Hollow Road to Quaker road.

Ordered Matthew MOORE overseer, new marked road from Quaker road to Coxs road.

Ordered a S.F. issued John HUDSPETHS Executors.

Account settlement estate of John THOMPSON, deceased, returned.

Inventory sale estate of William KIRKPATRICK, deceased, returned.

2nd Monday November 1788

Present: John RANDLEMAN, Esq.

2nd Tuesday November 1788

Present: Martin ARMSTRONG, John TALIAFERRO, John RANDLEMAN, Esqrs.

Last Will and Testament of Henry SPEENHOUR, deceased; oaths of Henry SHORE and Samuel STROOPE; Peter HOOSER and John Henry SPEENHOUR, Executors, quallified.

2nd Wednesday November 1788

Present: Martin ARMSTRONG, John TALIAFERRO, Constant LADD, Esqrs.

Grand Jury: David HUMPHRISS, Foreman; Michael HOOSER, Junr., Thomas WRIGHT, Airs HUDSPETH, Abraham DOWNEY, Robert MARKLAND, John FARMER, William LEWIS, Joseph NELSON, William HAWKINS, Patrick McGIBBONY, Thos. GOODE, Junr., Joseph BANNER and John HUTCHINS.

John Thomas LONGINO, John BOSTICK and Ambrous GAINES quallified as Deputy Sheriffs.

Deed from Philip DEATHERAGE to Edwin HICKMAN: oath William HARRIS.

Bill of Sale from Richard Henry DENNIS to James DOWNEY; oath Abraham DOWNEY.

Deed from Valentine REESE to William ZACHARY; oath Henry SPEER.

Deed from William DOUGLASS to William HOLLIMAN; oath William HARVEY.

Deed from John HARVEY to John HARVEY; oath William HARVEY.

William YORK vs Joshua K. SPEER. Jury: James DAY, Malcum CURRY, John BRAIM, John LYNCH, Joseph GENTRY, Justice REYNOLDS, John FARR, Charles WADDLE, William PRATHER, John APPLETON, Samuel CLARKE, Benjamin HUMPHRIS.

Edward LOVELL vs John HARPER; same jury except Lewis WHEELIS in room of Malcum CURRY; Elisha WIGGINS, witness for Plft., 8 days, 120 miles.

Daniel W. EASLEY vs James DOYLE: same jury except Richard HORN in room of James DAY; non suit.

William HERBEARTS Administrators vs William SHEPPERD; same jury except John BRISON in room of John LYNCH.

William NALL, Esq. vs William SHEPPARD, Esq. Jury: Richard HORN, Malcum CURRY, John BRAIM, John BRISON, Joseph GENTRY, Justice REYNOLDS, Gabriel JONES, Charles WADDLE, William PRATHER, John APPLETON, Samuel CLARKE, Benjamin HUMPHRISS.

Peter ONEAL vs Thomas SMITH (Jockey); same jury.

Benjamin MYERS vs William LANKFORD: same jury.

John BRISON vs John DUGLASS: John BRISON, Junr., witness for Pltf., 300 miles, 10 days.

2nd Thursday November 1788

Present: Martin ARMSTRONG, Joseph WINSTON, William DOBSON, William HUGHLETT, Esqrs.

Deed from Lazarus TILLEY to Shadrick PREWETT; acknowledged.

Deed from Lazarus TILLEY to Jesse SIMMONS; acknowledged.

Deed from Benjamin CORNELIOUS to Thomas BALL; oath Elijah GILLISPEE.

Deed from Henry TILLEY Senr., to Archelouis HUGHES and George HAIRSTON; oath of Reubin DOBBINS.

Deed from Jacob FREEMAN to William WHITAKER: oath Job BRAUGHTON.

Deed from Andrew RUDOLPH to Patrick BURNS; oath Henry SPEER.

Deed from Benjamin SPEER to Matthew STEELMAN; oath Henry SPEER.

Deed from William VENABLE to John VENABLE: acknowledged.

Deed from David MORROW and wife to Wm. DOBSON, Esq.; oath Archibald CAMBLE. (1)

Deed from David MORROW and wife to Wm. DOBSON, Esq.; oath Archibald CAMBLE. (2)

Deed from Richard WEBSTER and wife to William WALKER; oath of John MORGAN. (2 deeds).

Following appointed Collectors for 1788: Andrew ROBINSON, LADDS District; Michael HORN and John COOLEY, securities; Michael HOOSER, SHOUSES District, Andrew ROBINSON and John COOLEY, securities; Joseph ASHLEY, LOVELLS District, Edward LOVELL and John VENABLE, securities; Stephen K. SMITH, HUMPHRISS District, John TALIAFERRO and John BOSTICK, securities; John COOLEY, HILLS District, Andrew ROBINSON, Michael HOOSER and Jo. WINSTON, securities; John EVANS, McANALLYS District, (no securities); Charles BEAZLEY, BEAZLEYS District, Reuben DODSON and John FARMER, securities; Thomas GORDON, HUGHLETTS District, John RANDLEMAN and Jesse HORN, securities; Joseph PORTER, EDWARDS District, John TALIAFERRO and Gideon EDWARDS, securities; Jeff MORGAN, BOSTICKS District, Thomas NEAL and Joseph EASON, securities; Jeffrey JOHNSON, ATKINS District, William SILVIA and Wm. JOHNSON, securities.

Gibson WOOLDRIDGE vs Henry WORD; tried last term; Jeremiah RILEY, Garnishee, says he owes nothing.

State vs James LEFOY. Jury: Joseph EASON, Henry PATTILLO, Frank POINDEXTER, Lewis ELLIOTT, Wm. FREEMAN, Richard LINVILLE, Richard HORN, Adonijah HARBOUR, John APPLETON, Shadrack PREWETT, Daniel SCOTT, Matt. WARNOCK; find Deft. not guilty.

State vs Jonathan HARROLD; same jury except Wm. PHILLIPS in room of Wm. FREEMAN; Archelouis GIBSON, witness for Pltf., 80 miles, 5 days; Garrott GIBSON, 80 miles, 5 days; John GIBSON, 100 miles, 5 days; Aron LISBY, 120 miles, 3 days; James GIBSON, 80 miles, 5 days; Samuel PARKER, 72 miles, 3 days; Richard NUNNS, witness for Deft., 100 miles, 2 days.

Joseph WINSTON vs Joseph CARMICHAEL; James COFFEE, witness for Deft., 330 miles, 53 days.

Augustine BLACKBURN vs Wm. WAGGONER: appeal at November Court 1786; John APPLETON, witness for Pltf., 150 miles, 20 days.

Admr. Estate of Elisha DOBSON, Deceased, granted Nancy DODSON, widow and relict, William ASHEST (?) and Charles McANALLY, securities.

John BOSTICK, Collector, McANALLYS and GAINES Districts reports omitting returns; William MOORE, 1 poll, 100 acres; Russell CAIN, 1 poll as Insolvant 1787.

2nd Friday November 1788

Present: Martin ARMSTRONG, William DODSON, Zachariah RAY, Esqrs.

Deed from Mary EASON to Joseph EASON; oath James COFFEE.

Deed from Joseph CUMMINS to Nathan DILLON; oath Archibald CAMBLE.

Deed from Richard GOODE to Nathan DILLON, acknowledged.

Robert FULTON, orphan of Francis FULTON, deceased, chose Samuel CLARKE his guardian; Joseph WINSTON and Richard GOODE, securities.

Matthew MOORE, Assignee vs Daniel SHIP. Jury: John MORGAN, Thomas NEAL, Wm. BURRIS, Joseph EASON, James GIBSON, Wm. ALLAN, Edward CLANTON, Thompson GLEN, John BLALOCK, Jonathan HAINES, Lewis ELLITT, George HOLCOMB.

Joseph WILLIAMS vs William CHANDLER and Reubin DODSON; not tried; John COX, witness for Deft., 250 miles, 4 days.

John RANDLEMAN vs John SHELTON; same jury.

William LATHAM, Esq. vs Charles VEST; Deft. not guilty; Jane HOWARD, witness for Pltf., 100 miles, 7 days.

Joseph COLE Executors vs Justice REYNOLDS; not tired; James WHEALIS, witness for Pltf., 80 miles, 3 days.

Abner GREENWOOD vs John DOYLE; non suit; Edward CLANTON, witness for Deft., 220 miles, 31 days; Willis BRADLEY, witness for Pltf., 400 miles, 15 days.

Ordered George HOLDER overseer, road in room of Andrew BLACK.

Ordered Jesse STANLEY overseer, road in room of William CHILDRESS.

Admr. Estate of Abraham WOOD, deceased, granted to Jesse SCOTT, son-in-law of said WOOD; Obediah WOOD and James SCOTT, securities.

Ordered following appear as Jorors next County Court: Azariah DENNY, Edward LINVILL, Wm. CRITCHFIELD, John McMICKLE, Wm. WALKER, James GAMBLE, Wm. ELLIOTT, Frederick LONG, John PIPES, Richard WILBURN, Wm. N. COOK, Richard MURPHY, Jacob McCRAW, Wm. ARMSTRONG, Jesse McANALLY, John HALBERT, Frederick MILLER, Daniel HUTCHERSON, Samuel CARTER, Isaac SOUTHARD, James BADGET, John CARTER, Thompson GLEN, John RIGHTS, John MICKEY, Capt. Daniel SMITH, John LYNCH, James SANDERS, Senr., Wm. SILVIA, John SUMMERS, Senr., John HARVEY, Wm. HICKMAN, Wm. MARTIN, and Wm. SPARKS, Junr.

2nd Saturday November 1788

Present: Martin ARMSTRONG, Jo. WINSTON, William MEREDITH, Esqrs.

James TUCKER vs Jo. LANFIELD and others; ordered witness not allowed for more than one day in each Court as Saturday is appeal day.

Abner GREENWOOD vs John DOYLE; Joseph REAVIS, witness for Deft., 300 miles, 16 days.

George PETTIT vs Justice REYNOLDS. Jury: Lewis ELLIOTT, Wm. VENABLE, Thomas NEIL, Isham COX, Pleasant KERBY, Edward WOOLDRIDGE, Geo. HOLCOMB, John WEATHERFORD, Wm. BURRIS, Godfrey CODY, Henry PATTILLO, Levi SPEER, Samuel FREEMAN and John BROWN, witnesses for Deft. failed to appear, George HEAD, witness for Pltf., 77 miles, 5 days; Matthew BROOKS, 100 miles, 12 days.

John WILLIAMS vs John COLVARD; same jury.

Matthew McKINNE vs Abner PHILLIPS; Zachary RAY, witness for Pltf., 60 miles, 1 day.

John JERVIS vs William SILVIE; Zachariah RAY, witness for Deft., 60 miles, 1 day.

John LONGINO vs John and Thomas ROBERTS; Hugh MORRIS, witness for Pltf., 40 miles, 7 days.

William HUGHLETT vs Matthew MOORE; mistrial.

Arthur SCOTT vs Samuel CUMMINS: same jury.

Elizabeth HEATH vs Oliver CHARLES; James COFFEE, witness for Pltf., 60 miles, 5 days.

John and William ENGRAM vs Thomas HANDLEN; Gideon EDWARDS says he owes nothing nor had nothing in his hands but Michael MONTGOMERY told said EDWARDS he owed said Deft. Michael MONTGOMERY, Garnishee, was called and failed to appear.

Deed from Isaack WHITE to Moses LAWS; oath Joseph WINSTON.

Certificate signed by Joseph DUNNINGAN; oath Zachariah RAY, Esq. presented.

Ordered Jesse LESTER appointed committee employ person to raise floor Court House and repair same manner it was before (it gives away).

Arthur SCOTT appointed Constable, HUGHLETTS District; John KEER and Robt. SMITH, securities.

Ordered Mill already built on Forbis Creek belonging to Thos. HUTCHINS be deemed publick Mill.

Ordered Tavern Rates settled as follows: Good proof Whiskey, half pint, 1 shilling; Good proof Brandy, half pint, 1 shilling; Common Rum, half pint, 1 shilling, 9 pence; West India Rum, half pint, 2 shillings; French Brandy, half pint, 1 shilling 6 pence; Punch with W. India Rum, quart, 2 shillings; Punch with common Rum, quart, 3 shillings, 6 pence; Tody with W. India Rum, quart, 2 shillings, 6 pence; Tody with Common Rum, quart, 1 shilling, 8 pence; Malt Beer or Cyder, quart, 8 pence; Cyder Oil, quart, 2 shillings; Teneriffe Wine, half pint, 2 shillings; Claret, half pint, 1 shilling, 6 pence; Horse stabled and hay or fodder 12 hours, 1 shilling; Corn or oats, quart, 2 pence; Pasterage for Horse 12 hours, 1 shilling; Common Breakfast, 1 shilling; with Tea or Coffe, 2 shillings, 6 pence; Common Dinner, 1 shilling, 6 pence; with Hott Roast and Boiled, 2 shillings, 6 pence; Lodging night clean Bed and Sheets, 6 pence.

Ordered George HAUZER, William HUGHLETT, William THORNTON, Esq. and John Thomas LONGINO appointed committee to settle with Executors in James GLENS Estate.

Ordered William HUTCHERSON, James VERNON, Joseph READ, Robert CRUMP, John VAWTER, James MEREDITH, Junr., Anthony DEARING, Jesse GEORGE, Alexander JOYCE, Isaac JOYCE, James LANGHAM, George JOYCE, Wm. DAVIS, John ONEAL and Wm. HAWKINS view old and new roads leading from George JOYCES Cabbins to the Virginia line.

2nd Monday February 1789

Present: Martin ARMSTRONG, Esq.

2nd Tuesday February 1789

Present: Martin ARMSTRONG, Wm. T. LEWIS, Joseph WINSTON, George HAUZAR, Jacob BLUME, Esqrs.

Grand Jury: John HALBERT, Foreman; James SANDERS, Wm. WALKER, Jesse McANALLY, John RIGHTS, John LYNCH, Azeriah DENNY, Edward LOVILL, Frederick LONG, John PIPES, Wm. N. COOK, Richard MURPHY, Jacob McCRAW, William ARMSTRONG and Samuel CARTER.

Last Will and Testament of Gottfrey AUST; oath John RIGHTS, Gottlieb SHOBER and John MICKEY, Executors, quallified; Inventory Estate Gottfrey AUST, deceased; returned by Gottlieb SHOBER.

Last Will and Testament of Jacob GROETER: oath Peter HARRILL; Peter FRY, one Executor named came into Court and in proper person relinquished his right to said Exectorship; Mary Catharine GROETER, widow and relict of said deceased, one of the Executors named, quallified.

Deed from John George EBERT to Fredr. Wm. MARSHALL; oath John RIGHTS.

Deed from Joshua MIZE and wife to James SANDERS: oath Richard WOOTEN.

Deed from Thomas GLOVER and wife to Richard WOOTEN; oath Hardy SANDERS.

Deed from William JOHNSON and wife to Stephen HOBSON; oath Isaac STUBBS.

Deed from Stephen HOBSON and wife to Isaac STUBBS; oath Thomas VEST.

Deed from Stephen HOBSON and wife to Thomas VEST; oath Isaac STUBBS.

Deed from Charles PARKER to Samuel KERBY; oath John LYNCH.

Jesse LESTER, Thompson GLEN and Obediah Martin BENGE came into Court and quallified as Justices of the Peace.

James DAVIS has leave to keep Tavern at his dwelling house; John HALL and George DEATHERAGE, securities; Maj. GOODE to pay.

2nd Wednesday February 1789

Present: Wm. T. LEWIS, Jacob BLUME, John RANDLEMAN, Esqrs.

Ordered John GILES, John Thomas LONGINO and John COOLEY summond to attend upon Court as Constables.

Ordered Thomas RAPER exempt from payment Poll Tax in future.

Ordered James BURNSIDES overseer, road from Wilkes to Rowan County lines.

Ordered Gottfrey FIDLER overseer, road in room of Robert ELRODE.

Ordered Salethiel MARTIN overseer, road in room of Isaac SOUTHARD.

Ordered Abraham TRANSOU overseer, road in room of Gottlob CRAMMER.

Ordered Joseph WINSTON, James GAINES and Stephen WOOD appointed committee to settle estate of James GLEN, deceased.

Ordered Sheriff expose to sale perishable part of estate of Elisha DOBSON, deceased.

Deed from Isham THOMPSON to William SILVIE: oath Wm. T. LEWIS.

Deed from Roger GIDDENS and wife to Thomas MARTIN; acknowledged; Wife Elizabeth privately examined by Absalom BOSTICK, relinquishes her dower.

Deed from Dan HILL to Edward MERRIT; oath of John MERRITT.

Deed from John WILLIAMS (LT) to Grimes HOLCOMB; acknowledged.

Deed from Peter COLEMAN to Peter JEAN; acknowledged.

Joseph WINSTON vs John GOODE. Jury: Isaac SOUTHARD, William SILVIE, Joseph PHILLIPS, Godfrey CODY, Thomas RAPER, James LAWRENCE, Allen GROCE, Francis FORDNEY, Robert MARKLAND, John FARE, James BADGETT, William SPARKS; appeal prayed and granted; Samuel CLARKE, witness for Pltf., 80 miles, 5 days; Ann CLARKE, 80 miles, 4 days; Thomas MORRIS, witness for Deft., 35 miles, 2 days; Samuel WAKE-FILL, 48 miles, 5 days; James COFFEE, 60 miles, 6 days; John HALL, witness for Pltf., 80 miles, 3 days.

John TATE vs Leo DAVIS and Gid EDWARDS; Jury: Isaac SOUTHARD, Godfrey CODY, Thomas RAPER, Fredr. MILLER, William SILVIE, James BADGETT, Robt. MARKLAND, James LAWRENCE, John MICKEY, Allen GROCE, Francis FORDNEY and William SPARKS.

William T. LEWIS vs Mason COMBS; same jury.

Richard WILLIAMS vs Samuel CUMMINS to use Fredr. MILLER: same jury.

John WILLIAMS (LT) resigned his office as Constable and Ninian RILEY resigned as Constable; John WRIGHT appointed in room of

John WILLIAMS and Ninian RILEY.

Ordered Gid EDWARDS, Esq. released payment taxes 1788 on 5,000 acres, it appearing he owns but 550 acres and stands charged with 5,500.

Ordered Thomas RING exempt of 300 acres 1788, it being a mistake.

On motion Silvester THOMPSON, Ordered Sheriff summon jury to lay off dower to Mary KIRKMAN, now wife of George KIRKMAN, in Lands John THOMPSON died seized of, she being relict of said decedent.

Ordered Charles McANALLY appointed Trustee and William DOBSON, Stray Master.

2nd Thursday February 1789

Present: Martin ARMSTRONG, Absalom BOSTICK, William COOK, Esqrs.

Ordered Joseph WINSTON, Esq. released from committee to settle GLENNS estate and William THORNTON, Wm. T. LEWIS, Wm. MEREDITH, Esqrs. are added thereto.

Ordered Justice REYNOLDS be fined for an insult offered to Court; payment to Jo WILLIAMS, Clerk of Court.

Elizabeth LOGAN chosed John LOGAN, guardian; he accepted; Jo PHILLIPS and Joseph GENTRY, securities.

Deed from William SELBY to James MARSH; oath Miner MARSH.

Deed from James BRYSON and wife to William HILL; oath John BRYSON, Junr.

Deed from Thomas SMITH and wife to Benjamin BENSON; oath David HUMPHRISS.

Deed from Gray BYNUM to William COOK; acknowledged.

Deed from James DOAK and wife to Obed BAKER; oath Stephen K. SMITH.

Deed from Toliver DAVIS to Benjamin SPEER; oath Henry SPEER.

Deed from Henry SPEER to Frederick SHORE; acknowledged.

Deed from Henry SPEER to Standwick HOWARD; acknowledged; Gid EDWARDS to pay.

Deed from Abraham CRESON to James CAMBELL; oath Henry SPEER.

Deed from Richard LINVILL to David LINVILLE: oath Andrew ROBINSON.

State vs Benjamin HUMPHRISS; Basterdy Bond in 100 pounds to Wardens for maintenance of the child.

Matthew BROOKS vs Robert SMITH; Jury: Fredr. MILLER, Isaac SOUTH-ARD, James BADGETT, William SILVIE, William SPARKS, James BOLES, James MEREDITH, Benjamin BENSON, Charles DUDLEY, Wm. PRATHER, John MICKEY, Daniel SCOTT; appeal granted; Thompson GLEN, witness for Pltf., 114 miles, 44 days; Jos. GENTRY, 80 miles, 12 days.

John LATTON vs John TAYLOR: same jury; Joel LEWIS, witness for Pltf., 525 miles, 26 days; Wm. T. LEWIS, 510 miles, 32 days.

Ordered Noble LADD, William LADD, Almond GUINN, Joseph VAUGHN, John WEBSTER, Lemuel SMITH, Charles ANGEL, Lawrence ANGEL, Robert MAJORS, William SOUTHERLAND, George BRADLEY, Reuben ZIMMERMAN, John CRITENDON, Absalom BOSTICK, Esq. view road from said BOS-TICKS to Thompsons Blacksmith Shop, nearest way across Evans Creek, Absalom BOSTICK, overseer.

Ordered Matthias CARPENTER overseer, road instead of George PHILLIPS.

Ordered John BRANSON overseer, new road leads by William JEANS from forks roads near him to Thomas OWENS Shop.

Ordered Samuel YOUNG overseer, road from forks road where John BRANSON lives down to the Rockingham County line.

Ordered John ARMSTRONG, John Thomas LONGINO, William MEREDITH, Zachariah RAY, Lewis ELLIOTT, John RANDLEMAN, and Henry SPEER, Esqrs. appointed Jurors to attend next Superior Court.

2nd Friday February 1789

Present: Absalom BOSTICK, Wm. T. LEWIS, Obediah M. BENGE, Esqrs.

Ordered John HARVEY, William CRITCHFIELD, John McMICKLE, William ELLIOTT, Richard WILBURN, John SUMMERS, William HICKMAN, William MARTIN, James Raylor RILEY, John HUTCHENS, John CARTER, Samuel DOWNEY, Joseph CLOUD, Capt. Robert HILL, Joseph HAUZAR, John BRINKLEY, Windle CROUSE, John CROUSE, Daniel SCOTT, George PETTIT, Aron MOORE, Wm. LAIN, Airs HUDSPETH, Carter HUDSPETH, Nicholas HORN, Richard HORN, Henry COOK, Wm. COOK, Jr., John ANDERSON, John PARSONS, John MARTIN, Thomas SPENCE, Lazerus TILLEY, Thomas CARDWELL, William BRUCE and John BRANSON serve as Jurors next County Court.

Ordered Clerk secure Seal for County.

Mannering SUMMERS records his mark.

Ordered Jesse LESTER, Gid EDWARDS, James GAINES and Col. Martin ARMSTRONG appointed committee to settle estate of James GLENN, deceased.

Deed from Lewis ELLIOTT to Jacob ELSBERRY; oath Airs HUDSPETH; LONGINO to pay.

Deed from Richard GOODE, Sheriff, to John LYNCH; acknowledged.

Bill of Sale from Toliver DAVIS to Wm. T. LEWIS; oath James DOWNEY.

Bill of Sale from Richard Henry DENNIS vs William T. LEWIS; oath James DOWNEY.

Bill of Sale from Absalom BOSTICK to Wm. T. LEWIS; acknowledged.

Bill of Sale from Joseph PHILLIPS to Wm. T. LEWIS; acknowledged.

Deed from Thomas MOSBY to Philip HOWARD: oath Jo WILLIAMS.

Bill of Sale from George PRIDDY to Wm. T. LEWIS; oath James DOWNEY.

Ordered citations issued different Stray Masters and County Trustees to appear to settle with said court.

Copy LANIER & WILLIAMS agreement and affidavit presented; oath Wm. THORNTON.

John ARMSTRONG vs Samuel CUMMINS; John RANDLEMAN, Garnishee says he owes something but cannot ascertain sum, William HUGHLETT says he owes about 135 pounds but cannot exactly ascertain.

Ordered Supersedias issue vs George HAUZER, Esq. bring proceedings in suit Philip SNIDER vs Roger GIDDENS; Jo. BITTEN, Constable and Airs HUDSPETH, security for GIDDENS.

Jesse MAUPIN vs John SHELTON; Reuben DODSON, witness for Pltf., 390 miles, 25 days.

Ordered Charles BEAZLEY has leave to keep Tavern at his house; Matthew MOORE and John CHILDRESS, securities.

Ordered Sheriff sell 100 acres belonging to Daniel BARNETT to satisfy his taxes for 1787.

Charles VEST resigned his office as Constable.

On Petition of Joseph HAMM, ordered Grist Mill now building on Lick Creek by said HAMM be deemed public Mill.

Ordered Constantine LADD, James HOLBROOK, Andrew ROBINSON, Richard LINVILL, David LINVILL, Michael FARE, John HUTCHINS, Henry COOK, Patrick McGIBBONY, Henry HAMPTON, John LOW, James GAMBILL, Michael FULPS, Joseph LADD, Aron LINVILL and John FARE jury, road leading near James HOLBROOKS.

11 May 1789

Present: James GAINES, Jesse LESTER, Esqrs.

12 May 1789

Present: John TALLIAFERRO, James GAINES, Jesse LESTER, Esqrs.

Deed from James REAVIS and Mary REAVIS to John HUTCHINS: oath of John JOHNSON.

Grand Jury: Airs HUDSPETH, Foreman; William CRITCHFIELD, John McMICKLE, William ELLIOTT, Richard WILBOURN, John SUMMERS, Samuel DOWNEY, John BINKLEY, Daniel SCOTT, Carter HUDSPETH, William COOK, Jr., Lazerous TILLEY, John BRANSON, William HICKMAN, and John CARTER.

Account Sale Estate of Abraham WOOD, deceased, returned by John Thos. LONGINO, DS.

Last Will and Testament of Michael HOUZAR, deceased; oath Geo HOUZAR, Michael HOWZAR and Peter HOWZAR, Executors, quallified.

Admr. Estate of Thomas NORMAN, deceased, granted Thomas NORMAN, son of the deceased; John TALLIAFERRO and James GUNSTON, securities.

It appearing there is an error in return of the Imported Merchandize of John CUNRODE, amount 200 pounds 1788; ordered he be released from paying.

Joseph WILLIAMS, guardian KIMBROUGH Orphans vs Roger TURNER, a former Executor; Ordered William THORNTON, Henry SPEER and Thompson GLEN, Esqrs. be committee to settle the accounts of Marmaduke KIMBROUGH, deceased and Roger TURNER, a former Executor.

Temperance POCOCK, Admr. vs Samuel HUMPHRIS; mistrial; Jury: Richard HORN, Alexander MOORE, John HARVEY, John STONE, Meredith SMITH, James BOLES, John BAILEY, William VENABLE, Edward SMITH, John SHELTON, Justice REYNOLDS, and William FREEMAN.

Ordered Jonas REYNOLDS overseer, road in room of John JOHNSON.

John WELLS, HILLS District, was exempt some years ago from payment Poll Tax for himself, has by mistake, been charged tax for 1787; Ordered return of same to WELLS; also, he be allowed Insolvant Poll for 1788.

Ordered John HARVEY has leave to keep Tavern at his dwelling house; Robert SMITH, security.

Jacob MILLER has leave to keep Tavern at his house; Fredr. MILLER, security.

Anthony BITTING has leave to keep Tavern at his house; Wm. CAMBELL and James MARTIN, securities.

William DOBSON, Esq. has leave to keep Tavern at his house,

Peter HOWZAR, security.

Peter HOWZAR has leave to keep Tavern, Wm. DOBSON, security.

Jacob BLUME has leave to keep Tavern at his house in Salem; Joseph WILLIAMS, security.

Christian LASH has leave to keep Tavern at his dwelling house, Jo WILLIAMS, security.

13 May 1789

Present: William COOK, John TALLIAFERO, Constant LADD, Esqrs.

Robert WILLIAMS, Esq. produced Commission from Hon. Samuel ASHE, Samuel SPENCER and John WILLIAMS, Esqrs. Judges of Superior Courts of Law and Equity authorizing him to practice as an attorney in several County Courts, etc.

Hugh ARMSTRONG, Esq. elected Sheriff.

On petition of Matthew MARKLAND, ordered citation issued against Reason WILLIAMS and wife to appear and give fresh security for Admr. Estate of James DOUTHIT, deceased.

Ordered Joseph WINSTON, Absalom BOSTICK and Harry TERREL, Esqrs. appointed committee to settle with Charles McANALLY, County Trustee and William DOBSON, Esq., Stray Master.

Ordered William COOK, John RANDLEMAN and Jacob BLUME, Esqrs. be appointed committee to settle with Executors and Administrators during this term.

Richard JACKS, Executors vs Thomas EASTROP; Jury: John ANDERSON, Richard HORN, John CARTEY, West MOSBY, John HARVEY, William PRATHER, James BOLES, Matthew WARNOCK, Samuel FITZPATRICK, Robert MARKLAND, John RIGHTS, George HUDSPETH; non suit.

Robert MARKLAND vs John COLVARD: same jury except Edward SMITH in place of Robert MARKLAND.

John YOUNG vs Joseph PHILIPS; same jury except Robt. MARKLAND in room of Samuel FITZPATRICK; find Deft. guilty.

Benjamin McCRAW vs John FLEMING; same jury; William McCRAW, witness for Deft., 180 miles, 3 days; William BURRIS, 490 miles, 14 days.

Blizard McGRUDER vs Samuel FREEMAN, Senr.; same jury; William FREEMAN, witness for Deft., 18 days, 140 miles.

Thomas CARLIN vs Elijah GILLESPIE, bail for Wm. WHARTON; Jury: Richard LINVILL, John JONES, John EVANS, John MERREL, Nicholas HORN, William HOLLEMON, Justice REYNOLDS, Matthew BROOKS, Michael FRY, Charles HUDSPETH, John WILLIAMS, William BURRIS.

Robert SMITH vs Thomas SMITH (Jockey); same jury.

John DOYLE vs William BURRIS; same jury except James MARTIN and John CUMMINS in room of Nicholas HORN and William BURRIS; non suit.

Gideon WRIGHTS Admrs. vs James BADGETT; not tried; William FREE-MAN, witness for Pltf., 260 miles, 33 days.

Abraham CRESON vs Jane SCOTT; determined some years ago, writ of error made known; ordered proceedings be sent to next Superior Court.

Ordered Joel CHILDRESS, orphan of Benjamin CHILDRESS, deceased, bound to Stephen CHILDRESS until 3 March 1798 when he arrives at 21 years of age to learn Art and Mistry of House Carpenter and Joiner, said Stephen agrees to give him tools and clothes at his freedom.

Ordered John HOLLAND overseer, road in room of Tego NISSION, deceased.

Bill of Sale from Richard HEATH to Johnson HEATH; oath James COFFEE.

Deed from Richard GOODE, Sheriff, to Airs HUDSPETH; oath Wm. THORNTON.

Receipt from Ann Mary BONN to John RIGHTS; oath Jacob BLUME.

Receipt from Jacob BONN to John RIGHTS; oath Jacob BLUME.

Ordered Settlement Estate of Doctor Jacob BONN, deceased, with John WRIGHT, Surviving Executor.

14 May 1789

Present: Joseph WINSTON, William DOBSON, Jacob BLUME, Esqrs.

Ordered David RIGGS in EDWARDS District be released from payment overcharge 300 acres.

Ordered Abner BARNS in McANALLYS District be released payment Poll Tax 1788.

Ordered Nancy DODSON, same district released payment tax on 100 acres.

Ordered Humphrey COCKRAM in LEWIS District be released payment Poll Tax 1788.

Ordered William CHILDRESS in BEASLEYS District be released payment one Poll and 50 acres 1788.

Ordered Henry TILLEY same district be released payment of tax on 305 acres.

Enoch STONE resigned as Constable.

Commissioners appointed to settle Executors James GLEN, deceased; returned same: Depotition Thompson GLEN; oath Jesse LESTER; Covenant between Thompson GLENN and John LYNCH; oath said GLEN; Account sale estate of James GLEN returned by John LYNCH, Exec. in right of his wife; Bond from Thompson GLEN to John LYNCH acknowledged by oath said GLEN; Agreement aigned by Thompson GLEN between him and John LYNCH acknowledged; Receipt from Thompson GLEN to John LYNCH acknowledged by oath said GLEN.

Deed from Henry AIRS to Joseph HAGAMAN; oath said HAGAMAN.

Bill of Sale from Abraham CRESON to Wm. Terrel LEWIS: oath James DOWNEY.

Power of Attorney from Abraham CRESON to Wm. Terrel LEWIS: oath J. DOWNEY.

Deed from John ALLEN and wife to Zachariah SUGART: oath Abraham REESE.

Deed from Mary EASON to James THOMPSON; oath Adam MITCHELL.

Deed from Wm. and Susanah LAFFOON to Thomas BURRIS; oath Stephen K. SMITH.

Deed from John BLEDSOE and wife to John DAVIS; oath Michael AHEART.

Deed from Wm. SHEPPERD to Edmund KERLEY; oath said SHEPPERD.

Copy receipt from Wm. MEREDITH, County Trustee to Wm. SHEPPERD; oath of Jo WINSTON.

Ordered Thomas ALLEN overseer, road in room of Joseph SPARKS.

Ordered Wm. McBRIDE overseer, road in room of Wm. COOK, Junr.

Ordered Frost SNOW overseer, road in room of John COOK.

Joseph WILLIAMS vs William CHANDLER and Reuben DODSON. Jury: John ANDERSON, John LYNCH, Jonathan HAINES, Samuel VEST, Richard LINVILL, William BURRIS, Fredrick MILLER, Richard HORN, Peter HOWZER, Abner PHILLIPS, and Joseph GENTRY.

State vs Mary REYNOLDS. Jury: John ANDERSON, Jonathan HAINES, Samuel VEST, Eliphalet JARVIS, William BURRIS, Fredrick MILLER, Richard HORN, Peter HAUZAR, George HAUZAR, Abner PHILIPS, Frank POINDEXTER; Mistrial.

State vs Gideon REYNOLDS; same jury except Joseph GENTRY in room of Frank POINDEXTER; Deft. not guilty; Thomas HADLEY, witness for State, 70 miles, 2 days; Eunecy HADLEY, 35 miles, 1 day; Abraham REESE, 35 miles, 1 day; Aaron SPEER, 64 miles, 2 days; Jacob DOBBIN, 35 miles, 1 day; Reuben SHORES, 50 miles, 1 day; Susannah LAKEY, 80 miles, 2 days.

15 May 1789

Present: Gideon EDWARDS, Constant LADD, William DOBSON, Esqrs.

Deed from Wm. T. LEWIS to Abner PHILIPS acknowledged by said LEWIS; Gideon EDWARDS to pay.

Deed from Wm. T. LEWIS to Abner PHILIPS acknowledged by said LEWIS; Gideon EDWARDS to pay.

Deed from Amos LONDON to John LONDON; oath Reziah JARVIS; M. SUMMERS to pay.

Bill of Sale from Wm. HOLDERLEY to Abel CARTER: oath Edward SMITH.

Deed from Thomas RABOURN and wife to Nathaniel STEWART; oath Thos. NORMAN.

Deed from Thomas SMITH to Samuel KERLEY; oath Joseph WILLIAMS; also one other.

Deed from Jacob ROBINSON to Samuel KERLEY; oath James MARTIN.

Deed from John and Mary READE to Robert HAMMOCK; oath Jacob BURRIS.

Deed from Maj. WILKERSON to Peter HAIRSTON; oath James GAINES.

Deed from James and Sarah FIELDER to Peter MURPHY; oath Richard MURPHY.

Bill of Sale from Henry SPEER to James Martin LEWIS; oath John WILLIAMS.

Joseph WILLIAMS, guardian, vs James and Wm. BARNES; John McBRICE, Garnishee says he has of Wm. BATES one jack plain, 1 raising plain, 1 head, 1 wooden square, 1 wooden gauge and no more; that he owes James nothing.

State vs William HOLLEMAN. Jury: John ANDERSON, Richard HORN, John DUNNIGAN, Godfrey CODY, William CHILDRESS, Greenberry PATTERSON, Abner PHILIPS, Matthew CHILDRESS, Malcum CURRY, Michael HOUZAR, Gotlib KROUSE, Henry STARR; find Deft. guilty.

State vs Mark HOLLIMAN; same jury; find Deft. guilty.

16 May 1789

Present: Martin ARMSTRONG, William COOK, Hugh ARMSTRONG, Esqrs.

Ordered Thomas BURCH released payment taxes on 300 acres, 1 Poll in MEREDITHS District 1788.

Court appointed Justices and Constables list taxables 1789: LEWIS District: Zachriah RAY, James DOWNEY; SANDERS: Stephen WOOD, John WRIGHT; EDWARDS: Gideon EDWARDS, Joseph PORTER; MEREDITHS: William MEREDITH, Rezia JARVIS; ADKINS: William COOK, Jeffery JOHNSON; HUMPHRISS: James BRYSON, Stephen K. SMITH: LOVILLS: Jesse BUMPS, Enoch STONE; GAINES: James GAINES, Reubin GEORGE; BEASLEYS: James MARTIN, Reubin DODSON; McANALLYS: Charles McANALLY, James COFFEE; HUGHLETTS: William HUGHLETT, Charles VEST; GLENS: Thompson GLEN, John Thomas LONGINO; SHOUSES: Jacob BLUME, Joseph BITTING: HILLS: Jos. WINSTON, John COOLEY; BOSTICKS: Absalom BOSTICK, Joseph VAUGHN; LADDS: Constant LADD, Archibald CAMBELL; COLVARDS: Henry SPEER, Geo. KIMBROUGH.

Last Will and Testament of Thomas PETTIT, deceased; oath John SHORES; Admr. granted to Rachael PETTIT, widow and relict of said deceased; Isaac ALLEN and Wm. COOK, Esqrs. securities.

Hugh McCOLLUM vs John TATE; Jury: Thomas BURCH, Reubin SHORES, James LAWRENCE, George JOYCE, Abel CARTER, William WALKER, John CRITCHFIELD, Daniel MERREDITH, Joseph READ, Thomas ISBELL, Adam MITCHELL, and Godfrey CODY.

Francis COOMBS vs James TODD; dismissed; Jeffery JOHNSON, witness for Pltf., 160 miles, 4 days; William CRITCHFIELD, 80 miles, 2 days; Zachariah WRAY, 30 miles, 1 day.

Joseph WINSTON vs David OWEN; same jury.

Stephen WILLIFORD vs John JARVIS; same jury; James RAINWATER, witness for Pltf., 12 miles, 2 days.

David OWEN vs Thomas McCARREL; same jury except William WOOLDRIDGE in room of Thomas ISBELL.

Deed from Abraham WINSCOTT and wife to George LASH; oath Allen GROCE; ordered Mary WINSCOTT relinquishment of dower in said land be taken.

Power of Attorney from Nancy CURRY to Wm. DOBSON; oath Constant LADD.

Deed from Joel GURLEY to Ratliff BOON; oath David HUMPHRIS.

Ordered William DENNY, Samuel HUMPHRIS, George WATKINS, Benja. HUMPHRIS, Jos. ASHLEY, Jesse BUMPS, Robert HARRIS, Tyree HARRIS, Isaac COPELAND, Joshua FLIN, David HUMPHRIS, Azariah DENNY, John MARTIN, Jonathan HAINES, Obed MARTIN and Icabod BLACKELAGE view road best way from Hollow Road near the LOVILLES to the Iron Works.

Ordered Wm. SWEAT overseer, road in room of Joseph WILLIAMS.

On petition sundry inhabitants Surry praying that Edmund KERLEY have leave to errect public Ferry on Yadkin River near Yellow Bank ford; ordered said KERLEY have leave to errect and keep Public Ferry at said place.

Ordered Joel CHILDRESS, orphan of Benjamin CHILDRES, deceased, who was bound to Stephen CHILDRESS, still remain in possession of Abraham CHILDRESS until next Court and said indenture cancelled.

Ordered following appointed Jurors to attend next County Court, Court House at Richmond 2nd Monday August next: William SWAIM, John DOWLIN, Micajah OGLESBY, John FLEMING, David HUMPHRIS, John BRYSON, John PIPES, Thomas SPENCE, Abraham DOWNEY, John PERSONS, James RAILEY, Jeremiah RAILEY, Airs HUDSPETH, John ARMS, William SILVEY, Anthony DEARING, John MORGAN, Charles BEASLEY, John HUGHES, Joseph EASON, Isaac GARRISON, Samuel HAMPTON, Philip GREEN,

Joe HOWZAR, John BLAKE, John LYNCH, James REAVIS, Samuel ARNOLD, Daniel SCOTT, and Valentine MARTIN.

10 August 1789

Present: William Terril LEWIS; John RANDLEMAN, Obediah BENGE, Esqrs.

Deed from George PHILLIPS to George MESSICK; oath Josiah ROTEN.

11 August 1789

Present; Joseph WINSTON, William Terrel LEWIS, Henry SPEER, Stephen WOOD, Obediah BENGE, Esqrs.

Grand Jury: David HUMPHRIS, Foreman; John FLEMING, Philip GREEN, Wm. SILVIA, John PIPES, John ARMS, Thomas SPENCE, Abraham DOWNY, John PERSONS, James RILEY, Daniel SCOTT, Valentine MARTIN, Isaac GARRISON, Joseph HAUSER, and William SWAIM.

Ordered Sheriff summon jury 12 men to view old and new roads leading from near Joices Cabbins to Virginia line.

Ordered John HASKET overseer, road in room of Richard BEASON.

Ordered West MOSBY overseer, road in room John MARSH.

Ordered Abijah OLIVER overseer, road in room of Daniel SHOUSE.

Ordered hands of John HOWARD, John PAGET, Thomas FANNON, William HOWARD, John SMALLWOOD and James TAKEWELL work under Isaac COPELAND, overseer road.

Ordered Henry COOK overseer, road in room of Joseph LADD.

Ordered Henry HAMPTON overseer, road in room of William GIBSON.

Deed from Francis CALLOWAY and wife to Isaac WINFREY; oath Caleb WINFREY.

Deed from Abraham WINSCOTT and wife to George LASH: oath Henry SPEER; also relinquishment of Mrs. WINSCOTTS Dower to 100 acres heretofore recorded May Term 1789 returned by Henry SPEER and William THORNTON.

Deed from Christophar MONDAY to Matt BROOKS; oath George LASH.

Deed from Michael and Barnabas FARR to John FARR (Fare, Fair); oath Andrew ROBINSON.

Deed from James JOHNSON to Robert JOHNSON; oath Andrew ROBINSON.

Joshua JONES of LADDS District exempt payment Poll Tax for himself 1789.

Last Will and Testament of Peter EDDLEMAN, deceased; oath George RENNIGAR; Henry SPEER. Executor quallified; Margaret EDDLEMAN, widow and relict of deceased, enters her desent to said Will and prays her thirds and dower may be laid off; Ordered Sheriff summon Jury to premises and lay off her thirds and dower according to law.

Last Will and Testament of Samuel VANCE, deceased; oath John CUMMINS and Abraham ENDLSEY, also Aley VANCE, widow and relict of deceased and John LOWRY, Executors. qualified; Inventory of Estate Samuel VANCE, deceased; returned by Executors.

Account of Sales Estate of Jacob KRUDER, deceased, returned by Administrator.

Last Will and Testament of John STRUB, deceased; oaths John DAUB and Henry SPOONHOUR; Samuel and Adam STRUB, Executors, qualified.

Inventory Estate of Thomas PETTIT, deceased; returned by Admrs.

Ordered James LAURENCE appointed Constable, HUMPHRISS District; James BRYSON and John BOSTICK, securities.

Ordered William COLEMAN appointed Constable, LOVELLS District; Joseph ASHLEY and Samuel HUMPHRIES, securities.

Joseph CREWS proves to Court that in month June last at house of Wm. DOBSON, Esq. in a fight with William CLAYTON, he the said CREWS had part of his Left Ear bit off.

Ordered Sarah BOLES in GAINES District charged with tax on 100 acres 1788 when she has none, be released from payment of same.

Manassah McBRIDE proved satisfaction of Court to be an aged, infirm person, ordered he be released from payment Poll Tax for himself in 1788.

On petition of Wm. HOLDERLEY, ordered proceeding be brought up in case of Jos. ASHLEY vs said HOLDERLEY determined before Jesse BUMPS, Esq.; Richard KERBEY was Constable.

12 August 1789

Present: Joseph WINSTON, Henry SPEER, William COOK, Wm. T. LEWIS, Esqrs.

Ordered Jacob BLUME, Henry SPEER and George HOWZAR, Esqrs. appointed committee to receive County Claims, lists of taxables, allow insolvants and lay County Tax for 1789.

Ordered William COOK, Jesse LESTER and Stephen WOOD, Esqrs. appointed committee to settle with Executors and Administrators.

Ordered William BOYLES be released from payment 1 poll for year 1788 as has son was under 21 years of age.

Ordered James ROBERTS of HUMPHRISS District be released from payment tax on 200 acres 1788.

Ordered Alexander WESTMORELAND released from payment Poll Tax for himself in future.

Agreeable order last term to bring orphan Joel CHILDRESS to Court for further direction, ordered he be bound to Abraham CHILDRESS until age 21, he being now 12 years old 22nd last March.

On petition of Reason WILLIAMS and wife Mary, ordered Sheriff summon jury to lay off Dower of said Mary of estate of James DOUTHIT, deceased, she being relict of deceased.

Joseph COLES, Executors vs Justice REYNOLDS; Jury: Micajah OGLESBY, Aires HUDSPETH, Anthony DEARING, John MORGAN, John HUGHES, John LYNCH, Joseph LACEFIELD, Elijah GALLISBY, Job MARTIN, Alexander KERR, James MATTHEWS, Edward SMITH; John TALLIAFERRO, witness for Pltf., 350 miles, 12 days.

William BURRIS vs William ROSS; same jury.

Daniel HOUSTIN vs John ALLEN; bail for John KIMBROUGH; not tried; Thomas JINNINGS, witness for Deft. proves 240 miles, 1 day.

Robert LANIERS Executors vs Jiles HUDSPETH; not tried; John BLALOCK, witness (as he says) for Deft., 21 days, 300 miles before and 200 miles since he moved to Georgia.

On petition of John BRADLEY, Executor Terry BRADLEY, deceased, to bring up proceedings in case of Thomas McCARREL vs said BRADLEY before Joseph WINSTON, Esq.

Deed from John BLALOCK to Carter HUDSPETH; oath said BLALOCK. (2)

Deed from Peter MURPHEY to John FRANKLIN; oath Richard MURPHEY.

Deed from John BLALOCK to Thomas CLANTON; acknowledged by said BLALOCK.

Deed from John BLALOCK to Joseph HILL; acknowledged by said BLALOCK.

Deed from John LEFOY to Stephen HENDLEY; oath James LEFOY.

Deed from Moses PADGET to Nathaniel SCALES; oath John CHILDRESS.

Deed from Richard GOODE, Sheriff, to Peter FULP; acknowledged.

Deed from Gotlieb SHOBER to John RANCKE; oath Jacob BLUME.

Deed from Fredr. W. MARSHALL to Peter and Henry MOSS; oath Jacob BLUME.

Power of Attorney from John WHITEHEAD to Francis BITTICK; acknowledged by said WHITEHEAD.

Ordered road leading by Jam GOODES be turned to cross Lick Creek above Thos. GOODES Saw Mill Pond and below Thos. GOODE, Junrs. Plantation; Benjamin YOUNG, Junr., overseer.

Ordered John CARTY overseer, road in room of Darvy RYON.

Ordered Samuel HAMPTON overseer, road in room of Reuben SAMUEL.

Ordered John WILLIAMS overseer, road from Vanwords (?) Mill to Brooks road in place of Daniel BILLS.

Ordered Thos. WILLIAMS overseer, road from John WILLIAMS Mill to Richmond fork of Brooks road in place of Daniel BILLS.

Ordered William LOVE overseer, road in room of John BURCHAM.

13 August 1789

Present: Joseph WINSTON, William COOK, James BRYSON, Obediah BENGE, Esqrs.

Deed from William ALLEN to John ALLEN: oath of Jeffery JOHNSON.

Deed from John DAVIS and wife to Zaza BESHEARS: oath William GIBSON.

Bill of Sale from Joseph PHILLIPS to Jesse LESTER: oath Edmond KERBY.

Deed from Jos. and Samuel GENTRY to John RIDENS; oath Matthew BROOKS.

Deed from Richard GOODE, Sheriff, to John Thos. LONGINO; acknowledged by said GOODE.

Also same to same.

John MEAD vs Reuben DODSON; Thomas ISBELL, witness for Pltf., 2 days, 50 miles; Ambrose GAINS, 1 day, 60 miles; John Thos. LONGINO, 2 days; Matt MOORE, 3 days, 30 miles.

The State vs Thomas FLOYD, Junr. Jury: Airs HUDSPETH, John MORGAN, John HUGHES, John LYNCH, Micajah OGLESBY, Wm. GIBSON, Richard LINVILL, John BRANSON, Matt MARKLAND, Reason WILLIAMS, George HOLCOMB, Garner TUCKER: find Deft. not guilty.

The State vs Charles CLAYTON. Jury: John MORGAN, John HUGHES, John LYNCH, Micajah OGLESBY, Wm. GIBSON, Richard LINVILL, Richard HORN, Anthony DEARING, Reason WILLIAMS, Matthew MARKLAND, George HOLCOMB, Garner TUCKER; Thomas POINDEXTER, witness for State failed to appear.

Henry PATTILLO vs Jiles HUDSPETH; appeal; not tried; James CAMPBELL, witness for Deft., 1 day, 26 miles.

Jesse LESTER vs Bazzle RIDDLE. Jury: Charles DUDLEY, Edmond KERBY, John MORGAN, Airs HUDSPETH, Thomas McCARREL, John LYNCH, Micajah OGLESBY, Richard HORN, Anthony DEARING, George HOLCOMB, Garner TUCKER, and Reason WILLIAMS.

Peter DALEY, witness for MARKLAND, 40 miles, 2 days. (This is recorded here by itself, rta.).

Hugh ARMSTRONG, Esq. produced commission from his Excellency, Samuel JOHNSON, Esq., Governor of this State, appointing him Sheriff of this County; John BOSTICK and Martin ARMSTRONG admitted as Deputies; said Sheriff objects to the sufficiency of the Jail.

Account settlement estate of James DOUTHIT, deceased; returned by committee. Reason WILLIAMS, who intermarried the widow of James DOUTHIT, deceased, publicly assumes to maintain the children of said deceased without any expence to Estate of Orphans.

Account settlement Estate of Elisha DODSON returned.

A Marriage Covenant between Abraham CRESON and Mary LEWIS; oath of Henry SPEER.

Ordered Richard KERBY released from payment one Poll Tax 1789 on account of his son being under age when given in.

Ordered John COOK exempt payment Poll Tax for himself in the future.

Ordered John LYNCH has leave to keep Tavern at his now Dwelling House; William THORNTON, security.

Ordered Jesse LESTER has leave to keep Tavern at his house, Jo WILLIAMS, security.

Ordered William HOLDERBY has leave to keep Tavern at his house in Richmond; William MEREDITH and John CHILDRESS, securities.

Ordered Benjamin HUDSPETH overseer, road from fork near Capt. COLVARD and across Yadkin at HUDSPETH Ferry; thence to Speers Bridge on Deep Creek and following hands work under overseer: Jiles HUDSPETH, George HUDSPETH, Benjamin ARNOLD, Dudley PORTER, George HEAD, John CARTER, John COE and Abraham CRESON.

Ordered Francis POINDEXTER overseer, in room of John SATER.

Ordered Edmund KERBY, Joseph PHILLIPS, Senr. and Daniel SCOTT appointed Patrollers of Capt. HUGHLETTS District.

14 August 1789

Present: Joseph WINSTON, William MEREDITH, James GAINES, Esqrs.

The Governor in behalf of Richard GOODE, late County Treasurer vs John MORGAN and securities, Collector for 1788.

The Governor vs John COOLEY and Securities, Collector 1788.

The Governor vs Joseph ASHLEY and Securities, Collector 1788.

The Governor vs Charles BEASLEY and Securities, Collector 1788.

The Governor vs Stephen K. SMITH and Securities, Collector 1788.

Same Jury all cases: David BLACKWELL, Alexander MOORE, Robert HARRIS, Samuel HUMPHRISS, William HARRISON, Matthew BROOKS, James MATTHEWS, John ARMSTRONG, Aires HUDSPETH, William WEBB, William HOLDERBY, and Thos. FLOYD.

Inventory Estate of Michael HOWZAR, deceased; returned by Execrs.

Court appoints Collectors year 1789: HUMPHRISS District: James LAURANCE; GAINES: James GAINES; LOVELLS: Joseph ASHLEY; BEASLEYS: Charles BEASLEY; MEREDITHS; Rezia JARVIS; ADKINS: Jeffery JOHNSON; SHOUSES: Joseph BITTING; HILLS: John COOLEY; BOSTICKS: William WALKER; LADDS: Andrew ROBINSON; COLVARDS: John Thomas LONGINO; GLENS: same; SANDERS: John WRIGHT, Junr.; LEWIS; Isaac SOUTHARD; McANALLYS: John EVANS; HUGHLETTS: Joseph BITTING: EDWARDS: Joel MACKEY.

Ordered Henry SPEER, William COOK, Zachariah RAY, Constantine LADD, Joseph WINSTON, Charles McANALLY and John Thomas LONGINO appointed Jurors to serve next Superior Court of Law and Equity at Salisbury for District of Salisbury 15th September next.

Ordered William SPARKS, Ambrouse BRAMBLETT, Charles SMITH, Obed BAKER, Joseph ASHLEY, Isaac SOUTHARD, Lewis ELLIOTT, Moses WOODRUFF, Moses AIRES, Richard MURPHY, Richard HORN, Joshua FREE-MAN, Thomas EAST, Michael HOWZAR, John KROUSE, Leonard DAVIS, Wm. HUTCHERSON, Wm. WALKER (Evans Creek), Frederick LONG, Samuel HAMPTON, Charles BEASLEY, Hardy REDDICK, Matthew BROOKS, Joshua CRESON, Benjamin SPEER, Richard COCKS, Henry HAMPTON, William LAIN, Thomas BRIGGS and Lemuel SMITH appointed Jurors next County Court, Richmond Court House 2nd Monday November next.

Account Insolvants allowed several Collectors 1788; BOSTICKS: John MORGAN; MEREDITHS: John BOSTICK; SHOUSES: Michael HOWZAR; GAINES: Ambrouse GAINS; EDWARDS: Joseph PORTER; LOVELLS: Jos. ASHLEY; HUMPHRESS: Stephen SMITH; HUGHLETTS: Thomas GORDON; McANALLY: John EVANS; HILLS: John COOLEY; LADDS: Andrew ROBINSON; ATKINS: Jeffrey JOHNSON; COLVARDS: John Thomas LONGINO.

Following Releasements allowed at several courts; returned with Insolvants: John BOSTICK, error in his former Insolvant list; Gideon EDWARDS, error in acreage; Thomas RING, 300 acres; John WELLS, 1 poll; David RIGGS, 300 acres; John WELLS, 1 poll; David RIGGS, 300 acres; Abner BARNS, 1 poll, 50 acres; Henry TILLEY, 305 acres; Sarah BOLES, 100 acres; Mannassah McBRIDE, 1 poll; William BOYLES, 1 poll; James ROBERTS, 200 acres; James WRIGHT, 500 acres; Michael HOWZER, Collector for errors in lists.

Committee appointed to receive County Claims, List Taxables, Allow Insolvants and Lay County Tax for 1789 make following report: John GILES, warning part of SHOUSES District, attendance as Constable at November and February Courts; Wm. T. LEWIS, Juror September Superior Court; John RANDLEMAN, Juror March 1789 Court; Richard GOODE, Sheriff Exofficio service 1788 and 1789; James COFFEY, Constable attending Courts 1784 and 1785, warning Mc-ANALLYS District 2 days 1788 and 2 days 1789; Joseph PHILLIPS, serving Juror September Superior Court 1788, Ticket to issue Michael HOUZAR; Rezia JARVIS, warning MEREDITHS District 1789; Job MARTIN, Juror September Court 1788; William MEREDITH, Juror September Superior Court 1788 and March 1789; Wm. T. LEWIS, Juror September Superior Court 1784 for Wm. MEREDITHS use; Thomas POINDEXTER, Juror March Superior Court 1783 for Wm. MEREDITHS use; Zachariah RAY, Juror September Superior Court 1788; William COOK, Esq. Juror September Superior Court 1788; Stephen SMITH, Constable August Court 1788, warning HUMPHRISS District 1789; Joseph PORTER, Constable EDWARDS District 1789; John ARMSTRONG, Juror Superior Court; Thomas OWEN, making and putting on two pair handcuffs on John WILLIAMS and Robert BRIGGS; Henry SPEER, Juror March Superior Court 1789; Archibald CAMPBELL, Constable LADDS District 1789; John COOLEY, Constable attending November 1789 and February, May and August 1789; Philip GREEN, who acted Constable carrying Powel VAUGHN to Jail 3 years ago; Jos. BITTING, Constable carrying Daniel BAZDEL to Richmond Jail, attending May Court 6 days, warning

SHOUSES District; Thomas LOW, Constable attending Court 3 days February 1789; Jeffrey JOHNSON, Constable ADKINS District 4 days; William THORNTON, 2 books purchased for use Registers office; John Thos. LONGINO, Juror September Superior Court 1788, Constable August and November 1788 and February, May, August 1789, warning GLENS District at present; Jesse LESTER, mending and raising Court House Floor, underpinning, making steps. sweeping and finding candles two years, mending lock, making a chair, making and mending windows; James COFFEE, attending on Committee; Lewis ELLIOTT, Juror March Superior Court 1789 for use of Joseph WILLIAMS; Joseph WILLIAMS, Clerk for making out alphabetical lists taxable property for years 1785, 1786, 1787, 1788; Committee allowed what they call a State Charge: John COOLEY, Constable serving State Warrants on BRIGGS, John WILLIAMS and Clabourn GENTRY and taking them to Justice; Matthew BROOKS, furnishing COOLEY necessaries when in pursuit and return of being after John WILLIAMS; Ambrouse GAINES, conveying three prisoners with a guard to Salisbury Jail; Guards: Augustine SAMUEL, Thomas MOSBY, David FLINT, Samuel SCOTT, Edward COOLEY; Jacob BLUM, diets and lodging the prisoners one night with guards; Richard KERBY, conveying William DALTON to Salisbury Goal from Hugh ARMSTRONGS, Esqrs., committed for Horse Stealing; Charles VEST, carrying John LYNCH to Salisbury Goal 1786; Committee also Lay County Tax 1 shilling on each Poll, four pence each 100 acres land: James WRIGHT, overtax; John CUNROD, duty on 200 pounds worth of goods; Abner BARNES in McANALLYS District poll tax 1788; Nancy DODSON, same district, tax on 100 acres; William BOYLES, one Poll Tax; Gideon EDWARDS, tax on 5,000 acres; David RIGGS, tax on 300 acres.

9 November 1789

Present: Jesse LESTER, Esq.

10 November 1789

Present: William HUGHLETT, John RANDLEMAN, Jesse LESTER, Esqrs.

Wallace ALEXANDER, Esq. produced Commission from Hon. Judges Superior Court authorizing him to practice as an Attorney. Clerk of Rowan County having certified his taking several oaths, he is admitted to practice in this Court.

Robert WILLIAMS, Esq. appointed Protem Attorney for State in absence of Nathaniel WILLIAMS, Attorney.

Grand Jury: Matthew BROOKS, Foreman; Charles BEASLEY, William WALKER, Charles SMITH, Obediah BAKER, Joseph ASHLEY, Moses WOODROUGH, Michael HOUZAR, Thomas EAST, John KROUSE, William LAYN, Richard COX, Joshua FREEMAN, Joshua CRESON, Ambrose BRAMBLETT.

Last Will and Testament of Margeritt Barbary HAUN, deceased, by oath of Jeremiah ELRODE; Michael VOGLER, Executor, quallified.

Bill of Sale from Amos LONDON to John LONDON; oath Jabez JARVIS.

Deed from Isaac WILLIAMS to Owen WILLIAMS; oath Micajah WIESNER.

Deed from Isaac WILLIAMS and wife to Micajah WEISNER: oath Thomas MORGAN.

Deed from Joshua MIZE and Martha MIZE to John COPELAND; oath Rich. WOOTEN.

Robert SIMINGTON vs Richard BLALOCK, bail for James KELL. Jury: Wm. SPARKS, Richard HORN, Leonard DAVIS, Benjamin SPEER, Thomas BRIGGS, Wm. CHILDRESS, John HUGHES, Thomas GOODE, Jonathan VERNON,

Malcum CURRY, Jno. BLAKE and James BOLES.

Matthew MOORE, Esq. vs James LAWRANCE; same jury; John HUGHES, witness for Pltf., 120 miles, 5 days.

11 November 1789

Present: Richard GOODE, William T. LEWIS, Henry SPEER, Esqrs.

John SUMMERS records his mark.

Ordered Henry STARR overseer, road in room Matthew ESTERLINE.

Ordered Philip ROTHROCK overseer, road in room of Jacob BEROTH.

Ordered John MORGAN, William WALKER, William SOUTHERN, Reuben SOUTHERN, Boaz SOUTHERN, John WEBSTER, Joseph VAUGHN, Jonathan VERNON, Jr., and John DAVIS view and mark road from Rockingham County line into McANALLYS road and William WALKER, overseer.

Elisha SIMMONS vs John GLEN; nonsuit; Jury: Richard HORN, Leonard DAVIS, Benjamin SPEER, Thomas BRIGGS, Robert CLARKE, Airs HUDS- PETH, Joseph EASLEY, William BURRIS, John SHELTON, John HILL, James BOLES, and Isaiah COE.

Robert WALKERS Executors vs Jesse KNIGHTON; same jury; new trial granted.

Jesse MAUPIN vs John SHELTON; same jury except William SPARKS in place of John SHELTON.

Samuel CUMMINS vs William SHEPPERD, bail for Hezekiah ROBERTS; same jury; appeal granted.

ALLEN & POINDEXTER vs William SHEPPERD, former Sheriff, bail for David GORDON; same jury; David POINDEXTER, witness for Pltf., 115 miles, 67 days.

Howell HARGROVE vs Arthur TATE; same jury.

Petition of Thomas McCARREL, ordered proceedings in case of Benj. TROTTER vs Thomas McCARREL tryed before William DOBSON, Esq. and returned by Archibald CAMBELL, Constable and Thomas PETTIT, security; prosecute with effect.

Admr. Estate of George SHULTZ, deceased; granted Jacob SHULTZ and Gotleap RANK; Jacob BLUM, security. Inventory and Account of Sale above estate, returned.

Inventory Estate of John STRUB, deceased, returned by John and Adam STRUB, Executors; ordered perishable part of estate be sold.

Last Will and Testament of Thomas GOODE, deceased; oath Andrew ROBINSON; Richard and George GOODE, Executors, quallified.

Last Will and Testament of Hugh DENNUM, deceased; oath Charles McANALLY; Isaac CLEMENTS, one Executor quallified.

Ordered Charles McANALLY, James GAINES and John RANDLEMAN, Esqrs. appointed committee to settle Intestate Estates.

Jesse HORN in ADKINS District, failed to give his taxable property of 1 poll, 100 acres.

Ordered Reason WILLIAMS who intermarried Mary DOUTHIT, widow and Admrx. of James DOUTHIT, deceased, enter into new security for said Admr. and said REASON did.

Deed from John SCHAUB to John SCHAUB, Junr.; oath Jacob BLUME.

Deed from John McBRIDE to John TRUITT: oath Francis POINDEXTER.

Deed from Benjamin YOUNG to Benjamin YOUNG, Junr.; oath Richard GOODE.

Deed from John GOODE to Richard GOODE; oath William JEAN.

Deed from Lazerous TILLEY to Jesse SIMMONS: acknowledged.

Deed from George PRIDDY to Thomas GARNER; oath Argee GARNER.

Deed from Toliver DAVIS to Thomas GARNER; oath William COLVARD.

Deed from Toliver DAVIS to Argee GARNER; oath William COLVARD.

12 November 1789

Present: Henry SPEER, Jacob BLUME, Thompson GLEN, Esqrs.

Ordered Abraham STINER has leave to keep Tavern at his dwelling house in Bethabara; Jacob BLUME, security.

Deed from John HARVEY and wife to Joseph HALL; oath William THORN-TON.

Deed from Richard GOODE, Sheriff, to John Thomas LONGINO; acknowledged.

Bill of Sale from John GALLOWAY to Judith GALLOWAY; acknowledged.

Ordered John BRYSON overseer, road in room of Charles SMITH.

Robert LANIERS Executors vs Jiles HUDSPETH. Jury: William SPARKS, Leonard DAVIS, Benjamin SPEER, Thomas BRIGGS, Blunt GARRET, William BURRIS, Windle KROUSE, Joseph PHILIPS, Charles VEST, Henry BANNISTER, George SPRINKLE, and John JACKSON.

John MEAD vs Reuben DODSON, Deft. prays writ of error granted; Job MARTIN and William MEREDITH, securities.

Additional Inventory Estate of Terry BRADLEY, deceased, returned by John BRADLEY. Report committee settlement Terry BRADLEYS estate was returned.

David DAVIS of HILLS District failed to give in his taxables, 1 Poll, 177 acres.

Ordered Amasa DEAN, orphan of John DEAN, deceased, be bound to Joseph GENTRY until 21 years old, now aged 15 years 25 December next to learn Art and Mistry of Planter.

James DOWNEY resigns as Constable; Daniel LESTER appointed Constable; Jesse LESTER and James GAINES, securities.

13 November 1789

Present: William Terril LEWIS, Henry SPEER, Jacob SHEPPERD, Esqrs.

Ordered James LAWRENCE appointed Collector HUMPHRISS District.

Ordered Thomas MASON appointed Constable; Henry SPEER and John WILLIAMS, securities.

Ordered Samuel EDGEMAN bring next Court Silvia LOVILL, an apprenticed Girl bound to him so she may be dealt with according to law and Supen. Sarah HOLT, Matt BRIDGEMAN and Susannah GAINES in behalf of Orphan.

Ordered George KIRKMAN, guardian to John THOMPSON, orphan of John THOMPSON, deceased; Matthew BROOKS and John LYNCH, securities.

Copy order of Superior Court signed by Robert MARTIN presented; oath of Wm. MEREDITH and Henry SPEER that they believe to be hand said MARTIN.

Affidavit Jane SCOTT proved by oath Obediah Martin BENGE who swears he saw her sign freely; certificate also proved by oath

Wm. MEREDITH that he drew an original and this is true copy.

Admr. Estate of William WOOD, deceased, granted Jacob McCRAW, Hugh ARMSTRONG and William ARMSTRONG, securities.

Admr. Estate of Keziah DEAN, deceased, granted John DEAN who quallified; Joseph GENTRY and Job DEAN, securities.

Ordered Alexander MOORE of McANALLYS District is admitted to give in 350 acres, one Poll taxables.

William HUGHLETT vs Matthew MOORE. Jury: William SPARKS, Benjamin SPEER, Thomas BRIGGS, Obed HUDSPETH, James REAVIS, Windle KROUSE, Francis POINDEXTER, Richard HORN, Edmund KERBY, Lewis WHEALIS, Isaiah COE, and Reuben SHORE.

Lindsay CARLTON vs Justice REYNOLDS; same jury except David COOK in room of Frank POINDEXTER.

State vs John BOLES; Elizabeth POINDEXTER, witness for State, 4 days; John MEAD, 5 days.

Bill of Sale from John BREAM to Benjamin WATSON, oath Drury WATSON.

Deed from William WEBB to Samuel ERNEST; oath Ambrose GAINES.

Petition George KIRKMAN to appoint commissioners to divide 2/3 real estate of John THOMPSON, late of this county, deceased, between his two sons, Silvester and John, the dower of said land being heretofore laid off; ordered William THORNTON, Samuel MOSBY, Matthew BROOKS, John LYNCH, and John HARVEY, appointed.

Ordered John WILLIAMS (LT) be released, his being bound to Peace heretofore by John GOODE.

Andrew ROBINSON, Collector LADDS District made his return; Johnson CREWS and William CLAYTONS lands for taxes 1788-1789.

14 November 1789

Present: Henry SPEER, James GAINES, Wm. HUGHLETT, Wm. MEREDITH, Esqrs.

John MRAD vs Reuben DODSON; ordered DODSON not to pay for witnesses.

Ordered Giles HUDSPETH, George HUDSPETH, Joshua CRESON, John JOINER, John COE, Francis POINDEXTER, Benjamin SPEER, Charles HUDSPETH, Benjamin HUDSPETH, Samuel MOSBY, Thomas MOSBY, John CARTER, Henry PATTILLO and Henry SPEER view road from Speers Bridge on Deep Creek across at HUDSPETHS Ferry; thence into Salem road; Report returned of Jury appointed view old and new roads leading from near Joices Cabbin to Virginia line; Old Road is best way.

Ordered following attend next County Court as Jurors: William HARVEY, John HARVEY, John LYNCH, Airs HUDSPETH, William ELLIOTT, Frederick LONG, Thomas ALLEN, Aron MOORE, Nathaniel MORRIS, Isaac SOUTHARD, John PIPES, John ARMS, Wm. SILVIE, John SUMMERS, Joseph CLOUD, Samuel HUMPHRISS, Jacob McCRAW, Wm. ARMSTRONG, Valentine MARTIN, Joseph PHILLIPS, Henry WAGGONER, John MORGAN, Nicholas HORN, Andrew McKILLIP, Joseph NELSON, Frederick SHOUSE, William WEBB, Charles LAY, Younger BLACKBURN and Richard MURPHY.

INDEX

ABBERT, Geo.,044
ADAM, Robert,142
ADAMS, John Sr.,073
    , John,084,091,108,119,123
    , Richard,127 ,137
ADAMSON, Enias,141
ADDAMS, John,084
ADDAMSON, Enos,141
ADDIMAN, Thomas,013,038,052,053,
    089,118,132,136
    , Thos.,079
ADDIMON, Thomas,057,071
ADKIN, ,093
ADKINS, (Dist),088
    , ,072,109,115,116,117,118
    ,123,159,164,165
    , William,059,072,077,082,
    129,138
    , Wm.,033,070,103,120
ADLOMS, William,123
AHEART, Michael,157
AIRES, Elihu,117
    , Moses,164
AIRS, Elienor,090
    , Elihue,119
    , Henry,030,051,058,157
    , Nathaniel,090
    , Robert,052
ALBERTY, Frederick,071 ,146
    , Fredrick,062
ALDERSON, Benedic,079
    , Benedictus,009
    , Benjamin,054 ,059,081
    , Bennedick,059
ALDRIDGE, Daniel,098
    , Delilah,098 ,142
    , Elizabeth,098
ALEXANDER, Angus,004
    , Jesse,004
    , Wallace,165
ALFORD, Wm.,126
ALLAN, Wm.,149
ALLEN, ,166
    , Adnirum,016
    , Benjamin,034
    , Charles,004
    , D.,003
    , Daniel,106 ,129
    , David,036,051
    , Isaac,110,159
    , John Jr.,110
    , John,010,023,029,032,049,
    051,060,071,092,107,
    110,111,112,116,121,
    122,123,132,138,140,
    143,145,157,161,162
    , Joseph,047 ,106
    , Nathan,061 ,078,080,093
    , Thomas,030 ,116,157,168
    , William,111 ,138,162
    , Winneford,093
    , Winniford,131
ALLIN, ,005
    , Adnorirum,006
    , Adornirum,006
    , Benjamin,034
    , David,034,052,053,054,055
    ,067,072,087,56
    , John,021,028,029,053,058,
    062,070,078,080,087,
    096,099,102
    , Mary,028,078
    , Nathan,064 ,067,076,079
    , Valentine,054
    , Winneford,067,068,079
ALLINS, John,073
    , Volentine,096
ALTUM, Ann,065
    , Spencer,065
AMY, William,007
ANDERSON, Benjamin,054
    , John N.,087 ,121
    , John,137 ,154,156,158
ANGEL, Charles,153
    , James,120
    , Lawrence,120,153
    , Sebella,120
ANGLE, Charles,041 ,079,084,088,
    103,105,133
    , John,109,132
    , Laurence,055
    , Lawrence,057,084,088
ANGLES, Charles,036
ANTHONY, John,120
    , Thomas,050,052,053
APLING, Joel,144
APPERSON, William,042
APPLETON, ,066
    , John,019 ,047,050,060,
    076,078,081,086,092,
    095,096,138,148,149
ARMS, John,159 ,160
ARMSTRONG, (Colo.),083
    , Hugh,010,023,025,026,
    027,030,042,044,047,
    053,054,057,070,088,
    089,093,100,104,105,
    106,116,121,131,133,
    137,141,156,158,163,
    165,168
    , James,026,088
    , Jno.,134
    , John(Maj),019
    , John,003,004,005,006,
    041,045,061,062,067,
    071,082,083,108,111,
    113,116,123,131,133,
    134,135,154,163,164
    , Mark,035,050,057
    , Marten,004
    , Martin(Colo.),031,046
    ,049

ARMSTRONG, Martin,004 ,005,012,
    013,023,025,027,028,
    030,031,037,038,041,
    042,043,044,045,046,
    047,049,050,051,052,
    057,063,076,078,080,
    081,082,083,084,085,
    088,089,091,094,096,
    097,100,101,102,104,
    106,108,109,110,114,
    119,120,127,130,137,
    140,141,147
    , Martin,148 ,149,150,
    151,153,154,158,163
    , Richard,123
    , Robert,046
    , William,035 ,098,106,
    151,168
    , Wm.,147 ,150,168
ARNEY, Catharine,101
ARNOLD, Benjamin,163
    , Henry,136 ,141
    , John,125
    , Samuel,023 ,028,033,137,
    160
ASH, Samuel,027
ASHBY, Jo.,123
ASHE, Samuel,124,156
ASHEST, William,149
ASHLEY, Jo---,139
    , Jos.,159,161,164
    , Joseph,071 ,074,080,101,
    116,125,129,146,149,
    161,163,164,165
ATKINS, (Capt),057 ,070
    , (Capt.),082
    ,136,146,149,164
    , Capt.(Dist),074
    , William,057,130,132
    , Wm.,133
AUGUSTUS, Cesar,072
AUSLETT, Isaac,137
AUST, George,086,101
    , Gottfrey,151
AUSTIN, Isaac,093
AUSTON, Isaac,138
    , Valentine,003
AVERY, W.,001 ,002
AWLS, William,002
AYERS, (Mrs),034
    , ,034
    , Elihu,085,117
    , Elihue,142
    , John,086
    , Moses,100
    , Robert,016 ,017,021,027,
    029,032,034
AYRES, (Capt.),045
    , (Capt.),050 ,041
    , (Dist),034
    , Eleanor,073
    , Elihu,109,111,117
    , Henry,032
    , John,137
    , Joseph,032 ,058,101
    , Moses,065
    , Nathaniel,117
    , Robert,022 ,030,032,035,
    038,039,044,046,054,
    095,108
    , Thomas,087
AYRS, Robert,012
BACIN, Michael,030
BACON, Michael,030 ,033,034,037,
    040,041,061,093,095,
    107
    , Micheal,039
    , Thomas,082
BACONS, Michael,030
BADGET, James,024 ,026,034,037,
    039,040,045,050,052,
    053,077,078,107,108,
    111,125,134,135,150
    , John,136
BADGETT, James,019 ,076,086,089,
    152,153,156
    , John,070
BADGIT, James,014
BAGGE, Tragott,010 ,043,060,073
    , Traugott,023,042,044,045,
    046,047,049,050,053,
    054,057,060,079,088,
    090,091,092,095,101,
    103,143
    , Traugotte,076
    , Traygott,044
BAGGET, James,012
BAGGETT, James,014
BAILES, Daniel,082
BAILEY, Daniel,071
    , John,155
BAILS, Daniel,072
BAKER, Anna,035
    , Christian,050
    , David,117
    , Francis,040 ,044,051,089,
    56
    , Henry Jr.,135
    , Henry,050,102,135
    , Moses,012,016,017,058,064
    ,067,071,094,095,097
    ,098,101,106,112,129
    , Obed,140,144,153,164
    , Obediah,133 ,144,165
    , Wm.,054
BALDRIDGE, Jane,054
    , Wm.,054
BALDWIN, James,086
    , Thomas,027
    , Zeanos T.,087
    , Zeanos,030,032,051,061,
    064,066,088,090,092,
    093,096,101,107,146

BALDWIN, Zeanous,081
    , Zeanus,117
    , Zenas,104 ,114
    , Zenos,112 ,114,115,116,
    121,128,146
BALES, Wm.,146
BALEY, Gamaliel,073
BALKIUM, Thomas,071
BALL, Edmond,067
    , Spencer,020 ,023,048,126
    , Thomas,148
BALLARD, David,082 ,084
    , Mereman,100
    , Moreman,082,084
    , Thomas,025,026,082,107,
    110
BALLINGER, Jacob,132
BALWIN, Zeanos,078
BANNER, Benj.,038
    , Benjamin,059,139
    , Ephraim,059,100,106,138
    , Ephram,106
    , Henry,098 ,125
    , Jo.,114
    , Jos.,015,059,121
    , Joseph,014 ,023,037,038,
    052,082,087,094,095,
    096,114,118,124,125,
    138,147,148
BANNISTER, Henry,100,107,131,167
    , Mary,127
BARBAUGH, William,019
BARNARD, Francis,072,090,145
    , Trustam,090
    , Trustum,018,021,090
BARNES, Abner,165
    , James,158
    , Wm.,158
BARNET, Thomas,090
BARNETT, Charles,133
    , Thomas,063
    , Thos.,064
BARNITZ, Charles,136
BARNS, Abner,157,164
BARRAT, Abigail,004
    , John Sr.,004
BARRET, Joseph,109
    , Nathaniel,004
    , Sarah,003
BARRON, Thomas,028
BARTON, Henry,021
BARWONGER, John,140
BASKET, Jesse,103
BASS, ,067
    , Matt.,025
    , Matthew,007 ,010,019,021,
    025,033,039,043,067,
    068,070,087,088,098,
    107,108,114,127,56
BATES, William,075
    , Wm.,158
BATTEN, Stephen,044
BAXTER, Barnabas,016
BAZDEL, Daniel,164
BEAKET, Nicholas,012
BEALS, Barbara,052
    , Daniel,121
    , Mary,069
    , Matthew,069
    , Thomas,121
BEAN, Jno.,134
BEASLEY, ,157 ,159,164
    , Charles,127,146,159,163
    ,164,165
    , Richard,122
BEASON, Amaziah,141
    , Richard,138,160
    , William,021
BEATS, James,143
    , Mary,043
    , Matthias,043
    , William,143
BEAZLEY, ,136
    , Charles,129,130,132,134
    ,136,149,154
BEESLEY, Martha,033
    , Reubin,033
    , William,033
BEESON, Amaziah,141
BEIWZHAUS, George,073
BELL, Benjamin,076
    , James,076,076,110,112,128,
    132
    , William,087 ,107,120
BENGE, Obediah M.,152 ,167
    , Obediah,133 ,154,160,162
BENNET, Thomas,081
BENNETT, Benjamin,109
BENNIT, Benjamin,146
BENSON, Benj.,129
    , Benjamin,146,153
    , Chichester,065
BENTON, Jesse,001 ,002,003,005,
    039
    , Lazarous,035
BERNARD, Francis,072
BERNEY(?), William,055
BERNEY, William,106
BEROTH, Jacob,166
BERRYMAN, Chas.,123
BESHEARS, Zaza,162
BEVEHOUSE, George,069
BEVIGHOUSER, Geo.,060
BIARD(?), Thomas,019
BIGGS, Samuel,034
BILES, William Sr.,072
BILLATOR, Zebedci,065
BILLITER, Zebulan,125
BILLS, Daniel,162
    , George,117
BINGE, Benjamin,085
BINGHAM, William,095

BINGHAMAN, Thomas,086
BINKLEY, (Capt.),030
, (Dist),046
, Adam,033 ,047,141
, John,014 ,021,029,051,
110,155
, Peter,051 ,052,069
BINKLEYS, (Dist),034,054
BINKLY, John,043
BIRNEY, William,087,095
BITTEN, Anthony,138
, Bitten,129
, Jo.,154
, Joseph,133
BITTICK, Francis,162
, John,142
BITTIN, Anthony,137
, Joseph,123
BITTING, Anthony,084,101,106,107
,155
, Jos.,164
, Joseph,146,159,164
BITTINGS, Anthony,102
BITTINS, ,113
, Anthony,100
BLACK, ,119
, Adam,130
, Andrew,078 ,150
, Barbara,010
, George,013 ,071
, Jacob,010,013,095,140
BLACKBOURN, Ambrous,012,022,023
, Ambrouse,020,070
, Amrous,024
, Angus,030
, Augustine,025 ,034
, Younger,034
BLACKBURN, (Capt),045 ,057,099
, (Capt.),041
, (Dist),047
, ,093,102,103,107
, Amb.,146
, Ambrose,059 ,117
, Ambrous,007 ,008,012,
017,026,029,030,041,
045,046,047,057
, Ambrouse,017
, Augustine,016,019,046
,057,070,077,083,085
,121,136,149
, Auston,026
, Elizabeth,115
, John,011,017
, Newman,002
, Younger,014 ,022,027,
029,030,036,039,040,
045,047,063,069,097,
129,134,136,168
BLACKBURNS, (Capt),070
, (Dist),073 ,088
, Capt.(Dist),082
BLACKELAGE, Icabod,159
BLACKLEDGE, Icabud,113
, Jacabud,081
BLACKWELL, David,163
, James,011,032,037,038
,039,040
, John,008,040,044,054,
055,056
BLAKE, Jno.,166
, John,045,067,086,110,160
BLALOCK, John,010 ,013,015,027,
029,043,064,067,074,
075,076,078,083,119,
120,129,142,143,144,
149,161,162
, Lewis,072
, Richard,081,165
BLANKS, , Winney(Mulatto),043
BLAYLOCK, John,012 ,137
BLEDSOE, John,119
, ,103
, John,066 ,157
, Susannah,119
, William,135
BLEDSWORTH, Samuel,103
BLOOM, Jacob,059,069,070,110,113
BLOOME, Jacob,046
BLUM, Jacob,007,060,073,096,110,
113,119,125,131,137,
165,166
BLUME, Jacob,029,030,052,053,054
,055,056,057,091,094
,112,116,119,138,151
,152,154,157,159,161
,162,166,167
BLUMO, Jacob,088
BOATRIGHT, Daniel,127 ,141
, James,141
BOELING, Spence,012
BOHANNON, Andrew,002
, James,137,138
, John,091 ,131,132,144
, Sarah,113
BOLES, Alex,136
, Alex.,118
, Alexander,134,138,139,140

, Christopher,127
, James,047,138,153,155,156
,166
, John,014,083,084,112,115,
126,127,168
, Re(blurred),026
, Sarah,161,162
, Thomas,026
BOLLIJACK, John,101
BOMAN, Edward,135
BOND, Jacob,001,003
BONE, John,042

BONER, William,061 ,067
BONN, Ann Mary,157
, Anna Maria,032

, Jacob(Dr.),036
, Jacob,001,002,032,076,157
BOOLE, John,002
BOON, Ratliff Jr.,074 ,121,125
, Ratliff,121 ,125,159
, Thomas,099
BOONE, Ratliff,079
, Thomas,064 ,066,070
BOOTH, John,096
, Wm.,099
BOROTH, Jacob,143
BOSTICK, (Capt),045
, (Capt.),041,064
, (Dist),034,036
, ,093 ,103,112,116,123,
125,136,146,149,159,
164
, Absalom(Capt.),023
, Absalom,017,018,021,023
,027,029,041,042,045
,053,055,058,059,060
,062,063,070,071,079
,084,086,088,089,090
,091,093,094,098,101
,102,103,106,108,109
,110,112,115,116,118
,119,121,122,123,126
,127,131,133,134,135
,136,144,145,146,153
,154,156,159
, Absolem,010
, Elizabeth,018
, John,084 ,096,100,103,
117,123,127,130,148,
149,161,163,164
, Littlebery,023
, William Sr.,029
, William(Capt.),023
, William,020,023,034,035
,041,054,063,064,065
,068,071,084,088,096
,117
, Wm.,045,084
BOSTICKS, (Capt),057,070
, (Capt.),030 ,082
, (Dist),088
, Absalom,025 ,079,089
, Capt.(Dist),074
, Wm.,025
BOTHURNS(?), Thomas,010
BOUREN, John,073
BOWEN, Sarah,043
BOWIN, Sarah,002
BOWLES, Benajmin,023
, James,146
, John,085,086,124,144
, William,021
BOWLS, John,003,015,023,090,094
, Thomas,029
, William,003
BOWMAN, Peter,007 ,016
, Robert,007 ,098
BOYD, William,048
BOYE, Nathaniel,136
BOYER, Jacob,124
BOYES, Richard,106
BOYLES, ,003
, Eve,053
, William,010,024,053,107,
109,161,164,165
, Wm.,003,090,128
BOYLS, William,002
BRABBIN, James,111 ,119
, John M.,111
, Milley,115
, Sarah,111 ,119
, William,115
, Wm.,111
BRADLEY, Edward,044
, George,153
, John,018 ,039,059,064,
065,094,098,101,161,
167
, Joseph,107
, Len,043
, Leonard,017,055,144
, Pricilla,074
, Priscilla,077
, Terry,010 ,017,023,055,
059,064,143,161,167
, Will,062
, Willis,062,068,117,150
BRAIM, John,148
BRAMBLET, Ambrous,033 ,039,040,
041
, Ambrouse,138
BRAMBLETT, Ambrose,165
, Ambrouse,037 ,046
, Ambrouse,164
BRANCH, John,087
BRANDON, James,013
, John,065 ,096
, Mary,096
, Sarah,067
, William,065
, Wm.,067
BRANNON, William,074
BRANNUM, Benjamin,106
, Martin,117
BRANSOM, John,063
BRANSON, ,146
, John,029 ,084,088,090,
133,146,154,155,162
BRASHEARS, Robert,117
BRASILL, Samson,002
BRASWELL, Hannah,047
, John,047
, Sampson,016
BRAUGHTON, Job,148
BRAY, David,059,076,079,089,098,
100,101,107,111,115,
116,122,126,128,131,
133,138,140

BRAY, Davis,102
, William,138
BREAM, John,168
BREAZEL, Godfried,094
BREEDING, Spencer,022
, William,025
BREEDON, James,127
BRENON, Robert,098
BREVARD, John,121
BREWER, Burwell,024
, George,114
BREWERS, (Capt),014
BREZEL, Gottfrey,032
BRIDGEMAN, Matt,167
BRIDGES, Thomas,086
BRIGGS, Henry,111
, Robert,055 ,096,104,108,
128,164
, Robt.,082
, Thomas,014 ,016,017,021,
037,039,040,052,063,
094,095,100,110,121,
124,164,165,166,167,
168
, Thos.,040
BRINKLEY, (Capt.),041
, John,033 ,050,052,063,
154
BRISON, James,129 ,130
, John Jr.,066,141,148
, John Sr.,066
, John,141,148
BRITTAIN, Philip,110
BRITTEN, Joseph,112
BRITTENS, Anthony,100
BROCK, Richard,146
BRONE(?), ,055
BROOK, Matt,060
BROOKS, ,045
, Acquilla,108
, David,121
, George,129
, Mathew,125 ,138
, Matt,017,022,028,029,038
,041,046,092,160
, Matt.,048 ,067,110,114
, Matthew,005,006,010,012,
014,018,019,021,023,
024,025,026,029,031,
034,037,040,043,044,
045,046,049,050,054,
055,059,060,062,063,
066,067,068,072,077,
081,083,087,089,092,
094,095,099,105,106,
108,114,115,116,127,
128,131,136,137,140,
144,150,153
, Matthew,156,162,163,164,
165,167,168,56
, Matthews,034
, Wm.,001
BROWN, Gideon,017 ,124
, James,003,014,015,037,042
,044,066,119,120,143

, Jesse,003
, John,067,110,120,150
, Joshua,097 ,138,145
, Josiah,016 ,035
, Michael,074
, Randal,117
, Samuel,058
, Sarah,042
, William,089
BRUCE, ,118
, Charles,013
, George,071
, James,023
, Jno.,133
, John,049,051,054,055,059,
069,073,086,087,090,
092,100,103,114,115,
117,122,127,142
, Mary,023
, William,154
BRUMGER, Edward,067
BRUNSON, John,083
BRYAN, Battaly,123
, Daniel,066
, John,092
BRYANT, David,003
BRYSON, James,038 ,076,083,085,
086,089,090,108,121,
153,159,161,162
, Jno.,134
, John Jr.,090
, John Sr.,113
, John,103,105,126,140,141
,143,144,153,159,167

BUCHANNON, Philemon,147
BUFFINGTON, Joseph,039
BULLOCK, John,056 ,122
BULTSHECK, Joseph,051
BUMPS, Jesse,025,029,042,043,044
,052,070,071,072,098
,116,121,130,131,139
,144,145,159,161
, John,027
BURCH, Ben,112 ,114
, Ben.,061,073,112
, Benj.,051,098
, Benjamin,023,025,030,034,
063,069,080,106,107
, Henry,018,019,086
, John,023,024,026,034,037,
039,040,041,054,060,
061,063,064,067,069,
071,073,076,086,090,
092,094,095,102,112,
121,134,146
, Thomas,103 ,158,159

BURCH, William,023 ,029,030,055,
        115,139
      , Wm.,116
BURCHAM, Henry,147
      , John,139 ,162
BURCK, Ben.,114
      , Benjamin,029
      , John,099
BURGE, Alexander,007,114
BURGH, Woody,115
BURK, Benj.,082
      , Benjamin,014
      , James Jr.,098
      , James,050,053
      , John,026
      , Joseph,012
BURKE, David,021
      , Joseph,010 ,012,013,021,
        022,057
      , Josiah,124
      , Mary,124
      , Thomas,011
      , William,124
BURKETT, Joseph,007
BURNER, Sarah,126
BURNET, Thomas,077 ,081,086,087,
        117,118
BURNETT, Thomas,073,100
BURNS, Patrick,148
BURNSIDES, James,121,152
BURRIS, William,101
      , Jacob,158
      , Jesse,140
      , John,071
      , Martin,088 ,091,098,101
      , Nancy,140
      , Thomas,070 ,095,110,157
      , William,043,052,053,055,
        067,073,089,094,107,
        116,136,137,140,145,
        156,158,161,166,167
      , Wm.,027,068,090,106,106,
        115,122,133,149,150
BURROWS, John,082
BUSLEY, ,123
      , Charles,123
BUTLER, William,003,007
BUTNER, Sarah,043 ,089
BUTTERY, Abraham,118
BYNUM, (Capt),014
      ,017
      , Gray,002,008,014,021,024,
        029,046,057,059,069,
        071,074,082,086,089,
        099,103,124,138,142,
        153
BYRD, Robert,117
BYREHAM, John,086
CAIN, Hugh,006
      , Russell,149
      , Thomas,129
CALLEWAY, Samuel,139
CALLIHAN, William,092
CALLION, Thomas,074
CALLIWAY, James,050
      , Saml.,127
CALLOWAY, Francis,160
      , Richard,097
      , Samuel,097,101,102,115

CALVIN, John,049
CAMBELL, Archibald,090 ,131,159,
        166
      , James,121 ,153
      , William,023,053,058,059
        ,097,116
      , Wm.(Capt),046
      , Wm.,155
CAMBLE, Archibald,148 ,149
CAMERON, Isariah,066
CAMMERON, John,052
CAMPBELL, Archibald,164
      , James,162
      , William,014 ,042,052,
        118,131
      , Wm.,101
CAMPORLINS, (Capt),014
CAMRON, Ezeriah,063
CANBELL, William,061
CARBY, Joel,124
CARDWELL, Daniel,062
      , Thomas,008,009,154
CARLIN, Thomas,071 ,072,156
CARLTON, Blake,107
      , Elijah,137,142
      , Fload,107
      , John,100 ,116,125,133
      , Lindsay,119,168
CARMICHAEL, (Ford),055
      ,098,109
      , John,008,010,023,026
        ,029,065,074
      , Jos.,026,032,039
      , Joseph,021 ,026,027,
        029,035,051,054,065,
        068,143,149
      , Rebekah,065
      , Ruth,065
      , Sarah,018 ,020,021,
        029,124
      , William,005,018,020,
        033
      , Wm.,008,029
CARMICHALL, Wm.,014
CARPENTER, Matthias,153
CARR, James,118
CARRELL, George,089
CARRINE, John(?),005
CARROLL, Thomas,023
CARSON, 003,103,104,109,124
      , Capt. (Dist),088
      , James,005 ,054,055,103,
        108

CARSON, Thomas,005 ,012
CARSONS, (Capt),057,070
      , (Capt.),082
CARTER, Abel,158,159
      , Charles,066
      , Daniel,043
      , George,018 ,027,058
      , Jacob,062
      , Jno.,136
      , John,012,018,021,110,115
        ,123,134,135,142,150
        ,154,155,163,168
      , Joseph,008
      , Samuel,001 ,150,151
      , William,023,058
CARTEY, John,072,075,156
CARTY, John,162
CARVER, Anna M.,130
      , Christian,078
      , Christine,130
      , George,130
CASH, (Capt),070
      , Joshua,066
      , William,066
      , Zach,130
CASTON, Glass,072
CASWELL, Richard,006,123
CATE, Charles,003
CATES, Charles,003 ,016
CHADWELL, Lewis,044
      , John,018
CHAMBERS, Matthew,141
      , Nathaniel,120
CHAMPLIN, ?,011
CHANDLER, Daniel,014,016,020,075
        ,077,106,107,112,118
        ,120
      , John,162
      , Timothy,072
      , Willam,093
      , William,114 ,117,149,
        158
      , Wm.,070 ,112
CHAPMAN, James,072
CHARL(?), James,014
CHARLES, James,020 ,028
      , Oliver,028,132,141,150
CHARLTON, Lindsay,074
CHAVES, Elizabeth,038
      , Stephen(Mulatto),040
CHEAVAS, Stephen(Mulatto),040
CHEAVES, Elizabeth,040
CHEEK, Bartlett,145
      , Richard Sr.,072
      , Richard,005
      , William,101
CHILDRES, John,068
CHILDRESS, Abraham,142 ,159,161
      , Ann,065
      , Benjamin,156,159
      , Joel,156,159,161
      , John,008,010,012,023,
        028,035,054,059,061,
        062,065,067,070,072,
        073,080,093,100,106,
        112,132,134,135,136,
        137,145,154,162,163
      , Joseph,124
      , Matthew,109 ,158
      , Rich.,062
      , Richard,012 ,014,017,
        065,140
      , Stephen,156 ,159
      , Thomas,140 ,142
      , William,121 ,150,157,
        158
      , Wm.,143 ,165
CHILDRISS, William,124
CHIPMAN, Parris,062,120
CHITTY, Benjamin,141
CHURCH, Mary,144
      , Thomas,114
CLAMPET, Samuel,135
CLANTON, Edward,046,083,118,137,
        142,144,147,149,150
      , Thomas,024,026,063,083,
        086,137,162
CLARK, David,019,023
      , Macajah,015
      , Micajah,011 ,015,023,030,
        048,057,064,077,093,
        094,100
      , Samuel,059 ,060,063,094
      , Thomas,061
CLARKE, Ann,152
      , Boling,079 ,117
      , David,027 ,084,130
      , Jonathan,030
      , Luranny,113
      , Macajah,023
      , Micajah,023,041,043,044,
        065,078,113
      , Robert,166
      , Samuel,057 ,082,083,088,
        095,106,109,148,149,
        152
      , Thomas,056 ,080
CLASBY, Chas.,090
CLATON, Edward,062
      , William,122
CLAYTON, Charles,063,070,071,116
        ,162
      , Elizabeth,028 ,032,038
      , John,111 ,119
      , Mary,038
      , Phil,028
      , Philip,028,038,041
      , Stephen,008,010,014,015
        ,028,037,039,040,042
        ,058,065,097,134
      , William,017,028,032,038
        ,041,117,161,168

CLAYTON, Wm.,020,117
CLEAVELAND, John,110
CLEAVLAND, John,092
CLEMENTS, Isaac,166
      , Jesse,013
      , Reubin,013
CLEMMENTS, Reubin Jr.,013
CLEMMINS, Peter,117
CLEVELAND, Benjamin,144
CLIFTON, George,093
CLOUD, (Capt.),023
      , Catharine,127
      , Isaac,074,079
      , Jo.,024
      , Jos.,039
      , Joseph Jr.,012
      , Joseph,007 ,008,016,027,
        051,034,037,040,041,
        057,060,065,079,094,
        098,099,103,108,111,
        122,123,138,154
CLOUDS, ,025
CLOUS, Joseph,086
COARSE, ,107
COB, Abial,016
COBB, Abel,014
      , Abial,017,024,026,029,032,
        052,053,081
COBBS, (Capt),030
      , Wm.,111
COCHRAM, Wm.,030
COCKER, Wm.,016
COCKERAM, William,138
COCKRAM, Daniel,059,098
      , Hezekiah,117
      , Humphrey,030 ,157
      , Moses,064 ,067,069
      , William,030,168
      , Wm.,108
COCKRAN, Moses,064
COCKS, Richard,164
CODY, ,076
      , Godfrey,089 ,102,125,128,
        136,138,140,143,150,
        152,158,159
      , Thomas,003,067,069,075,076
        ,083
COE, Isaiah,142,143,166,168
      , Jno.,136
      , John,008 ,011,023,036,055,
        060,067,070,071,087,
        163,168
      , Timothy,059
COFFE, James,064
COFFEE, ---nes,006
      , James,015 ,018,024,029,
        038,040,047,054,062,
        064,068,102,108,111,
        124,132,137,139,141,
        143,144,149,150,157,
        159,165
COFFEY, James,097 ,164
COFFIN, Aaron,099
      , Seth,009,010,012,018,021
        ,052,064,069,073,086
        ,090,092,102,109,133
COGGBURN, Henry,067,068
COKER, Ann,019
      , Joseph,035
      , Robert,025
      , Solomon,016 ,035,037
      , Thomas,014 ,019
      , Thos.,048
COLBERSON, David,068
COLDEASURE, Philip,012
      , Phillip,010
COLDEASURES, Philip,012
      , Phillip,010
      , Phillip,010
COLE, Job,069
      , Jobe,139
      , John,004 ,011
      , Joseph,150
COLELEASURE, Philip,017
COLEMAN, ,007
      , Fredrick,080
      , Joseph,071,080,101
      , Peter,152
      , William,161
      , Wm.,080
      , Younger,071
COLEMANS, Younger,007
COLES, Joseph,161
COLLINS, Anthony,070,100,117
      , James,108
      , Obediah,118
      , Thomas,020,117
      , William,055
COLVARD, (Capt),163
      , 123 ,128,146,159,164
      , John B.,022,023,041,043
        ,054,070,077
      , John,014 ,025,030,034,
        045,061,081,082,087,
        099,102,103,107,117,
        123,132,139,150,156
      , William,004
      , Willliam,167
      , Wm.,078,094
COLVERISS, John,126
COLVERT, ,136
      , John,120
COLYER, John,089
COMBES, Thomas,073
COMBS, John Sr.,143
      , John,051,055,056,062,070,
        072,079
      , Lucretia,001
      , Mason Jr.,060
      , Mason,064,070,079,136,152
CONANT, Hardy,058
CONDON, James,013 ,040

CONLEY, Enoch,122
CONNEL, John,008,009,100,114
CONNELL, John,045 ,056,137
CONNELLY, David,094
CONNELY, David,117
CONNER, Lewis,014 ,016,052,072,
080,095,107,111
, William,062,118
, Wm.,049
CONROD, ,125
, John,131
CONRODE, Christian,131
COOK, (Capt),123
, (Dist),088
, ,093,103,118
, David,168
, Henry,013,014,034,048,054,
058,084,086,154,155,
160
, John,040 ,051,052,086,126,
158,163
, Joshua,086
, Nicholas,016
, Nichols,034
, Robert,020,022
, Thomas,086,100,124
, W.N.,132
, Willam N.,141
, Willam,164
, William Jr.,030 ,111,135,
155
, William N.,017,057,064,068
078,112
, William Sr.,116
, William,008 ,023,024,025,
026,030,031,032,035,
036,039,042,043,044,
050,051,052,057,061,
062,065,067,069,070,
073,074,076,077,078,
085,089,093,094,102,
103,105,106,114,115,
116,121,122,127,130,
131,132,138,144,145,
153,156,158,159,161,
164
, Winston,162
, Wm.,006 ,031,033,040,041,
045,073,084,088,092,
098,118,119,137,138,
159
, Wm.Jr.,107,108,131,134,154
158
, Wm.N.,027,074,075,076,087,
088,090,096,107,118,
120,128,143,143,146,
147,150,151
, Wm.Nicholas,014
, Wm.Nichols,023,025,027,030
045,051
COOKER, Joseph,034 ,043
, Robert,043 ,043
, William,040
COOKS, (Capt),045 ,056,057
, (Capt.),041 ,082
, (Dist),090
, (Dist.),085
, (Capt.Dist),071 ,085
COOKSEY, Andrew,034
COOLERY, John,083
COOLEY, Abraham,019
, Edward,062 ,063,083,087,
088,165
, John,014,015,018,023,025
030,034,045,054,057
063,065,070,082,083
084,088,093,103,109
117,123,123,125,133
138,144,146,149,152
159,163,164,165
, William M.,085
, William,109
COOLY, John,004
COOMBS, Francis,159
, John,56
COOMER, Richard,146
COOMES, Richard,146
COOPER, Leven,018
, Levin,041
, Thos.,117
COPELAND, Isaac,094,139,147,159,
160
, John,165
CORBIN, ,103,109
, Peter,103
CORNELIOUS, Benjamin,148
CORNELIUS, Benjamin,037
, Rowland,030
COSSART, Christian F.,104 ,129
COTTERAL, William,096
COUNCIL, Jesse,021 ,022,046,076,
113
COX, (?),059
, Frederick,003 ,008,009,028
, Fredrick,020 ,032,085
, Isham,150
, John,054 ,072,073,103,121,
137,149
, Joshua(Capt),014
, Joshua,017,021,022,034,035,
036,043,045,054,061,
067,078,079,081,083,
084,086,103,105,114,
120,134
, Mary,127 ,137
, Matthew,042,073,095,135,141

, Milly,028 ,085
, Richard,016,019,024,026,037
039,040,041,050,052
053,079,134,135,165

COYLE, James,003

CRAFFORD, David,102,129
CRAMMER, Caleb,141 ,147
, Gotlieb,131
, Gottlob,152
CRANE, John,023
CRASON, ,117
CRAUSS, William,022
CRAWFORD, William,082
, Wm.,072
CREED, Bartlett,143,145
, Bennett,135
, John,135
, Margit,135
, Matthew,135
CREEK, Bartlett,145
CRELL, Thos.,114
CRESON, Abraham,005,006,009,010,
012,013,016,017,022,
052,067,076,087,093,
153,156,157,163
, James,024
, Joshua,032 ,109,116,122,
134,164,165,168
, Thomas,035
, Johnson,168
CREWS, Johnston,135
, Jonathan,141
, Joseph,161
CRITCHFIELD, Amos,122
, John,159
, Joshua,102,138,139
, Rebekah,104,113
, William,094,124,154
,155,159
, Wm.,095,121,150
CRITENDON, John,153
CRITZWITCHER, Mary,085
, Philip,085
CROCKET, Samuel,045,047,049,118,
119,132,134,139,140
CROCKETT, Samuel,132
CROOK, William,138
CROSS, -----uel,059
, Asail,141
, Azael,124
CROUCHER, Anthony,080 ,082
CROUDER, Stephen,025
CROUSE, ,123,136
, John,013,119,154
, Windle,029 ,129,154
CROWDER, Stephen,049,055,114,136

CRUMP, Robert,034 ,086,111,151
CULCLASURE, Philip,130
CULCLEASURE, Philip,56
CULDEASURE, Philip,014
CULDEUSURES, Phillip,019
CULELEASURES, ,031
, Samuel,006
CULLEASURES, Phil,017
CUMMINGS, Samuel,006
CUMMINS, (Capt.),030
, (Dist),034
, ,034 ,132
, John,009 ,018,020,043,
054,066,080,081,083,
085,086,103,105,109,
111,112,121,138,143,
144,156,160
, Joseph,149
, Samuel,009,010,015,019,
023,024,025,030,031,
033,034,037,039,043,
044,045,046,048,050,
056,062,068,069,070,
072,081,086,088,089,
110,120,123,130,141,
150,152,154,166
CUNNINGHAM, Jane,032
, John,019,032
, Samuel,014 ,015,032,
037,093
CUNNINGHAN, Thomas,043
CUNROD, Christian,095 ,115
, John,102,103,165
CUNRODE, Christian,132
, John,138 ,155
CUNRODES, Christian,136
CUPPLES, William,124
CURD, James,113
CURREY, Malcom,081
, Malcum,005
CURRY, John,117
, Malcom,045 ,046,062
, Malcomb,072
, Malcum,005 ,012,019,023,
024,025,027,034,035,
041,050,057,069,076,
082,086,089,096,097,
098,103,105,127,130,
138,141,142,148,158,
166
, Nancy,159
CURY, Malcom,029

DALEY, Peter,163
DALTON, William,165
, Wm.,003
DAMMERSON, John,111
DANIEL, John,017,088,091,098,109

, William,020,023,036,114
DANNER, Frederick,128 ,130
DAUB, John,101 ,160
DAUSE, Matthew,135
DAVID(DAVIS), Leticia,007
DAVID, Toliver,066
, Wm.,017
DAVIS, Charles,048 ,065,069,133
, Dan,137
, Daniel,063 ,097,111,136
, David,004,007,010,063,089
,167
, Edmund,111

DAVIS, Evan,076,118
, James,007,008,052,053,055
058,073,089,090,095
101,106,121,123,131
152
, John,054,072,085,093,094,
106,112,123,131,132,
135,157,166
, Leo,152
, Leonard,065 ,138,142,164,
165,166,167
, Littisha,082
, Lutisha,085
, Matthew,008 ,074,102,107,
125,129
, Morgan,023 ,065,134
, Philip,089 ,111
, Phillip,007 ,009,082
, Samuel,069 ,075,097,137
, Stephen,115 ,131
, Thomas,030 ,063,117
, Toliver,066 ,080,087,090,
153,154,167
, William,055 ,063,121,137,
138
, Wm.,106 ,151
DAY, James,148
, Thomas,060
DEAN, Amasa,167
, Job,055 ,168
, John,055 ,129,167,168
, Keziah,126,168
DEARILNG, Anthony,019,029,035,037
039,040,041,052,083
,085,086,087,088,108
,111,129,130,134,146
,151,159,161,162,163
,56
, John,140
, Robert,085
DEATHERAGE, Arkillis,058
, Arkilus,083
, Geo.,038
, George,008 ,019,030,
037,039,041,043,045,
046,051,058,077,114,
129,152
, Jno.,127
, John,029,034,035,043
,045,052,055,067,069
,071,072,074,076,086
,091,095,096,114,115
,125,127,131,136,145

, Phil,114
, Philip,148
, Phillip,071
, Wm.,091
DEATHERIDGE, George,014,026,027
, John,016 ,026,027
DEAVENPORT, Wm.,043
DEES, Jesse,117
DEITZ, Jacob,029
DENNEY, William,043
DENNIS, Henry,154
, Richard H.,148
DENNUM, Hugh,001,032,065,166
DENNY, Azariah,150 ,159
, Azeriah,151
, Benjamin,019
, John,018,019
, Samuel,139
, William,159
DENTON, Arthur,003 ,014,016
DEPORTER, John,134
DESERN, Frederick,120 ,132
, Fredr.,043
DEVENPORT, William,142
DICKERSON, Ann,129
, Griffith,129
, Thomas,117
DICKS, Susanah,035
, Wm.,035
DIER, John,087
DILLARD, James,095
DILLEN, Nathan,056
DILLION, Nathan,062
DILLON, Nathan,002 ,006,149
, William,105
DIX, John,044
DIXON, Joseph,097
DOAK, David,119
, James,008,010,024,025,026,
027,029,032,034,045,
050,058,064,086,092,
097,103,108,110,111,
120,132,133,153
, Robert,022
DOBBIN, Jacob,158
DOBBINS, Alexander,142
, Reubin,148
, William,132
DOBSON, ,011
, Alexander,016
, Elisha,149 ,152
, Reuben,136
, Reubin,020
, William,008,009,014,020,
021,029,038,041,047,
048,049,054,057,065,
066,069,073,075,082,
085,094,095,096,116,
131,139,148,153,155,
156,157,158,166
, Williams,144
, Wm.,009,013,014,018,023,
068,074,093,099,102,
109,111,133,137,148,
156,159,161
DOBSONS, (Dist),025
DODSON, Charles,116,134,135
, Elisha,163

DODSON, Joshua Sr.,098
, Joshua,091 ,095
, Nancy,149 ,157,165
, Reuben,045 ,087,093,095,
096,107,112,149,154,
158,162,167,168
, Reubin,014 ,023,024,026,
028,030,034,035,039,
042,044,046,062,070,
094,112,146,149,159
, William,045,149
DOKE, James,014,015
DOLEN, John,054
DONALD, William,018
DONALSON, Ann,129
, Francis,129
DONELEY, John,047
DONOHO, Thomas,126
, Wm.,126
DOOLING, John,104
DOSS, Matthew,118 ,131,134,144
DOTSON, Reuben,041
DOUB, John,047
DOUG, John,090
, Marthy,090
DOUGHORDY, James,076
, Michael,076
DOUGLAS, Alexander,049
, John,066
, William,058,148
DOUGLASS, Alexander,117,145
DOUTHIT, Abram,104
, Alex,102
, Ann,079,084,128
, Isaac,084 ,110
, Jacob,128
, James,042 ,047,079,084,
128,130,156,161,163,
166
, John,079 ,084,128
, Mary,042 ,118,166
, Thomas,102,128
DOVE, Thomas,065
DOWDEN, Zephaniah,070 ,112,127
, Zepheniah,134
, Zepheriah,126
, Zephiniah,082
DOWDIN, Zepheniah,070
DOWLIN, John,159
DOWNEY, Abraham,030,093,098,116,
147,148,159
, James,077 ,144,145,146,
147,148,154,157,159,
167
, Peter,098
, Samuel,128 ,154,155
DOWNY, Abraham,160
, Peter,069,100
DOYAL, James,014
DOYL, John,080
DOYLE, James,058,081,107,119,120
125,127,133,148
, Jno.,132
, John,087,094,097,104,116,
117,119,122,140,145,
150,156
DOYLIN, John,142
DRAM, ,146
, Jacob,146
DRAYTON, Thomas,041
DROUSE, John,086
DUASE, Matthew,134
DUDLEY, Charles,029,030,040,043,
067,071,079,080,081,
085,086,105,112,115,
118,124,127,128,129,
130,132,133,139,140,
142,147,153,163
DUGGONS, Thomas,008
DUGLASS, David,114
, John,148
, William,128
DULL(DOLL?), Nicholas,010
DULL, Nicholas,135
, Nicholass,090
DUNAHOE, Thomas,093
DUNCAN, Eve,145
, James,106 ,136
, John,001
, Winnna,115
DUNLAP, James,112 ,145
, John,007,008,052,053,055
063,069,071,072,074
076,088,102,112,112
, Margeret,007
, Samuel,007
DUNN, (Colo.),044
, John,047
DUNNAGAN, Isaac,139
, Thomas,139
DUNNIGAN, John,047 ,053,158
, Thomas,018,052
, Thos.,047
DUNNIGIN, Thomas,029
DUNNINGHAM, Joseph,150
DUNTHER, James,130
DURGINS(?), John,058
DURHAM, James,100
, John,039,069,142
DURROM, John,073
DWIGGINS, John,138
DYALL, John,068
DYAR, John,090
, Samuel,020,033
DYARE, (Capt.),045
DYARS, (Capt.),030 ,041
, (Dist),034
DYCKES, Agnes,011
, John,011,042,044
DYER, John,022 ,072,121
DYKES, John,035
EASLEY, Daniel,039 ,043
, Joseph,166

, Warham,090
EASON, James,036,052,091,098,114

, Joseph,003 ,010,052,053,
063,065,071,094,095,
096,097,103,109,111,
134,147,149,159
, Mary,010,145,149,157
, Thomas,001 ,005
EAST, Isham,109,113,121
, Joseph,039,086,089,105
, Thomas,052,054,090,100,111
118,121,124,127,130
141,164,165
, Wm.,053
EASTERLINE, Matthew,101
EASTOP, Thomas,143
EASTROP, Thomas,156
EASTS, William,036
EBERT, George,050 ,052,053
, John George,051
, Martin Sr.,079
, Michael,073
EDDLEMAN, Margaret,160
, Pepter,087
, Peter,071,072,078,134,
160
EDDLEMON, Peter,128
EDGEMAN, Samuel,167
EDLEMAN, Peter,078
EDMUNDS, William,072
EDWARDS, ,146 ,149,157,159,164
, Edward,127
, Gid,152,153,154
, Giddeon,108,130
, Giddion,138
, Gideoin,111
, Gideon,064,069,075,086,
089,103,111,114,119,
129,135,136,137,142,
144,145,146,149,150,
158,159,164,165
, Priscilla,039 ,042
EKMORE, Thomas,121
ELDER, Peter,043,082
ELLESBERRY, Isaac,013
ELLIOR, William,037
ELLIOT, William,094
, Wm.,040
ELLIOTT, Ben,132,136
, Lewis,013 ,029,058,114,
116,118,119,120,121,
144,147,149,150,154,
164,165
, Mary,118
, Thomas,036,057,100,118,
126,133,136
, Thos.,132
, William, 096 ,039,064,
066,067,068,076,078,
097,098,101,107,116,
119,154,155,168
, Wm.,092,095,110,118,119
,120,121,150
ELLIS, Christopher,086 ,139
, Evan,058
, Sarah,058
ELLITT, Lewis,149
ELLROD, James,083
ELLSBERRY, John,014,023,033,041,
054,059,083
ELLSBURY, Isaac,029
, John,084
ELMORE, A.,140
, Abejah,144
, Abijah,049 ,062,113
, Elijah,119
, Thos.,018 ,121
, Thos.,144
ELROD, Adam,067,103
, Robert,008 ,009,071
ELRODE, Adam,086
, Jeremiah,165
, Peter,110
, Robert,130 ,152
, Samuel,039
ELSBERRY, Jacob,154
, John,013
ENDLSEY, Abraham,160
ENDSLEY, Andrew,009
, Hugh,009
, James,009
, Jane,009
, John,009
, Mary,009
ENGLAND, John,005 ,012,021,022,
023,033,046
, Joseph,005,012
ENGRAM, David,055
, John,150
, William,150
ENOCHS, Gabrial,136
ENYART, Silas,101
ENYERT, Abraham,055
, Silas,105
EPPERSON, Robert,077,087
ERNEST, Samuel,168
ESTERLINE, Matthew,109 ,166
EVANS, Ann,057
, David,028,095,105
, Edward,014 ,038,100
, Elijah,127
, James,071
, John,100,120,121,127,132,
146,149,156,164
, Nicholas,005
, Phil,139
, Philip,097 ,098,114
, Thomas,007 ,010,011,012,
014,020,023,029,048,
057,063,067,071,085,
087,089,097,099,101,
108,109,111,127

EVANS, Thos.,034,082
EVERTON, Thomas,072
FAGIN, John,062,074
FAIN, Charles,028
FAIR, Barnaba,144
, Barnabas,009 ,010,014,015,
112,126,131
, Barney,006
, John,122 ,143,160
, Michael,126 ,130
FANNON, Thomas,160
FARE, Archelus,044
, Archilas,044
, Barnabas Jr.,102 ,127
, Barnabas,018 ,065,102,122,
127,130
, Barnby,026
, Barney,002
, John,069 ,152,155,160
, Michael,102 ,122,130,155
, Peter,131
FARGESON, John,050
FARGISON, Rebekah,050
FARGUSSON, John,047
, Rebekah,047
FARMER, Benj.,079
, Benjamin,017
, John,069,071,094,100,134
,136,147,148,149
FARNER, Geo.,137
FARR, Barnabas,054
, Barnabas Sr.,054
, Barnabas,133 ,160
, Barnabus,106
, Barney,110
, John,079 ,148,160
, Michael,054 ,077,160
FAW, Jacob,109
FENDER, Gabrial,137
FEREE, Jacob,012
, Michael,141
FERREE, Jacob,036 ,040,134
FIDLER, Godfrey,076,116
, Gottfrey,152
FIELD, John,130
FIELDER, James,076 ,083,158
, John Jr.,037 ,039,040,
041
, Sarah,158
FISHEL, Adam,097
, John,141
FISHER, Adam,056
, Andrew,100
, Casper,014 ,022
, Elizabeth,085
, James,008 ,080
, John,072
, Thomas,008
FISKET, Adam,109
FISLER, Andrew,014
, Peter,119
FITZPATRICK, Andrew,017
, John,017 ,109
, Samuel,097,111,156
, Thomas,002,017,037,
039
FIZPATRICK, Thomas,006
FLANERY, John,004
, Thomas,003,004
FLEMING, John,018 ,034,035,050,
051,052,054,066,077,
100,103,107,112,114,
115,116,156,159,160
FLEMINS, John,023 ,057
FLEMMING, John,134
FLETCHER, John,110
FLIN, Joshua,159
FLINN, Laughlin,048,052,071,077
, Thos.,076
FLINNS, Len,037
FLINT, David,165
, John,135
, Thomas,088
, Thos.,092
FLOYD, Thomas Jr.,162
, Thomas,002 ,019,021,055
, Thos.,163
FLYN, Jacob,107
, Laughlin,088
, Theophilus,050
FLYNN, George,044 ,142
, Laughlin,051,055
, Thomas,044
, William,044 ,082,142
FOCKLE, Samuel,095
FOGLER, Samuel,131
FOLGER, Latham,012
, Lathan,010 ,090
FOLKNER, John,008
FOLLIS, William,106,114,115,123
, Wm.,115
FORBIS, Robert,023 ,026,029,052,
063,066,067,069,071,
096,106,108,110,111,
112,116,122
FORDNEY, Francis,152
FORKNER, Francis,062
, John,040 ,081,095
, William,003,060,061,133

, Wm.,003,058,059,111,144

FORRESTER, James,142
FORRISTER, John,101
FORSTER, William,005
, Francis,130
FORTNER, William,126
, Wm.,128
FOSTER, James,117 ,145
FOTH, ,125
FOUNTAIN, Stephen,063 ,120,137
FOWLER, Mary,041
, Molley,047

FOWLER, William,041,105
, Wm.,047
FOX, Samuel,109
FRANCE, Henry,054
FRANCIS, Joseph,054
, Lucee,058
, Samuel,010,024
FRANKLIN, Edmund,089
, Jesse,077,137
, John,056 ,076,162
FRAZER, Wm.,117
FREEMAN, Amos,051
, Jacob,148
, James,014 ,020,027,034,
050,052,053,094,096,
112,138,143
, Joshua,058,086,088,112,
113,121,129,164,165
, Josiah,142
, Polly(Mulatto),043
, Samuel,012,014,023,041,
042,043,053,074,130,
131,150,156
, William,024,026,027,041
,058,059,080,085,086
,087,101,130,132,155
,156
, Wm.,014,022,030,042,046
,079,083,088,112,121
,124,125,143,149,149
FREEMANS, (Capt.),023
,025 ,037
FRETWELL, Mary,061 ,066
, Samuel,066
FREY, Barbara,023
, John,071
, Michael,050 ,098,124
, Valentine,023,116
FROHOCK, Thomas,066,124
FROST, ,119,120,126
FROUSE, ,112
FRY, Henry,008 ,014,017,100,102,
105,114,138
, Michael,004,008,010,014,017
,050,063,078,081,087
,090,092,106,108,131
,138,144,156
, Michial,123
, Peter,151
, Valentine Jr.,078
, Valentine,014 ,054,078,138
FULERMAN, John,141
FULK, Adam,036 ,092,100,109,127,
141
, William,078
FULKS, Adam,109,113
FULP, George,071,106
, Michael,050 ,073
, Peter,073,102,120,162
, Valentine,072
FULPS, George,100 ,109
, Michael,112 ,144,155
, Peter,107,111,112,122,133
,137
FULTON, Francis,149
, Robert,149
FULTZ, Peter,085
FURCHASE, Tobias,140

GAINES, (Dist),044 ,088
,093,116,117,123,136,146
,149,159,161,164
, Ambrose,138,168
, Ambrous,148
, Ambrouse,147,165
, James,011 ,026,058,071,
080,082,085,090,
091,092,094,096,097,
103,104,105,108,111,
112,114,115,117,122,
127,129,130,136,137,
138,140,152,154,155,
158,159,163,164,166,
167,168
, Robert,134 ,136,138
, Susannah,167
, Thomas,085 ,086,088,108,
131,138
GAINS, (Capt),045 ,057,070,101
, (Capt.),030 ,041,082
, (Dist),034 ,073
, Ambrose,162
, Ambrouse,109,164
, James,011,016,031,033,034
,035,040,042,045,048
,051,053,060,061,072
,074,076,077,095,096
,103
, John,049
, Robert,095
, Thomas,035 ,083,086,087,
098
GALLASPY, Elijah,012
GALLAWAY, Richard,079
GALLION, Mary,020
, Thomas Jr.,137
, Thomas,007,022,052,053,
068,071,076,077,078,
102,103,114,128,130,
141
, Thos.,114
GALLISBY, Elijah,161
GALLOWAY, John,167
, Judith,167
GAMBALL, James,023
GAMBELL, James,024 ,026,027
GAMBILL, James,155
GAMBLE, James,010 ,021,099,105,
150
, William,112
, Wm.,099
GAME, John,117

GAMEL, James,069
GAMIL, James,073
GAMMEL, James,058 ,103
GAMMIL, Robert,117
GAMMON, Esaih,123
, Isaac,031
GARNAND, Adam,097
GARNER, Arge,115
, Argee,107 ,167
, John,134,140
, Thomas,167
, Wiatt,071 ,099,118
, Wyatt,016 ,018,024,030,
045,047,051,064,069,
077,087,093,141
GARRET, Blunt,167
, John,080,117
GARRETT, Isaac,125
, John,037 ,039,040
GARRISON, Elizabeth,026
, Isaac,009,012,026,048,
054,063,083,088,102
120,121,132,133,159,
160
, Issac,008
, Joseph,020,023,089
GARROT, Blont,133
GARROTT, Blunt,141
GENTRY, ,113
, Clabourn,165
, Clabourne,099
, Jos.,153,162
, Joseph,010 ,075,082,083,
084,100,102,121,124,
148,153,158,167,168
, Lucey,005
, Nicholas,068
, Sam'l,050
, Samuel,055 ,056,067,076,
078,079,080,081,086,
088,093,162
GEORGE, Jesse,021 ,058,063,151
, Reuben,021 ,022,059,063,
070,082,090,093,099,
102,107,112,134
, Reubin,018 ,030,057,059,
063,146,159
GERBER, Anna Magdalin,051
, Gerber,051
GIBSON, (Blank),061
, ,146
, Archelouis,149
, Catharine,059
, Elizabeth,038
, Garrel,019
, Garrot,124
, Garrott,149
, James,019 ,059,072,149
, John,008,059,068,099,149
, Joseph,008 ,011,037,090
, Mary,061
, Phebe,059
, Thomas,129
, William Sr.,069
, William,063,071,073,132,
133,135,146,160,162
, Wm.,061,083,133,135,162
GIDDENS, Francis,047
, Richard,075,100
, Roger Sr.,075
, Roger,062 ,076,089,100,
101,103,125,132,133,
136,141,152,154
GIDDEONS, Roger,068
GIDDIN, Joseph,108
GIDDINS, (Capt.),025
, James,024 ,048
, Roger,014 ,023,025,030,
034,057,078,094,132,
133,145
GIDDIONS, (Capt.),023
GIDIONS, Roger,044
GILBERT, John,012 ,021,039,048,
072,105
, Michael,126
GILES, John,021,022,084,091,112,
123,152,164
, Thomas,003 ,012
GILL, William,075
GILLESPIE, Elijah,156
GILLION, Thomas,063
GILLISBY, Elijah,091
GILLISPEE, Elijah,148
GIMET, James,122
GINNAND, Adam,141
GINURARY(?), Joseph,050
GITTENS, James,066 ,067
, Richard,079
GITTINS, James,034 ,055
, John,068
, Margarett,105
, Richard,105
GLADDEN, Geoard,123
GLEN, ,116,123,136,146,147,159,1
64,165
, James,010,012,012,013,016,
022,024,032,036,039,
043,067,090,152,157
, John,166
, Patience,032 ,055,059,115
, Thomas,119
, Thompson,055 ,058,059,064,
067,074,081,086,087,
088,089,103,114,116,
118,119,121,143,149,
150,152,153,155,157,
159,167
, Thompsonn,114
, Tyree,008
GLENN, ,153
, Elizabeth,131
, James,024,129,136,145,154

GLENN, Martha,131
, Nancy,131
, Patience,131
, Sarah,131
, Thompson,055,078,115,124,
128,130,131,136,143
GLENS, Hanes,125
, James,089,143,151
GLOOM(Blum), Jacob,016
GLOVER, Reuben,039 ,042
, Thomas,039 ,080,151
GOINES, Thomas,120
GOING, Joseph,061
GOOD, Richard(Major),024
GOODE, (Maj.),152
, (Major),065 ,088,100,109
, Edward,125
, George,166
, John,032,065,071,100,123,
145,152,167,168
, R.,123
, Richard(Maj.),065,084,085
, Richard,015 ,016,017,018,
019,020,023,024,026,
029,030,033,038,039,
041,042,044,047,055,
057,058,061,064,071,
081,083,084,085,088,
090,091,099,100,101,
103,106,108,109,113,
120,122,123,130,133,
137,138,141,144,147,
149,154,157,162,163,
164,166,167
, Thomas Jr.,052 ,053,081,
088,109,133,144
, Thomas Sr.,060 ,109
, Thomas,102 ,133,147,165,
166
, Thos.Jr.,148
, Thos.Sr.,088
GOODES, Jam,162
, Richard,091,102
, Thos,162
GOODNER, John,047
GOODS, (Major),026
GOOLESBY, Druary,052
GORDON & STEWART, ,014
GORDON, ,146
, David,002 ,016,043,055,
166
, Seth,060
, Thomas,123 ,149,164
GORMAN, Sarah,049
GOSLIN, Samuel,141
GR(Blurred), Zachariah,026
GRACE, George,141
GRAGG, William,143
GRAHAM, James,059 ,060,077,094
, Thomas,111 ,138,142
, Thos.,073
, William,136
GRAMMER, Caleb,133
GRANT, John,050,068,096,132
GRAVES, David(Daniel?),007
, David,023 ,057
GRAY, William H.,115
, William,009
, Wm.Hargus,023,029
, Wm.Harguss,049
GRAYHAM, James,088
, Thomas,107
GRAYHAMS, Thomas,075
GREEN, David,050
, Frederick,003,009,016
, George,047
, Jesse,052
, John,011
, Lucy,047
, Meshack,051
, Phil,057,107
, Philip,012 ,021,044,120,
121,138,159,160,164
, Thomas,067
GREENWOOD, Abner,046,061,062,063
068,080,089,090,096
,097,104,114,115,116
,118,150
, Samuel,070 ,071,134,
135
GRIFFETH, Benjamin,079
GRIFFITH, Benj.,103
, ELizabeth,012
, John,008 ,012,016
, Jonas,008
GRIMES, Thomas,097
GRINES, James,090
GROCE, Allen,152,159
, Deval,118
, George,031 ,052
, John,154
, Simon Sr.,118
, Simon,063,118
GROETER, Jacob,151
, Mary C.,151
GROSE, John,010
, Simon,010
, Simond,066
GROSS, Garret,005
, Garrot,005
, Gerrett,002
GRUDGE, Wm.,111
GRYMES, Thomas,065 ,069,138
GUILBERT, John,066
GUIN, Almon,122
, Almond,096
, Deborah,060
, Samuel,060
GUINN, Almon,024,036,084,131
, Almond,026 ,034,035,153
, D.,066
, Deborah,125

GUINN, Samuel,066 ,125
GUNSTON, James,074 ,155
GURLEY, Joel,029,126,159
GUTTERY, Charles,117
GWIN, Sarah,001
HADLEY, Eunecy,158
  , Simon,010 ,014,026,103
  , Thomas Jr.,026
  , Thomas,102 ,105,134,158
HADLY, Thomas,134
HAGAMAN, Joseph,157
HAGGARD, Samuel,006,080,138
HAGGOOD, Samuel,138
HAGWOOD, Samuel,012
HAIET, John,124,131
HAINES, John,107
  , Jon.,129,131,136
  , Jonathan,069,077,079,080
    081,088,090,091,092
    093,094,097,104,105
    108,112,114,118,120
    121,126,127,129,137
    139,145,146,149,158
    159
  , Nathan,137
HAINS, John,075
  , Jonathan,060,063,066,072,
    078,098,101,102,104
HAIRSTON, Geo.,135
  , George,148
  , Peter,091,102,109,122,
    127,131,133,145,158
HAIS, Bethany(Male),004
HAIXL, John,049
HAIXT(?), John,076
HALBERT, Joel,008 ,029,058,063,
    088
  , John,003 ,007,009,014,
    017,037,039,040,047,
    063,085,086,088,089,
    103,105,109,122,147,
    150,151
  , Wm.,079
HALBERTS, (Capt.),023
  , ,025
HALE, Francis Sr.,137
  , John,118
HALL, ,066
  , David,087
  , John,057 ,059,061,063,089,
    091,125,152
  , Joseph,167
  , Robert,063
  , Thankful,015
  , William,003 ,005,006,008,
    009,015,024,028,031,
    055
  , Wm.,003 ,008,014,015,016,
    025,027,050
HALLS, John,088,098
HAMBLIN, Job,117
HAMILTON, F.,005
  , Garden,004
  , John,003
HAMM, Jos.,133
  , Joseph,058,155
  , Mordicai,144
  , Mordical,083
  , Thomas,086,092
  , William,089
  , Wm.,086
HAMMET, Robert,080 ,089
HAMMOCK, Robert,158
HAMPTON, Collins,027,057,060,063
    066,108,127
  , Henry,020 ,023,074,087,
    098,102,111,123,133,
    134,135,137,140,155,
    160,164
  , James,017 ,020,041,046,
    047,060,082,089,092,
    095,102,109,111
  , Jamies,138
  , John Sr.,131
  , John,132
  , Preston,037
  , Samuel,114,134,135,138,
    159,162,164
  , Thomas,060
HANBY, Jonathan,089
HAND, Henry,016
HANDLAN, Thomas,114
HANDLEN, Thomas,150
HANES, Jonathan,088
HANISH, Adam,141
HANKINS, ,033
  , John,023
  , William,007,030
  , Wm.(?),006
  , Wm.,011,014
HANLIN, Thomas,119
HANN, John,029 ,033
  , Susannah,029
HANNA, John Doak,070
  , John,119
HANNAH, Andrew,021 ,023,058,099
  , Doke,014
  , John,010,012,013,018,021
    024,026
HANOM, Mordicai,109
HARBOUR, Ado.,144
  , Adonijah,051 ,070,071,
    083,088,105,108,111,
    124,132,134,135,149
  , Adonjah,087
  , Moonijah,063
HARCILLE, David,063,064
HARDEN, Wm.,120
HARDIN, (Capt),011
  , (Dist.),011
  , Mark Jr.,042,045
  , Mark,020,021,023,038,040

    ,041,042,045,046,055
    ,085,131
HARDIN, William,007
HARDING, Mark,027
HARDY, John,016
HARGROVE, Howell,166
HARKWELL, John,055
HARMOND, John,005
HARPER, John,019,031,049,056,072
    089,098,107,120,148
HARREL, Jonathan,018
HARRILL, Peter,151
HARRIS, John,032,067,108,122
  , Robert,011 ,016,020,023,
    024,027,041,043,045,
    048,053,060,068,069,
    071,076,080,082,086,
    087,094,095,103,136,
    159,163
  , Robt.,020 ,098
  , Tyree,159
  , William,148
HARRISON, Jeremiah,016
  , John,005
  , Joseph,014,048,125
  , Nathaniel,119
  , Robert ,054
  , Robert,029,039
  , William,008 ,139,163
HARROLD, John,078 ,079,095
  , Jonathan,021 ,062,067,
    082,149
HARSTON, (Major),114
  , Peter,091 ,102,109
HART, Joseph,123
  , Michael A.,119
HARVEY, John Jr.,014,051,076,083
    084,099,117,129,133
  , John Sr.,010,012,050,136
  , John,010,014,041,043,050
    051,116,117,129,156
    148,150,154,155,156
    167,168
  , Lem,118
  , Lemuel,029 ,033,068,118,
    125,128
  , Lemul,124
  , Leon,123
  , Samuel,080 ,118
  , William,095,133,148,168
HARVILL, David,118
MARVY, John,125
HASKET, John,160
HAUN, Margeritt B.,165
HAUSER, George Jr.,110
  , George Sr.,063 ,100
  , George,015 ,059,064,066,
    067,068,075,094,095,
    099
  , Joseph,070 ,160
  , Martin,063 ,064,066,067,
    068
  , Michael Jr.,070
  , Michael,059,064,099,103,
    110,123
  , Mickel,015
  , Peter,102
HAUZAR, George Jr.,044
  , George,020 ,021,022,023,
    054,056,085,093,124,
    125,151,158
  , Jo.,143
  , Joseph,124 ,154
  , Michael,079,082
  , Peter,020 ,056,079,158
HAUZER, George Jr.,126
  , George,097 ,129,136,137,
    142,151,154
  , Michael,092,097,101
HAWKINS, Alex.,065
  , Alexander,030 ,143
  , Ben,134
  , James,143
  , Joseph,014
  , Nicholas,125 ,143
  , William,063,138,148
  , Wm.,147,151
HAWKS, William,106
HAWLEY, Dice,124
  , Sheba,124
HAWN, Barbary,144
  , George,144
HAWZAR, George,041
HAY, Matthew,076
HAYBURN, John,117
HAYNE, James,141
HAYNES, Francis,055
  , Jonathan,072,087,088
HAZELET, Moses,122
  , Robert,016
HAZELETT, Moses,023
HAZELWOOD, Richard,015 ,068
HAZLET, Moses,017 ,055,091,122
  , Robert,020 ,022
HAZLETT, Moses,062 ,088,135
  , Robert,145
HAZLEWOOD, Richard,121
HEAD, George,128,132,150,163
  , William,010 ,011,020,022,
    023,025,057,127,141,
    142
  , Wm.,014 ,018,019,142
HEARNDON, Ben,113
  , Benjamin,075 ,077,081,
    088,094,115,118
HEATH, Elizabeth,132,141,150
  , John,106
  , Johnson,090 ,109,157
  , Richard,097 ,134,157
  , Thomas,013 ,064
  , William,137
HEITH, Cornelious,129

HELSABECK, Fredrick,033,063
  , Jacob,141
  , Patrick,050
HELSBECK, Fredr.,116
HELSEBECK, Frederick,040,100
  , Fredrick,033,050
  , Jacob,100
HELSIBECK, Frederick,014
HENDERON, David,117
HENDERSON, Archibald,142
  , George,138
  , John,098,105
  , Michael,054 ,055,062,
    088,093,112
  , Micheal,036
  , Michel,052
  , Samuel,039 ,098
HENDLEY, Stephen,162
HENDRICK, Henry,056
HENDRICKS, Henry,017
HENFIELD, Jo.,133
HERBEARTS, William,148
HERBST(?), Henry,020
HEREMAN, David,095
HERNDON, Benjamin,062 ,063,076,
    131
HERRIN, Delaney,033,078
HERRING, Edward,005
  , Henry,135
HERRYMAN, David,093
HESABECK, Jacob,127
HESTER, John,139
HIATT, John,082
  , Joseph,094
  , Wm.,082
HICKMAN, (Capt.),045
  , (Capt.),041
  , ,011 ,093,103,105,116
  , Eddy Sr.,016
  , Edward Sr.,034
  , Edwin,011 ,022,035,050,
    148
  , Thomas,070
  , William,023,024,026,029
    034,035,045,086,089
    136,154,155
  , Wm.,050,121,124,134,150
HICKMANS, (Capt),014,057,070
  , (Capt.),030 ,082
  , (Dist),034,088
HIDE, George,113,118
HIGHSMITH, Thomas,057 ,039,040
  , Thos.,051
HILL, (Capt),123
  , ,093,103,109,116,117,118,1
    23,136,146,149,155,1
    59,164,167
  , Barlet,124
  , Dan,125 ,152
  , Daniel,106,116,124,138
  , Dann,079
  , Isaac,112
  , Jesse,105
  , John,100 ,131,166
  , Joseph,066,162
  , Phil,102 ,104
  , Robert,002,035,069,083,084,092
    097,103,105,106,109
    154
  , William Sr.,111
  , William,007 ,020,032,059,
    106,153
  , Wm.,004
HILLS, (Capt),045 ,057,070,104
  , (Capt.),030 ,041,082
  , (Dist),034 ,054,088
  , (Dist.),084
  , Capt.(Dist),076
HINE, Jacob,107,141
  , John,053 ,069,097,124,125,
    126,127
HINMAN, William,133
HINSHAW, Joseph,129
HIRE, Rudolph,109
HOBBS, Anna,106
  , Joseph,106
HOBSON, Stephen,152
HOCKKETT, Nathaniel,011
  , Rachel,011
HODGES, Bartholemew,069
  , Barthomew,075
  , Edmund,069 ,075
HOGGALL, Rachel,011
HOL(?), ,059
HOLBROOK, George,018,021,023
  , James,079,102,122,155
  , John,084 ,133
  , Susannah,127
  , William,065
  , Wm.,127
HOLBROOKS, (Dist),026
  , ,024
  , James,155
HOLCOMB, Drury,104
  , Geo.,043 ,077,104,132,
    133,150
  , George,030,033,034,036,
    039,040,045,046,047,
    055,059,060,062,063,
    068,071,076,077,078,
    080,094,107,113,125,
    129,133,140,141,143,
    149,162,163
  , Grimes,018,081,129,152
  , John,009 ,026
  , Laurance,069 ,074
  , Laurence,073 ,074,077,
    101
  , Lawrence,121
  , Phil,030 ,034,040,055,
    097,101,117,118,120,
    128,132,133,141

HOLCOMB, Phil.,072 ,077
, Philamen,062
, Philamon,126
, Phileman,118
, Philemon,061 ,062,063,
074,077,087,096,107,
110
, Philiman,118
, Philip,011,012,033,046,
079
, Philm.,063
, Thomas,125,142
HOLDER, Charles,021,022,023,024,
044
, Geo.,124
, George,095 ,132,150
, Henry,096 ,135
, Joseph,049 ,078
HOLDERBY, William,163
HOLDERLEY, Wm.,158 ,161
HOLECOMB, Philemon,080
, Phillemon,142
HOLECOME, Phil,088
HOLEMAN, Daniel,105
HOLIMAN, William,078,130
HOLLAND, James,102
, John,044 ,157
HOLLBROOK, William,085
HOLLEMAN, William,107 ,158
HOLLEMON, William,156
HOLLIMAN, Mark,158
, William,049 ,087,148
, Wm.,116
HOLLOMAN, Wm.,125
HOLMANS, William,069
HOLME, George,107
HOLSCLAW, Henry,101
HOLT, Ambrose,136
, Edmond,008
, Edmund,080
, Francis Jr.,048
, Francis,024 ,026,049,054,
072,075,077,124,133
, Frank,060
, Molley,033
, Sarah,167
, William,024
, Wm.,033
HOLTON, Hugh,008
HOLTSCLAW, Henry,127
HONS(HANES), Mark,079
HOOF, Daniel,059
HOOPER, James,019
, Michael,107
, Richard,074
HOOSER, George,112 ,122,131,132
, Michael Jr.,147,148
, Michael,112,118,121,124,
138,141,146,149
, Peter,108 ,113,137,138
HOOTS, Jacob,083
HOPPAS, Daniel,083
, George Sr.,112
, George,137
HOPPIS, Daniel,137
, John,137
HORN, Jesse,100,124,125,130,149,
166
, John Jr.,021
, John Sr.,008 ,009,034,054,
083,086
, John,022 ,024,029,085,087,
089,090
, Michael,149
, Nicholas,059 ,107,125,154,
156,168
, Richard,017 ,023,062,063,
067,073,077,079,081,
086,087,090,112,131,
132,143,144,148,149,
154,155,156,158,162,
163,164,165,166,168
, Thos.,134
HORNE, Richard,081
HORNS, (Capt.),023
, (Dist),025
, ,025
, Richard,141 ,142
HORTON, Abraham Jr.,072
, Abraham,072
HOUSAR, George,026
HOUSE, David,091
HOUSER, George Sr.,050
, George,027
, Henry,097
, Martin,067
, Michael,026
HOUSTIN, Daniel,142,161
HOUZAR, ,011
, Geo.,054,155
, George Jr.,045
, George,042 ,043,050,051,
052,055,057,078,083,
092,136
, John,054
, Martin,016 ,054
, Michael Jr.,023
, Michael,030,078,146,155,
158,164,165
, Peter,016 ,091
HOWARD, (Wid),138
, Abraham,004,012,038,049,
052
, Ann,044
, Barna,048
, David,130
, James,035 ,043,051,074,
075,077,087,116,130,
133,138,140
, Jane (Mrs),038
, Jane,049,068,074,077,087,
116,140,150
, John,112,119,130,160

HOWARD, Joshua,106
, Lucy,087
, Mary,033
, Phil,026,050,117,123,125
, Philip,012 ,014,024,050,
082,084,086,089,106,
154
, Phillip,010
, Sarah,077
, Stanwick,153
, William,033,115,128,130,
133,140,142,160
HOWEL, David,063
HOWELL, Alse,118
, Daniel,108
, David,041 ,050,061,066,
067,068,076,083,086,
111,120,126,127,129,
131,132,134,138,140
, James,021 ,022,029,034,
037,039,040,041,050,
083,091,094,134
, Thomas,010 ,016,020,021,
022,041,050,099
, William,077
HOWZAR, George,009 ,014,019,036,
037,039,047,161
, Jacob,008
, Joe,160
, Martin,010 ,012
, Michael Jr.,019,021,022,029
163,164
, Peter,014 ,155,156
HOWZER, Michael,006,164
, Peter,158
HUCTHINS, John,048
HUDSON, Hall,037
HUDSPECK, John,142
HUDSPETH, ,117
, Aires,104,161,163
, Airs Jr.,062 ,126,139,
140
, Airs,026 ,030,033,034,
043,046,048,056,059,
062,065,067,071,073,
074,076,077,078,081,
087,089,091,093,095,
101,104,106,113,115,
116,118,119,122,127,
128,130,131,132,138,
139,140,140,142,144,
147,148,154,155,157,
159,162,163,166,168
, Ayres,035,086,096
, Ben.,116
, Benjamin,163 ,168
, Carter,046,104,116,154
155,161
, Catherine,061
, Charles,156 ,168
, Daniel,049
, David,015,051,052,053,
118
, Davidd,126
, George,116,125,156,163
168
, Giles,015,116,168
, Jiles,049,161,162,163,
167
, John,006 ,007,008,009,
011,012,013,014,
015,016,018,019,023,
025,026,028,051,140,
145,161
, Joseph,117,126
, Mary,057
, Milly,132,140
, Obed,168
, Samuel,138
, Wm.,015
HUFF, Daniel,059,060,096,102,144
HUFFINDS, D.,005
HUFFINES, Daniel,119,122
HUFFMAN, George Jr.,135
, Lewis,119
HUGH, Archelouis,148
HUGHES, Archelus,135
, Archelois,136
, Archelus,085
, Edward,137
, John,098,103,105,118,129
,134,135,136,159,161
,162,165,166
, Joseph,004 ,016
, Leander,010,012,014,016,
020,049,056,117
, Thomas,036 ,051,052,056,
090,110,139
, Thos.,068
HUGHLET, William,043,062
, Wm.,034
HUGHLETT, (Capt.),163
, ,115 ,116,118,123,136,
146,149,151,159,164
, William F.,108
, William T.,136
, William,031 ,036,049,
052,066,069,070,088,
096,104,110,115,116,
124,128,129,133,134,
141,142,148,150,151,
154,159,165,168
, Wm.,056 ,094,096,113,
120,168
HUGHLETTS, (Capt.),139
HUGHS, Thomas,063
HUGLETT, William,066
HUITT, Nancy,053
HUMPHRES, Benjamin,061 ,076
, David,061,103

HUMPHRES, John,103
HUMPHRESS, ,139,164
, David,147
HUMPHREY, (Capt),070
, David,071,074
HUMPHREYS, (Capt),045 ,105
, (Capt.),064 ,082
, (Dist),066
, ,103
, Benj.,036
, Benjamin,048,078,079
, David,048,079
, John,022
, Samuel,036 ,037,038,
048,051,054,079,161
HUMPHRIS, (Capt),057
, (Capt.),030 ,041
, (Dist),034,066,088
, ,093 ,116,117,123,146
, Benj.,058
, Benja.,159
, Benjamin,043 ,090,094,
148
, Daniel,090
, David,069,086,089,090,
105,126,159,160
, Jack,021
, John,083 ,100,105
, Samuel,025,029,040,044
,097,155,159
HUMPHRISS, ,149,159,161,164,167
, Benjamin,148,153
, David,023,129,148,153

, John,129,134,138,140
, Saml.,132
, Samuel,128 ,163,168
HUNT, Crispen,078 ,141
, John,114 ,116
HUNTER, George,027
, James,135
, John,071
HURST, George,126
, James,095
HURT, John,030 ,058,069,070,071,
138,143
HUSBANDS, ,005
HUSK, George,107
HUSTON, Hall,120
HUTCHENS, John,147 ,154
, Smith,006
HUTCHERSON, Daniel,147 ,150
, William,083,084,151
, Wm.,164
HUTCHINGS, Benjamin,124
, John,065,108,111,133,
147
, Libby,065
, Strangeman,112
HUTCHINS, John,014 ,015,029,103,
148,155
, Nicholas,074
, Thos.,151
HUTCHINSON, John,102
HUTCHISON, Daniel,147
HUTHENS, John,058
HUTHERSON, Daniel,039
, William,043
HUTHINS, John,054
HUTTON, James,042
HYDE, George,062
, Stephen,079

INGRAM, John,119
, William,119
IRON, Darby,064
IRONS, Peter,039,044,055,068,074
, William,062
ISAACKS, Godfrey,126
ISBEL, Jason,106
ISBELL, ,133
, Benjamin,035,053
, Jason,035 ,039,072,087,
090,131,133
, Thomas,055 ,061,073,076,
081,130,131,133,159,
162
, Thos.,035 ,133
ISSBELL, Christopher,030
JACKS, Richard,009 ,092,146,156
, Thomas,093
JACKSON, Andrew,124
, Jacob,072
, John,111 ,124,167
, Martha,111
, Samuel,080,088
JACOBI, Adam,091
JAMES, Abraham,124 ,139
, David,106
, James,117
, John,080
, William Sr.,069 ,127
, William,015 ,024,026,059,
063,088,127,133
, Wm.,014
JANNAWAY, Jos.,135
JARVES, Jabez,043
JARVIS, ,005,011
, Daniel,108 ,116
, Elephalet,114
, Elephalet,091
, Eliphalet,069 ,072,075,
114,119,137,158
, Elophalet,024
, Jabez,001 ,006,012,014,
017,023,048,060,124,
165
, John,003,060,067,069,119
,139,159
, Lewis,140
, Rexia,054
, Rezia,043 ,045,059,066,
095,102,103,159,164

JARVIS, Reziah,045 ,112,123,127,
141,146,158
, Stephen,112
JASON, James,023,030
JAYNE, Nathaniel,071
, Stephen,071 ,124
JEAN, Na(blurred),038
, Stephen,018 ,036
, William,050 ,144,167
, Wm.Jr.,065
JEANS, William,154
JEFFERY, Wm.,117
JENKINS, William,006
JEPFERT, George,095
JERVIS, John,141,150
JESSOP, Joseph,082 ,100,101
, Timothy,144
JESSUP, Joseph,094 ,121
JETT, James,004
JINKINS, John,120 ,121
, Thomas,117
JINNINGS, Thomas,161
JOHNSON, ,058 ,072,123
, Alexander,051
, Ashley,059,107,126,146
, Benjamin,026
, David,114
, Isaac,080
, James,017 ,107,126,160
, Jason,144
, Jeffrey,036,037,039,040
,112,128,146,159,164

, Jeffrey,005,111,123,146
,149,164,165
, John,051 ,069,070,071,
072,073,075,096,121,
142,155
, Joseph,006,122
, Moses,005
, Robert,121,160
, Samuel,071,163
, Thomas,009,012,014,016,
017,020,023,128
, Thos.,010
, William,005,016,059,063
,096,138,152
, Wm.,036,046,149
JOHNSTON, Jeffery,141
, John,124
, Joseph,011
, Robert,018
, William,148
, Wm.,131 ,136
JOICE(JOYCE), Alexander,009
JOICE, Alexander,063,114,116,134

, George,062 ,072,107,146
, Isaac,087,101,107
JOIN, George,139
JOINER, John,014,116,168
JOLLEY, James,035
, Nansey,035
JONES, ,139
, Alexander,008
, Cad.,038
, Charles,141
, Evan,117
, Gabriel,139 ,144
, Gabriel,024 ,054,099,131,
148
, Isaac,082
, Jacob,120
, James Jr.,069,073,142
, James,048,102,136,138,142

, Jno.L.,118 ,125
, John,039,108,156
, Joseph,030 ,044
, Joshua,127 ,160
, Lemuel,002
, Levy,002
, Philip,071
, Samuel,011
, Thos.,048
, William Sr.,071
, William,117
JOYCE, Alexander,151
, George,151 ,159
, Isaac,028,101,151
KAYSER, John,105
KEEL, Robert,075
KEELINGS, Wm.,121
KEEN, (?),059
, Gilbert,030 ,032,051
, Josiah,032
KEER, John,088 ,151
KELL, Esebella,110
, James,132,165
, John,071
, Robert,078,079
, Thomas,110
, Thos.,078
KEMP, Aaron,042
KENNADAY, Charity,003
KENNEDY, Charity,001
KENSLEY, Benjamin,119
KERBEY, Richard,161
KERBY, Edmond,064 ,162,163
, Edmund,014 ,069,071,099,
108,139,163,168
, Francis,126
, Henry,024,037,039,040,050
052,053,054,116
, Joel,064,069,071,090,099
, Martin,108
, Pleasant,150
, Richard,074 ,090,112,139,
163,165
, Samuel,018 ,028,029,037,
047,099,136,141,152
KERLEY, Edmund,015 ,157,159
, Joel,090

KERLEY, Richard,090
, Samuel,158
KERR, Alexander,161
KETCHAM, John,56
KIDNER, Francis,114,131,132
, Frank,125
KIDNOW, Francis,010
KIGER, Adam,117
KIMBROUGH, (Orphs),155
,076
, Geo.,123,128,159
, George,028 ,112,123,
146
, Goldman,028 ,121,128
, John,093,115,125,142,
161
, Marduke,028
, Marmaduke,028,074,076
,077,155
, Mary,028
, Orman,028
, Widow,076
KIMMON, John,021
KINE, John,121
KING, Benajah,107
, Joseph,120
, Mary,067
, Richard,067
, Samuel,061
KINGHTON, Jesse,101
KINMAN, Drury,103
, William,063,084,103,138
, Wm.,105,134,142
KINSELL, Fredrick,117
KIRKMAN, Elijah,073
, George,143,153,167,168
, Mary,153
, Thomas,079
KIRKPATRICK, Sarah,143
, William,040,147
KIRSHNER, Christopher,037
KLEIN, Christopher,101
KNIGHT, James,071 ,143
, Thomas,115 ,143
, Thos.,118
KNIGHTEN, Jesse,062,077,108,116,
138,56
KNIGHTON, Jesse,087,090,106,114,
127,128,129,139,140,
166
, Jessee,144
KNOTT, William,144
KONLE, Enoch,122
KRAUSE, Windle,027
KREEL, Thomas,098
KRIMSHAW, John,118
KROUSE, (Capt),097 ,141
, (Dist),044 ,049
,103,108,116,118,121,123
,146
, Gotlib,158
, John,061,076,080,081,094
095,100,105,111,112
,127,129,130,138,142
,143,164,165
, Windel,119 ,132
, Windle,070 ,096,130,132,
133,167,168
KROUSES, (Capt),045,070
, (Capt.),082
, (Dist.),066,073,088
, (Dist.),084
,093
KRUDER, Jacob,160
KRUGER, George,127
, Henry,127 ,145,146
, Jacob,047 ,127,145

LABERRT, Joel,122
LACEFIELD, Joseph,161
LAD, Noble Sr.,016
LADD, (Capt),141
,116,123,131,137,139,146,1
49,159,160,164,168
, Amos,020 ,023,037,038,039,
040,042,052,055,065,
079,091,094,097,098,
102
, Con.,133 ,139
, Constantine,055
, Constant,030 ,040,043,046,
054,057,095,097,101,
102,106,108,111,121,
123,131,133,136,146,
147,156,158,159
, Constantine,055 ,061,065,
096,098,108,109,111,
114,129,130,133,135,
138,146,156,164
, Jos.,110
, Joseph,053,155,160
, Judith,053
, Noble Jr.,050
, Noble Sr.,010,018
, Noble,003,047,050,051,053,
054,055,084,086,089,
102,134,135,153
, Richard,143
, William,153
, Wm.,053
LAFFOON, Susanah,157
, Wm.,119,120,157
LAGFORD, Thomas,003
LAIN, William,116 ,164
, Wm.,050 ,154
LAKEY, Elizabeth,057
, John,068
, Susannah,158
, William,016
LANCASTER, John,049,061
, William,058
LANCHESTER, John,054,078
LANE, John,008

LANE, William,009 ,070
LANFIELD, Jo.,140 ,150
LANGHAM, James,099 ,151
LANIER & WILLIAMS, ,012,013,043
LANIER, ,051,079,097,102,111,154

, Jane,099
, Lewis,121
, Robert(Colo.),009 ,031
, Robert,003 ,005,006,010,
011,013,015,014,015,
016,021,022,024,025,
026,027,039,041,042,
044,049,050,051,053,
054,065,082,096,097,
104,106,126,129,139,
161,167,56
, Thomas,096 ,143
LANIERS, ,145
, Robert,116
LANIUS, John,060
LANKASTER, John,095,103,117
LANKESTER, John,107,117
, William,117
LANKFORD, (Wid),019
, Henry,044
, James,055,072
, John,044 ,054,073,112,
115
, Richard,008
, Sarah,038,044
, Thomas,011,044
, Thos.,035,038
, William,148
, Wm.,090
LASH, Adam,013 ,076
, Christian,113,137,156
, Geo.,020
, George,010,024,026,052,053
,060,083,125,159,160
,56
, John C.,110
, Nath.,065
LASSFIELD, Joseph,069 ,075
LASSWELL, Joseph,129
LAST, Abraham,119
LASTER(?), Micheal,044
LASWELL, Joseph,134
LATHAM, William,116,150
LATHANS, William,080
LATTON, John,153
LAURANCE, James,105,164
, Richard,074
LAURENCE, James,161
, Richard,058
LAW, John,084
LAWRANCE, James,166
, Richard,008
LAWRENCE, Claiborne,105
, Isobell,113
, James,105,113,117,123,
152,159,167
, Jos.,118
, Joseph,015,036,118,119

, Rich,079
, Richard,010 ,024,026,
052,105,113,121,144
LAWS, Moses,150
LAWSON, David,051
, Jonas,078
LAXON, Charles,095,101,168
LAY, Chris.,051
LAYN, William,165
LEASH, Jacob,052
LEDFORD, Nicholas,098
LEE, Richard,076
LEFOY, James,127,136,149,162
, John,162
LEINBACK, Catharine,029
, John,029
LESTER, Daniel,167
, Jesse,123 ,128,129,131,
138,146,151,152,154,
155,157,161,162,163,
165,167
LEWIS, (Capt),057 ,070,099
, (Capt.),082
, (Dist),066 ,068,088
,069,093,116,117,118,123,
136,146,157,159,164
, Capt.,103
, Elkanah,053
, J.M.,078
, James M.,063,069,075,076,
104,114
, James Martin,081,088,093,
128
, Joel(Maj.),045
, Joel,030,031,053,064,068,
071,074,077,079,080,
082,087,092,093,099,
112,114,115,143,144,
153
, Martin,158
, Mary,108,126,163
, Micajah,076
, W.T.,112
, Walter,046
, William T.,030 ,031,033,
037,041,057,060,064,
070,074,075,076,084,
087,088,091,093,094,
098,101,105,108,110,
113,116,126,132,136,
144,152,154,160
, William Terril,057 ,062,
064
, William,091 ,098,109,138,
148
, Wm.(Capt),046
, Wm.,073 ,147

LEWIS, Wm.T.,031,034,061,062,065
,067,068,074,075,076
,087,090,091,093,094
,095,098,099,102,103
,104,108,110,111,112
,114,115,118,121,124
,126,128,131,143,144
,145,146,151,152,153
,154,157,158,161,164
,166,167
, Wm.Teril,034
, Wm.Terrel,022,023,027,081
,084,085,086,087,088
,089,106,108
, Wm.Terril,031,032,033,044
,049,081,143,145
LIBERTINE, Daniel,125 ,139,140
LICK, Martin,138
LIMEBURG, Barbara,007
, Benjamin,007
LINDSAY, C.,146
, Carlton,052,055,079,087
,105,107,110,118,120
,124,126,127,128,132
, Charlton,063
, James,124 ,142
, Reuben,145
, Reubin,123
, Thomas,093,126
LINDSEY, Carlton,069,071
LINEBACK, Abraham,126
, Joe,145
, John,122
, Lewis,130
LINEBECK, Abraham,095
LINESAY, Carlton,091
, James,142
LINSTER, Moses,114 ,143
LINSTOR, Moses,125
LINVELL, David,101
LINVIL, Richard,018
LINVILL, Aaron,111 ,133
, Aron,155
, David,021 ,091,106,111,
143,153,155
, Edward,025,038,150
, Richard,054,069,071,106
,111,112,133,143,144
,153,155,156,158,162
LINVILLE, David,102
, Moses,058
, Richard,021 ,149
LINVILLS, (Capt),057
LINVIILL, Moses,127
LINZY, James,012
LISBY, Aaron,021,027,145
, Aron,022,149
LITTLEPAGE, Epps,144
LIVILLE, Richard,020
LOBLIN, Elizabeth(Mrs),051
LOCKENOUR, George,107
LOGAN, Elizabeth,153
, John,153
, Patrick,018
LOGANS, John,119
, Patrick Sr.,069
, Patrick,060
, William,002
LOGEN, John,119
LOGINO, John Thos.,062
LONDON, Amos,012,058,079,136,138
,142,158,165
, John,158,165
, William,111,137
LONG, Frederick,046,100,111,150,
151,164,168
, George,121
LONGINO, ,073 ,123,154
, J.T.,126
, John T.,050,109,110,112
,136
, John Thomas,007,009,014
,037,096,103
, John Thos.,015,017,023,
025,030,033,034,040,
045,046,047,051,057,
068,070,071,075,076,
081,082,093,103,104,
108,117,118,124,134,
142,143,144,145,147,
148,151,152,154,
155,159,162,164,165,
167
, John,150
, Thos.,124
LOUFIELD, Joseph,132
LOUVILLS, (Dist),034
LOVE, James,065,101
, John,021 ,061,065,082,101,
117,123
, Ruth,101
, William,021 ,117,162
LOVELL, ,103,123,136,149,164
, Edward,039 ,070,071,074,
076,078,095,096,097,
116,139,148,149
LOVELLE, (Capt),076
LOVELLS, (Capt),070
LOVEN, Thomas,084
LOVILL, (Capt),047
,114,116,131,146,159
, Edward,037 ,040,043,051,
054,076,080,094,108,
116,135,151
, Silvia,167
LOVILLE, ,093 ,159
LOVILLES, (Capt.),038
, (Dist),088
LOVILLS, (Capt),045
, (Capt.),082
LOVILS, (Capt.),030
LOVIN, Thomas,058
LOVING, Presley,004

LOVINS, Thomas,134 ,139
LOVINS, Presley,004
LOVORN, Thomas,083
LOW, John,084 ,111,112,130,131,
155
, Thomas,137,146,165
LOWE, John,100 ,101,106
LOWREYS, Jacob,036
LOWRY, Andrew,038 ,039
, Eve,065
, Jacob,065
, John,160
LOYD, Thomas,011,024,039,095
LUDWICK, Peter,077
LYNCH, John Jr.,086,124
, John,009,010,012,014,022,
027,029,040,041,052,
058,060,076,087,097,
102,108,121,124,125,
131,136,138,144,145,
148,150,151,152,154,
157,158,160,161,162,
163,165,167,168
, Patience,136
LYON, Robert,025
, Susannah,025
MA(Blurred), Joel,038
MAAB, Patrick,100
MACAY, Spruce,056
MACKEY, Joel,072,142,164
, John,134
MACKMILLION, Andrew,106
MACY, Gwyn,090
MADHIFF, Isaiah,144
MAINS, Henry,106
MAJORS, Robert,098 ,153
MANAHA, Joseph,136
MANAKEY, Joseph,107
MANNERING, Jordan,075
, Jordin,093
MANNING, Jordan,077,083,139,140,
147
MANUEL, Issact,096
MARKHAM, Matthew,137
MARKLAND, ,163
, Matt,162
, Matthew,012 ,042,045,
092,131,132,156
, Robert,119,128,141,148
,152,156
, Robt.,152,156
MARKLEN, Robert,147
MARKLIN, Mathew,008
MARLATT, John,082
, Rebekah,082
MARR, John,112
MARS(MYERS?), Foil,072
MARSH, James,153
, John,138,142,144,147,160
, Miner,153
MARSHALL, Frederick Wm.,144
, Fredr.,110
, Fredr.W.,162
, Fredr.Wm.,042,070,071,
079,095,101,104,110,
119,129,151
, Frederick Wm.,048 ,090
, Wm.,095 ,137
MARTAIN, Moses,006
MARTIN, (Capt.),030,041
, (Colo.),010,016
, ,011,024
, Abraham,010,014,017,059,
082,106,134,139
, Alex.,029
, Alexander,007 ,094
, Andrew,034 ,072,074
, David,008 ,012,016,018
, James(Colo.),023
, James(Ferry),023
, James,006 ,015,017,019,
023,028,044,048,051,
057,059,060,061,063,
075,090,094,096,097,
112,114,116,124,126,
128,132,135,136,145,
155,156,158,159
, Job(Capt),014
, Job,008,019,020,026,027,
039,041,045,046,047,
052,053,054,055,057,
064,067,069,071,074,
076,077,085,086,087,
089,090,092,095,096,
099,103,105,114,129,
129,138,143,144,145,
161,164,167
, John,020,023,030,031,037
,038,048,051,054,054
,056,060,061,072,083
,087,088,096,102,103
,105,108,113,124,129
,145,154,159
, Jon,024
, Joseph,009 ,017
, Mary,012,048,126
, Moses Jr.,017 ,088
, Moses Sr.,017 ,069
, Moses,001 ,008,011,016,
017,020,023,033,073,
097,109,125,126,135,
138
, Obed,159
, Obediah,050,052,053,116,
136
, Robert,094 ,167
, Salathia,029
, Salathiel,012 ,030,033,
034,099,134,137
, Salathiel,043 ,044,069,
070,072,075,082,092,
094,095,112,114,146
MARTIN, Salethiel,152

, Thomas,128 ,146,152
, Valentine,009 ,019,064,
066,067,068,069,071,
099,160,168
, Volentine,008
, William,054,092,122,124,
135,136,147,154
, Wm.,035,065,121,140,150
, Zacariah,017,019
, Zach,128,133
, Zach.,133
, Zachariah,018 ,019,021,
022,040,126,127
MARTINA, Moses,017
MARTINS, (Capt),045
, (Capt.),023
, (Dist),027
, Salathiel,025
MARTON, Salathiel,099
MASH, John,036
, William,075
MASON, Thomas,069
MASTERS, Joseph,028,072
, Nicholas,120
MATIN, Job,103
MATTHEW, James,009 ,032,108
MATTHEWS, (Dist),037
, Aquila,126
, James,016,022,027,029,
030,045,047,054,095,
107,116,119,120,134,
136,138,139,140,141,
142,143,161,163
, Mary,054
, Reuben,043,044,055,056
,079,117,128
, Reubin,006,008,009,025
,031,033,039
, Robert,116,136
MATTHIS, James,064 ,065,072
, Matthew,071
MAUPIN, Jesse,094 ,095,154,166
MAYER, Jacob,121
MAYO, Williamson,008,051
MCAFEE, William,075,142
MCAFFEE, Wm.,016
MCANALLY, ,097 ,116,123,127,136,
137,141,146,149,157,
159,164,166,168
, Charles,001 ,009,014,
015,018,020,021,023,
024,028,030,032,033,
038,039,041,042,044,
047,048,051,052,052,
055,057,059,059,063,
064,065,070,073,074,
075,082,085,090,091,
093,096,097,098,103,
108,112,120,122,123,
127,133,134,135,136,
144,146,149
, Charles,153 ,156,159,
164,166
, Chas.,035,088,127,134
, Jesse,014,015,017,096,
120,121,129,134,147,
150,151
, John,015 ,017,059,082,
137
MCANALLYS, Charles,101
MCANNALLEY, Charles,081
MCANNALLY, Charles,002 ,004,116
, Jesse,023
MCANNALY, Charles,043
, Chas.,012
MCBAIN, Elizabeth,009
, Sarah,009
MCBRICE, John,158
MCBRIDE, Wm.,158
, John,103 ,119,123,166
, Manassah,161
, Mannassah,164
, William(Capt),045
, William,030,054
MCCAREL, Thomas,112
MCCARREL, Isbell,020
, Nathaniel,083
, Thomas,052,086,087,114
,130,159,161,163,166
MCCARRELL, Thomas,088 ,124,127
, Thos.,068,126
MCCARROL, Nathaniel,002,006,018,
020
MCCARTER, John,069
MCCAY, ,120
, John,022
, Spruce,013 ,019,027,062,
096,120
MCCLOUD, Caty,143
, Katey,087
MCCOIN, James,102
MCCOLLUM, Elizabeth,063,066
, Hugh,159
, John,068
MCCOLLUMS, John,049,063
MCCONNEL, John,141
MCCRAW, Benjamin,156
, Jacob,044 ,048,066,090,
120,137,141,145,147,
150,151,168
, Samuel,090
, William,156
, Wm.,066,100
MCCRAWS, ,084
MCDANIEL, ,102
MCFEE, William,018 ,069
MCGEE, Martha,009
MCGIBBONEY, Patrick,083
MCGIBBONY, Patrick,083 ,084,088,
100,102,105,109,121,
124,132,133,140,147,
148,155

MCGIBONEY, Patrick,061
MCGIMSEY, John,062
MCGRAW, Jacob,090
       , Samuel,025
MCGRUDER, Blizard,156
MCHAND, Matthew,058
MCKILLIP, Andrew,168
        , Hugh,021
MCKILLUP, Andrew,054
        , Hugh,054
MCKINNE, James,124
       , Matthew,150
MCKINNEY, Elizabeth,032
        , John,007 ,032,050,068,
          095
        , Patrick,039
MCKINNY, James,065
MCKOIN, James,016 ,040,048,059,
        086,106,109,113
MCLEMORE, Ephraim,090 ,106,114,
         125
MCLIMOR, Ephraim,028
MCLIMORE, Ephraim,028 ,120,126,
         127,137,138,144
        , Sterling,043 ,061,120
MCMICKLE, John,100 ,150,154,155
MCMILLON, Abraham,082
MCNAIRY, Francis,068,126
       , John,066 ,093
MCPHARSON, Joseph,137
MEAD, John,167 ,168
MEALE, John,143
MEDDLEN, Anna,068
MEEKS, William,064
MEERS, Thomas,112
MEIRS, Moses,047
MELTON, David,008 ,009,111,118
      , Richard,104
MELVIN, Ellerd,084
MENADUE, Henery,003
MENDEHALL, Mordicai,059
MENDENHALL, Joseph,059
          , Mordicai,059,062,067
           ,084,088,107
MEREDETH, ,024
        , James,035
MEREDETHS, ,025
MEREDITH, (Capt.),024
        , ,065 ,127,146,159,164
        , JOhn,115
        , James Jr.,151
        , James,122,135,153
        , John,030
        , Martin,015
        , William,008 ,011,014,
          015,018,019,021,023,
          025,029,030,031,033,
          038,041,061,062,063,
          065,066,077,095,102,
          103,113,116,130,132,
          136,137,138,144,145,
          146,150,154,159,163,
          164,167
        , Wm.,015 ,018,028,033,
          045,065,075,099,111,
          120,127,134,138,153,
          157,167,168
MEREDITHS, (Capt.),023
MEREITH, William,038
MERIDETH, William,007 ,008,011,
         130
MERKLY, Christopher,095
MERREDITH, Daniel,159
         , William,038 ,039,042,
           054,056,078,084,088,
           089,090,091,095,105,
           106,116
         , Wm.,034 ,046,054,078,
           081,083,095
MERREL, John,156
MERRET, John,146
MERRIDETH, Ann,057
         , William,057 ,058
         , Wm.,042
MERRIDITH, (Capt.),046
MERRIL, John,020
MERRIMAN, John,058
MERRIT, Edward,152
      , James,117
      , John,152
MERRYMAN, John,054
MERRYMANS, John,056
MESSICK, George,160
METALL, John,048
      , Rebakah,048
MEYERS, Jacob,056
MICKEY, John,029,038,069,073,101
       ,109,150,151,152,153
MIDDLEN, Anna,115
MIDDLETON, James,101
MIDLEN, Anne,087
MIER, Peter,115
MIERS, Moses,045
MILLER, ,132
      , Andrew,069 ,073,117
      , Ann,062
      , Christian,063 ,121
      , Frederick,008 ,010,012,
        017,023,027,029,034,
        045,054,091,097,098,
        105,120,121,124,125,
        131,132,133,139,144,
        147,150
      , Fredick,058
      , Fredr.,040 ,079,097,120,
        133,144,152,153,155
      , Fredrick,024,052,060,062
        ,081,086,089,093,098
        ,107,108,116,158
      , Godfrey,008,014,019,026,
        039,056,062,081,088,
        123

MILLER, Jacob,072 ,103,105,137,
        141,155
      , John,010,062,063,064,066
        ,067,068,105,125,141
        ,145
      , Joseph,010 ,012,014,056,
        127
      , Randal,069
      , Randol,136
      , Randolph,121
MILLS, Aaron,107
     , Sarah,119
MILLWOOD, James,139
MIRES, Jacob,068
MITCHEL, Adam,011
       , Moses,013
MITCHELL, Adam,007 ,010,029,082,
         085,088,093,114,134,
         157,159
MITCHELS, Moses,095
MIZE, Isaac,079,117
    , Joshua,151,165
    , Martha,165
    , Mary,120
MOBBS, Jesse,120
MONDAY, Christophar,160
      , Christopher,142
MONTGOMERY, ,005
          , Michael,150
MOOE, Alexander,146
MOONAHAN, Shadrack,124
MOORE, ,027
     , Aaron,065,122
     , Al (Blurred),037
     , Alex,039,040,124,125
     , Alex.,035,038,086,092
     , Alexander,008,014,022,035
       ,054,056,058,059,090
       ,097,101,138,142,155
       ,163,168
     , Andrew,057 ,083,084,111
     , Ann,120
     , Anna,111
     , Aron,154,168
     , Edward,010 ,021,022,049,
       062,063
     , Geo.,077
     , James,111,120,141
     , John,012,023,024,025,030,034,
       045,057,058,077,083,
       121,124
     , M.,088
     , Matt,070,162
     , Matt.,045
     , Matthew,009 ,014,015,018,
       018,022,023,024,025,
       026,028,031,042,043,
       045,047,048,049,050,
       052,057,061,062,071,
       073,075,086,087,088,
       092,094,097,098,105,
       115,116,118,120,122,
       128,132,137,140,141,
       144,147,149,150,154,
       166,168
     , Robert,031
     , Samuel,005
     , Thomas,068
     , William,149
     , Wm. Sr.,070
     , Wm.,036
     , Wm.Jr.,070
MOOT (MOTT), Lidia,047
MORE, Samuel,005
MORELAND, William,086 ,092
MORELY, Samuel Jr.,008
MORES, Samuel,005
MORGAIN, Antony,004
MORGAN, ,067
      , Jeff,149
      , John,014,025,029,030,031
        ,032,034,041,054,055
        ,063,088,108,116,123
        ,124,146,149,159,161
        ,162,163,164,166,168
      , Orman,049 ,056,086,088,
        098,107
      , Ormand,034
      , Thomas,165
      , Valentine,117
MORPHISS, Richard,129
MORRIS, George,001
      , Hugh,071,104,121,124,141
        ,150
      , Nathaniel,030 ,086,107,
        144,148
      , Richard,030,040
      , Thomas,125 ,152
      , Wm.,104
MORRISON, William,132
MORRISS, ,138
MORROR, David,133
MORROS, David,076
MORROW, ,109,146
      , Daniel,109
      , David,020 ,021,027,057,
        060,069,076,080,081,
        086,090,092,097,098,
        102,107,148
MORROWS, David,018 ,069,073,096,
        102,103,107,115,125
MOSBEYS, (Capt.),023
MOSBY, (Capt.),099
     , (Capt.),041 ,082
     , (Dist),022 ,034
     , ,093,103,116,117,118,123,
       125,139
     , Damuel,050
     , Daniel,004 ,054
     , Herucia,023
     , Jacob,139
     , Samuel Jr.,023 ,024,026,
       028,029,036,039,086,
       089,097,108,129

MOSBY, Samuel Sr.,028 ,029
     , Samuel,023 ,028,030,032,
       050,051,057,067,074,
       111,112,113,117,123,
       125,131,168
     , Susannah,113,131
     , Thomas,125 ,134,135,154,
       165,168
     , Thos.,123
     , West,146,156,160
MOSBYS, (Capt),014 ,045,057,070
      , (Dist),088
      , ,025
MOSELEY, Jacob,069
MOSER, ,056,065,075
     , Leonard,047 ,056
     , Peter,127
MOSLEY, ,011
MOSS, Henry,162
    , Matthew,019
    , Oze,003 ,004
    , Peter,162
MOSSER, Francis,141
      , Leonard,042,092
      , Peter,042 ,101,109
MOSSERS, Catharine,101
MOTT, Moses,047,117
MOTTS, Mary,035
MOUSERS, Leonard,017
MOXLEY, Nathaniel,005
MOYER, Peter,002
MRAD, John,168
MULATTO, Poll,037
MULL, Henry,117
MURPHEY, ,073
       , Joseph,006
       , Keziah(Mrs),034,037
       , Keziah,033
       , Peter,162
       , Richard,003,015,024,033
         ,034,037,040,062,075
         ,162
MURPHEYS, (Mrs),036
MURPHY, Joseph,067 ,112,129
      , Keziah,060 ,061,077
      , Peter,134 ,158
      , Richard,043,085,096,119,
        126,134,147,150,151,
        158,164,168
MURRAY, John,076
MYARS, Hannah,055
     , Jacob,029,091
     , Peter,071,094,109
MYER, Jacob,129
MYERS, Benjamin,148
     , Jacob,055
     , Joseph,013
     , Peter,055,143
NALL, William,148
NAUL, Wm.,003
NEAL, Thomas,149
    , Rudolph,076
NECT, Bartlet,053
NEGRO, Jacob,040
     , Jenny,087
NEIL, John,063
    , Thomas,062,134,150
    , William,063
    , Wm.,063
NELEY, James,117
NELSON, Joseph,079 ,084,094,100,
       102,129,133,147,148,
       167
      , Margaret,095
      , Marget,105
      , Margret,110
      , Solomon,028,032,095
NELSONS, Wm.,030
NICHOLD, Becket,111
NICHOLS, ,063
       , Becket,056,104,113,118,
         120
       , Bickel,094
       , Burket,077
NIEL, John,120
NISSION, Tego,157
NOLAND, John,005
NOLIN, Mary,013
NOLL, Jacob,090
NORMAN, Eli,129
      , Peter,113
      , Thomas,042 ,056,068,095,
        155,56
NORMANS, Henry,020
NORTH, Edward,078
NORTING, Matthias,126
NOWLEN, Mary,010
NOWLIN, David,019
      , James,016
      , Mary,014,016,029
      , Sarah,016
      , Susan,016
NULL, Christina,078
    , Jacob,076,083,084,108,125
    , John,078 ,081,089,124
    , Michael,068 ,073,095,103
    , William,068 ,089
    , Wm.,089
NUNN, Richard,016
    , Whorton,025
NUNNELY, Edward,132
NUNNS, Richard,149

OBARR, Robert,044 ,062
OGILSBY, Micajah,134
OGLESBY, Micajah,085,114,135,159
        ,161,162,163
OLDHAM, Richard,060
OLIVER, Abijah,133 ,160
      , Ahijah,127 ,141
      , Elijah,098 ,140
      , Ezekiel,100,141
      , James,117

ONEAL, John,151
, Peter,148
ORMAN, Thomas,068
OSBORN, (Blurred),015
, (Colo.),009
, Jonathan,016
OSBORNE, Stephen,050
OSBURN, Adlai,120
OSBURN, Abraham,072
, Jonathan,003
OVERBY, William,117
OWEN, Daid,085
, David,016,033,046,038,048,
049,052,062,078,159
, Solomon,052
, Thomas,164
, Wm.,083
OWENS, David,072,077
, Edward,127
, John,117
, Thomas,154
PADGET, James,015
, John,116,140,142
, Moses,162
PAFF, Peter,100,105
PAFFORD, John,089
, Samuel,089
PAG--(?), Abraham,008
PAGET, John,160
PAGOTT, Benjamin,071
PAIN, David,048
, Mary,048
PAINIEL, Benjamin,007
PANNIEL, Benjamin,009
PARFORD, John,096
, Rachel,096
PARIS, ,013
PARISH, Henry,011 ,022
PARKER, Charles,049,058,141,152
, Elisha,117
, John,067,094,118
, Jonathan,142,144
, Samuel,149
PARKS, Benjamin,030,044,144
PARMER, Nathan,123
PARRIS, Geo.,005
, George,056
PARRISH, Henry,040
PARSONS, James,093
, John,093 ,106,154
, Richard,093
PARTICK, John,025
PATARICK, John,117
PATRICK, (?),059
, ,072
, John,025 ,027,029,034,
042
, Samuel,070,072,099
, William,054
PATTERSON, ,013
, Charles,008
, Greenberry,102 ,131,
139,158
, Greenburry,142
, Greenbury,138,142,143

, Grenberry,003
, Joseph,018 ,051,081
, William,044
PATTILLO, Henry,115,123,127,149,
150,162,168
PEARCE, Elisha,016
PEARIS, Elisha,019
PECOCK, Abel,015
, Abraham,014
PEDYCORD, William,062
PEGGS, Matthew,124
PENDLETON, Wm.,076
PENN, John,067
PENROY, John,120
PEPES(PIPES), Silvanus,080
PEPES, John,080
PEPPER, Samuel,053
PERKINS, Peter,032 ,090,122
, Valentine,044
PERRY, James,058
, John,159
PERSON, John,141
PERSONS, John,128 ,145,160
PETERS, Edmund,088 ,091,098,122,
127
PETIT, George,085 ,131,141
PETREE, Jacob,023 ,097,102,104,
138
, John,035,138
PETTICOAL, Wm.,008
PETTICORD, William,008
PETTIE, Benj.,003
, Benjamin,089
, Thomas,114
, William,034
PETTIR, Benj.,046
, Benjamin,008,056,085
, Geo.,133
, George,089 ,114,125,127,
128,132,150,154
, Judith,084 ,092
, Rachael,159
, Thomas,003,020,021,084,
086,089,092,114,116,
118,119,127,133,143,
159,161,166
, Thos.,126
, Wm.,132
PETTITT, Henry Jr.,099
, Henry,102
PETTY, William,033
, Wm.,083 ,106
PETTYJOHN, John,105
PETTYJOHNS, John,063
PETTYS, William,033,086
, Wm.,083
PFAFF, Peter,129

PFAW, Jacob,109
PHELPS, Thomas,024
PHILIPS, (Major),017
, (Wid)017
, ,045
, Abner,060 ,104,114,158
, George,114
, Jo.,017,118,136
, Jos.,096
, Joseph(Colo.),055
, Joseph,013,014,015,043,
045,046,049,050,054,
058,061,067,079,080,
081,092,118,156,167
, Mark,070
, Richard,055,062,092
, William,041,048,062,085

, Wm.,082
PHILLIPS, (Major),031
, Abner,112,126,144,145,
150,158
, Cornelius,126
, Elias,126,144
, George,153,160
, Jo.,153
, Jo.,133
, Joseph,002,010,019,021
,022,024,026,031,033
,034,079,127,134,136
,143,144,152,154,162
,163,164,168
, Mark,032 ,115,131,133
, Richard,034
, Wm.,143 ,149
PICHET, William,126
PICKET, Judy,003
PIKE, Nathan,082,128,137
PIKES, Joseph,105
PILCHER, James Jr.,138
, James,069 ,071,077,094,
104,113
PILCHERS, James,073
PILGRAM, William,117
PILGRIM, Amos Jr.,117
, Amos,117
, William,005
PINKLEY(BINKLEY), John,010
PINKLEY(BRINKLEY), John,012
PINKLEY, Adam,101 ,110
, John,108 ,111
, Peter,051 ,052
PINKSTON, (Mrs),119
, Baswell,090 ,103,119
, Bazel,099
, Bazwell,117
PINSON, Richard,082
PIPES, ,005
, John Jr.,029,030,051
, John,003,064,067,069,074,
076,077,078,081,087,
088,090,093,098,099,
106,112,114,115,147,
150,151,159,160
, Pricilla,098
, Silbanus,078
, Silvanue,078
, Silvanus,051,064,069,074,
076,077,081,087,088,
090,093,097,099,104,
112,114,115,116,129,
134
, Susannah,001
, Sylvanus,061
POAGE, Robert,060
POCOCK, Temperance,155
POINDEXTER, ,166
, David,035 ,115,139,
144,166
, Elizabeth,168
, Frances,097,102,114,
117,121,136,139,163,
166,168
, Frank,114 ,115,128,
143,149,158,168
, Jane,097
, Thomas,004 ,029,034,
035,052,064,074,085,
098,104,124,131,138,
162,164
PORTER, Dudley,163
, Jane,078
, Joseph,059 ,069,070,071,
074,076,077,078,112,
120,124,146,149,159,
164
, Wm.,078
POTTER, Abraham,076,119
, John,076
POTTIT, Thomas,133
POWELL, Abraham,007,021,024
, Joseph,024
POWERS, Jesse,132
, Joseph,125
, Thomas,125
PRAEZEL, Gottfried,110
PRATHER, William,033,081,148,156

, Wm.,121,153
PRESTON, David,003 ,004
, William(Colo.),018
PREWETT, Shadrack,149
, Shadrick,148
PRICE, Angus,029
, John,140
, Joseph,061
, Matthew,018
PRIDDY, George,087 ,128,129,154,
167
PRIEM, John Fredr.,095
PRIME, Ben,005
, Benjamin,004
PRITCHETT, Moses,055

PRUET, Micajah,072
, William,076
PRUIT, Levy,029
, Michael,105
PUKET, Wm.,089
QUILLEN, James,072 ,087
, John,058
, Teague,118
, Wm.,052
QUILLIN, James,024
, John,058
, William,033,054
QUINN, John,021,022

RABOURN, Thomas,158
RABURN, Silkend,135
, Thomas,135
, Thos.,135
RAILEY, James,159
, Jeremiah,159
RAINWATER, James,072,159
RAMEY, ----ck,059
, James,068
, John,096,117,119,132,133
, Joseph,028 ,034,037,039,
040,041,061,067,068,
075,076,077,078,083,
085,132,138,140
, Js.,128
, William,067 ,116,119,132,
140
RAMSEY, Jane,038
, William,038,087,097,133
RANCK, John,130
RANCKE, John,162
RANDLEMAN, (Doctor),058
, ,115
, John,051,069,070,075,
078,081,087,094,095,
096,097,103,107,110,
112,114,116,120,122,
124,125,129,133,135,
136,140,141,142,147,
149,152,154,156,160,
164,165,166
RANK, Gotleap,166
, Michael,053 ,116
RANSOME, Holday,045
, Mary,045
, Simon,045
RAPER, Thomas,083 ,120,123,133,
152
, Thos.,137
RATCLIFF, Wm.,050
RATLIFF, Richard,032
RAY, Zachariah,147
, George,055,091
, Reubin,055
, Thomas,033,039
, Urseley,040
, Zac.,112
, Zach,128 ,139,144,146
, Zach.,128
, Zachariah,050 ,051,052,068,
082,086,093,097,099,
103,104,120,121,123,
124,136,139,146,149,
154,164
, Zachary,150
, Zachriah,159
RAYNARD, Sophia,102
REACE, Abraham,063
REACH, John,117
READ, James,091,094,105
, John,040 ,096
, Joseph,011,100,101,151,159

, Wm.,067
READE, John,158
, Mary,158
REAPER, Thomas,063
REASE, Abraham,066
, Valentine,063
REASOR, Christian,085
REATHERFORD, Griffith,076
REAVES, Edmond,110
, Edward,105
, James,049
, John,044
REAVIS, David,021 ,022,023,039,
044,067,080,093,105,
107,113
, Edmund,077 ,080,105
, Edward,087 ,097,145
, Henry,077 ,080,086
, James,007 ,020,028,048,
061,067,081,086,107,
113,137,155,160,168
, John,013,056,062,067,080
,096,111,112
, Joseph,020 ,048,101,140,
150
, Mary,155
REDDICK, Hardy,052 ,069,097,099,
123,134,164
REDEFURD, John,004
REDICK, Hardy,116
REDIN, James,140
REED, George,062
, James,098
, John,002 ,003,005,048,091
, Joseph,008,011,014,017,047
,063
REEDS, John,005
REES, James,029
REESE, Abraham,067 ,068,069,073,
129,142,157,158
, Absalom,102
, Valentine,066,068,074,077
,148
, Volentine,060
REICH, Christian,132
REID, Joseph(B.I.),086

REID, Joseph,023
RENNIGAR, George,160
RENNONGER, ,070
REYNARD, Ben,143
  , Joel,143
  , William,102
  , Wm.,143
REYNOLD, Suffiah,121
  , Wm.,121
REYNOLDS, Ezekiel,044 ,129
  , Francis,003 ,004
  , Gideon,158
  , James,009,109
  , Jonas,069,073,090,124,
    155
  , Justice,060 ,061,067,
    068,069,077,080,081,
    087,093,094,102,103,
    107,115,116,118,119,
    119,128,131,133,133,
    139,140,141,148,150,
    153,155,156,161,168
  , Mary,158
  , Micheal,094
  , Micheal,036
  , Nathaniel,082
  , William,006 ,007
  , Wm.,082
RHOTEN, David,110
RICE(?), ,027
RICHARDS, Leonard,142
RICHARDSON, Matthias,111
RIDDICK, Hardy,017 ,020
RIDDLE, Basdel,063
  , Basil,026
  , Baswell,123
  , Bazel,070
  , Bazwell,101
  , Bazzell,100
  , Bazzle,163
  , Boswell,052,112
  , Brasseell,066
  , Brazzlo,133
  , John,068
  , Randol,134
RIDENS, Jno.,136
  , John,038,059,072,074,076
    ,078,111,162
  , Milley,038
  , William Jr.,012
  , William,002,008,009,038
RIDGE, Elizabeth,064 ,092
  , Mary,064 ,092
  , Seth,064
  , Sythe,092
  , Thomas,064 ,092,131
  , William,021 ,064,067,078,
    092
  , Winneford,078,092,131
  , Winnefred,064
  , Winniford,057
  , Winnifred,060
  , Wm.,064 ,078,079,092,093,
    100,131
RIDING, ,080,081
  , John,090
RIDINS, John,016,049,070,080,108
    ,111
  , Milley,042
  , William,042,051
RIDONS, John,060
RIFFE, Peter,107
RIGGS(?), Edward,062,063
RIGGS, David,032,059,066,075,113
    ,121,124,129,134,157
    ,164,165
  , Edward,001 ,003,006,067
  , Iram,134
  , Isam,129
  , R.,003
  , Reuben,004 ,005,006
  , Reubin,002 ,007,032
  , Reuin,007
  , Samuel,029 ,034,069,072,
    075,091,129,134
  , Silas,129,134
  , Zadoc,069
  , Zadock,055 ,075,091,129,
    134,138,142
RIGHT, John,119,124
RIGHTS, John,032,036,057,070,071
    ,074,138,145,150,151
    ,156,157
RILEY, James R.,154
  , James,160
  , Jeremiah,080,143
  , Jermiah,149
  , Ninian,143 ,152,153
RING, John,041 ,062,072,078,085,
    087
    Thomas,073,085,153,164
RINGGOLD, James,069,073,107
RINGOLD, James,054
RITES, Jno.,137
  , John,144
ROADH, Judd,124
ROAS, John,008
ROBERSON, Andrew,035,061,065,141
  , George,071,078
  , Jacob,049
  , John,008 ,014,020
  , William,016
  , Wm.,003 ,082,083,086
ROBERTS, Elijah,122
  , Elizabeth,037
  , George,005
  , Hezekiah,068 ,081,166
  , James,061 ,088,111,161,
    164
  , Jno.,133
  , John,008 ,022,037,041,
    114,150
ROBERTS, Lanier,005

  , Mary,120
  , Micael B.,092
  , Michael B.,128,140,143
  , Olive,016 ,027,030,033,
    034,038,043,044,052,
    055,076,085,087,088
  , Phillip,019
  , Thomas,150
ROBERTSON, Andrew,073 ,121
  , Butler,013
  , George,084
  , John,068,138
  , Wm.,128
ROBESON, Andrew,141
ROBINSON, ,123
  , A.,100,146
  , Andrew,047,079,081,083
    ,084,085,088,098,100
    ,101,102,103,106,107
    ,108,117,122,123,124
    ,126,127,130,132,133
    ,137,144,146,149,153
    ,155,160,164,166,168
  , Jacob,158
  , John,016 ,116,142
  , Nancy,102
  , Thomas,106
  , Wm.,111 ,117
ROBISON, William,001,002
ROGER, Jacob,140
ROGERS, Jean,011
  , John,008,018,079,107
  , Thomas,011
  , William,032
ROLES, Christopher,068
ROMINGER, Elizabeth,020
  , Jacob,063,069,070,071,
    097,098,099,119,146
  , Martin,020,046,098
  , Michael,095
ROOPE, Michael,130
ROSE, Abner,060
  , Brasilia,010
  , Brazalia,010
  , Hannah,089,102,138
  , Peter,069
ROSEBERRY, William,105 ,132
ROSS, Charles,141
  , David,047
  , James,014
  , Thomas,037,072,094
  , Thos.,072
  , William,161
ROTEN, Josiah,160
ROTH(?), Andrew,053
ROTHROCK, Eve Eliz.,079
  , John,008
  , Peter,021,085,097,107,
    143
  , Phil,050 ,107
  , Philip Jr.,053
  , Philip Sr.,053
  , Philip,079,126,166
ROTHWELL, John,026
ROUARK, Michael,052
ROWAN, John Johnson,072
ROWARK, (Capt),011
    ,027
  , Barna,033 ,051
  , Barney,061
  , Chris.,061
  , David,015 ,016,017,019,
    072
  , Elisha,016
ROWE, Thomas,107
ROWLES, Christopher,108
RUDLEDGE, William,078
RUDOLPH, Andrew,029,148
RULPP, Isaac,146
RUNELS, Francis,003
RUNNELS, Michael,019
RUSSEL, Buckner,077
RUSSELL, Buckner,107
RUTHLEDGE, Mary,107
RUTLEDGE, (Wife of Wm.),028
    ,110
  , Isaac,092
  , James,092
  , Joel,092
  , John,092
  , Johnston,005
  , Mary,027 ,041,077,081,
    093,104,105
  , William,024 ,058,062,
    093,105,107
  , Wm.,028 ,076,086,092,
    104
RUTLEG, Johnston,005
RYAN, Carby,121
RYON, Darvy,162
SALLE, Peter,085,119
SALLEY, Jacob,047
  , Peter,047
  , Petter,045 '
SALLY, Peter,054
SAMPFORD, Thomas,117
SAMPSON, Benjamin,096 ,119
SAMUEL, Augustine,132 ,133,165
  , Reuben,139 ,162
SAMUELL, Foster,002
  , (Capt.),124
SANDERS, (Capt.),046,082
    ,011 ,093,103,116,117,
    118,123,136,146,159,
    164
  , Hardy,151
  , Jacob,126
  , James Jr.,013 ,067,074,
    077,080,082,103,105,
    114,116,134,137
SANDERS, James Sr.,080 ,108,137,
    150

  , James,009 ,010,012,013,
    016,020,033,043,046,
    050,054,059,063,064,
    067,068,073,074,076,
    080,081,087,096,100,
    103,105,123,129,137,
    138,147,151
  , Joel,144
  , John,013 ,021,033,034,
    045,046,050,059,065,
    081,107,121
  , Joseph,097
  , Matthew,022
  , Sarah,087
SANDFORD, James,079
SANFORD, James,079
SATER, John,106,114,115,117,128,
    143,163
SAVAGE, Leavin,057
  , Levin,050
SAXTON, Robert,110 ,116
SAYERS, Richard,073
SCALES, Nathaniel,162
  , Peter,131
SCAMERON, Alexander,112
SCHAUB, John Jr.,166
  , John,017,112,166
SCHINIDER, Cornelius,107
SCHNIDER, Cornelius,073
SCOTT, (Capt),124
  , Aaron,127
  , Arthur,037 ,039,040,041,
    113,118,128,139,141,
    150,151
  , Auther,019
  , Ben,134
  , Benjamin,069,075,129
  , Charles,143
  , Daniel,045 ,047,059,149,
    153,154,155,160,163
  , David,101
  , Gabriel,022
  , Happy,013,108,126
  , Jacob John,024
  , Jacob Joseph,014
  , Jacob,044
  , James,150
  , Jane(Negro),009
  , Jane,087,156,167
  , Jean,013
  , Jemima,013
  , Jeremiah,126
  , Jesse,108,113,118,125,126
    140,141,150
  , John Jacob,023 ,025
  , John,069,075,119
  , Keziah,013
  , Mima,108
  , Pricilla,108
  , Prisilla,013
  , Prisscle,126
  , Robert,006
  , Samuel,165
  , Sarah,013,108,143
  , Wm.,005
SCOTTS, (Capt.),023
  , (Dist),025
  , ,025
SCRITCHFIELD, John,003
    Palmer,103
SCURRY, Eli,025
SEIDEL, Nathaniel,048
SELBY, William,153
SELL, Jonathan,065
SENTER, Zachariah,105
SEWARD, Samuel,100
SEWEL, Edward,134
SEXTON, Robert,141
SHADWICK, John,053
SHAMBLE, John,079
SHAMBLIN, William,049
SHAR, Matthew,059
SHARPE, (Mr.),088
  , John Jr.,014
  , William,057,080
SHAW, James,028
SHEARMON, Peter,128
SHEARMOUR, Peter,042
SHEEKS, Adam,145
SHELTON, David,094 ,095,112
  , Edward,047,050,066,076,
    078,092
  , John,020 ,026,043,093,
    094,107,112,144,149,
    154,155,166,166
  , Mary,047 ,076
  , Ralph,114
  , Susannah,114
  , William,024,026
  , Wm.,043
SHELTONS, (Will),060
  , William,060
SHEPERD, Jacob,041
SHEPHERD, William,020
SHEPPARD, Jacob Sr.,123
  , Jacob,114
  , James(Capt),011
  , James,036
  , William,005 ,148
  , James,015
SHEPPARDS, (Capt),045
SHEPPERD, (Capt.),041
  , (Colo.),034 ,046
  , (Dist),054
  , Elizabeth,019
  , Jacob,040,050,060,069,
    072,081,083,084,086,
    112,124,136,144,146,
    167
  , James(Capt),015
  , James,019,026,028,030,
    031,045,049,050,061,
    067,076,083,090,114,
    119,125,136

SHEPPERD, John,125
, William,003 ,004,005,
006,007,011,014,015,
017,019,020,021,023,
024,025,026,030,031,
034,035,036,037,041,
042,044,045,046,049,
051,060,067,068,076,
077,087,094,098,107,
118,120,123,125,132,
136,148,166
, Wm.,004 ,005,028,030,
031,034,037,045,046,
061,067,095,123,157
SHEPPERDS, ,025
, James(Capt),014
, Wm.(Capt),014
, Wm.,019 ,131
SHERMON, Peter,062
SHERPHEDS, (Capt.),023
SHEPHERDS, (Dist),025
SHIELDS, Abel,111
SHINN, Samuel,104 ,116
SHIP, Daniel,036,044,072,079,107
,149
, Jos.,038
, Mack,008
, Thomas,035,038,053,063,134
,135
SHOAF, Jeremiah,095
SHOBER, Gottlieb,162
, Gottlieb,101,151
SHOEMAKER, Adam,029,097
SHORE, Frederick,071,153
, Henry,012,013,020,021,022
,029,030,038,042,043
,045,047,055,059,063
,064,066,067,068,134
,136,139,140,141,147
, Jacob,105
, Reuben,043 ,121,168
, Reubin,024 ,029
SHORES, Daniel,113
, Henry,010 ,024,040,100,
111,136,138
, John,080,086,090,094,095
,096,116,159
, Reuben Jr.,100 ,134
, Reuben Sr.,094
, Reuben,041 ,046,052,053,
057,095,116,124,158
, Reubin,026 ,027,159
, Simeon,116
, William,055
, Wm.,051
SHORT, James,010,012,013,019,043
,053
SHOUB, John,007
SHOUSE, Henry,127
, ,146,149,159,164,165
, Christian,103
, Daniel,085 ,100,107,116,
127,160
, Frederick,127 ,168
, John,075,141
, Madalene,103
, Philip,011 ,014,015,031,
036,052,053,053,100,
105,127
SHULL, Samuel,008
SHULTZ, George,166
, Jacob,166
SHUTT, Jacob,107
SIDE, John,119
SIDES, Michael,097 ,107
SIGILL, John,080
SILLS, Jonathan,107
SILVA, William,136
SILVEY, William,159
SILVIA, William,149
, Wm.,150,160
SILVIE, William,150,152,153
SIMINGTON, Robert,132 ,165
SIMMONS, Elisha,166
, Jesse,148 ,167
, John,007
, Peter Jr.,067
SIMPKINS, James,031
SIMPSON, John,067
SIMS, John,045 ,047
SITES, Michael,063
SIZEMORE, William,109
SKEEKS, Adam,145
SKIDMORE, Abraham,105 ,116,134
, Elijah,013
, John,041 ,055,058,105,
134
, Thomas,058,105
SKRIMSHAW, John,112
SLATEN, George,007
, John,007
SLATER, Henry,073 ,084
SLATTEN, John,008 ,081,086
SLATTON, (Major),063
, John,100
SLAUGHTER, John,100
SLAVE, Abner,103
, Bob,127
, Charles,144
, Cudger,103
, Jim,133
, Nan,127
, Nora Bird,103
, Phebee,127
, Stephen,103
, Titus,103
, York,080
SLIDER, Valentine,022 ,024
SMALL, Elijah,123
SMALLWOOD, Elijah(Capt),014
, Elijah,003 ,014,015,
016,034,070,094,095,
105,106,123,133,140

SMALLWOOD, John,160
, Sarah,094
SMALLWOODS, ,025
SMILEY, George,56
SMITH, Stephen,112
, (Capt.),041
, Benj.,060
, Bennet,113 ,127
, Charles,027 ,052,053,084,
164,165,167
, Christian,007,100,125,126
, Christopher,076 ,083,095
, Daniel Jr.,118
, Daniel,135 ,150
, David,062
, Edward,042 ,051,110,142,
155,156,158,161
, Edwin,072
, George,101
, Grizilla,108
, Henry(Capt.),023
, Henry,021,042,050,056,061
,067,068,071,094,095
,108,110,114
, James,041
, Jno.,041
, John,026,036,047,049,055,
057,059,060,070,073,
074,076,097,098,099,
112,137
, Joseph,050
, Laurence,073
, Lawrence,003
, Lem,065
, Lemuel,058 ,071,083,084,
090,091,109,121,122,
124,153,164
, Marth,050
, Meredith,143,155
, Minor(Capt.),037,039
, Peter,100,101
, Philip,108
, Reubin Jr.,062
, Robert Jr.,076
, Robert,062 ,080,099,100,
112,131,140,142,143,
153,155,156
, Robt.,151
, Samuel,147
, Sarah,013
, Stephen I.,089
, Stephen K.,070 ,146,149,
153,157,159,163
, Stephen R.,123
, Stephen,086 ,097,110,111,
121,146,164
, Thomas,010 ,012,013,014,
018,025,030,036,041,
042,048,049,056,057,
058,061,062,064,068,
069,070,071,074,076,
077,079,080,081,082,
086,088,089,093,094,
099,115,118,119,125,
130,143,148,153,156,
158
, William,026
, Wm.,080
SMITHERLAND, Daniel,117
SMITHS, (Capt),014
, ,025
SMITY, Daniel,112

SNEAD, John,012,014,019
SNEED, Charles,016 ,043,061
, Chas.,047
, John,014,020,027,029,031,
043,050,054
SNIDER, Cornelious,119
, Elizabeth,144
, Martin,074
, Melchour,095
, Peter,141
, Philip,085 ,122,154
, Phillip,144
, Simon,012
SNOW, ,119,120,126
, Ebenezer,103
, Frost,158
, Henry,025
, Wm.,053
SOUTHARD, Henry,076,083,084,121,
124
, Isaac,069,071,112,113,
123,144,145,146,150,
152,153,164,168
SOUTHERLAND, Phil,139
, Sarah,033
, William,034,058,111
,127,153
SOUTHERN, Boaz,166
, Gibson,114
, Reuben,166
, William,041 ,047,078,
105,136,166
, Wm.,105
SOUTHERS, Henry,116
SPACH, Gottlieb,110
, Martha,110
SPANHOWER, Henry,097
SPARKS, John,118
, Joseph,113 ,157
, Matthew,007
, Solomon,092
, Thomas,147
, William,007,152,153,164,
166,167,168
, Wm.,113,165
, Wm.Jr.,123 ,150
, Wm.Sr.,123
SPARPOINT, Joseph,097
SPEANHOUR, Michael,070

SPEAPOINT, Jo.,143
SPEENHOUR, Henry,147
, John Henry,147
, Jowde,141
SPEER, Aaron,038,124,125,127,158

, Andrew,008 ,010,012,013,
024,026,039,043,044,
048,050,058,064,083,
121,136
, Ann,048
, Aron,012
, Ben,134
, Benj.,140
, Benjamin,084,148,153,164,
165,166,167,168
, Elizabeth,039
, Henry(Capt.),040
, Henry,018,021,023,026,027
,028,029,030,031,032
,033,034,035,037,038
,039,041,044,049,050
,052,057,058,059,061
,061,062,064,065,068
,069,070,073,074,075
,076,077,078,079,080
,081,082,083,084,085
,086,087,088,089,090
,091,092,093,094,095
,096,097,098
, Henry,099,100,101,102,103
,104,105,106,108,109
,110,112,113,115,116
,118,119,121,122,123
,125,126,127,128,129
,131,132,133,134,136
,138,140,142,143,146
,148,153,154,155,158
,159,160,161,163,164
,166,167,168
, Jacob,010,012,027,046,071
,084,090
, John,071,140,143
, Joshua H.,125,132
, Joshua K.,121,148
, Joshua,039
, Leroy,130
, Levi,008,150
, Levy,050
, Robert,010 ,030,031,039,
043,047
, Thomas,073
SPEERS, Aaron,073
, Henry,073 ,117
, Rhody,048
, Robert,048 ,051
SPENCE, David,093 ,128
, Davis,122
, Thomas,032 ,037,039,040,
086,089,093,095,106,
116,121,128,154,159,
160
, Thos.,095
SPENCER, Moses,074
, Samuel,027,135,156
, William,117
SPENHOWER, Henry,098
SPIRGIN, Samuel,139
, William,139
SPOON, Adam,049,123
SPOONHOUR, Henry,014,020,021,046
,047,092,109,160
, Jacob,036,100,101,102
,109
, Warner,039
SPOONOUR, Warner,125
SPRINKLE, Geo.,077
, George,010,012,014,031
,061,076,088,094,167

, Peter,074
, Henry Jr.,125
, Jacob,127
SPUNHOUR, Henry Jr.,125
SPURLOCK, John,042 ,070
STAFFORD, William,008
, Wm.,003
STAMPER, Jonathan,003 ,004
STAMPS, Thomas,098
, Timothy,032
STANDLEY, Christian,117
, Christopher,068
, Elijah,038
, John,127
, Joseph,041
, Strangeman,064
, William,041
STANLEY, Jesse,150
, John,124
STANTON, Christopher,055,068,071

, Judith,071
STARR, Henry,069,073,158,166
STATEN, John,083
STATTEN, John,085 ,086
STEEL, William,064 ,132
STEELMAN, Charles,144
, George,115,131
, Mathias,028 ,070
, Matthew,148
, Matthias Jr.,041 ,047
, Matthias,028 ,028,041,
047,091,100,111
, William,028
, Wm.,120
STENTON, Christopher,021,078,084

, Judith,084
, Thomas,086
STEPHENS, George,033
, James,117
, Jno.,136
, John,127 ,141,142
, William,032

STEWARD, Benjamin,014 ,106
, Charles,013,117
, David,009 ,070
, Elizabeth,106
, Joseph,014,106
, Nathaniel,074
, Sarah,106
, Steward,038
STEWART, Benjamin,010 ,012
, David,029 ,078,101,119,125
, George,013
, James,129
, Joseph,010,016,017
, Nathaniel,107 ,158
, Reubin,125
, William,134
, Wm.,129
STINER, Abraham,167
STINSON, Elijah,092
STINTONS, Thomas,013
STOE, Abraham,090
STOLTIS, Samuel,134
STOLTZ, Samuel,097 ,138
STONE, Enoch,131,157,159
, Jacob,020
, John,058,067,136,155
, Litleberry,041
, Litleberry,054
, Marble,017
STONER, Jacob,023
STONES, Marble,008
STRAWN, Larkin,074
STREALE, Fredrick,094
STROOP, Samuel,014 ,017,022,033
, William,033
STROOPE, Samuel,147
STROPP, Samuel,013
STRUB, Adam,160,166
, John,160,166
STRUPE, Samuel,124
STUBBS, Isaac,152
STULTZ, Philip,089
SUGART, Zachariah,157
SUMMERS, (widow),015
, James,117
, John Sr.,150
, John,012 ,154,155,166
, Johnson,096
, M.,158
, Mannering,123 ,154
, Thomas,099
, Weightman,012
SUMNER, Boarter,124,129
, Boater,078 ,082,113
, Boeter,105
, Joshua,064
, Phebe,072 ,130
, Robert,078
SUMNERS, Boater,095
, Boawater,064
, Boeter,101
, John,131
, Manning,124
, Robert,064
SUTHER, William,091
SUTHERLIN, Phil,102
SUTHERN, Gibson,091
SUTON, John,077
SUTTEN, John,094
SUTTON, Dread,061
, Etheldred,049 ,056,062,063,073,131
, Jacob,052
, John Etheldred,072
, John,049,056,063,069,072 ,078,081,088,094,114 ,115,118,122
SUTTONS, John,073
SWAIM, John,114
, Moses,093
, William,107 ,126,139,144,159,160
SWARTZ, Adam,090
SWATZ, Andrew,085
SWEAT, Edward,123
SWEAT, Wm.,122 ,123,159
SWIM, John,100
, William,065 ,097
, Wm.,065
SWINEY, Daniel,122
SYSEMORE, William,136

TAKEWELL, James,160
TALBOT, Thoushuway,110
TALIAFERRO, ,093
, Charles,099
, John,085,088,112,147 ,149
TALIAFERRO, John,046,049
TALLIAFERO, John,070,156
TALLIAFERRO, Charles,071
, John,071 ,073,074,077,155,161
TALLIEFERRO, Richard,034
TALLIFERRO, Dorcas,031
, John,031,041,060
, Richard,031
TANNER, Frederick,145
, James,135
TATE, ,005
, Adam,035 ,048
, Arthur,048,054,056,083,086 ,109,113,118,127,132 ,166
, John,053 ,126,133,152,159
, Rachael (Mrs.),040
, Rachel (Mrs),056
, Rachel,039
, Robert,012,021,034,039
, Samuel,098
TATES, (Adars.),060
, Arthur,075

TATES, John,064
TATUM, Absalom,027
TAYLOR, Edward,069 ,075
, John Luis,135
, John,072,153
, Matthew Sr.,112
, Robert,012
, Sarah,066
TEAGUE, John,018,021,045,047,053 ,065,081,083,084
, Martha,065
TERREL, Harry,084 ,086,088,156
, Henry,094
TERRELL, Harry,107
TERRIL, Harry,091 ,112,114,118
, Henry,095 ,110
, Timothy,040
TERRILL, Harry,114 ,118,119,120
, Henry,102
THOMAS, ,093
, Deborah,132
, Evan,132
, John,123
THOMASON, Richard,060
THOMERSON, John,064
, Richard,014 ,017,031,042,046,064,087,093,117
THOMPSON, Adam,021 ,022,055
, Alexander,102
, Ave,038 ,041
, Catharine,091
, Edmond,134,135
, Edward,042,055,084,088 ,089,091,110,112,126
, Elijah,091
, Fredrick,107
, Isham,064,065,091,117,152
, James,039,122,131,157
, John,026 ,041,063,070,082,084,088,091,098,100,107,123,130,140 ,143,147,153,167,168
, Joseph,072,086
, Justice,110
, Mary,042 ,100,143
, Pegge,135
, Silvester,153,168
, William,038 ,041,042,112,125
, Wm.,038 ,042,122,134
THOMSON, John,014
THOMURSON, Richard,017
THORNBERRY, Jo.,141
, Joseph,018 ,141
, Thomas,141
, Thos.,141
THORNTON, William,014 ,017,027,059,060,065,067,076,077,078,098,107,112,121,126,127,133,136,145,146,151,153,160,163,165,167,168
, Wm.,040 ,068,073,081,090,103,105,106,122,123,125,126,154,157
TICKER, James,119
TILLELY, Henry,164
TILLERY(TILLEY), Joshua,029
TILLERY, Joshua,041,048,055
, Susanah,041
TILLEY, Henry Sr.,148
, Henry,089 ,095,102,132,157
, James Sr.,016
, James,047 ,099,122
, Jane,089,095
, John,139,147
, Joshua,023 ,144
, Lazaros,021
, Lazarus,030,078
, Lazarus,022,076,081,148
, Lazerus,155,167
, Lazerus,154
, Martha,099
TILLY, Henry,106
, Lazarous,008
TINSLEY, Tabitha,065
, Thomas,019,065
TLOVIRD(?), Thomas,081
TODD, James,056,057,062,070,075,081,099,102,112,116,118,119,132,138,159
TOLIVER, John,066
TOMERSON, Hannah,086
, Richard,093 ,117
TOMMERLIN, Alexander,144
TOWN, Sorry,138
TRANSOU, Abraham,152
TROTTER, Benj.,166
TROY, Matthew,013
TRUBEL, Christian,095
TRUITT, John,166
TUCKER, Brench,087 ,145
, Garner,126 ,127,162,163
, James,038 ,072,087,097,119,127,133,140,143,150
, John,145
, William,059
, Wm.,143
TULL, Nicholas,039 ,136,140
TURNER, Catherine,035
, ELias,028
, Elias,008 ,058,076
, Rhody,032 ,035
, Robert,032 ,035,043
, Roger,008 ,016,023,027,028,035,066,076,077,155
, Thomas,003 ,076

TUTTLE, Thomas,074 ,118
UNDERHILL, John,025
UNDERWOOD, William,029 ,030,031,033,036,044,060,066,074,139
, Wm.,014 ,034,036
UNDERWOODS, (Capt.),030
, (Dist.),043 ,034
UPTHOGROVE, Isaac,132
UPTIGROVE, Isaac,075
VAN VLECK, Henry,094
, Jacob,094
VANCE, Samuel,160
, Aley,160
, Samuel,160
, William,059
VANDEFORD, Charles,092
VANDEPOOLE, Abraham,142
VANDERFORD, Charles,082
VANDEVER, Charles,095
VANHOY, John Jr.,122
, John,122
VANHOZER, Valentine,002
VANNOY, Andrew,003
, John,058
VARNAL, Richard,007,015,018,019,020,021,022,023,025,027,028,031,050
, William,010,019
VARNALS, Richard,073
VARNEL, Richard,025
VAUGHN, David,068
, John,098
, Jos.,085
, Joseph,091 ,125,153,159,166
, Milly,140
, Powel,164
, Samuel,027
VAWTER, John,090,151
VENABEL, John,149
VENABLE, John,132 ,139,148
, William,036,048,132 ,148,155
, Wm.,043,087,150
VENABLES, William,002
VENDERMAN, Jacob,004
VERNON, James,134 ,147,151
, Jonathan Jr.,166
, Jonathan,079,106,165
VEST, Charles,087 ,102,112,113,116,150,155,159,165,167
, Chas.,099
, Samuel,140,146,158
, Sarah(Mrs),080
, Thomas,152
VEVENDER, John,108
VOGLER, Lorenz,012
, Michael,165
, Philip,073
, Samuel,107
VOLK, Andrew,095
WADDAL, Charles,006
WADDEL, Charles,006
WADDILL, Charles,138
WADDLE, Charles,008,046,079,091,127,130,142,148
, Chas.,079
WADKINS, George,059,090
, Henry,059 ,097
WAG(blurred), John,033
WAGGNON, John,055 ,061,062,081,087,120
WAGGONER, (?),060
, ,005 ,119
, Adam,110
, Gabrial,138 ,143,144
, Gabriel,008 ,014,015,026,040,086,121,124,143
, Henry,009,083,084,168
, John,048
, Joseph,052,054
, Philip,048
, Samuel,009,010,047,059
, Thomas,076
, William,084 ,037,038,059,063,087,088,111,127,130
, Wm.,072 ,111,112,125,127,149
WAGNON, John,023,033,036,056
WAGNOR, John,017,021
WAGON, John,040,041
WAGONER & BROOK,012
WAINSCOTT, Abraham,136
WAKEFILL, Samuel,152
WALDROON, Joseph,065
WALKER, David,005 ,107,137,139
, David ,137
, James,134 ,136,139
, John,015,135
, Joseph,028 ,029
, Mary,067,090,096
, May,021
, Robert,007
, Robert Jr.,010 ,012,024,033,053,069,073
, Robert Sr.,033
, Robert,001 ,002,003,007,008,009,011,012,014,015,017,018,019,021,022,023,025,026,028,030,031,034,037,043,044,045,046,050,052,056,057,064,067,070,075,076,078,079,080,082,084,085,088,090,092,095,096,104,107,109,110,115,119,123,128,131,166

WALKER, Thomas,068
, Warren,029
, William,014,017,018,021,
032,033,050,071,082,
084,090,107,149,159,
164,165,166
, Wm.,017,083,150,151,164
WALLACE, William,010,022,032
WALLER, Henry,053
, Sarah,053
WALTERS, John,123
WALTON, Jesse,003
WARD, ,110
, Elizabeth,001,028
, Henry,013,093,096,104,107,
140
, John,013 ,095
, Leven,122
WARNER, Wiatt,027
WARNICK, Matthew,039
WARNOCK, ,108
, James,062
, M.,005
, Matt.,149
, Matthew,005,008,010,016
,020,024,026,027,029
,051,067,068,069,081
,084,095,098,106,107
,108,111,118,121,124
,125,130,138,139,144
,156
, Robert,007,010,011,017,
023,043,052,055,112
, Robt.,026
, Samuel,017,079,091,095,
098,134
WATERS, George,072
, John Allen,114 ,136
, John,072
WATKINS, George,040,062,139,144,
159
, Henry,134
WATSON, Ben,038,057,064
, Benj.,012 ,048,070
, Benjamin,008,011,013,018
,019,021,023,024,026
,028,030,039,041,042
,043,044,053,054,079
,168
, Claibourn,144
, Drewry,086
, Drurey,030 ,081
, Drury,168
, John,071,138
, Nathaniel,038 ,055,120
, Nathenial,049
, William,074
WATT, William,116
WATTERS, John,087
WEATHERFORD, John,139 ,150
WEATHERMAN, Christian,137
WEAVER, William,036
WEBB, Martha,039
, William,029 ,039,069,071,
105,116,134,136,139,
163,168
WEBSTER, John,131 ,132,153,166
, Richard,032,091,149
WELL, John,164
WELLS, Daniel,006 ,007
, John,016,017,063,072,086,
087,089,090,100,109,
132,133,136,155
, Thos.,134
, John,100
WESTMOND, Isham,012
WESTMORELAND, Alexander,161
, Isham,072
WHARTON, Wm.,156
WHEALIS, James,150
, Lewis,168
WHEELIS, Lewis,148
WHELES, Benjamin,100
, Lewis,100
WHELTON, Edward,096
WHITAKER, William,148
WHITE, ,072
, Bennedict,124
, Isaack,150
, James,017,055,106
, William,038 ,040,072
, Wm.,040 ,070,081
WHITEHEAD, Ann,057
, John,162
WHITEWORTH, Samuel,115
, Thomas,115
, Wm.,115
WHITLOCK, Charles,045
WHITNEY, Francis,076
WHITTICOR, Johnson,121 ,123
, Mary,121
, Thomas,090 ,121
WHITTON, William,058
WHITWORTH, Samuel,093 ,125
, Thomas,093 ,125
, William,125
, Wm.,093
WHORTON, William,071
WIESNER, Micajah,165
WIGGINS, Elisha,145,148
WIL-S(?), John,005
WILBURN, Richard,155
WILBURN, Edward,100,115
, Martha,047
, Moses,047 ,052,053
, Richard,150,154
WILES, Thomas,142
WILEY, William,013
WILKERSON, (Maj),158
, John,089
, Major,098
WILKINS, John,008 ,095
WILLEFORD, Stephen,039

WILLIA, Robert,041
WILLIAM, ,005
, John(L.T.),066
, John,116
, Joseph,047
, Nathaniel,115 ,118
WILLIAMS, ,051 ,079,097,111,154
, Drerey,070
, Druary,082,084,129
, Drury,091,098,108,109,
111,129,147
, Isaac,117,165
, Jacob,002
, James,081
, Jane,055
, Jo,153,154,156,163
, Jo.,003 ,021,023,025,
031,035,050,077,091,
102,121,131,134
, John(L.T.),069,074
, John(Lt.),077
, John (little),074
, John,006 ,008,014,015,
016,017,020,023,027,
029,030,033,034,039,
044,045,046,049,056,
056,057,062,066,070,
071,073,076,080,082,
083,087,093,099,100,
101,102,103,104,105,
111,112,112,113,124,
125,129,133,134,135,
137,141,147,150,152,
153,156,158
, John,162 ,164,165,167,
168
WILLIAMS, Jos.,032 ,051,053,056,
103,123,126
, Joseph,006,009,010,013
,015,017,025,028,029
,030,031,033,034,046
,049,056,060,061,065
,068,075,085,091,093
,094,096,097,099,103
,104,108,113,116,119
,121,124,133,143,146
,147,149,155,156,158
,159,165
, Lisha(Lt),013
, Major,003
, Mary,079 ,102,161
, Moses,129,134
, Nathanial,018
, Nathanial,011,013,023,
038,110,132,165
, Owen,165
, Reason,079,102,156,161
,162,163,166
, Rebecca,126
, Rebekah,108
, Richard,152
, Robert,107,156,165
, Thomas,038,071,073,074
, Thos.,069,162
, Timothy,059
, William,076
WILLIFORD, Stephen,159
WILLIS, (Capt),070 ,123,141
, (Capt.),082
, (Dist),088
, ,093,103,116,123,124,136
, Robert,014 ,015,023,030,
037,071,075,077,077,
081,091,108
WILLLIAMS, ,102
WILLS, John,132
WILSON, ,005
, Abraham,076
, Benjamin,024
, George,003
, John,006,117
, Mary(Mulatto),038
, Mary,042
, Phil,040,095,134
, Phil,016
, Philip,022 ,043,052,059,
065,094,097,107
, Richard,147
, Thomas Jr.,117
, Thomas,055 ,117
, Whitfield,003
, William,061,101
, Wm.,106,111
WINFREY, Caleb,160
, Isaac,160
WINSCOTT, (Mrs),160
, Abraham,016 ,041,051,
065,159,160
, Jacob,056
, Jos.,051
, Joseph,056
, Mary,159
WINSE, Abraham,040
WINSOTN, Joseph,091
WINSTON, (Major),017,024
, James,119
, Jo,157
, Jo.,021,023,035,088,149
,150
, John,138
, Jos.,099 ,119,123,159
013,014,016,020,021,
022,023,030,035,036,
037,040,041,043,051,
052,053,054,055,057,
059,060,061,062,063,
064,065,066,067,068,
070,071,072,082,089,
090,091,092,093,094,
096,100,101,102,104,
105,106,108,110,112,
114,115,116

WINSTON, Joseph,121,122,125,130,
131,133,136,143,144,
148,149,150,151,152,
153,156,157,159,160,
161,162,163,164
WINSTONS, (Major),014
WOLDRIDGE, Gibson,033
, William,136
WOMACK, Matthew,074
WOOD, Abraham Jr.,062
, Abraham,072 ,087,092,124,
142,143,150,155
, Edmund,096
, Obediah,150
, Richard,041 ,062,078,085
, Samuel,106
, Stephen,094 ,108,116,118,
119,121,122,131,136,
144,152,159,160
, William,168
WOODRIDGES, (Capt),014
WOODROUGH, Gideon,088
, Joseph,054
, Moses,086,088,093,165
, Nathaniel,013,027,089
,130
, Samuel,089 ,116
, Thomas,026
WOODRUFF, Gideon,062,095,106
, Joseph,070
, Moses,061,074,076,078,
164
, Nathaniel Jr.,069,099
, Nathaniel,069,071,096
, Samuel,108
, Thomas,071
WOOF, John Adam,076
WOOLDRIDGE, (Capt),027
, Edward,150
, Gibson,025 ,029,031,
032,033,034,044,052,
057,077,081,088,093,
094,104,110,113,114,
116,138,140,143,146,
149
, Gilbert,093
, Martha,029
, William,029,052,077,
159
, William,016
WOOLDRIDGES, (Capt.),023
, (Dist),034
WOOLDRIGE, Gibson,034 ,098
WOOLF, Adam,013,016,023,024,034,
035,042,044,050,075,
084,092,101,105
, Daniel,141
, Elizabeth,085
, John Adam,084,085
, Lewis,029,030
, Wm.,005
WOOLRIDGE, ,063
, Gibson,046 ,062,063,
068,071,118
, Martha,065
, Thomas,073
, William,065
, Wm.,065
WOOLRIDGES, (Capt.),030
, Gibson,030
WOOTEN, George,013 ,139
, Rich.,165
, Richard,013,137,151
, Thomas,071 ,080,130
, Thos.,050
WOOTON, George,071
WORD, Charles,010 ,018,038,048
, Elizabeth,036,038
, Henry,076,077,081,138,140,
143,149
, John,060
, Susannah,128
, Will Charles,036
, William,141
, Wm.,128
WORK, Charles,025
WRAY, Zachariah,090,107,159
, Zachs.,070
WRIGHT, (Capt),070
, (Capt.),041
, (Colo.),037
, Aaron,066
, Catharine(Mrs),049
, Catharine,046
, Daniel,048 ,055,112
, Elizabeth(Mrs),036
, Elizabeth,048 ,052,058,
113,125
, Gideon(Colo.),004
, Gideon,001 ,003,004,008,
009,010,012,014,016,
018,019,024,025,036,
043,048,052,054,156
, Gidion,001
, H.,098
, Hezekiah,001,004,005,008
,013,016,020,040,045
,046
, Hezih(Hezekiah),058
, Isaac,027
, James,130 ,135,164,165
, John Jr.,164
, John,016,020,023,028,030
,033,041,046,057,066
,074,080,109,121,152
,157,159
, Moses,113
, Samuel,003
, Thomas,013 ,033,041,046,
146,147,148
WRIGHTS, (Capt),045,057
, (Dist),088

YANCY, ,076
YARBROUGH, Edward,041
YARNEL, Peter,110
YARREL, Peter,044
YEOMANS, Stokes,053
YOMANS, Stokes,032
YORK, James,012,072,086,132
    , John,077 ,117
    , William,079 ,148
YOUNG, ,093
    , Benj.,088
    , Benjamin Jr.,109,144,162,
        166
    , Benjamin, Jr.,090,010,017
        ,078,090,166
    , Edward,047 ,051,085,112,
        142
    , Edwards,092
    , Ezekiel,017 ,063
    , James,111,134
    , John,099,124,156
    , Joshua,091
    , Josiah,117
    , Rebecca,004
    , Samuel,154
    , Thomas,095
ZACHARY, William,148
ZEIGLER, George,130
ZIGLAR, Christopher,032
ZILLMAN, Henry,095
ZIMMERMAN, Reuben,153
ZINE, Margarett,005